# WALKING BLUES

University

of

Massachusetts

Press

*Amherst*

# WALKING BLUES

Making Americans from Emerson to Elvis

*Tim Parrish*

Copyright © 2001 by University of Massachusetts Press
All rights reserved
Printed in the United States of America
LC 00-054392
ISBN 1-55849-302-6
Designed by Mary Mendell
Set in Janson with Poster Bovine display by Keystone Typesetting, Inc.
Printed and bound by Sheridan Books, Inc.
Library of Congress Cataloging-in-Publication Data
Parrish, Tim.
    Walking blues : making Americans from Emerson to Elvis / Timothy L. Parrish.
        p. cm.
    Includes index.
    ISBN 1-55849-302-6 (alk. paper)
    1. National characteristics, American. 2. Pluralism (Social sciences)—United States.
3. United States—Civilization—Philosophy. 4. Popular culture—United States—
Philosophy. 5. United States—Intellectual life. 6. Blues (Music)—Social aspects—
United States. 7. Pragmatism. I. Title.
E169.1 .P234 2001
973—dc21
00-054392
British Library Cataloguing in Publication data are available.

FOR LIBBY

# CONTENTS

■ ■ ■ ■ ■ ■ ■

# ACKNOWLEDGMENTS

■ ■ ■ ■ ■ ■ ■

Writing a book of this sort is something you do alone but nonetheless requires the help of many people.

To Ross Posnock I owe an unpayable debt of thanks for introducing me to pragmatism, especially that of William and Henry James, as well as for his advice and support during the completion of this book. Donald Kartiganer deserves special recognition for his wit as a teacher and scholar and for sitting me down one afternoon and explaining to me what I needed to do to get a decent academic post.

Too many years ago Vicki Aarons and Char Miller encouraged me to believe that a life made out of reading and study was worth pursuing. This book is a tribute to their faith.

Two faculty grants from the College of Arts and Sciences at the University of North Texas and a course release from the English Department were instrumental in helping me to complete this project. I especially thank James T. F. Tanner, whose indefatigable support as chair of the English Department kept me on track whenever obstacles seemed to appear. I am grateful to Bruce Bond and Barbara Rodman for providing much needed moral support and friendship. Thanks also to Cool Bean's for giving me space to read and think.

Gena Caponi-Tabery, Nicholas Bromell, and Charles Mitchell each read the manuscript and offered crucial suggestions. My editor, Clark Dougan, has made working with the University of Massachusetts Press a pleasure. Jocelyn Moore and Maria Murphy provided invaluable help in helping to prepare the manuscript.

Brian Evenson, Cindy Phillips, Dianna Pope, Mark Wiebe, and Brett Zalkan were always present while I was writing the book. I cannot imagine having done it without their company.

Some time ago my father began asking how the book was coming along. Mom and Dad, here at last is the answer to your question. Thanks for helping me along the way. Though you are too young to understand why I say this, Samantha and Matthew, you helped to make this book too. I look forward to sharing the music and books that made this book with you.

When I began this project I had no way of knowing that I was writing it for Elizabeth Spiller. This book and my heart are hers.

An earlier version of chapter 1 appeared as "Whose Americanization?: Self and Other in Mary Antin's *Promised Land*," *Studies in American Jewish Literature* 13 (1994): 23–32, and is reprinted here in revised form by permission of Daniel Walden and *SAJL*. A portion of chapter 3 appeared as "Ralph Ellison, Kenneth Burke, and the Form of Democracy," *Arizona Quarterly* 51.3 (Autumn 1995): 117–48, and is reprinted here in revised form by permission of The Regents of The University of Arizona. A portion of chapter 4 appeared as "Imagining Jews in Philip Roth's 'Operation Shylock,'" *Contemporary Literature* 40.4 (Winter 1999), and is reprinted here by permission of the University of Wisconsin Press. An earlier version of chapter 5 appeared as "Our White Whale, Elvis; or, Democracy Sighted," *Prospects* 20 (1995): 329–60, and is reprinted here in revised form by permission of the editors.

Extracts from "Elvis Is Dead" Copyright (c) 1990 by Famous Music Corporation and Dare To Dream Music. Reprinted by permission.

Extracts from "Blind Willie McTell" Copyright 1983 by Special Rider Music. All rights reserved. International copyright secured. Reprinted by permission. (Thanks, Bob.)

T. P.

# WALKING BLUES

# INTRODUCTION  Practicing American Identity

■■■■■■■

> I used to stare at the Indian in the mirror. The wide nostrils, the thick lips. Starring Paul Muni as Benito Juárez. Such a long face—such a long nose—sculpted by indifferent, blunt thumbs, and of such common clay. No one in my family had a face as dark or as Indian as mine. My face could not portray the ambition I brought to it. What could the United States of America say to me? I remember reading the ponderous conclusion of the Kerner report in the sixties: two Americas, one white, one black—the prophecy of an eclipse too simple to account for my face. (1)

With these words, Richard Rodriguez begins his *Days of Obligation* (1992), an eloquent meditation on the hybridity of his American identity. Rodriguez's self-description recalls Henry James's oft-quoted observation that being an American is a complex fate. The complexity of that fate derives from the suspicion, even the knowledge, that as Americans we do not know who we are; moreover, we may even lack access to the history which would bring us to self-knowledge. Rodriguez notes that it took over three hundred years for us to elevate the truism that America is a nation of immigrants to the level of cliché: "We are a nation of immigrants—most of us say it easily now" (165). His use of the dash conveys the pause of a punch line: it transforms this cliché into a joke "we" Americans have played on ourselves, or perhaps have had played on us. Assuming cultural unity despite the chaos of our immigrant heritage, individual Americans—of whatever heritage—are easily and often shocked by who claims solidarity with them. "Our" resistance to the cliché begins with the Puritans. Unlike the Spanish priests who came to America to convert the Indians to Catholicism, the English Puritans, who through the vagaries of historiography preceded even the Native Americans in being known as the "first" Americans, never risked such an intimate relationship with the Indians. The Puritans did not grant the "savage" the honor of having a soul; hence they preferred to ignore and finally kill him. Today this history is greeted with guilt and even belated outrage—an irony that the legacy of a Puritan conscience confers upon us. As we are learning to account for the complexity of Rodriguez's face, the *Pure*-itan experience has been replaced with invocations to something called "diversity."

Today we challenge the very assertion that American history springs directly from the Puritans, like some Athena from the head of Zeus. We are suspicious of an identity that seems so narrow, an entire history reduced to the designs of a few white men. Henry Adams, a spiritual descendant of those white men, divined the coming of diversity at the beginning of this century and offered up his prayer to unity in the name of the Virgin. W. E. B. Du Bois hazarded a prophecy at roughly the same moment that was not so much a prayer but an assertion of fact: "the problem of the Twentieth Century is the problem of the color line" (*Souls* 3). It seems unlikely that Adams read Du Bois, but I cannot help but wonder if he would have seen Du Bois's work, which announced the rise of the descendants of slaves into visibility within American society and culture, as an instance of the multiplicity he feared.[1] Where Adams looked backwards to find his American heritage, Du Bois looked to the American future that seemed likely to sweep Adams's view away—the future that we have become. Rodriguez notes that the national injunction is to "celebrate diversity"; but how to do it? If once we sought to celebrate the unity of American experience, Rodriguez suggests that now "the dilemma of our national diversity becomes (with a little choke on logic) the solution to itself. But diversity is a liquid noun. Diversity admits everything, stands for nothing" (*Days* 169). By a peculiar American calculus, "diversity" becomes the reverse image of the monolithic America it would replace: an all-encompassing construct that at last does justice to the pluralistic ideal that prior versions of American identity and history have denied. Now we pray to multiple gods—each with an American claim.

Many now ask, Why even speak of America as if it were a coherent subject? A mainstream view among current scholars of American culture is that "America" exists only as a mythic ideal that does more cultural harm than good. The idea of "Americanness" as either a subject to be known or an ideal to be realized has been challenged because in the guise of representing unity, it actually conceals the many diverse cultural heritages and practices that exist within the United States. In the introduction to the influential anthology *Cultures of United States Imperialism* (1993), Amy Kaplan writes that "Americanness" as a subject for university study is a form of cultural enslavement. When Perry Miller stood on the shore of the Congo and received his epiphany that the "meaning of America" begins (and in a sense ends) with the Puritans, he invented "a coherent America by constructing Africa as an imperial unconscious of national identity" (5). In other words, America as a coherent subject was created by repressing the image of black Africa. By excluding Africa and hence "an alternative narrative of [American] beginnings in slavery," Miller established a paradigm for American studies that echoes the paradigm of American history that Rodriguez alludes to above: the Puritan extinction of the other in order to create what Crèvecoeur called "this new man," the American who would remain somehow both ever new and ever prior to all other identities, whether black, white, brown, yellow, or red.

Kaplan is one of a number of recent Americanist scholars who suggest that the paradigm of Americanness be replaced with a "decentered cosmopolitanism" that emphasizes American culture as an assortment of "borderlands" (17, 16). Implicit in this call is a dream persistent within our history, one that culminated most obviously with the Civil War: the desire to disssolve our national identity altogether. As Gregory Jay and William Spengemann have each suggested that we have reached "the end of American literature," so Carolyn Porter has argued that there is no American culture so much as a collision of various "cultural forcefields" ("What" 468).[2] Informing these critical perspectives is the idea that because American history comes out of so many different cultural heritages there is no way to articulate a collective American history without doing a disservice to the uniqueness and originality of the component American groups. The term "borderlands" derives from Chicano studies and can be read as a response to the kind of identity dilemma that Rodriguez describes above. More specifically, it is a response to the incontestable fact that much of American history has been concerned not only with excluding others from the national saga of America but with denying that the descendants of Africans, Mexicans, and untold Indian tribes have had any impact on what it means to know oneself as an American. Within Chicano studies, "borderlands" is a supple term that does justice to a specific set of cultural contradictions and ambiguities; once the term is translated to the field of American studies broadly conceived, however, its specific cultural relevance is lost. Redescribing the United States as the Untied States does not alter the fact that one cannot claim a "border" identity without invoking the unified American identity one would deny. No longer subject like Rodriguez to the repressive ideology of "the myth of America," America is merely a—its study a kind of—Higher Geography (Bercovitch, *American* xiv).[3]

Rodriguez explores the contingency of American identity when he looks in the mirror as an American only to find an Indian's eyes looking back at him. He wonders how to account for such complexity, especially when America is so often seen as being black and white. Borderlands approaches would tell Rodriguez that despite his suspicion that the image he perceives contains multitudes, what he really sees is the identity that his Americanness has suppressed. From this perspective, recovering and preserving his Indian identity requires not an act of Rodriguez's individual imagination so much as the denial of an American self that has suppressed this prior Indian identity. The image of Rodriguez before the mirror confronting the mystery of his heritage stands in opposition to the recent drift of academic Americanism because it suggests that America's multiple histories and shifting borders may be that contained in one person's face. Rodriguez knows very well the difficulty of representing such a possibility. In his earlier work, *Hunger of Memory* (1982), Rodriguez portrays a different mirror image, one more consonant with those arguments that suggest the repressive nature of American history. Aware that his dark skin marks him as different from the "gringos" who define America, Rodriguez confronts his *cara fea*, his ugly face:

> One night when I was about eleven or twelve years old, I locked myself in the bathroom and carefully regarded my reflection over the sink. Without any pleasure I studied my skin. . . . With a bar of soap, I fashioned a thick ball of lather. I began soaping my arms. I took my father's straight razor out of the medicine cabinet. Slowly, with steady deliberation, I put the blade against my flesh, pressed it as close as I could without cutting, and moved it up and down my skin to see if I could get out, somehow lessen the dark. (124)

Rodriguez contemplates an act of self-mutilation in response to being situated precisely on the border of identity between Mexican and American. As if his American identity cannot withstand the anger of his Mexican past, he picks up his father's tools to scrape off the physical evidence of his parents' heritage and to disfigure his American one. Physical and psychological self-effacement merge in the unchangeable fact of his racial identities.

This moment before the mirror underscores how difficult it will be for Americans to overcome the history of racism that has defined so much of our history. If Rodriguez's first glance in the mirror seems consonant with the cultural assessments of borderlands critics, he has subsequently resolved his dilemma by learning to account for his otherness as a condition of being American. Rodriguez's fiercest critics, however, say that what he could not manage with a razor, he has accomplished with his pen in *Hunger of Memory* and *Days of Obligation*—the Mexican Indian confined to the role of "interpreting the writing on the wall to a bunch of cigar smoking pharaohs" (*Hunger* 4). This critique is misguided because it fails to take into account that in these works Rodriguez dramatizes the inevitable futility of trying to escape the legacy of one's cultural heritage. For all of his bitterness in *Hunger of Memory* regarding his inability to avoid being labeled a minority and hence given advantages in school and employment that he does not believe he deserves, Rodriguez cannot write his story except as an immigrant child who has succeeded in making himself visible within American culture. The solution lies in a journey that begins with his exchanging the intimacy of his family's private language, Spanish, for the anonymity of the country's public language, English. In America, English becomes the medium for expressing his Mexican-Indian identity. This is not to say that becoming American means surrendering his Indian or Mexican cultural ancestry, but that those ancestries accrue an added dimension by virtue of his becoming American. To Rodriguez, the experience of becoming an American, of placing his story within the story of American history, enables him to voice the conflict he experienced as a Mexican immigrant. Mastering his American identity allows him to recreate his Mexican and Indian heritage and make them constitutive of his Americanness. Moreover, precisely because he foregrounds his own regret that the terms of his success cannot be separated from others' perception of his racial identity, his work continually confronts its readers with the difference that his racial heritage has made in his fashioning of his American identity.

Just as Rodriguez cannot escape the destiny of his skin, neither can the America to which he makes himself visible escape the transformative fact of Rodriguez's visibility. Rodriguez's example suggests that reconfiguring America as a loose ordering of borderlands or border cultures emphasizes our multicultural identity, but at the expense of seeing how these border identities take their meaning only in the context of American identity. Changing the dominant critical paradigm from "America" to "borderlands" or "cultural forcefields" will not replace a belief in America as an ideal to be realized. Indeed, these kinds of arguments can only reinforce "Americanness," for at the heart of these discussions remains the most familiar of American themes: identity. The cultural uniqueness that earlier generations of scholars found in exemplary Americans such as Franklin, Emerson, and Douglass is now attributed not to individuals themselves but to discrete ethnic or cultural groups. Consider this passage from Gloria Anzaldúa, often pointed to as representative in raising the kinds of border identity issues that received narratives of American identity have suppressed:

> I am a border woman. I grew up between two cultures, the Mexican (with a heavy Indian influence) and the Anglo (as a member of a colonized people in our own territory). I have been straddling that *tejas*-Mexican border, and others, all my life. It's not a comfortable place to live in, this place of contradictions. Hatred, anger, and exploitation are the prominent features of this landscape. (n.p.)

Anzaldúa defines her identity in terms of ethnicity and gender, and her self-representation unquestionably challenges conventional models of American identity. On the other hand, the appeal of her ethos is that it is autobiographical, and although her prose is enlivened with Spanish language phrases that underline her sense of cultural difference from mainstream and mostly monolingual Americans, she is nonetheless writing in English to an American audience. As Franklin, Emerson, and Douglass did before her, she addresses other Americans in order to present her individual experience as emblematic of the experience of America. Anzaldúa's assertion of identity accrues its extraordinary power precisely because her words and experience implicitly challenge the American ideology of inclusiveness—*e pluribus unum*. Yet without an ideal of *e pluribus unum* to work against, her words would have no appeal. Rather than discarding the myth of America, she writes a new one.

Contemporary Americanist scholars have been rewriting the work of earlier academics such as Perry Miller or F. O. Matthiessen because they cannot write the legacy of Puritanism out of American history—or, more crucially, out of their own historical perspectives. Injunctions to celebrate diversity rather than Americanness are really attempts to rescue the utopian dream of American history that we have inherited through the Puritans from the racist and even genocidal practices that have been committed in the name of that utopia. I see no reason why we should surrender the self-evident "truth" that "all men are created equal" that defines us as Americans even if that truth is highly provisional and has had to be rewritten so as to encompass those outside of its original address. Nor do I see any reason why we should not continue to write histories that explore the contradictions inherent in founding a nation based on equality when its economic basis was slavery. It is likely that our conception of ourselves as Americans can never get past this contradiction. What our desire to confront this contradiction requires of us is that we articulate perspectives that enable us to think about American identity in ways that account for our cultural diversity and its consequences without either insisting that we are all the same or denying that we share crucial ties that unite us as Americans. Inspired by the examples of such Americans as blues singer Muddy Waters and Elvis Presley, *Walking Blues* identifies and traces those ties: I examine how Americans of diverse cultural backgrounds talk to and make one another over *as Americans*. In so doing, I discuss how these figures re-create their identities as Americans not through some heroic process of self-individuation but through their interactions with other Americans. Be it Elvis or Emerson, each figure is considered as a maker of America among other American makers.

The process of America-making described in this book adapts its language from the pragmatist tradition lately revived by Richard Rorty. Put simply, a pragmatist approach to discussing American culture means examining American identity as an act rather than as an entity. Borrowing the language of pragmatism enables us to ask how American culture gets created rather than ask what American culture is—to talk about American cultural creations without fetishizing their Americanness. The language of pragmatism asks not what is American identity, but how does American identity get expressed? How do previous acts of American identity inform future ones? How do existing acts transform our understanding of previous ones? The advantage to taking a pragmatist stance toward American identity is that it avoids framing American culture as some transcendent or exceptional entity and thus allows us to focus on often overlooked points of cultural intersection that represent more practically how American identity gets created.

By my reading, Ralph Waldo Emerson was advancing an incipient pragmatism in *The American Scholar* when he said that for the student of American culture "the one thing in the world, of value, is the active soul" (*Essays* 57). In locating American identity in the language of pragmatism as first advanced by Emerson, I want to make clear that I am not claiming that American culture springs full-blown from Emerson's head. It is tempting to agree with Harold Bloom that virtually all of American litera-ture creates itself in an agonistic collaboration with Emerson, but such a claim inevitably risks trivializing the subject matter it addresses in the guise of elevating it ("Power" 148). The hyperbole of such a claim is a reaction to the recent trend to make Emerson and the transcendent or ahistorical American self with which he is associated the scapegoat for the failures of the liberal tradition. John Carlos Rowe's *At Emerson's Tomb* (1997) is an example of this tendency insofar as it suggests that "the important task" of learning to "coordinate the several traditions of literary and cultural expression now available to us" can only be done if we bury Emerson as a defining American thinker (15). Thus a work that would attend to the social and political implications of classic American litera-ture cannot begin without a kind of ritualistic invocation and dismissal of Emerson. To Rowe, Emerson's usefulness is outmoded because his aes-thetics are "complicitous" with the political and cultural practices his work presumes to challenge, just as the borderland critics equate "Amer-icanness" with cultural destruction. "Emersonianism" is "subject to trans-formation into an aesthetic ideology in the service of the very social forces for which Emerson had the greatest contempt" (5).[4] For Rowe and others, to reject Emerson involves not only the disavowal of some version of the American literary tradition but also ridding ourselves of the ideology that has supported slavery, sexism, U.S. imperialism, and so forth.

A curious form of essentialism underlies the belief that by rejecting Emerson one can also reject the evils of American liberalism. It seems to me that we will have escaped Emerson's relevance only when we have quit talking about him. If he must be invoked to justify "the efforts to construct independent cultural traditions for women and African-Americans," then his relevance to these issues is perhaps not wholly negative (Rowe, *Emer-son's Tomb* 8). Rowe acknowledges that for his time Emerson was very concerned about questions of race and gender but also argues that his well-intentioned personal politics could not overcome the blind spot of his liberal aesthetic ideology. The blind spot to this kind of critique, though, is its own startlingly Emersonian quality: in arguing against Emerson, critics remain true to his challenge in *The American Scholar* to remember that books "are for nothing but to inspire" and that one "had better never see a book, than to be warped by its attraction clean out of [one's] orbit" (*Essays* 57). If rejecting Emerson only underscores the at-traction of his thought, this is because one of the impossible tasks that our commitment to democracy demands of us is that we strain to listen to every voice as if it were whole unto itself. The truly dangerous element of Emersonianism is in this respect the impulse to separate the self's creations from the other selves who have made those creations possible. This logic enables us to say that one American stands for all Americans just as surely as it allows us to say that any given minority tradition is separate from a mainstream (Emersonian) American tradition.

Against those who see Emerson as emblematic of a kind of identity thinking that separates and excludes in the name of transcendence are scholars such as Richard Poirier and Cornel West, who have argued that Emerson's chief value lies in having established the groundwork for the pragmatism of William James and John Dewey. Not surprisingly, this attempt to challenge the entrenched view of Emerson has been met with critical skepticism. In his history of pragmatism, Paul Jay notes that "claims for Emerson's pragmatism are accurate in a very general kind of way" but are compromised because "rarely do the pragmatist Emersonians make an attempt to reconcile the so-called pragmatist side of Emerson with his mystical, transcendental side" (11). Jay's point is accurate to the extent that one is interested merely in placing Emerson within his own cultural-historical context. Of course this is an important task but if pursued too narrowly it risks becoming a kind of curio-keeping—the creation of an alcove for necessary straw men. If thinkers of the past are too enmeshed within their own epochs, though, how do we ever move past what once was desirable but no longer is considered to be so? The significance of making Emerson a link in the pragmatist tradition goes beyond intellectual history because it points to a way for transforming Emerson's thought into a vehicle for contemporary use. The value of Emerson is that he articulates a way of thinking about identity that is useful to understanding how a country of diverse cultural origins creates a recognizable American identity. However, Emerson is no more the inventor of a specifically transmissible American identity available to all than is Benjamin Franklin, Frederick Douglass, or Gloria Anzaldúa.

Besides a commitment to the value of self-creation, what connects these authors is not their belief in the possibility of positing a transcendental self for other Americans to copy but how they challenge present and future Americans to understand American culture as an ongoing collective creation. Americans are not and cannot be connected by a single racial identity; rather, we are connected only though a shared commitment to explore as fully as possible what it means to be "equal" to other Americans.

This aim does not imply, obviously, that all Americans are equal in fact or circumstance but that our belief in the possibility of equality becomes the basis for how each of us, regardless of race or class, has the opportunity to act out what it means to be an American. If Anzaldúa's self-description is considered from an Emersonian pragmatist perspective, she can be seen as a representative part of shared tradition of experiencing American identity as multiple and contingent.

By discussing American identity in pragmatist terms, I hope to avoid the kind of essentialism that so often polarizes discussion of American culture. In this respect, my work in ways almost too minute to specify responds to the kinds of arguments that Rorty has been making about pragmatism for the last twenty years. It seems to me that Rorty's central achievement has been to transform the work of Dewey and James into something relevant to the postmodern, poststructural era by demonstrating how arguments about epistemology end up being circular. Rorty notes that attempts to determine "whether the pragmatist view of truth—that it is not a profitable topic—is itself *true*" are irrelevant except insofar as we argue "about whether a post-Philosophical culture is a good thing to try for." Hence Rorty concludes that "there is no way the issue between the pragmatist and his opponents can be tightened up and resolved according to criteria agreed to by both sides" (*Consequences* xliii). Though there is no question that, even without Rorty, James and Dewey should be read as antifoundational thinkers, I think it is fair to say also that Rorty's transformation of James and Dewey has been a creative act on his part. Rorty has called for "all-purpose intellectuals" striving to live in a "post-Philosophical culture" in which the search for a single, unifying "Truth" has been abandoned for a realm that consists of competing descriptions, and redescriptions, of the society in which one wishes to live (xxxix). The question that Roty's work now raises is inevitably pragmatist: What do we do with pragmatism? In my mind, the best answers will not be those that rehearse the limitations of Rorty's argument but those that capitalize on the possibilities that his work opens up.

To date, though, pragmatists and critics of pragmatism have been mostly interested in defining either what pragmatism is or what a pragmatist orientation toward culture might look like. Richard Poirier, Ross Posnock, and Cornel West have significantly expanded our understanding of the pragmatist tradition by creating original and provocative pragmatist genealogies.[5] Giles Gunn, Paul Jay, and John Diggins have provided thoughtful reexaminations of the neopragmatist movement by placing it within the context of American intellectual history.[6] To these intellectual historians, attempts to use pragmatism have suffered from what Jay calls "the contingency blues"—the notion that one's arguments "cannot get beyond rehearsing how we have gotten to an epistemological and ethical impasse stemming from our realization that all knowledge is contingent" (7).[7] Rorty is frequently criticized for being unable to provide a methodology that will solve any given social, cultural, or political crisis to which it might be applied. Thus Gunn remarks that Rorty's perspective fails "to furnish us with sufficient mastery of our postmodern predicament" because it "does not show us how to enhance it" (*Thinking* 116). This criticism of Rorty duplicates the one that Randolph Bourne made of John Dewey eighty years ago.[8] Against Dewey's pragmatist justification of U.S. involvement in World War I, Bourne argued that Dewey had actually surrendered his intellectual perspective to the perspective of the warmongerers.[9] Critics of pragmatism point to Bourne as the one who revealed the fatal weakness inherent in pragmatist thinking: it has no transcendent ideal from which to critique the positions it endorses. The point of Bourne's critique, however, was not that Dewey should have been a pacifist as Bourne was, but that Dewey was naive about how easily his endorsement of the war could be co-opted to sanction acts that he would presumably rather not have endorsed.

Rorty's response to this line of thinking when it is applied to his own work has been to say that there is no transcendent justification to any intellectual answer; hence our answers can only emerge from the cultural context at hand.[10] In this respect I agree with Jay—and indeed with Rorty himself—that there is no compelling reason to perpetuate these types of epistemological debates. On the other hand, examining the contemporary interest in identity politics from the antifoundational perspective that pragmatism provides might go a long way toward helping us to understand how malleable American identity can be. To think that a pragmatist approach can solve all dilemmas in advance or guarantee a desired future, as many seem to do, is both naive and a distortion of pragmatism's aims. Although I would stop short of declaring the American commitment to equality a transcendent ideal, its promise whether realized or not is a given in all discussions of American culture.[11] John Dewey was making this kind of argument when he said that instead of asking, "What permits us to argue for democracy?" we should ask, "What serves democracy?" (qted. in Rorty, *Objectivity* 2:183 n. 19). Dewey's point was that since democracy had over the course of hundreds of years become our cultural and political frame of reference, emphasizing the former question was just a way of avoiding the latter. By Dewey's logic, if people want to argue for a potentially better political system than democracy, then that was certainly their right; nevertheless, one still cannot answer the question what permits us to argue for democracy without answering the question what serves democracy. Likewise, instead of arguing about whether this or that definition of America is correct, or whether this or that version of pragmatism is right, we should examine American identity in terms of the acts undertaken in the name of being (or not being) American.

Along with reconceiving how questions of American identity are traditionally understood, I hope to reframe how pragmatism is understood, or, more practically, how it is used. This book essays something very different from other pragmatist projects because it connects the pragmatist tradition to figures who would be included in no conventional intellectual history of pragmatism. Rather than writing a history of pragmatism, I understand myself to be writing about pragmatism as a form of American cultural history. Neither a reassessment of pragmatism nor an assessment of others' reassessments of pragmatism, *Walking Blues* is an attempt to use pragmatism to examine the ways in which seemingly disparate American acts are often connected and even mutually constitutive. For pragmatism, truth is not a priori, absolute, or essential but functional and contextual. A pragmatist orientation toward American culture requires a willingness to derive one's insights from American experience rather than framing American experience through an a priori critical perspective. In particular, I want to show how a pragmatist approach toward questions of identity is virtually identical with the practice of American culture. Because pragmatism identifies truth as an act rather than as an entity, pragmatism offers a tool for understanding how different creators of American culture constitute themselves—and by extension all of us. Not just intellectual history, pragmatism provides a vocabulary for identifying an American practice of identity making.

The figures I discuss—Mary Antin, James Brown, Kenneth Burke, Ralph Ellison, Elvis Presley, Ralph Waldo Emerson, Son House, Henry James, William James, Horace Kallen, Memphis Slim, Philip Roth, Bessie Smith, Muddy Waters, Jackie Wilson—conceive their American identity as a kind of practice. What makes them compelling as pragmatists and as theorists of American identity is that they derive their understanding of their identities as Americans from their practice rather than from some transcendent ideal. They share a belief that their critical and creative acts dramatize their experience as Americans: each knows that he or she is making American culture out of others' creations. Each brings to his or her work the understanding that the making of American culture implies a certain intellectual orientation and that that intellectual orientation implies a certain kind of culture creation. Since their creations are also critical acts, these figures thus do not divide easily into opposed disciplines of critics and artists. Rather than insisting that their version of American identity is the only one or even that American identity must be unitary, they recognize that their version of American identity is contingent, a provisional creation that is also the outgrowth of others' possibilities. They understand their art as they do their identities as Americans: unfinished works to be recreated by those who come after them.

Emerson asks a question at the outset of his essay "Experience" that is perfectly suited for a discussion of American identity: "Where do we find ourselves?" It is a question that Americans continually ask of themselves even if they have never heard of Ralph Waldo Emerson. I hear one answer in Son House's version of the Mississippi blues standard "Walkin' Blues," which gives this book its title. As if he were responding to Emerson's question in "Experience," House begins his "Walkin' Blues" with this observation: "Woke up this morning feeling around for my shoes / Know by that I got them old walking blues." As with Emerson's question, House's journey to truth begins uncertainly. Knowing that the blues is a form passed down through others, the singer, Son House, sets out on the road to create himself by wearing the shoes of his predecessors. He does not invent himself solely by his personal or ancestral history but through the action that he calls his "walking blues." House's "Walkin' Blues" confirms Emerson's claim in "The Poet" that "all language is vehicular and transitive, and is good, as ferries and horses are, for conveyance, not as farms and houses are, for homestead" (*Essays* 463). For the Emersonian pragmatist as for the Mississippi blues singer, identity exists as material under transformation; it is a practice and not an essence. As such, it provides an appropriate metaphor for my own exploration of the American Walking Blues: the blues that results from the understanding that our American identity is never realized except through a process of shared creation.

*Walking Blues* makes companions of an unlikely group—philosophers, blues singers, literary artists, popular musicians, and cultural critics—as a way of taking seriously our cultural multiplicity. It is not my intention, however, to provide a comprehensive discussion of American identity—pragmatism itself makes it clear that no such study can be written. Beginning with Crèvecoeur and continuing through Rodriguez, stories about America imply their universalism but their central pronoun has been implicitly male. Although my book to a certain extent reflects this tendency, it is my hope that by discussing American identity as an ever-changing practice, we will continue to change our understanding of how American identity is created and re-created.

I have written the chapters so that they develop out of one another, rather than piecing together five discrete arguments. Four of the chapters are paired—chapters 1 and 4 and chapters 2 and 5, respectively—with chapter 3 serving as the bridge that holds the book together. I begin with a reconsideration of Horace Kallen, a student of William James who came up with the theory of American identity known as cultural pluralism. A forerunner of today's multiculturalism, Kallen's cultural pluralism was arguably the first attempt to explain and justify American identity as a collection of cultural differences and to do so in pragmatist terms. Writing during the height of the heaviest period of immigration in U.S. history (1880–1924), Kallen identified the repressed racial component of American identity when he remarked, "Men can change many things, but they cannot change their grandfathers." Though subsequent commentators have used this remark to identify Kallen as a racist thinker, he was actually trying to show how naive—and racist—assimilationist arguments often were. Noting that American identity, as a collection of laws, could be understood only as an abstract entity, Kallen argued that Americans would define themselves culturally in terms of their ancestral heritages. Kallen has been criticized for arguing that culture must be defined by race—a consequence of his pointing out the ways in which discussions of American identity were already racist. Working from his premises rather than his conclusions, I critique Kallen from within the pragmatist tradition in order to resituate our discussions of American identity in terms of cultural practices rather than as a preconceived ideal. Kallen identified the manner in which our diverse American pasts would resurface to redefine our American present. The result is not, as he claimed, a federation of cultures living together in peaceful coexistence, but an American culture being continually re-created by different perspectives that make the past over into a version of the present.

In chapter 4 I look at the postmodern fiction of Philip Roth to examine how prophetic Kallen's theory of American identity making continues to be. Like Kallen, Roth assumes that every American has a potentially dual identity: an abstract, civic, "American" one and an inherited ethnic one.

Whereas Kallen argues that becoming American involves reclaiming one's ethnic ancestry, Roth explores how ancestral memories are re-created as American discoveries. In this respect, Roth is one of many contemporary American writers whose fiction is animated by the kind of identity logic that Kallen first explored. Indeed, no contemporary writer has explored as thoroughly as Roth how our ethnic pasts are remade into contemporary American identities. With *The Counterlife* (1986) and *Operation Shylock* (1993), he playfully returns to the putative origin of American Jewish identity, Israel, doubling back—literally and figuratively since in the latter novel the protagonist is named Philip Roth—to explore how, despite himself, he has been unable to escape the sense that his authentic self is somehow inherently Jewish. Ultimately, I argue, he goes to Israel not to find a pure point of cultural origin, but to confront how his American identity is invented from his desire to find an origin where none exists. In this way he explores fully the competing claims that our ethnic pasts and our American present make on us as Americans.

The other chapters attempt to unite American intellectual traditions that until now have been considered apart. I begin by suggesting that Emerson's attempt in *The American Scholar* (1837) to found an intellectual tradition consonant with our democratic ideals finds one of its incarnations in the tradition of the blues. Building on the arguments of Stanley Cavell and Richard Poirier, I suggest that Emerson's thought be understood as a provisional starting point for comprehending how American culture comes into being. Thanks to the valuable work of many historians and folklorists, we have come to understand the blues as a reflection of African American history, yet we have not done justice to the ways in which the blues is an expression of mainstream American thought. I see the blues in terms of a representative pragmatist cultural practice that invents us as Americans. Originating as a language of acculturation, the blues is concerned with how experience gets translated into action. Because its intellect is so rooted in everyday experience, it can be said to out-pragmatize Emerson or James. Like pragmatism, the blues does not offer particular solutions so much as a process that can be adapted to particular situations. The blues thus depends on inherited traditions while recognizing the contingency of its own identity making. A common blues line runs, "My first name is . . . and I can't tell my second name." Arguing that the blues is a form of American culture that is also a meditation on how American culture is made, chapter 2 makes Emerson the medium through which the blues speaks its second name.

Chapter 3 focuses on Ralph Waldo Ellison, who was named after Emerson. I suggest that Ellison's *Invisible Man* (1952) makes explicit the implicit connection between Emerson and the blues. Most readers have understood Ellison's work in the context of a traditional Emersonian self-reliance. By contrast, I resituate Ellison as a reader not just of American transcendentalism but of pragmatism by way of the blues. Beginning with the narrator's realization that Louis Armstrong's trumpet playing "demanded action," *Invisible Man* finds in the Jeffersonian principle that all men are created equal a principle of action that underwrites American culture's ceaseless explorations and inventions. Connecting Ellison also to the pragmatist thinking of Kenneth Burke, I argue that *Invisible Man* formulates Ellison's understanding of democracy as active, living practice. Read in this context, the hero of the book is not an invisible man—or any individual; rather, the hero is the principle of democratic action that he embodies. Ellison makes us see not only an invisible man but the ways in which we too have been invisible to the ongoing transformation of American identity. Playing on Emerson's famous "ballad in the street," Ellison's narrator converts the "languid blues" he hears on the street into a "true history of the times, a mood blared by trumpets, trombones, saxophones, and drums" that swings by virtue of the words that he finds to tell his story (*Invisible* 436).

These issues of culture, identity, and being American come to a turbulent conclusion with my discussion of Elvis Presley. Along with the makers of the blues, Elvis is this book's representative pragmatist critic. Using the 1991 Living Colour single "Elvis Is Dead" and its inventive structure to organize my own essay, I argue that both Elvis and the blues work to make visible a practice of identity making that unites us as Americans. The experience of the blues constitutes Elvis's secret history, just as one secret embedded in the history of the blues is the eventual arrival of Elvis Presley. As I suggest, coming to terms with Elvis means coming to terms with the sense that as Americans what we have been is not what we are, and that what we are is not what we will be.

# 1     What Difference Does the Difference Make?

We can see that there is a profound difference in racial, ethnic tone between America and France. In America the violent mixing of multiple European nationalities, then of exogenous races, produced an original situation. This multiracialism transformed the country and gave it its characteristic complexity.—Jean Baudrillard

## I

Horace Kallen first met Alain Locke in a class he was teaching at Harvard for William James and George Santayana. Nearly seventy years later Kallen remembered this meeting as the genesis of the theory of American identity that he would later call cultural pluralism and that today we might recognize as a version of multiculturalism:

> It was in 1905 that I began to formulate the notion of cultural pluralism and I had to do that in connection with my teaching. I was assisting both Mr. James and Mr. Santayana at the time and I had a negro student named Alain Locke, a very remarkable young man—very sensitive, very easily hurt—who insisted that he was a human being and that his color ought not to make any difference. And, of course, it was a mistaken insistence. It *had* to make a difference and it *had* to be accepted and respected and enjoyed for what it was. (qtd. in Schmidt 49)

Kallen reformulates Locke's humanistic understanding of identity into specifically American terms. For Kallen, Locke's American identity is expressed through what we would now call his African American identity. Although critics have attacked Kallen's cultural pluralism because, in Werner Sollors's words, "it did not have any room for Afro-Americans"

(*Beyond* 262) the complicated origins of Kallen's cultural pluralism reveal how deeply he was concerned with the African American's predicament.[1] Even if Kallen did not specifically discuss African Americans in *Culture and Democracy in the United States* (1924), his argument clearly responds to the conflict between being American and being black.[2] Indeed, in an essay written in 1957 to commemorate the life of Alain Locke, Kallen explicitly connected cultural pluralism with African American experience.[3] There he argued that "without the affirmation of Negro as Negro in terms of what cultural and spiritual production Negro as Negro can achieve, without the development of inner strength based on self-knowledge, developing without the tutelage from anybody, the Negro cannot begin to accept himself as a act instead of a problem" ("Alain Locke" 125). Kallen is not trying to reduce Locke or any other black merely to his racial or cultural identity, but to find an intellectual framework that can account for Locke's presence as an American that does not diminish his identity as an African American.

Two years later Kallen and Locke resumed their discussion on this issue while both were on a fellowship to Oxford, England, seemingly far away from the practices of racism that inspired their initial exchange. This time, though, their conversation was prompted by a specific act of racism committed by other Americans. Some southern Harvard Rhodes Scholars had insisted that Locke not be invited to their Thanksgiving dinner because of his color. Although "students from elsewhere in the United States outnumbered the gentlemen from Dixie," Locke was not invited (Kallen, "Alain Locke" 120). Though Kallen was outraged, Locke was, according to Kallen, philosophical. "[Locke] said, 'I am a human being,' just as I had said it earlier. What difference does the difference make? We are all alike Americans. And we had to argue out the question of how the differences made the differences, and in arguing out those questions the formulae, then phrases, developed—'cultural pluralism,' 'the right to be different'" (qtd. in Schmidt 49). Kallen remembers this conversation vividly because Locke's stubborn universalism seemed to be ill-equipped to confront the reality of the situation. Certainly, Kallen understood the appeal of Locke's argument: if universally accepted, differences in race and heritage would not matter and America would be the utopia it has so often been dreamed to be.[4] Yet even when Locke and Kallen take their argument outside of America, Kallen does not appeal to a universal humanity, a sameness that can transcend cultural and racial difference. For Kallen, such debates are always explicitly American in nature. To the

American, cultural difference is not minor, not something that becomes unimportant in the face of other shared qualities. In fact, difference is what we as Americans share, and this is the basis of our common identity.

As distressing as the stance of the "Dixie" men to Kallen and Locke is, perhaps more troubling is the willingness of the other Americans to join the sons of Dixie in their refusal to include Locke. Kallen's logic recognizes that he is implicated in this scene as an American, so he responds as an American. Consequently, he chooses the only honorable option available: he refuses to attend out of respect for Locke. Next, Kallen writes Barret Wendell, the Harvard professor from whom Kallen "got the key concepts regarding the spirit of this country," to ask that his old teacher show support for Locke (Toll 65, n. 22). Kallen tells his mentor that Locke "has a definite claim on me," but Wendell sides with those Americans who agreed with the "Dixie" contingent (Sollors, "Critique" 271). Unable to persuade either Wendell or Locke to change their views, Kallen ultimately seeks intellectual redress for this situation years later in the theory of American identity that he would identify as cultural pluralism.

At the time, Kallen could find no intellectual sustenance from either Locke or Wendell. Wendell refused Kallen's request to aid Locke on racial grounds—if I won't meet blacks at my table, then I cannot very well condemn others for doing the same, he tells Kallen. Kallen acknowledges that he has "neither respect nor liking for his race—but individually they have to be taken, each on his own merits and value, and if ever a negro was worthy, this boy is." Werner Sollors uses this scene and Kallen's letters to Wendell about it to intimate that Kallen is less interested in the tolerance of cultural difference than preserving a race-based orientation toward cultural identity, going so far as to suggest that those who follow in Kallen's tradition risk becoming "well-intentioned practitioners of Pluralism Klux Klan" ("Critique" 263). Kallen's characterization of Locke's race is certainly troubling. Almost equally disturbing is the bias implicit in his suggestion that Locke represents an exception—confirmed by his status as "a Harvard man." Kallen's comments are likely dictated by the audience he was trying to persuade: he certainly did not want to offend his professor. What is more important, though, is how Kallen's recognition of Locke's racial difference becomes the basis for his commitment to Locke's (and his own) fundamental rights as an American. Like another famous student of James's, W. E. B. Du Bois, Kallen ever felt his twoness, as Jew and as American. Kallen himself was an immigrant to this country from Silesia—his father was a rabbi—and by the time he met Locke he was trying to reconcile the conflict he experienced in being both a Jew and an American.[5] As a Jew who had experienced racism (and who was no doubt familiar with Wendell's anti-Semitism) Kallen identifies with Locke as an American whose "Americanness" is questioned because of his racial heritage.

In the case of the Oxford dinner, Kallen respects Locke's claim for a universal identity, but nonetheless wants to account for the racism of his Harvard peers, Wendell perhaps included. From the perspective that Kallen was working out, Locke's argument, admirable as it is, smacked of the ivory tower—as if Kallen wondered how can a black man, of all Americans, be making this argument to me? In the classroom—the "kingdom of culture," Du Bois called it—everyone may be equal, but what about outside the classroom? If people who call themselves "Americans" will not sit down to the table with you or hire you or allow you into their clubs because you are a Jew or a Negro, then perhaps their claims to a pure, race-free American identity are not so pure after all. Indeed, in his 1957 reminiscence of this scene, Kallen suggests that those Americans who chose not to respect Locke's difference by excluding him from their dinner were "inauthentic Americans" ("Alain Locke" 122). From Kallen's perspective, the insistence on a universal American identity that transcends racial and ethnic heritage is really only a form of whitewashing in the guise of democratic grandiloquence. Where Du Bois felt like "two souls, two thoughts, two unreconciled strivings" and "two warring ideals in one dark body" that created a kind of "double consciousness" which allowed him "no true self-consciousness," Kallen experienced and even celebrated his "double consciousness" as emblematic of everyone's American identity.[6] Kallen adapted Locke's premises to argue that difference was an experience that characterized all Americans.

Although Kallen's exchange with Locke is now rarely discussed, it predicts and in a certain sense establishes the terms of contemporary debates about American identity. In an influential essay, "What We Know That We Don't Know," Carolyn Porter basically reduces Kallen's argument to its essential components when she suggests in a widely cited essay that perhaps the term "American" is no longer a useful or even desirable one since it threatens to suppress the richness of minority and broader identities that exist within the geography of the United States.[7] In *The Disuniting of America* (1992) Arthur Schlesinger Jr., the epitome of liberal tolerance, coming on like Locke to Kallen, argues that "the cult of ethnicity has reversed the movement of American history, producing a nation of minorities" that "inculcates the illusion that membership in one or another ethnic group is the basic American experience" (112). Despite the apparent incompatibility of his and Porter's positions, they share an assumption that there is some core American identity which is incompatible with ethnic and racial difference. As I suggested above, Kallen's position avoids the sorts of arguments that ensue from this assumption by insisting that one's American identity is expressed through one's ethnic identity. Kallen has been misread, or at least misappropriated, precisely because critics have failed to recognize the importance of his insistence that cultural difference is what Americans share.

Schlesinger is right to suggest that since "America was a multiethnic country from the start," Americans have confronted an inevitable and constant question: "What is it then that, in the absence of a common ethnic origin, has held Americans together over two turbulent centuries?" (11). The familiar answer, one that undergirds most universalists' arguments, belongs to Crévecoeur. After marveling in *Letters from an American Farmer* (1782) over the many ethnic strains contained within the geography of America, Crévecoeur asks What, then, is this new man, the American? Crévecoeur was not interested in investigating what "American" means in the context of so many nationalities; rather, he was imagining the possibility of a "new man" who would embody a transcendent and unified American identity. As seductive as this formulation is, it cannot account for the persistence of ethnic and cultural differences. To say, as Schlesinger does, that immigrants came here "to forget a horrid past and that their goals were escape, deliverance, assimilation" (13) is simply wishful thinking that denies past and present history. Can anyone really believe that escaping a bad national or cultural situation is the same thing as assimilating into a new one? Schlesinger's logic does not account for slaves, for the experience of many immigrant groups at the turn of the century, for the many today who come from Mexico looking less to become Americans than to make money with which they can rebuild their homes in Mexico.[8] Arguments that look to Crévecoeur as a model duplicate his unexamined assumptions; they overlook the fact that you cannot assimilate into an American identity without changing the meaning of the "American" identity into which you assimilate.

The occasional stridency of Schlesinger's argument reflects his understandable frustration with those who would argue that "American" is an empty term, a catch-all for a nation of fundamentally separate peoples. Horace Kallen's thought can be distinguished from most multiculturalist arguments (with which it is often equated) in that he insists that you define your ethnic identity as a possibility of your American identity. Kallen would say to Schlesinger and Porter that Americans are connected neither by a single racial identity nor by a shared commitment to becoming "American," whatever that is, but by our commitment to explore as fully as possible the promises written into the Declaration of Independence and, to a lesser extent, the Constitution. This view does not imply that all Americans are equal in fact or circumstance but that our belief in the possibility of equality becomes the basis for how each of us, regardless of race or class, has the opportunity to act out what it means to be an American. The question to ask regarding American identity is not Crèvecoeur's but the one that drove Kallen's thesis: What difference does the difference make? Rather than thinking of the American as a fixed entity to which all must assimilate, this question prompts us to understand American identity as an act that leads to other acts. For Kallen, the racial and cultural diversity that so obviously mark American experience become the medium by which we are continually remaking ourselves as Americans. His value to a society that will be American only so long as it is multicultural is that he helps us to understand how people from our past have come to identify themselves as Americans in ways that have changed both them and us.

In reexamining Horace Kallen, I am not offering a defense of cultural pluralism or even an attack on universalism, nor am I discussing Kallen as a theorist of minority cultures. Other scholars have already ably staked out those issues.[9] Situating Kallen's work in relation to the thinking of his teacher and acknowledged master, William James, I examine Kallen as a pragmatist cultural theorist. Milton Konvitz has rightly suggested that "William James came to fruition in Horace Kallen" in that Kallen did not try "to build systems" but "affirmed the reality of identity and change, of continuation and mutation, of the confluence of the past and the future" (62–63). Though Kallen was sometimes prone to define ethnic identity in essentialist terms, his account of American identity as a process rather than an entity remains thoroughly pragmatist. Kallen's critics have overlooked this point; in the guise of criticizing his account of American identity, they have been objecting to his definition of ethnic or minority identity. That Kallen failed to realize certain contradictions inherent in his conclusions, though, does not discount the usefulness of his critique of American identity, nor does it undermine his recognition that our American culture is continually being transformed by our diverse ethnic heritages. If the incident involving Alain Locke at the Rhodes Scholars dinner encapsulated for Kallen a whole history of racism that no longer could be squared with American ideals, Kallen's cultural pluralism meant less to fix identity than to recognize it—as memory, not biology.

The remainder of the chapter is divided into three sections. In the first I examine how Kallen's cultural pluralism adapted the thought of William James to intervene in a cultural debate that had become staunchly racist in its expression. In so doing, my aim is to recover and reconstruct through Kallen a pragmatist lineage relevant to contemporary debates about race in American identity. In the concluding two sections, I read Kallen's ideas against the experience of two of his contemporaries who were also deeply concerned with these issues: the Jewish immigrant Mary Antin and the American emigrant, Henry James. In Antin's *The Promised Land* (1912) and James's *The American Scene* (1907), both writers answer Locke's question, What difference does the difference make?, by challenging the notion that American identity can be inherited rather than made. While Antin discovers the meaning of her Jewish identity through her ascension into the empyrean realm of the "American," James rediscovers his American identity in conflict with the alien "other."

*II*

In his 1924 review of *Culture and Democracy* for the *New York Times*, Nicholas Roosevelt responded to Kallen's assertion that America should be seen as "a federation of cultures" by charging that "Kallen proposes to Balkanize America" by "pretend[ing] that there is no American race and there are no American people" (3). Subsequent critics of Kallen have been more nuanced in their analyses, but Roosevelt's premise still informs current views of Kallen. David Hollinger says that Kallen's work is representative of "a protoseparatist extreme" (*Postethnic* 93). Recognizing that Kallen was a formidable thinker, Orlando Patterson nonetheless argues (borrowing from Milton Konvitz) that Kallen's conception of ethnic identity was basically Jewish and hence was not applicable to other groups, particularly African Americans (167). Other critics have suggested that Kallen's understanding of minority cultures was limited by its reliance on the belief that they would preserve their cultural uniqueness or authenticity. Milton Gordon argues that Kallen's conception of the ethnic group was misleading since it would lose its distinctive culture while keeping only its associational life (151–52). More sharply, Philip Gleason maintains that Kallen "shared the kind of romantic racialism represented by Anglo-Saxonism before it was absorbed into biological racism" ("American" 44). Isaac Berkson had already made this critique in 1920, and Werner Sollors entrenched it when he labeled Kallen's understanding of cultural identity as "descent"-driven.[10]

Making what amounts to a summary judgment of Kallen's thought, Walter Benn Michaels asserts that "it makes no sense . . . to see Kallen's cultural pluralism as opposed to racism" (*Our* 64). Michaels argues that Kallen's pluralistic understanding of cultural identity privileges what one inherently is over what one does. Kallen is representative of how pluralism "transforms the substitution of culture into the preservation of race" (14). To Michaels, any attempt to define identity in terms of an ethnic or cultural group assumes a racial or in any case essential identity. By Michaels's logic, though one's past, particularly if it has been defined in terms of race, is not relevant to how identity is defined. Kallen, by contrast, understood identity in terms of one's cultural history. Recognizing that the racist attitudes of some Americans had influenced the *actions* undertaken by other Americans, Kallen knew that he could not enjoy the luxury of rejecting racially oriented definitions of identity without also rejecting the notion that the past influences the present. Thus African Americans such as Locke became Americans not only by rejecting racist pasts in which others had defined them as not worthy to be known as American, but by re-creating their present identity in opposition to those past acts of definition. As Kallen observes in "Alain Locke and Cultural Pluralism," "race" or "color constitutes no problem when it is not appraised in racist terms" (125). Kallen argues that African Americans are "aware of the immemorial African past" and that their task is to "render it presently a living past." Thus "he must needs create that memory, by means of exploration and study" (124).[11] Instead of rejecting the idea of an American identity, as Michaels's argument implicitly does, Kallen's work actually helps us to understand the ways in which American identity is made by what we do as Americans.[12]

Though Kallen understood cultural differences as the crucial factor in the creation of American identity, many critics have seen them as a threat to a common American culture. In a series of books and essays stretching over nearly twenty years, David Hollinger has consistently used Kallen as a foil to argue for a perspective that is able "to *transcend the limitations* of any and all *particularisms*" (*American Province* 59, emphasis mine). As Hollinger's language suggests, critics of Kallen have seen a commitment to

ethnic identity as something to be overcome.[13] Kallen's value, however, is
that he helps us to rethink the idea that ethnic allegiances are atavistic,
leftover identities of the past that distract us from realizing an enlightened
shared identity. Kallen, no less than Michaels or Hollinger, questioned
the desirability or possibility of a transcendent American identity. His
pragmatist response was to ask instead how these "particularisms," that is
to say, specific ethnic histories, provide the context in which American
identity is created. One person's quixotic, if misguided, quest to authenticate one's identity by affiliation with an ethnically defined cultural group
would not be worthy of careful scrutiny, though, if it were not indicative of
larger cultural patterns.[14] In my reading of Kallen, distinctions between
real and symbolic ethnicity become irrelevant since what matters is how
one's chosen ethnic affiliation becomes the process by which one uses (or
invents) one's ethnicity to reorient oneself as American. Adopting this
perspective allows us to broaden the scope of his argument so that it
includes the non-European groups that he did not directly examine.

Understanding his work to provide a rationale for comprehending both
the manifest diversity of American culture and how that diversity shapes
our collective identities as Americans, Kallen transformed the thought of
William James into working cultural theory. Although many have noted
that Kallen's description of America as a "federation of republics" emerges
from James's similar language in *A Pluralistic Universe* (1909), William
Toll is nonetheless right to assert that Kallen's critics have not explored in
detail "the pragmatic revolution in philosophy out of which [Kallen's cultural pluralism] grew" (58).[15] That he was beginning to see American
identity through James's pluralistic vision can be seen as early as his first
book, *William James and Henri Bergson* (1911), where he characterizes
James's philosophy having as "its principle . . . that of direct democracy" (11). What is telling about this formulation is how Kallen understands James's thought itself to be an expression of democratic principles.
Whereas this early work reads James through certain assumptions about
democracy, Kallen's later essays on cultural pluralism interpret democratic assumptions through James. Just as James was suspicious of how
abstract principles betrayed the multitudinous and often contradictory
nature of experience, so was Kallen of how the all-encompassing term
"American" betrayed the richness of the many ethnic experiences that
made up American culture.

Kallen's critique of American identity clearly mirrors James's pragmatist theory of truth.[16] Instead of positing a truth that exists prior to experi-

ence, James argues that truths are created in the flow of experience. In *The Meaning of Truth* (1909) James mocks "the vulgar notion of correspondence" whereby "the thoughts must copy the reality" (869). Rather than finding the correct description that will line up with an already existing ideal of truth, James said that we can only invent descriptions that we later agree to be true.[17] "The truth of an idea is not a stagnant property inherent in it," runs one of James's most provocative statements. "Truth *happens* to an idea. It *becomes* true, is *made* true by events. Its verity is an event, a process" (574). For James, truth is neither absolute nor transcendent. Truth as such is really multiple: we live among competing truths. Truth is not something we inherit but something we make; it is contingent. If what we call "truth" is actually a description, then it is most likely a description that we find useful in some way. Thus not only does truth comprise contingent points of view, but those points of view become the means by which we orient ourselves in experience. Our truths make our experience even as our experience is the ground of our truth making.

James clinches his argument that truth is never stagnant with words that could not have been lost on Kallen: "There can *be* no difference anywhere that doesn't *make* a difference elsewhere" (508). According to James, to follow "the pragmatic method" meant that one "must bring out of each word its practical cash-value, set it at work within the stream of your experience. It appears less as a solution, then, than as a program for more work" (509). For James as for Kallen, we make new truths out of old truths. The truth as we create it is never either wholly new or wholly separate from previous truths. Any given truth, James said, is always an adhesive, "a go between a smoother over of transitions" (*Writings* 513). Recognizing that thoughts are also acts and that truth is transitive does not mean that we are doomed to whatever passing fancy seizes power, but that society could legitimately hope to improve itself through the best of "its own intrinsic promises and potencies" (601). Oriented toward acts rather than metaphysical essences, James's pragmatist theory of truth is concerned with the social consequences that accrue from choosing and acting on a particular definition of identity. In this respect, James's thought was ready-made to be translated by Kallen into a way of understanding the cultural consequences of the diversity of American culture.[18] James's assertion that "there can *be* no difference anywhere that doesn't *make* a difference elsewhere" became for Kallen a way of answering the question, What difference does the difference make? Just as James's pragmatist critique of truth led him to explore how we perceive truth as multiple in *A Pluralistic*

*Universe*, Kallen's pragmatist reading of American identity led him to explore how American culture allowed multiple possibilities for identity-formation. Compare James's definition of the pluralistic world with Kallen's definition of American identity. James concludes:

> The pluralistic world is more like a federal republic than like an empire or a kingdom. However much may be collected, however much may report itself as present at any effective centre of consciousness or action, something else is self-governed and absent and unreduced to unity. (*Writings* 776)

Now Kallen:

> [The United States's] form would be that of the federal republic; its substance a democracy of nationalities, cooperating voluntarily and autonomously through common institutions in the enterprise of self-realization through the perfection of men according to their kind. . . . The political and economic life of the commonwealth is a single unit and serves as the foundation and background for the realization of the distinctive individuality of each *natio* that composes it and of the pooling of these in a harmony above them all. (*Culture* 124)

In his earlier work on James, Kallen had argued that James's main message is that "the 'total,' always exceeding itself from moment to moment, is not a whole, but an aggregate of eaches, each with a vote that it casts primarily for itself, each involving novelties, chances, mutations, and discreteness as well as necessities and continuities and uniformities" (*William James* 11, 28). Here Kallen interprets American identity in terms of James's frequent observation that the "whole" of experience could never be equal to its parts. Our manifest diversity makes it impossible to see America as a cultural whole; "we" are Americans by law, yes, but as Americans we are also something else—in James's language, a variety of "ands" and "ifs" and "buts" and "bys." Where James argued against assertions of dogmatic "monism," Kallen deplored the then-prevalent notion that all potential Americans, or more specifically immigrants, had to undergo a process of assimilation or "Americanization." Where James celebrated "finite multifariousness," Kallen celebrated a democracy which embraced the "the perfection and conservation of differences" in the form of each "*natio*."[19]

Kallen called his cultural pluralism a "psychology of the American peoples." James's key psychological insight in *The Principles of Psychology* was that "whatever things are thought in relation are thought from the outset in a unity, in a single pulse of subjectivity" (268). In other words, even a single thought—and one may question whether in the Jamesian universe there is such a thing as a single thought—contained a multitude of interacting possibilities. James could never divide a whole into parts without imagining the commingling of those parts. He insisted that "no part absolutely excludes another, but that they copenetrate and are cohesive; that if you tear one out, the roots bring more with them; that whatever is real is telescoped and diffused into other realms; in short, every minutest thing is already its hegelian 'own other,' in the fullest sense of the term" (754–55). From a Jamesian perspective, the problematic phrase in Kallen's formulation is "the perfection and conservation of differences." Kallen dismantled the whole to separate its constituent parts. By Kallen's logic, ethnic identity was the "something else [that] is self-governed and absent and unreduced to unity" that James spoke of. James, however, either would have prompted Kallen to reconfigure his definition of ethnic identity in light of its conflicting parts or enjoin him to "dive into the flux" where issues of unity no longer matter. Thus, Ross Posnock notes, "in using James's thought to sanction multiple, discrete ethnic groups, Kallen stayed within the identity logic that James had repudiated" (*Color* 24).[20] On the other hand, James, for all of his insistence that thoughts are also acts, was responding only to the history of the mind; Kallen, by contrast, was formulating his thought in response to specific historical and cultural attitudes.

To understand how and perhaps why Kallen falls short of realizing the full implications of James's thought, we need to revisit the cultural context in which he was writing. His essay "Democracy and the Melting Pot" first appeared in 1915. The book in which the essay appeared, *Culture and Democracy in the United States*, was published in 1924, the year which saw the passage of the final anti-immigration law that put an end to the most intensive period of immigration in American history. The passage of this law climaxed a period of hysteria and fear of the foreigner-alien which began with the 1886 Chicago Haymarket riot and reached its peak during World War I. As immigrants, particularly immigrants from eastern Europe, seemed to take over the eastern seaboard cities, assimilation became less a comfortable assumption than a cultural threat.[21] Americans were even willing to restrain civil liberties to allay their fears of foreigners, particularly German Americans.[22] Among those who had occupied American soil for three generations or more there was a cry for "Americanization," and this cry betrayed the fear that there were some prospective Americans—chiefly southern Europeans—who lacked the cultural chemistry to be properly melted. For perhaps the first time in our nation's history (blacks were up until that time not thought of as being assimilable material), a notion of a hyphenated American identity became public currency—and nightmare. Woodrow Wilson declared that "any man who carries a hyphen about him carries a dagger that he is ready to plunge into the vitals of this nation" (qted. in Vaughan 448).

In his landmark study of American nativism, *Strangers in the Land* (1955), John Higham notes that traditionally "Americans [have] fashioned an image of themselves as an inclusive nationality, at once diverse and homogenous, ever improving as it assimilated more types of men into a unified, superior people" (21). Arthur Mann has argued that this inclusive nationality began when the founders turned their backs on their own ethnic identities. To become, literally and figuratively, the *new* men their principles promised, the American revolutionaries severed the emotional bonds that tied them to England. Mann notes that "they broke the century-and-a-half old hyphen in the Anglo-American duality, thereby releasing the force of American nationalism" (57).[23] Gradually, as Higham and Gleason and others have shown, our abstract American identity did discover its material host: the bodies and brains of Anglo-Saxons.[24] This discovery led to two related movements—Americanization and Anglo-Saxonism. The Americanization movement emphasized the need for cultural assimilation. Sharing republican ideals was not enough to be an American; one had to adapt to "American" manners, morals, language, and religion—whatever those may be. This fairly mild form of nativism gave way to the more extreme Anglo-Saxonism. Gleason observes that by the first quarter of this century "a commitment to liberty and republicanism was no longer regarded merely as the political heritage of the Anglo-Saxons, but as their native genius ("American" 41).[25] It became increasingly difficult to tell where one movement left off and the other began; out of this context arose virulently nativist works such as Madison Grant's *The Passing of the Great Race* (1916), "100% Americanism," and Wilson's ominous remark.

The suppression of difference in the guise of protecting American political liberty became the determining motive in defining what the American was at the very moment that "American" could no longer be confidently defined.[26] The German Jewish immigrant intellectual Ludwig Lewisohn described the atmosphere of "Americanization" as the "unbreakable instinct of intolerance" which denied "all qualitative distinctions—even in themselves" (164). "We are submerged beneath a conquest so complete that the very name of us means something not ourselves," wrote Barrett Wendell to his former student in a letter that Kallen would later include in the text of *Culture and Democracy in the United States*. Wendell's letter perfectly captures the logic of the Americanization movement: it defines the Truly American in terms of what it is not. To be foreign-born is not to be American; to be American is never to be able to accommodate the culture of the foreign-born. In this context, Kallen's cultural pluralism could be read as an attempt to convince both Alain Locke and Barret Wendell that the American scene could use a little more color. Pointing to the incontrovertible presence of so many nationalities other than "American," Kallen turned Wendell's chauvinistic Americanist argument on its head. If others were going to define the Truly American by what it was not, then he would show how that negative definition also canceled out any American identity that was not purely theoretical. Thus Kallen's cultural pluralism sought to imbue the idea of American identity with a saving notion of difference, even—especially—if that meant making "100% Americans" choke on the meaning of their identity. Exploring what happened when American identity was understood as something that was made rather than posited, Kallen made his antagonists into what they claimed not to be: partial Americans.[27]

Kallen notes that for the "essential American" or the "typical American," "whoever failed to acknowledge and conform to this type was somehow alien, a different order of being, not admissible to the benefits of democracy, and fit at best to be a hewer of wood and a drawer of water to the true American" (*Culture* 127). Ironically, for the "typical" American, the need for more hewers of wood, or more precisely, industrial laborers, was what brought so many immigrants to America. Kallen's seeing the immigrant alien as servant to the American ideal is more than bitter irony. As he observes throughout *Culture and Democracy in the United States*, the rise of immigration went hand in hand with the rise of industrial capitalism; thus the proliferation of immigrant cultures that turn-of-the-century America experienced was in effect sanctioned by the American's most sacred right, the right to make a buck. Kallen writes that "for the sake of wealth and power ['typical' Americans] drew the peoples of Europe and Asia to these shores" (17). The large manufacturers who owned the factories profited from the immigrants' labor; the immigrants, frequently from European villages that did not allow them a sense of national identity, were given the opportunity to seize for themselves a place more secure and promising than what they would have had in Europe. Both parties, immigrant and manufacturer, alien and "American," were dedicated to what Tocqueville called the doctrine of self-interest rightly understood, or that combination of Lockean self-interest and Horatio Alger greed which in a very real sense unites all Americans.[28] In pursuing his self-interest by coming to this country, the immigrant was just as "typically" American as his putatively native employer.

Whatever differences that existed between the "pure" and the "impure" American were ones of culture rather than ideology. As Kallen suggests, "the 'Anglo-Saxon' American, constituting as he does, the economic upper class, would hardly have reacted to economic disparity as he has, if that had been the only disparity. In point of fact *it is the ethnic disparity*, which has reenforced the economic, that troubles him" (89, emphasis mine). Not only is Kallen saying that the conflict over the definition of American identity is cultural rather than political, but that in American society (and history) cultural difference may be more significant than ideological, class, and even economic difference (especially given that economic conflicts are often the legacy of racial ones). In this respect Kallen anticipates the crucial but regrettably overlooked argument of Louis Hartz in *The Liberal Tradition* (1955). Hartz helps us to understand why Kallen was right to suggest that our American cultural conflicts stem in part from our lack of genuine ideological conflict. Usually grouped with the consensus historians of the 1950s who championed the exceptionalist view of American history with its emphasis on the continuity and originality of the American character, Hartz actually was the most astute critic of the sort of American exceptionalism that Kallen seems to embrace.[29] At the same time that Daniel Boorstin was celebrating America's rejection of the European political tradition, Hartz was relentlessly attacking the monotony of a political tradition that risked "not the danger of the majority, . . . but the danger of unanimity" (11).[30]

To demonstrate his thesis, Hartz, like Kallen, emphasizes Tocqueville's "storybook truth" about American history, that Americans were "born equal" (3). Our sense of equality derives from what Hartz calls the American interpretation of John Locke and "the master assumption of American political thought: the reality of atomistic social freedom" (62). Contrasting the European interpretation of Locke with the American one, Hartz notes that for European thinkers Locke's thesis that man is a free being existing in a state of nature justified the necessity of having a strong state.

By this logic, absolutist forms of government were a better choice than allowing the social chaos that an unleashed peasant class would bring. In the American version, however, the breakdown of the authority of social institutions, be they class- or government-oriented, was never seen as threatening; indeed, any such breakdown mirrored America's "state of nature." As a result, the American version of Locke stressed the need to limit government.[31] The irony, Hartz observes, was that the American conception of Locke had so thoroughly absorbed the idea of an atomistic social freedom that there was hardly a need to limit the power of government. Hartz drily suggests that the complicated series of checks and balances formulated in the Constitution, meant to keep the nation united, could only work in a nation that was already united.[32] Concerning the landmark document of American politics, Hartz remarks with characteristic wit: "The Founding Fathers devised a scheme to deal with conflict that can only survive in a land of solidarity. The truth is, their conclusions were 'right' only because their premises were wrong" (86).

Hartz's achievement was to reveal the impossibility of getting outside the liberal tradition. He reveals why in America communitarian-oriented political movements generally fail unless they can link their rhetoric to the appeal of Lockean individualism. From a Hartzian perspective, the success of the Civil Rights movement, for instance, is due less to its communitarian ideals than to Martin Luther King's ability to adapt the Lockean rhetoric of Jefferson (life, liberty, and the pursuit of happiness) to his cause.[33] That this cause was an African American one is almost incidental, since George Wallace could also claim that he was protecting the individual rights of his constituency (as Barret Wendell defended the right to exclude Locke from a gathering of Harvard men). By Hartz's logic, there is no ideological difference between King and Wallace, which is why he argues that whatever the Civil War was, it was not an ideological conflict. Writing during the peak of the McCarthy terror, Hartz saw at the end of the American liberal tradition another Tocquevillean conclusion: the tyranny of the majority. Ironically, Hartz felt trapped within the pattern he so brilliantly traced; he could only look longingly to Europe for genuine political traditions that by his own argument could not flourish here.

Looking for ideological difference and finding only monotony, Hartz closed his study with a question that slightly reworded might also have been asked by Horace Kallen. The dominance of the liberal tradition, he concluded, "raises the question of whether a nation can compensate for the uniformity of its domestic life by contact with alien cultures outside it" (14). Hartz's answer was bleak. He saw no way out of the logic of American liberalism except through a kind of willed "transcendence"—but what this transcendence might be he could not specify. Kallen, however, offers Hartz a way out, though it requires using the assumptions of Hartz's argument to explore different possibilities. Regarding King's quarrel with America, though, Kallen would point out that there is a quite obvious way of identifying the differences between King and Wallace: race. I do not mean that Wallace is white and King is black, but that their attitudes toward race and racial heritage necessitated different understandings of who should be included within the American liberal tradition. Hartz might respond that since King and Wallace share the same ideological assumptions, King has no perspective from which to unseat his antagonist. Kallen, however, would counter that the promises of the liberal tradition, however co-optable, must also be seen as *opportunities to be realized.* Like King, Kallen sees the liberal tradition as providing the only possible means for protesting those systems of belief that exclude his cultural point of view. At the deepest level, Hartz and Kallen have the same fear: the potential for a crushing conformity, the erasure of a saving difference that William James so admired and without which the impulses of "typical Americanism" are prone to run rampant. Reformulating Hartz's question in terms of Kallen's argument enables us to examine how our "alien cultures" within have by their very existence created an American identity that moves forward by being in conflict with itself.

By implicating the "typical" American with the loathsome alien, Kallen sounded the keynote of his pluralism: the ontological instability—in the cultural if not the ideological sense—of the term "American." Politically stable, America was nonetheless culturally volatile. That the "typical" American could not distinguish his political ideology from that of the newly arrived alien was certainly ironic. However, that irony had unpredictable consequences which meant that the same country that could be united by an unwavering commitment to the pursuit of self-interest could also be fragmented by the variety of cultural traditions which gathered around this shared political ideal. Even if "typical" Americans had the power both to bring the immigrant over with the lure of their factories and cities and to curtail the immigrant's tide once those factories had done their work, they did not have the power to control the enormous cultural changes brought on by the flood of immigrants: "['Typical' Americans] got wealth and power. They made America great. But their instrumentalities and their ends had each their by-products, by-products of social and intellectual life, by-products of *culture*" (*Culture* 17, emphasis mine).

Kallen shrewdly emphasizes the cataclysmic effect that immigrants had on American culture by noting that it was only as the fear of the alien increased that "typical" Americans felt constrained to define what was typically American. Kallen makes the point with a rhetorical question his audience probably would rather not have answered: "More and more emphasis has been placed on the unity of English and American stock. . . . If this is not ethnic nationality returned to consciousness, what is it?" (99). By suggesting that the onus of defining the American is as much a concern for the "typical" American as it is for the immigrant, Kallen demonstrates that in the realm of culture *there was no single standard of American identity to apply.* Every American was potentially alien, at the very least ethnic, and invariably hyphenated. Even "typical" Americans were "multicultural." Following the pragmatist imperative to view truth as a process-in-the-making, Kallen emphasized just how provisional American identity is. Just as Kallen's teacher, William James, observed that "truth *happens* to an idea" (*Writings* 574), so did Kallen insist that to be an "American" is to acquire an identity, not to inherit one.

James saw truth as additive and, in principle, Kallen's use of James should have caused him to see American ethnic identity in the same way. To a certain extent, James's notion of truth as additive or go-between can be aligned itself with Kallen's hyphenization of American character. Kallen's hyphen is the bridge which connects your past self to your American one. By James's logic, however, the truth that one discovers both becomes a part of and transforms all previous truths. Applying James's thinking to Kallen's hyphen means that one cannot reclaim one's connection with one's grandfather without transforming that prior identity into something else. Thus when Kallen argues that in the realm of culture the American will discover that his " 'inalienable liberty' is ancestrally determined" and that the "political autonomy" of the American is in "the spiritual autonomy of his group," his language contradicts his Jamesian orientation (*Culture* 123, 117). Kallen's understanding of identity is at times frustratingly static: he famously observed that citizens can change everything from their clothes to their religions, but "they cannot change their grandfathers" (122). John Dewey offered Kallen this Jamesian reading of cultural pluralism: "The typical American is himself a hyphenated character. This does not mean that he is part American and that some foreign ingredient is added. . . . The point is to see that the hyphen connects instead of separates" (qted. in Kallen, *Culture* 131–32). If Kallen's early and most famous articulation of these issues did emphasize that part of the hyphenation which precedes the term "American," in subsequent years he was able to agree with Dewey and assert that "the hyphen unites very much more than it separates" (qted. in Konvitz 67).

Granting that Kallen was initially too strong in asserting that every American would realize himself through his ethnic heritage (for it surely is an American possibility to ignore one's ancestors), then the cosmopolitan-universalist perspective risks going too far by denying the logic that enables one to invent his other identity in response to one's ancestry. One may argue, as Higham does, that Kallen's cultural pluralism represented his effort to halt the sway of American life—to preserve an ethnic heritage that was already being transformed into something else. One can just as easily claim, however, that Kallen's cultural pluralism is the attempt to find a "home" in a society dedicated to transformation for its own sake. This need is especially imperative in a culture that promises social and political equality while contradicting those promises through its racism. Perhaps Kallen pressed his grandfather argument too hard because he was trying to come to terms with what he saw as the cultural consequences of our ideological sameness—our abstract identities as Americans. Kallen recognized how strangely distinct American culture can be from American politics. Our shared commitment to an ideology of equality means that our cultural gestures, even when made in the name of politics, can assume meanings independent of political processes. It is not that politics and culture do not affect each other. Martin Luther King's march on Washington was certainly a political act. Nonetheless, given that our political rights were set into place shortly after the American Revolution, we have had little to do politically but sort out the consequences of these principles. Of course our interpretations of the principles have mattered and have taken form in our amendments and, most spectacularly, in our Civil War. Extending political liberty to include those previously passed over does not insure cultural acceptance, just as political repression does not prevent the politically marginalized from exerting an influence on the creation of American culture. Kallen recognized that even if immigrants were denied by law or custom certain inalienable rights (such as the right to live in whichever part of city one wanted), what could not be legislated was their cultural impact. Simply by being here, immigrants would seek self-definition. If the "typical" American culture could not accommodate them, then they would go on inventing themselves anyway.[34]

Kallen's assertion that "whatever else [the immigrant] changes, he cannot change his grandfather" has, as I have said, often been read as a kind of cultural determinism: one cannot escape one's racial ancestry. Understanding Kallen's attitude toward the constitution of cultural identity as a philosophical consequence of James's theory of truth, however, demands that Kallen be read in a fuller context. Kallen's remark comes from a longer and rarely cited passage in which he says, "The America he comes to, beside Europe, is Nature virgin and inviolate: it does not guide him with ancestral blazings: externally he is cut off from the past. Not so internally: whatever else he changes, he cannot change his grandfather" (*Culture* 94). Kallen's point is not merely that one cannot escape one's ancestral heritage; rather, he is emphasizing that in this new landscape Americans must create a history relevant to their situations *as Americans*. He underscores both the potential emptiness of American identity and the opportunity for cultural improvisation this emptiness allows. Virtually in a single moment one can become an abstract American—one need only accept the Declaration of Independence and the Constitution. But, as Kallen suggests, this acceptance does not abolish one's past. The very fact that these words have not always included all people living within American boundaries compels many to seek ways to make their past part of the American present.

Writing in response to Kallen, Randolph Bourne emphasized that the immigrant who comes to America finds no true native American culture. Bourne notes that the original settlers "did not come to be assimilated in an American melting-pot." It is more accurate to say that "they brought over *bodily* the old ways to which they had become accustomed" (*War* 109, emphasis mine). The remark is striking because, perhaps unintentionally, it reminds us that cultural identity inheres in a body. Negative reactions to immigrants were also reactions to the physical person of the immigrant: skin color, facial features, hair, and so on. The language of the body as much as the language of the tongue is the bearer of cultural identity. The negative reactions of "typical" Americans toward these so-called alien cultures could not repress the cultural impact that was a physical reality in the clothes, the food, the music, the language, and the very person of these immigrants. Ironically, this was the argument that Kallen was trying to get across to Alain Locke in the conversation with which I began this chapter. Whereas Locke wanted to transcend the racism that prevented him from being seen as just another American, Kallen knew that racism, if not its practice then its history, had to be a part of his cultural pluralist equation. "How does it feel to be a problem?" was the question with which Du Bois memorably summed up the status of the African American in American culture at the turn of the century (*Souls* 7). Kallen of course was never "the problem" that Du Bois or Locke were, but he did feel keenly the inadequacy of this question. Kallen knew—as Du Bois did—that "the problem" was not really Du Bois or Locke: it was America itself. Kallen understood that equality was a promise that included every body—black, white, or foreign—that inhabited this country. As "equality" became a word that anyone could claim, more Americans would insist that their denied heritages must be accepted as integral to the American story. Retrospectively, slaves can become Americans and Galicia a precursor to New York's Lower East Side. Here, then, is the hard truth behind Kallen's grandfather aphorism: even as we work to eliminate race from our thinking, it continues as a kind of forgotten bank account, on which any subsequent American, using whatever ethnic history available, can draw to define himself or herself and, potentially, redefine the rest of us who are committed to his or her self-realization. Kallen knew that "difference" could not be an inalienable right in and of itself without Locke's ideal that "we are alike all Americans," but he amended Locke to argue that the recognition of difference is what binds us together as Americans.[35] As Locke forced Kallen to re-Americanize himself, so did Kallen try to re-Americanize the "typical" American.

Michael Walzer, who, along with Milton R. Konvitz, is Kallen's most sympathetic critic, notes that by Kallen's logic merely to be American is in some sense to be anonymous. "America is a word," Kallen writes, and "as a historic fact, or as a democratic ideal of life, it is not realized at all" (*Culture* 95). Consequently, "American is an adjective of similarity applied to English, Welsh, Scotch, Irish, Jews, Germans, Italians, Poles and so on" (92). Walzer further points out that "the hyphen works, when it is working, more like a 'plus sign'" ("What" 611). If the hyphen is a plus sign, to what entity is one's ethnic identity being added? Must those Americans who claim no ethnic affiliation be called "American-Americans"? What happens when we drain the argument of the "British-Americans," as Kallen calls them, of its racism? What if, instead of saying that Americans are Anglo-Saxon in origin and everyone else better adapt to this culture, Americans called themselves the inheritors of the British political system and asserted that those who come to America will invent themselves according to this shared but acquired tradition? From Kallen's pragmatist perspective—one that we will see also in Emerson and Ellison—equality is not a thing, an abstract quality to be prized and possessed, but a process that is realized only in particular situations and only through the expression of difference. Without a plurality of different, and even conflicting, identity choices, the exploration of equality is meaningless. Thus we will not always be sure of who we are as Americans since inherent in our commitment to equality is the recognition that to be American is also to be in the process of becoming American.

James said that "for pluralistic pragmatism, truth grows up inside of all the finite experiences. They lean on each other, but the whole of them, if such a whole there be, leans on nothing. All 'homes' are in finite experience; finite experience as such is homeless. Nothing outside the flux secures the issue of it. It can hope salvation only from its own intrinsic promises and potencies" (*Writings* 601). For the pragmatist, the intrinsic promises and potencies of American life come to fruition in its capacity to unsettle. No one's American identity is stable—even, perhaps especially, in a postethnic America. As Walzer suggests, "America is still a radically unfinished society, and for now, at least, it makes sense to say that this unfinishedness is one of its distinctive features" (*What* 48). In other words, American identity properly understood involves a kind of metaphorical homelessness. Kallen, too, described the homelessness of American experience, and his argument helps us to understand the extraordinary pull that ethnic pasts have on our American present. Building your ethnic identity is a way of making a home in our multicultural America. These multiple (and multicultural) homes, however symbolic, mark the most likely roads Americans may use in their shared effort to create a place of rest and communal belonging. Understanding why so many Americans are compelled to redefine their American identity in light of a prior ethnic heritage is only half the story, though. What of those Americans who feel displaced by the redefinitions of American identity that Kallen offered or that multiculturalists offer today? Or what of those who want to trade their ethnic heritages in for a less particularized identity? These questions are crucial because if we accept census predictions that show a vastly transformed composite America by 2050, then they will be faced by every American, regardless of his or her prior American identity.

In the next sections I explore these questions by turning to Mary Antin and Henry James. In *The Promised Land* (1912) Antin writes from the perspective of a Jewish immigrant who seems to embrace her identity as an American because it allows her to transcend her history as a Jew. In *The American Scene* (1907) Henry James speaks as one of Kallen's "typical" Americans to say that he has seen the aliens and they are us. Though each writer shares Kallen's sense that American identity is a process of transformation, neither succumbs to Kallen's need to posit an essential cultural identity. To the question what difference does the difference make, Antin and James can only respond with another question: When considering American identity, which is not the alien?

*III*

Mary Antin's *The Promised Land* addressed the same audience and issues that Kallen did three years later with "Democracy Versus the Melting Pot." The year before her book was published the Dillingham Commission recommended that immigration be restricted. This recommendation would not achieve its full momentum until the 1924 Johnson-Reed act; Antin, however, wanted to prove to suspicious "typical" Americans that immigration was good for America.[36] Judging by the reviews her book received, if not subsequent acts of Congress, she succeeded. The *Bookman* said that her work "will do much to dissolve the gentle cynicism we take toward our so-called democracy," providing "encouragement as to our inherent possibilities" (419). The *New York Times* reviewer was grateful for an articulate view from the Old World. Though some later critics seemed to echo these reviewers, many viewed her story with more suspicion. Antin came to be understood not as a plucky immigrant who overcomes all obstacles to become a free American but as a Jew who had to sacrifice her cultural heritage in order to be accepted as an American.[37] Curiously, it was Horace Kallen who was perhaps the first critic—certainly the first critic who also conceived himself as a protector of ethnic perspectives—to castigate Antin for the ease and ardor with which she made herself into an American. Antin is mentioned by name three times in Kallen's *Culture and Democracy*, each time in a way that condescends to her defiantly optimistic "Americanization." Despite the fact that both were Jews thinking through questions of American identity in response to changing immigration laws, he saw her as a perverse instance of the Americanization movement he critiqued—worse that "typical" Americans because as a Jew who had experienced discrimination firsthand she should know better than to pretend to be one with "typical" Americans.[38] Kallen describes *The Promised Land* "as the climax of the wave of gratulatory exhibition," the work of a "successful and happy" product of "the melting pot" who is more "self-consciously flatteringly American than the Americans" (155, 22, 86). Nonetheless, Antin often echoes Kallen. Not only does she base much of her work on a reading of the Declaration of Independence similar to Kallen's, but her language at times seems to anticipate Kallen's own: "We are the strands of the cable that binds the Old World to the New," Antin proclaimed; had she said "hyphen" instead of "cable," her affinity with Kallen could not have been more pronounced (Antin, *Promised* xxi). Because Antin's story implied that abandoning her Jewish identity was the happy result of her becoming an American, however, Kallen thought she catered to the very audience he meant to unsettle.[39]

Antin's story is much more complicated than Kallen's formulation suggests. Indeed its lesson, no less than Kallen's cultural pluralism, is that she can be neither American nor Jewish without being both American and Jewish. Randolph Bourne recognized the complexity of Antin's story and used her as the jumping-off point for his 1916 response to Kallen, "Trans-National America."[40] Bourne suggests that Antin does not merely adapt herself to America but absorbs America within her story. Such a claim may appear to reinscribe the very celebration of "Americanization" that Kallen attacked and subsequent commentators have lamented. Yet in trying to position her assimilated audience so that they would identify with her story, Mary Antin challenges what "assimilation" is conventionally understood to mean. To participate in Antin's alleged triumph of assimilation, her audience is made to identify with one she calls a "curly-headed little Jew" (*Promised* 238).[41] Indeed, to the mixed dismay and approval of her audience, Antin wanted to convey not merely that "she" was one of "you" but that "you" were also one with "her."

Antin signals the complexity of her Americanization in her Introduction, where she announces that her story is nothing so much as a narrative of discarded selves:

> I was born, I have lived, and I have been made over. Is it not time to write my life's story? I am just as much out of the way as if I were dead, for I am absolutely other than the person whose story I have to tell. [I] could speak in the third person and not feel that I was masquerading . . . for she, and not I, is my real heroine. My life I still have to live; her life ended when mine began. (*Promised* xix)

At first glance Antin seems merely to be alerting the reader that her story will explain the protagonist's transformation into the person who writes the narrative they are reading. By this view, the story this later person tells of her "third person" would actually be a justification of the third person's extinction and subsequent rebirth as fully "Americanized" American. Antin's narrative is driven by her recognition of her own "otherness" and by the discrepancy that exists between the self of the story and the self that tells it. In this way, Antin is both writer and reader of her own story. Though her story may indeed become a kind of justification for the self who writes the story, she does not insist upon this interpretation. Rather, she invites the reader, who is also herself, to marvel at how this "other" creature is also somehow affiliated with the author. Only one paragraph into her story and Antin has managed at once to cancel and to preserve this "as if" dead person. She creates the distance between her authorial self and her third-person self, between her Americanization and her prior "otherness," only so that she may collapse it. Antin's story of her Americanization is also the dramatization of her own otherness.[42]

Antin structures her autobiography so that its first half is concerned exclusively with her "as if" other, the little girl who grew up in a Polish village called Polotzk located in the outer Russian territories. Also known as "the Pale," this area defined the boundary of where Jews were allowed to live in Czarist Russia. During the time that little Mashke, as she was known then, lived there (1881–91), nearly 94 percent of the Jews in Russia were quartered there (Howe, *World* 7). Identity in Polotzk was rigid. As Antin says over and over, "one was a Jew, leading a righteous life; or one was a Gentile, existing to harass the Jews, while making a living off Jewish enterprise" (122). At once a Jew confined to the Pale and a woman constrained by the patriarchal Jewish law, Antin had an identity defined only in terms of race and gender. Whereas male Jews at least had the opportunity to transform the Czar's regulation of their bodies into a joyous expression of religious spirit, Antin had no such opportunity. In such an environment even a headstrong Mashke who chafed against the strictures imposed by the Jewish law could do nothing but think of herself as a Jew. Antin therefore occupied a sort of double identity, each one a form of repression to Mashke who knew in her heart that "a greater life . . . dawned in me" (87). "Can this be I?" Antin asks at the outset of her story (79). In her existence as a Russian Jew, this question intimates the bewilderment with which her inner being confronts the facts of her outer life; as an American, it reflects her ability to refashion the seemingly immutable principles of race and gender into an identity that embraces the self's capacity to be transformed.

Ultimately, the contrast between her experience in America and her life in the Pale enabled Antin to recognize and express the nearly buried inner conflicts she experienced in Polotzk. My present point, however, is that even while in Polotzk she futilely sought a means to reconcile this conflict. Were she an American-born child she could simply deny her parents, their heritage, and run away from home. Granted, as novels as diverse as Dreiser's *Sister Carrie* (1901) and Anzia Yezierska's *The Bread Winners* (1925) have indicated, this would not have been an easy task. But to make this break from within the Pale would have required her transgression of the most sacred (even in a secular sense) cultural boundary there was: she would have to become Gentile. Such an escape would have been impossible anyway since even outside the Pale she would still be identified as a Jew and either would have been returned to the Pale or killed. No wonder she writes, "By the time I fully understood that I was a prisoner, the shackles had grown familiar to my flesh" (5).

These thoughts are not available to the young Mashke, but they certainly frame the perspective of the Mary who is telling Mashke's story. These two seemingly distinct Antins, Mashke and Mary, become one in their mutual need for outward recognition. Reaching out to her American audience, Antin knows that unless she finds a material host for her spiritual rebellion, her self-fashioning will have to remain entirely hidden. Indeed, without an audience her self-fashioning will remain hidden even to herself. As Antin presents the story, the sense of personal transcendence that Mashke experiences could only be satisfied through Mary's American identity. Understanding this point helps us to appreciate fully Antin's admittedly boisterous tribute to her Americanization. More perhaps than even Benjamin Franklin in his *Autobiography*, the idea and reality of America provides Antin with the opportunity to create not only her present identity but her past one as well.

As I suggested earlier, Antin's work was written against the rising tide of anti-alien fear that was overwhelming the nation and that prompted the passage of several anti-immigration laws. Yet as hard as she tries to impress upon her readers that she is a Jew who is also an American, she acknowledges that "it is doubtful that the conversion of the Jew to any alien belief is ever thoroughly accomplished" (249). Antin is not talking simply about religion but also culture. Hence she distinguishes between the "kernel" and the "husk" of Judaism and suggests that it is possible to drop the kernel and retain the husk (244). Antin comes to America as a Jew who has gratefully dropped her husk but retained the kernel, admittedly a peculiarly free-floating one. Her hero, Emerson, probably best expresses the consequences of her "new" identity, which is not so much new as it is in continual transformation. In "The Oversoul," he writes that "the soul looketh steadily forwards, creating a world before her, leaving worlds behind her" (*Essays* 338). Crossing the boundaries of transformed identities, she lands in America to discover Kallen's truth that in her self's expansion she could suddenly shape her Jewish identity to an extent never before allowed to her. She remains Jewish, but the meaning of her Jewishness has become transformed.

I suspect that it is this unapologetic Antin who provokes the resentment of those critics, including—ironically—Kallen, who think that she somehow sold out her cultural identity. The other side to this criticism is, of course, to ask what else was Antin supposed to do? Would readers be happier with a bloodied and bowed Antin whose story traced only the jagged edges of her loss? Perhaps the more difficult question is what was there either in her Judaism or her history for her to sell out? If it was the world of the *shtetl*, then some readers would have Antin silent; if not the *shtetl*, then the only voice available to the immigrant would be Jeremiah's, that of lamentation. Kallen of course predicted these responses but in truth Antin was—in Kallen's words—an unintended by-product of his thesis. Instead of arguing for a pure cultural identity, Antin revealed how malleable identity—even ethnic identity—is. In this respect, she exemplifed that part of William James's thinking that Kallen neglected: the desire to abolish the logic that requires identity be understood as a fixed entity. At the same time, Antin's example reinforces Kallen's argument to Locke that exploring the meaning of cultural differences was the logical consequence of our situation as Americans. Like Kallen, Antin recognizes that the very existence of immigrants like her transformed the identity of those whom she had joined. More subtly than Kallen, though, Antin invites her audience to accept her story and therefore partake of this recognition. Insofar as the audience accepts the American claims of this irreducibly Jewish woman, the American identity of both Antin and her audience has been complicated and altered.

At the very least, Antin forces the "typical" Americans to distinguish where their American identity differs from hers. In other words, Antin knows as well as Kallen that she can only be rejected on account of her physical person, since certainly her words and their reliance on the Declaration of Independence can only reinforce familiar American pieties. But of course the issue is not just repeating the words but recognizing that these words entail certain consequences, one of which is the arrival of the former Mashke, with all her dreams and memories, on these shores. Recognizing that defining herself as an American is itself an act that will require re-actions, Antin implies that her audience must likewise question the nature of their own established but nonetheless ceaselessly changing identity as Americans. Noting how "the public school" has "made us [foreigners] into good Americans," Antin identifies explicitly the demands that her narrative makes of its "American" readers.

> You should be glad to hear of [my becoming a good American], you born Americans; for it is the story of the growth of your country; of the flocking of your brothers and sister from the far ends of the earth to the flag you love; of the recruiting of your armies of workers, thinkers, and leaders . . . a rehearsal of your own experience.
>
> How long would you say, wise reader, it takes to make an American? (222)

Antin here addresses directly the audience whom she elsewhere figures as her jury. She posits, again, her fundamental situation of "otherness": the immigrant who is no longer a foreigner but not yet an American, betwixt and between. Her audience, born Americans, are secure in their position. Yet, in posing the situation in the form of a question, Antin tries to undermine the audience's presumption to security by implying that they participate in the process that is her transformation. She never directly answers her question, though it is the topic sentence for her next paragraph. Instead, the question hovers over her narrative, unintegrated and unsettling. How long *does* it take to make an American?

This question provides the frame for understanding the story she tells of the immigrant child who falls in love with Parson Weems's George Washington. The devotion she could never offer a rabbi she lavishes on Washington.[43] "Never had I prayed, never had I chanted the songs of David, never had I called upon the Most Holy, in such utter reverence and worship as I repeated the simple sentences of my child's story of the patriot" (223). To commemorate her devotion to Washington she writes a poem which the teacher reads before the awestruck class. As inspired as Mary is by Washington, she admits her fear that even if she never told a lie she still could "not compare myself to George Washington" (224). Antin locates her inferiority in her sense that she can never match Washington's bravery or political office. The self-revision this thought induces breeds another, more revolutionary one: no matter her shortcomings, she and he were "Fellow Citizens" (224). Using the Declaration of Independence to justify her ability to define George Washington as an ancestor to her Russian Jewish self, Antin suggests the power that accrues to her upon realizing that she can employ the phrase "*my country*" and feel it, as one *felt* "God" or "myself" (225).[44] This poem that so moves her classmates is eventually published in the Boston newspaper. Antin's published piece of writing anticipates and mirrors the autobiography she now writes, through which she enacts the process by which she becomes American.

Antin's appropriation of an American identity is not complete until the class hears her poem, just as her autobiography has not completed its work without her larger audience's approbation. She writes, "I must tell them what George Washington had done for their country—for *our* country—for me" (230). Reading her poem aloud, she has this opportunity. She confides that "there ran a special note through my poem—a thought that only (the Jewish) Israel Rubinstein or Beckie Aronovitch could have fully understood, besides myself." As the spokesperson for the " 'luckless sons of Abraham,' " she declaims:

> Then we weary Hebrew children at last found rest
> In the land where reigned Freedom, and like a nest
> To homeless birds your land proved to us and therefore
> Will we gratefully sing your praise evermore. (231)

Although the first three verses deal predictably with the uncommon heroism of our Founding Father, this last verse exemplifies how immigrants such as Antin transform their own pasts into a history shared by all Americans. Antin cannot express her assimilated message without insinuating her Jewish identity into her grateful praises; hence telling the story of her past changes the story of America's past. Perhaps, then, the point is not that Israel Rubinstein and Beckie Aronovitch have a privileged understanding of the poem, but that Antin's Jewish perspective allows her to rewrite the story of George Washington so that she and Israel and Beckie are as much a part of the story as are the rest of her classmates.

That Antin invites this interpretation is confirmed by the fact that she identifies one Lizzie McDee as her intended audience. Lizzie was Antin's rival for the teacher's approval, the only other student verse-maker whose skills rivaled Antin's own. The thought of Lizzie's approbation meant more to her than that of the "august School-Committeeman," the "teacher from New York," with whom she later found herself "shaking hands" (240). Why? Because when Antin looked at Lizzie, she recognized that her rival "knew her as a vain boastful, curly-headed little Jew" (238). This was the point Antin wanted her "born Americans" to stumble upon when they joined her teachers and her classmates in praising her story, her Americanization. Swallow my universal story, she seems to say, and you have swallowed your own multicultural identity—whoever you are. The point is not that Antin had renounced her Jewish identity, though theoretically she is free to do so. Rather, in her achievement of an identity she calls "American," she exercises what we might call the right of self-hyphenation, or the opportunity to construct the meaning of her Jewish heritage. The cultural uncertainty which secures her right of interpretation necessarily gives her stance a feeling of ambivalence. That she can go either way, that she can be Jewish or American or a combination, means that her interlocutors will not always know how to take her; moreover, she may not always know how to take herself.[45]

Antin's "assimilation" suggests that if our commitment to an egalitarian ideology is what allows each person to express herself as she pleases, then our shared anonymity as Americans is indeed a kind of identity. Without it, we would not be free to rewrite the histories of how we came to be the Americans that we are. The embodiment of Walzer's claim that "the hyphen works, when it is working, more like a 'plus sign,'" Mary Antin added her life—and "the scores of unwritten lives" she represented—to that heady anonymous multitude that was and is America (xxi). And only then was she content to disappear, having altered the number she joined.

## IV

Eleven years before Kallen wrote the essay that would first define cultural pluralism, Henry James had already experienced the tensions of Kallen's argument in his own portentous person. Resisting "homesickness" for his adopted land of England, James returned to "the long-neglected and long unseen land of one's birth" in 1904 to find that "the land affects one as such a living and breathing and feeling and moving great monster as this one is" (Edel 332). He left a record of this experience in *The American Scene* (1907). Twenty-five years earlier in his critical biography of Nathaniel Hawthorne, James had defined his relationship to his native land in terms of what it lacked—kings, queens, popes, and all that made up his famous list of "absent things" (*Hawthorne* 42–43). As James was well aware, his removal to Europe occurred as America was being transformed into an industrial twentieth-century empire, for which New York in 1904 was the babbling prophet. When James stepped off the boat that fateful 1904 day, he returned to America as the "restored absentee" and sought to determine what relation he could preserve, if any, with his native land. James's oxymoronic description of himself is telling because it suggests not only the uncertainty with which he approached America, but also the uncertainty that America enforced upon him.[46]

The most famous moment of this uncertainty occurs while James is visiting his "ruthlessly suppressed birth-house" to find it replaced by a building that "proclaim[ed] its lack of interest with a crudity all its own." Shocked, James declares the effect was as if he had been "amputated of half my history" (91). James's response would seem to recall Barret Wendell's letter to Kallen in which he confessed that the inundation of immigrants made him feel as if his country no longer belonged to him. Though James too experiences nostalgia and bitterness for the lost past, he comes to recognize that homelessness is a condition of American identity. Unlike Wendell, James, to his surprise, incorporates the alien's perspective into his own. Taking advantage of his homelessness to forge the sort of flexible, improvisatory critical perspective that his brother's pragmatism implied, Henry James experiences in his unorthodox position the cultural fluidity that Kallen's argument implied.[47] Like Mary Antin, James chooses to make the "alien perspective" constitutive of his renewed relationship with his old native land. In this respect, *The American Scene* reveals James as the ideal audience for both Kallen and Antin. An established American who could take his identity as an American for granted, he nonetheless recognizes that the arrival of each new immigrant unsettles the settled American. James sees that Americans were absorbing the immigrants only to the extent that the immigrants were absorbing America.

Commentators on *The American Scene* have generally understood James to be washing his hands of America. Leon Edel says that the "burden of the impressions that James set down" showed that he "found America terribly wanting" (317).[48] Yet, as Edel admits, mixed with this alleged disappointment was the "eagerness for experience that James brought with him to America" (227). He knew that America was sloughing off the old skin, and this is what intrigued him. He wrote his brother William (who had begged him not to come for fear of his disappointment) that "he wanted to see everything." He says in his Preface, that he was "as 'fresh'" and as "acute as an inquiring stranger" (*American* xvii). He wrote Edmund Gosse that he was "seeing so many charming things for the first time I quite thrill with the romance of elderly and belated discovery" (*Letters* 4:332). Far from having a preconceived notion of America, James, the "restless analyst," returns to America with a sense of expectancy and openness that is almost vulnerable.

Where this thrill and vulnerability are most palpable, I think, is when James confronts the spectacle of the arriving and recently arrived Jewish immigrants on New York's Lower East Side. The usual response to these passages has been that James is at best a snob and at worst a racist.[49] Saul

Bellow speaks of how "James was alarmed by the Jewish immigrants he saw, appalled by their alien, ill-omened presence, their antics and their gabble" (*It* 152). Acknowledging that he himself is a descendant of East European Jews, Bellow chides James for his vulgar anti-Semitism and, understandably, takes issue with James's fear that the alien would corrupt America's future culture. When James observes that "there is no claim to brotherhood with aliens in the first grossness of alienism" (120), he seems to substantiate Bellow's remarks. Yet, as Ross Posnock argues, James's interest in the alien went beyond the easy desire to wash his hands of them. Instead of agreeing with the prevalent view that James's troubling language reveals a latent racism, Posnock persuasively says that in *The American Scene* generally, and in his remarks on the alien specifically, James is "conversant and conversing with one of the major intellectual debates of its era and beyond: the philosophical opposition to identity logic" (*Trial* 81). Posnock connects Henry's analysis of the alien with William's rejection of "the logic of identity" in *A Pluralistic Universe* in that Henry understands that "truth requires the subject's yielding to the alien object" (156). Posnock connects James's thinking on identity primarily with other critics of modernity such as Theodore Adorno, Walter Benjamin, and John Dewey. James speaks not as a philosopher, though, but as an American.[50] Like Kallen or even Antin, James's interest in the alien was stimulated not only by the strangeness of the alien's presence, but by the recognition that the alien's existence offered a potential challenge to the smug complacency of the "typical" American.

Because James's account of the alien is so unsettling, readers have tended to read his commentary in isolation from the rest of the book. Read on their own, with no surrounding context, they are much more troubling than when read in context of James's other, more pointed reflections regarding homogenizing cultural tendencies that he found to be endemic in certain kinds of American experience. As he makes clear throughout *The American Scene*, the chief threat to his native land was not the alien but the sweep of the "huge democratic broom" that threatened to remove anything that might unsettle the American's unified—and hence unexamined—identity (55). As we shall see James's remarks about the immigrant are meant to contrast with the disturbing will to homogeneity that he witnessed elsewhere and which he thought was contaminating American culture. Defining his visit in terms of the opportunity to inquire into the progress of "the working of democratic institutions," James identified the "narrowed margin" of "the vast crude democracy" which "fail[ed] to involve conspicuously or to explain, any creature, or any feature not turned out to pattern" (55, 67, 156).[51] Against a crushing sense of sameness, James looked to the alien to find examples of cultural incongruity and difference. Hence James is astonished—and a little pleased—to encounter everywhere democracy's "huge white washing brush" on the same streets, if only a few blocks down, from where he also encountered "the general first grossness of alienism," or the great variety of potential Americans who seemed impenetrable to the homogenizing effects of the brush (127, 126). In this tension between a society that created and pursued an ethic of homogeneity and one that encouraged the proliferation of the heterogenous alien, James worked out the principal themes of his inquiry into "the working of democratic institutions."

. James's saving critical and cultural principle would be "the general law of *all* relief from the great equalizing pressure: it took on that last disinterestedness which consists of getting away from one's subject by plunging into it, for sweet truth's sake, still deeper" (126). This remarkable declaration, rich in contradiction and ambiguity, contains, I think, the core of James's project.[52] The word "relief" suggests how monotonous James found the surface of American experience to be; the word "plunge" suggests his willingness to "dive into the flux" of American identity. As I see it, James exploits these two competing forces of democracy, the desire for homogeneity versus an identification with the alien, to complicate Kallen's notion of the hyphenated American. Whereas Kallen at times imagined a hyphenated identity equally balanced on both sides, James sees "the great equalizing pressure" of democracy subsumed and transformed by the "general law of *all* relief." Himself a "restless analyst," James recognizes a larger American identity never content with its own assumptions. He identifies his analysis as "restless" in tribute to his determination to adapt to his subject's capacity for ceaseless transformation. Indeed, were James familiar with Dewey's letter to Kallen, he would have qualified Dewey to assert that the hyphen not only connects but detaches and reconnects elsewhere.

William James suggested that our consciousness was as interesting for the thoughts that we could not pursue as for the ones we could identify, and James's restless analysis is reflected in a prose style that at times seems to be a self-conscious attempt to enact his brother's theory. In registering his impressions of the American scene, Henry describes with an astonishing energy and precision the fleeting sensations of conflict, transition, and transformation that he experiences. The reader—and James too—is

sometimes left with the feeling that James cannot record all that he perceives. He frequently notes the "chaos of confusion and change" into
which his impressions are "thrown" (1). He finds himself "up to his neck"
in his subject, floating in "innumerable questions" in which he felt himself
to "sink beyond his depth" (5, 33). He speaks of "the numerous hours at
which one ceased consciously to discriminate, just suffering one's sense to
be flooded" (173). The restless analyst finds it "thrilling" to be where
"everything directly contributed, leaving no touch of experience irrelevant" (3). So dense are his impressions, "swarming" like the streets he
describes in the Lower East Side, that James confesses that his "curiosity
had been greater than I knew" (7). His actual openness to his "chapters of
experience," causes him to confess that "there was something of a hundred of those [memories] I may not note" and can only "pluck but a fruit
or two from my branch (422). Confronting an America which insisted on
its "universal" character in the face of its multiple and multicultural reality, James asks: "What, in such a show of life, may take the place of
amusement, of social and sensual margin, overflow and by-play"? (45).

If James was stimulated even as he was disturbed by the turbulent immigrant culture of the street, he was depressed by the hotel culture he experienced in New York's Waldorf-Astoria and Florida's Breakers. Well before the triumph of chain franchises such as McDonald's or Wal-Mart,
James finds in the "hotel world" the same powerful leveling force that
would make these late twentieth-century empires so successful. Even one
as skeptical—and as marginal—as James is surprised to find how easily he
can be absorbed into the monotonous harmony of the hotel world. Thus
when James falls into that world, comprising Kallen's "typical" Americans, he emphasizes his entrance's lack of transition. "Projecting the visi-
tor with force," this "amazing hotel world closes around [James]" (100).
Leading lives in perfect equilibrium with their desires, the anonymous
Americans of the hotel world are as unaware of the "gross aliens" that
move among them outside the hotel as they are of themselves. Of course
James's point is that there is no "outside" to the hotel world once one is
sucked in. Rushed so suddenly into its ethos, James seems to marvel at
how easily a perspective as cultivated as his could be blotted out. James
cannot avoid lamenting the absence of transition, since it is only the
moment of transition which makes him aware of his identity, or in this
case the absence of transition which makes for the absence of identity.[53]
James is most struck by the sense that the "hotel-spirit" conveyed "the
ache of envy of the spirit of a society which had found there, in its pro-

digious public setting, so exactly what it wanted" (104). Disconcertingly, James wonders if he has not found "the American spirit" in the hotel-spirit of the Waldorf-Astoria.

James fears the hotel-spirit as the nightmare culmination of democracy's leveling tendencies at their worst. Anticipating Louis Hartz, he suggests that the "beguiled and caged" denizens of the hotel-spirit have no way of registering their implication within a system that is "blissfully exempt from any principle or possibility of discord with itself" (441, 104). In the hotel's ministering force James detects an insidious desire which caters less to want or desire than it obliterates desire by total fulfillment. "The hotel spirit lies in wait for [its citizens], anticipates and plucks them before they dawn, setting them up prematurely and turning their face in the right direction" (440). Initially, James suggests that the people whom he sees going in and out of the hotel with such felicity of purpose are manipulated like puppets by the hotel-spirit, but so deftly that they think they are moving "free and easy" (107). James modifies this view when he has occasion to study the hotel-spirit operating in Florida as smoothly as it did New York. Since both places represent "the lubrication of the general [democratic] machinery" which "includes everyone," the only "outside" or generating power to the hotel-spirit is democracy itself (108).

Critics normally identify James's fascination with the "organic" production of the hotel with his own aesthetic principles. Such readings, however, overlook that the crucial point for James is that to be outside of the hotel-spirit is not to exist.[54] To be totally excluded, utterly absent—this is the legacy for the marginalized, the alien, those left outside the hotel-spirit's perfect harmony. To James, what distinguished the "typical" Americans, whose logic Kallen mocked and Antin tried to co-opt into her own way of defining America, was their complete indifference to the sort of arguments that Kallen and Antin and James might try to make. His response was despairing: "Definitely, one had made one's pilgrimage but to find the hotel-spirit in sole *articulate* possession and, call this truth for the mind an anti-climax if one would, none of the various climaxes [James's other disappointments with America] struck me as for a moment dispossessing it" (442). In this remarkable moment, Henry James, the great American novelist of manners, who never subscribed to the liberal distinction between self and society, finds himself, while seeking to establish a relation with his native land, utterly and completely alone. And like other archetypal solitary American heroes to whom James condescended to or simply ignored—Emerson, Thoreau, Huckleberry Finn—he protests this horrid manifestation of a tyrannical democracy in the name of a better, truly fluid democracy by shouting his version of "NO! in thunder." Adopting the voice of the perpetually marginalized, James challenges the complacency of Kallen's "typical" American in words would that conjure all the chaotic energy of democratic culture:

> You are not final, complacently as you appear so much of the time to assume it—your inevitable shaking about in the Margin must more or less take care of that. . . . Distinct as you are, you are not even definite . . . you are perpetually provisional, the hotels and the Pullmans [represent] the stages and forms of your evolution, and are not a bit, in themselves, more final than you are. (407–8)

Mixed with James's curse, then, is a hope for the future. A little later he says that "your actual stage will be short" as if he were some sort of American Prospero who could call forth a "democratic culture" that would create itself through the continual bursting of its own provisional boundaries. In the end, James agrees with Antin that the hotel-spirit is defined by the Margin that it would exclude, and thus cannot absorb that Margin without its own equilibrium being overturned. James knows that the hotel-spirit, left by itself, cannot recognize the provisional status he wishes to confer upon it; but the expression of marginal voices would inject a saving sense of difference to an otherwise serenely indifferent and unaware ethos. James insists that the "great equalizing force of democracy" the hotel-spirit represents is ultimately divisible by the incalculable Margin which surrounds it. No less than Horace Kallen or Mary Antin, Henry James, perfect symbol of the genteel white American male, sought to contaminate pure "Americanism" with a sense of difference.

The saving sense of difference that James seeks in American culture he finds at Ellis Island, where he witnesses a "visible act of ingurgitation on the part of our body politic and social," prompting in him, not surprisingly, "a thousand more things to think of than he can pretend to retail" (84). James, like Bourne, recognizes that the physical presence of the foreign bodies entering America will have cultural consequences. As if to assault the conventions of his "anonymous" American audience, James's insistently corporeal language flaunts the uneasiness he feels. James forces his audience to keep down the thought that his haphazard look into the jaws of this ingurgitation is representative of a process that is occurring every day on a national scale, forcing untold changes on how American identity is practiced. It is possible that his use of the word "ingurgitation"—with its association with swallowing and, eventually, defecating—

is James's way of displacing his own anxiety about what he describes onto his audience. I think it more likely, though, that James uses the word to subvert his audience's assumptions while seeming to assuage their worst anxieties. Twenty years later James's audience would try to resolve the issues and misgivings that his account raises by stopping the flow of immigrants that he witnessed at Ellis Island. James, by contrast, searches for a perspective that will enable him to view the arrival of these foreign bodies as an opportunity for cultural renewal. He writes that "the simplest account of the action of Ellis Island on the spirit of any sensitive citizen who may have happened to 'look in' is that he comes back not at all the same person as he went" (85). In making this observation James is not merely commiserating with an audience who fear the loss of their American identity, but communicating the identification he felt *as an American* who had returned to his native land only to find himself an alien. James knew, in other words, that you did not have to leave the country and then return twenty years later to discover that homelessness was a condition of being American. The audience whom he addressed were already experiencing a version of this displacement.

Antin writes to temper this discovery; James flaunts it. Indeed, being altered by an encounter with "the inconceivable alien" is completely consonant with one of James's cherished principles of novelistic composition, addressed in the preface to *The Princess Casamassima*: "The agents in any drama, are interesting only in proportion as they feel their respective situations; since the consciousness, on their part, of the complication exhibited forms for us their link of connexion with it. . . . Their being finely aware . . . makes absolutely the intensity of their adventure" (*Literary Criticism: European* 1088). "Intensity of adventure" best describes James's reaction to the figure of the alien. He probes the "affirmed claim" the alien has on him to its bottomless depths. Thus he describes himself as a "*questionably* privileged person" whose encounter "shakes" him "to the depths of his being" (emphasis mine). James is shaken because he realizes "that it is his American fate to share the sanctity of his American consciousness, the intimacy of his patriotism with the inconceivable alien. . . . I like to think of him, I *have* to think of him," James confesses in a mixture of horror, fascination, and exhilaration (*American* 85).

Here James's thoughts and identity almost unanchor themselves, as he drifts in what he elsewhere called the "terrible *fluidity* of self-revelation" (*Literary Criticism: European* 1316). James's identification with the alien is all the more remarkable because as "intimate" as he feels toward the alien, he refuses to water down what remains "immeasurably alien." Rather than draw back from the alien, James identifies with the alien's "otherness." Adrift in the stream of American identity, James, for a moment only, reaches to secure a notion of universal American character: "One's supreme relation, as one had always put it, was to one's country—a conception made up so largely of one's countrymen and countrywomen" (85). Following the flow of his thoughts, as if trying to buoy himself up, James wonders if this "instinct is not sound," for "to pull it about" too much would risk "weakening it." However, this thought cannot stand the alien's insistent undercurrent, so James once again drifts into a queer identification with what so unsettles him. Indeed, he settles for "unsettled possession" and comes to the stunning thought that "we, not they, must make the surrender and accept the orientation" (86). Later, walking along the Lower East Side, James unleashes the most profound question our multicultural American experience can enforce upon the Americanist, one that replaces and recasts Crèvecoeur's famous question. Surveying America's diverse terrain, seeking his own shifting identity in the strange faces of "others," James asks of them and himself: Which is not the alien?

Just as Kallen attacked the notion of the melting pot by arguing that everyone was in some sense a hyphenated American, so does James destabilize American identity by making it irreparably "alien." William Boelhower observes that James had "dislocat[ed] the fixed point of view [by] making the relation rather than the immobile subject central" (*Through* 23). This is precisely the stance that Kallen's cultural pluralism borrowed from William James. If Kallen did not imagine how ethnic cultures would interact, James recognizes that in America the fluidity of one's identity can potentially transgress any supposed cultural or ethnic boundary. James understands that without a sense of cultural difference there could be no possibility for the kind of cultural transgression he embraces; yet he does not consider how these cultural differences are defined. He more or less groups Italian immigrants and Jewish immigrants together in their composite ability to estrange Henry James. Insofar as the existence of immigrants surrounds and suffuses him, James is unconcerned with the potentially enormous differences between the Italian laborers that so startle him while strolling about what he takes to be Hawthorne's New England and the Jewish immigrants he seeks out in the Yiddish quarter. The point, though, is not that James defines their cultural identity but that he allows their cultural otherness to redefine his own relation to the country. He dramatizes how mutual strangeness can be a form of mutual inclusiveness.

James recognizes that however one defines one's hyphenated cultural identity, this definition is provisional and subject to change. "The great thing" about the immigrants he observes is that "they were all together so visibly on the new, the lifted level—that of consciously not being what they *had* been" (126). In this observation, James finds the ground where his partial American identity overlaps with that of others: a shared sense of displacement. Compared with the hotel-spirit, James finds this sense of displacement liberating, just as he observes that the immigrants are emboldened by their new relation to their American selves. In this context, James's own name for himself, "the restored absentee" describes that anonymous entity "the American," investing its anonymity with a sense of unresolved conflict, a feeling of being always at odds with itself. As an American, James moves among the company of other "restored absentees," or, perhaps, absentees restored.

James thus addresses those who would claim that there is no communion with the alien "in the first grossness of their alienism." Such critics point to the "common school and the newspaper" as "agents of uniformity" which will wash the "greasy" stuff of "alienism" in the "cauldron of the 'American' character" (120, 121). James disrupts the potential serenity of this washing away of character on two levels. In the first place, he asks what becomes of the "various positive properties" of "the installed tribes," "into what do they so provisionally, and so indiscoverably all melt?" In a magnificent metaphor, James likens Americanization to the washing of clothes in a tub of hot water where "if the stuff loses its brightness the water of the tub is more or less agreeably dyed with it." Reversing the logic of the then-building Americanization movement, James announces that "the new subject begins to tint with its pink azure his fellow-soakers in the terrible tank" (129, 128). James takes a supposedly unchangeable, if still volatile, concept—racial identity—and touches it up. James's image is rich in irresponsible humor, both for his day and ours. Placed in the context of "jazz singer" Al Jolson or contemporary comedians such as Richard Pryor and Eddie Murphy, who often have lightened their faces and dialects to act and mock "white," James's remark elicits the same laughter of uneasiness about our American identity which these other performers have exploited so ingeniously. Puckishly, James blackens or "pinkens" or "azurens" the American's face for an always ongoing national minstrel show, where the roles, as it were, are always shifting actors. James overturns the figure (and the meaning) of Crèvecoeur's melting pot and pours it over the heads of his audience to wash them over anew, whatever their cultural and ethnic background, whatever their "color," in the national bath of fluid identity.

James's second level of response further undermines the confidence that Kallen's "anonymous" Americans take in the "white washing brush" of the public schools. Along with Antin, James recognizes these presumed "equalizing forces" give a voice to the very marginal forces they are supposed to convert.[55] At the same time, the assimilation machine of "the common schools and the newspaper" can only convert so much, James argues. James speculates on the "obstinate, unconverted residuum" of the alien, which, if not overtly expressed, still remains latent in every American. An indefinable "something" remains and it is perhaps this something that lingers in the ring left around America's "terrible tank." What is this unconverted residuum but the impulse within Americans to fix their American identity on one side of the hyphen or the other? But where so many wish to cling to the idea of "an unconverted residuum," there always exists the possibility that a merely free-floating American can attach himself to the remains of *someone else's* residuum. This is the greatest significance of James's identification with the alien. For the American, ethnic identity exists both as cultural presence and as a possibility for self-transformation. In *The American Scene* James bathes in the "fluidity of appreciation" that "floated me, my wave, all that day and the next," that "rendered me of various penetrations, charming coves of still blue water, that carried me up into the subject, so to speak, and enabled me to step ashore" (3). Like his brother's more famous "stream of thought," Henry's cultural and critical voyage teaches him that the "charming coves" of his thought, or his identity, are formed and washed ashore in the incoherent rush, one might almost say debris, of sensation that his perception of American experience comprises. The shores upon which James moves— the cultural identities that Kallen seemed to think were permanent—are only islands of rest. These islands have no fixed place or name and are themselves moving anyway; they belong to anyone, or any combination of anyones.

# 2   Thinking in Blues

■■■■■■■

We have had no genius in America, with tyrannous eye, which knew the value of our incomparable materials. . . . Our log-rolling, our stumps and their politics, our fisheries, our Negroes and Indians, our boats and our repudiations, the wrath of rogues and the pusillanimity of honest men, the northern trade, the southern planting, the western clearning, Oregon and Texas, are yet unsung. Yet America is a poem in our eyes; its ample geography dazzles the imagination, and it will not wait long for meters.—Ralph Waldo Emerson, "The Poet"

I got a new way of spelling Memphis, Tennessee
I said I got a new way of spelling Memphis, Tennessee
Double M, Double E, Good God! XYZ
—Furry Lewis

*I*

In the lexicon of the blues, "the crossroads" designates a place where unlikely and sometimes dangerous meetings occur. Such encounters may result in either joy or fear, but a crossroads experience is invariably one of transformation. In American intellectual history, the traditions of Ralph Waldo Emerson and the blues meet at a crossroads that few have encountered and even fewer have identified for others. One such traveler is Bob Dylan, whose 1983 work "Blind Willie McTell" is about one poet whom Emerson might have summoned. Dylan's song is both a tribute to artists whose brilliance remains unknown to most Americans and an attempt to account for the blues as a historical force that continues to define American cultural possibility. Hence "Blind Willie McTell" marks a fit point of entry for considering the blues as an instance of the kind of pragmatist cultural work that Emerson called for in *The American Scholar* (1837).

Before recording "Blind Willie McTell," Dylan's indebtedness to the blues was well established. He named his first electric rock album *Highway 61 Revisited* (1965) in tribute to the road that runs from New Orleans to Chicago and on which the blues was created by African Americans as they journeyed from slavery to freedom. What is startling about "Blind Willie McTell" is not that Dylan again acknowledges the blues as an influence, but that he represents his own artistic identity as a consequence of slavery and more specifically of the world the descendants of slaves created after the Civil War. In the crowning achievement of his career, Dylan conjures a nearly forgotten blues singer, William Samuel McTell, to recover the history that created the blues and through it the bond that ties Dylan to McTell. On one level, Dylan brings McTell's heritage into the present: he maps the unlikely road that leads from nineteenth-century Georgia where McTell was born to the late twentieth-century Minnesota hotel room in which Dylan sets the song. Yet "Blind Willie McTell" is also for Dylan a form of self-effacement; it is a way of situating his identity as a performer within the same tradition of largely anonymous people that created McTell. In this respect, the work that McTell or Dylan made is less important than the work that made each of them. Dylan's song makes us recognize that American culture can often best be understood as the embodiment of African American experience, and it challenges us to revise our understanding of American culture through this perception.

Crucially, Dylan neither reveals anything of McTell's biography nor sings the song as the kind of blues McTell sung. Each verse ends with a pointed statement of humility before McTell's power: "I know no one can sing the blues like Blind Willie McTell." Repeatedly, Dylan raises his subject only to back away. He does this because he wants the entire tradition of the blues to speak through the figure of McTell. To sing a blues in McTell's own style would be a gesture of disrespect, an expression of mastery masked as tribute. That no one can sing the blues like Blind Willie McTell does not mean that the history of the blues must end with McTell. Dylan's song does more than preserve McTell's legacy: it makes it over into something else. Dylan offers McTell's memory the ultimate maker's gift: another creation. In the process, Dylan effects a neat shift on a familiar blues stance that highlights the anonymity that goes with being black in white America. "My first name is so and so," one blues line runs, "and I can't tell my second name." In Dylan's mini-history of the blues, the singer speaks McTell's name to frame the vignettes that each verse comprises. Without referring to McTell's songs or to his life, Dylan

thereby speaks McTell's as if it were the signature to each verse. As the end
to which each verse leads, McTell figures as both an unknown blues singer
and as the song's author. He is understood to be among those of whom the
singer thinks while he "traveled through East Texas where many martyrs
fell" if only because their lost histories are contained within the music that
McTell made. Making the phrase "Blind Willie McTell" stand for the
nameless thousands whose lives found form through the blues, Dylan
restores to McTell his name by making it stand for the history of the blues.

Except as a voice, Dylan does not enter the song until the last verse
when he reveals that the singer is "gazing out the window of the St. James
Hotel." This is both a sly reference to Dylan's native state—the St. James
is located in Minneapolis—and to the fact that Dylan has adapted his
song's melody from the jazz standard "St. James Infirmary." In that song
an inconsolable singer confronts the fact of his lover's death. In "Blind
Willie McTell" a distraught singer confronts a world doomed by endless
cycles of "power and greed and corruptible seed." To the singer, who in
the opening lines faces a deserted mansion with a doorpost that reads "this
land has been condemned / all the way from New Orleans to Jerusalem,"
this knowledge belongs to the blues since it was spawned by the corruptible seed of slavery. Like the shattered mansions in Faulkner's *Absalom,
Absalom!* (1936) or Toni Morrison's *Beloved* (1987), Dylan's apocalyptic
image calls attention to the difficulty of confronting and therefore imagining a past that has been cursed, abandoned, and made too horrible to
know and remember. Dylan renders the landscape of slavery in images
simultaneously terrifying and beautiful: "See them big plantations burning / Hear the cracking of the whips / smell the sweet magnolias bloom-
ing / See the ghosts of slavery ships." Here the sweet smell of the trees is
the seductive perfume that might naturalize slavery's horror into nostalgia, a beautiful post card of Scarlet O'Hara's Tara in the moment of its
destruction. By pointing to slave ships and the destinies contained within
them, however, Dylan conveys no longing for lost mansions. The images
are not meant to be perceived sequentially but experienced whole, the
result being a recognition that the plantations were doomed to destruction from the moment the slave ships arrived.

"Blind Willie McTell" moves beyond images of lost material wealth to
recover the secret and virtually lost history through the singer's desire to
"hear them tribes moaning" and hear "the undertaker's bell." For if the
undertaker's bell tolls for the unrecorded deaths of uncounted slaves, the
tribes' moans provide the voice through which the slaves and their de-

scendants created an identity separate from their enslavement. Dylan traverses the fields that the freed slaves trod, encountering "gypsy maidens" who "strut their feathers well" and "a woman by the river with some fine young handsome man" who is "dressed up like a squire, bootleg whiskey in his hand." Just as the women decorate themselves with flamboyance and skill, the young man wears what are likely his former master's clothes to project a world that is changing. These people construct selves out of the fragments of prior identities. This squire could also be a wily version of Dylan who is turning the blues inside out to enact his own identity as a musician through this song. The singer places himself among the women dancing in their feathers to hear "the hoot-owl singing as they were taking down their tents." With the woman by the river, he hears voices coming from "the chain gang on the highway." Beautiful in their own right, Dylan's poetic images function primarily to call forth the music that in a sense creates this lost world. Ordinarily, we think of music accompanying other activities—dancing, card-playing, or, for the chain gang, road-building—but in this case the music *is the history*. "Them tribes moaning" in one verse takes the form of the chain gang's "rebel's yell" in another verse to convey the continuity of the slaves' expression. The feathers, the squire's clothes, the chains that once bound the prisoners together are gone, but the history associated with the experience of these things inheres in the music. To Dylan, singing over a century after slavery legally ended, the music is the work that remains.

If the historical Blind Willie McTell appears in the song at all, it is as the owl's voice singing as "they were taking down the tents / The stars above the trees were his only audience." What is at first striking about this line is that, against historical evidence, it romanticizes the singer as one condemned to perform without an audience. According to available accounts, McTell rarely lacked for an audience and could pretty much depend on finding places to play throughout the South and in Atlanta especially. More important, the nameless singers dating back to slavery for whom this shadowy figure stands sang to each other about their shared experience. The form that chronologically preceded the blues, the work song, came out of the experience of groups working and singing together, just as the spirituals emerged as the slaves' collective attempt to imagine and then create a place that transcended the world of slavery. If we think of Dylan's song as being about the mysterious passages of cultural inheritance, then it is clear that Dylan invokes the romantic image of the artist singing only to the barren trees and the stars above them in order to identify a nation unwilling or unable to listen to its own story. In this way the singer of "Blind Willie McTell" transforms its subject from that of a great artist who has not received his due to a kind of unknown bard who carries within his art a version of our national, American story.

## II

When Emerson apostrophized the American poet of the future, he was playing on a variation of a theme he had first announced in his landmark 1837 address, *The American Scholar.* There he challenged an audience of would-be American scholars to prepare themselves for the time "when the sluggard intellect of this continent will look from under its iron lids and fill the postponed expectation of the world with something better than the exertion of mechanical skill." Yet this mechanical skill is a crucial part of Emerson's pragmatist, action-oriented aesthetic; when he localizes the attributes of his ideal poet, he thinks in terms of physical labor. This labor involves acts of making that are analogous to the work of the American poet. Inevitably, Emerson understood this poetic making as the material expression of our revolutionary democratic principles, as if to say that what he could not conjure forth, *American experience itself* would. "Events, actions arise," he prophesies, "that must be sung, that will sing them-selves" (*Essays* 53). But what will these actions be and who will sing them? In the reverie from "The Poet" quoted above, Emerson struggles to name the events that will be sung and out of which an American poetry will be created. That Emerson could not create the poetry himself matters less than his attempt to be consistent with his admonition in *The American Scholar* that the most highly valued component of the successful scholar is a commitment to action. For Emerson as for Dylan, the acts cannot be separated from the words that these acts will inspire.

One reason *The American Scholar* remains alive as something more than an artifact of literary history is that instead of worrying why American culture had failed to live up to its democratic promises, as others were, Emerson is directing his audience's attention to those places where culture is created. For Emerson, culture is not produced in the poet's study but by the experience acquired outside of it: Emerson's American scholar, like his ideal poet, would thus be someone who had come to know "the meal in the firkin" and "the milk in the pan" and "the ballad in the street" (*Essays* 69) as ingredients for future creations. To know them requires labor—be it cooking or farm labor or singing. This critical Emersonian idea—that culture should be understood as a series of actions—animates his opening remark that the anniversary the scholars have gathered to celebrate "is one of hope," but "not enough of labor" (53). By stressing the value of labor over hope, Emerson warns his audience that those who would participate in the creation of a recognizably American culture should concern themselves with the work that creates the artifacts of culture rather than with the artifacts themselves.

Emerson's ideal American Scholar takes for granted William James's crucial pragmatist assertion that "truth *happens* to an idea" (*Writings* 574). Where James sees the discovery of truth as an act, Emerson sees action itself as the invention of truth, for "without it thought can never ripen into truth" (*Essays* 60). Emerson's characterization of "Man Thinking" describes exactly the pragmatist philosopher James would argue for. To Emerson, the true American Scholar is a switchboard between thought and action: "The mind now thinks, now acts, and each fit reproduces the other" (62). The pun on "fit" suggests exactly how Emerson makes the central pragmatist tension between experience and perception the constitutive issue for understanding how American experience becomes American culture. Emerson plays with two meanings of "fit": (1) proper size and shape, and (2) a sudden period of vigorous activity. Thus his pun reflects the pragmatic sense that thinking and acting are interchangeable. As the gerund "thinking" suggests, there is never a moment where thought can be distinguished from action. Alive to all currents of experience, Man Thinking is a master improviser, whose quick wit and keen eye encompass more than the mere books of the typical scholar. Lamenting the "notion that the scholar should be a recluse" who is "unfit for any handiwork or public labor as penknife for an axe," he states that "action is with the scholar subordinate, but it is essential" (59–60). We are wrong to suggest that Emerson perceives thinking to be an end to itself; rather, he enjoins us to understand our thoughts and acts to be made through a process of perpetual conversion.

In seeing Emerson as a pragmatist thinker, I am revising and extending the work of Richard Poirier and Cornel West, who have argued that before the term was coined Emerson inaugurated the tradition of pragmatism. Both men identify Emerson as the starting point for a pragmatist intellectual tradition centrally concerned with how action is converted into thought. West looks to Emerson specifically and pragmatism generally for an American intellectual tradition that will provide a call for "serious thought and moral action" consonant with his ideals of political activism, whereas Poirier finds in Emerson a pragmatist literary source for

William James as well as for figures such as Robert Frost, Gertrude Stein, Wallace Stevens, and Kenneth Burke.[1] Poirier's literary Emerson would seem to have little to do with West's political Emerson, yet both critics in their different ways seek to prove, in Poirier's words, "how powerful Emerson's impingement" can be on "larger cultural, social, and critical issues" (*Poetry* 6). Poirier rightly observes that Emerson's only real value to us is in how he helps us to imagine "possibilities of personal and cultural renewal" (11). As persuasive as Poirier's pragmatist genealogy is—I think it absolutely convincing—it can only go so far, to paraphrase Poirier, in putting Emerson to cultural work. By insisting that the past is primarily a linguistic creation and "that language is too agitated a medium ever to allow any such fixity of meaning or value," Poirier almost unconsciously privileges those worlds elsewhere where only literature can take us (11).[2] Emerson was of course interested in writing as writing—he could polish a period as well as anyone. But as an orator as well as a writer, Emerson was also concerned with how words become acts. Poirier correctly says that for Emerson "every text is a reconstruction of some previous texts of work, work that itself is always, again, work-in-progress" (17). Emerson conceived his work-in-progress as part of a broad democratic work-in-progress. To be true to his democratic and intellectual ideals, we need to seek those moments when his work is understood to be addressing more than a book-bound audience.

Somewhat along the same lines, Stanley Cavell argues that American intellectuals have neglected the cultural-philosophical inheritance that Emerson tried to establish.[3] Though Cavell claims for Emerson the role of neither pragmatist nor blues philosopher, he does show how Emerson conceived of his work as an initial step in the creation of a recognizably American culture. A philosopher, Cavell hears in Emerson "a call for philosophy" and he discovers through Emerson a path to Wittgenstein and Heidegger (*This New* 28). I think it significant that Cavell says Emerson is making a call for philosophy rather than offering a particular philosophy. By "call" I take Cavell to mean that Emerson is offering a description of the kinds of intellectual and cultural activities that he will demand of himself and his audience. "I am ready to die out of nature," Emerson writes, "and be born again into this new yet unapproachable America" (*Essays* 485). America remains unapproachable for Emerson because it is understood only as a rarefied idea, an abstract philosophical construct. Emerson proposes to inhabit this unapproachable America, but this can only be accomplished through the work of others.

Cavell emphasizes that Emerson's work truly founds a nation, but I think that this observation neglects Emerson's awareness that America is an entity in perpetual transition. America is unapproachable for Emerson because he cannot know exactly what future acts his work will inspire—or which future acts will claim his for their own. Thus, Emerson would "found" this "new yet unapproachable America" but only as a provisional finding, as it were. What he makes must be remade. Emerson would find, rather than found, America by defining his philosophy according to its *practice*. Where this practice leads depends on the understanding that the ground on which it is provisionally built might shift also. In *The American Scholar* Emerson asserts that the "revolution [in human aspiration] is to be wrought by the gradual domestication of the idea of Culture. The main enterprise of the world for splendor, for extent, is the upbuilding of man. Here are materials strewn along the ground" (*Essays* 67). "Ground" in this passage signifies not a bottom or place of absolute origin since the ground is already being made over at the point we identify it as "the ground." Indeed, the material with which we make over the ground becomes part of the ground we make. "Domesticating the idea of culture" obligates us to understand culture as something that is in the process of being created. The ground that we uncover we also raise; in other words, the ground moves as we build (on) it.

Because one can act only on certain provisional findings or foundations, Emerson knew that a founder could not name his successor—hence his emphais on the renewal of language. Out of our work of building an American culture true to our democratic promises, new languages will be created. How and from whom? At the outset of *The American Scholar* Emerson gives us a clue when he notes that we have not exerted ourselves in the creation of letters. Hence he characterizes the occasion of the gathering as "one of hope and, perhaps, not enough of labor" (*Essays* 53). On one level, he means that our labors have been devoted elsewhere, but he also suggests that we do not know what kind of labor produces letters. Labor is of course an act—whether it be with a pickaxe or a pen—but it is also a form of thinking. In "The Poet" Emerson suggests what it means to labor over letters so that the creation of letters become one's labor when he asserts that "words are also actions, and actions are a kind of words" (*Essays* 244). But how do acts become words?

Emerson is drawn to "log-rolling" and "the southern planting" and "the western clearing" because he recognizes that a new American language will emerge from these actions. If there is poetry in the act, then words will emerge that are true to the poetry of the acts undertaken.

Describing a theory of language, Emerson chooses metaphors to convey how language is made through an encounter with some prior act, and he adds, "As the limestone of the continent consists of infinite masses of shells of animalcules, so language is made up of images or tropes, which now, in their secondary uses, have long ceased to remind us of their poetic origin" (*Essays* 457). In a cryptic utterance, Emerson says that "language is fossil poetry." The poet is a kind of archaeologist-artist, his pen also a pick, working over the materials that have already been shaped into prior forms. The poet inherits his language, but nonetheless creates a new language by excavating the remains. Taking what others may perceive to be final and transforming it into something new will also create an inheritance for others to make over. With each new cycle of creation the poet's new work still bears an imprint of some other work's remains.

Dylan's "Blind Willie McTell" identifies slavery's heritage as the ground of future cultural renewals in a way that Emerson obviously could not. As an American Scholar, Dylan reveals the poetry of the blues encrypted in the bones of slavery. It would be quixotic and even perverse to argue that Emerson could foresee how the history of the slaves' path to freedom would become a way of creating a new American culture. As a cultural theorist, though, Emerson has much to tell us about the way we create ourselves as Americans. From this perspective, Emerson matters to us today not because of what he said about race relations in 1850, but because he gives us a way of accounting for the difference that the ex-slaves' presence has made in creating the America we have inherited today. In any case, Emerson did recognize that the abolition of slavery offered an opportunity to create a language by which American culture might be excavated and rebuilt. He aptly observes that "language must be raked, the secrets of the slaughter-houses and infamous holes that cannot confront the day, must be ransacked, to tell what Negro slavery has been" (quoted in Gates, *Loose* 23). Emerson himself would provide the rake, but he could not see what would come of the raking. In fact, he had already himself become an instance of how the African presence had influenced American culture. As David Reynolds has shown, Emerson's own speaking style had been influenced by the styles of black preachers.[4] Though this connection could be viewed as ephemeral, it takes on resonance by the end of the twentieth century when a white president of the United States is seen as a clear expression of African American style.[5] Though less obviously, Emerson also is a product of the sort of cross-cultural inventions that have made the tradition of the blues, among other American forms, possible. Thus Emerson's example—both as a historical figure and as one who left a record of his thoughts in language—matters primarily because he helps to render these cross-cultural inventions visible.[6]

In bringing together Emerson and the blues, I am not arguing for a direct causal connection between the two. Rather, I am suggesting that we see the blues tradition as providing answers to the sorts of questions Emerson asked, answers that also transform our understanding of Emerson. It may be fair to say that Emerson would not have recognized the language quoted from Furry Lewis above, words that come from deep within the blues tradition and the culture of slavery that preceded it, as answering the questions he raised in *The American Scholar* and "The Poet." Emerson himself suggested, though, that "one must be an inventor to read well," which means that we cannot limit either Emerson or our understanding of him strictly to what his work meant in 1837 or 1845 (*Essays* 58). A creative reading of Emerson allows us to recognize that his distance from Lewis is evidence of how successful the tradition of the blues has been in achieving precisely those acts of aesthetic and cultural transformation that Emerson hoped for. Furry Lewis's work is not just a new way of spelling Memphis, Tennessee, or a new use of old metaphors, but as Emerson intimated, a wholly new language created out of Lewis's participation in a changing American experience. Without the perspective that comes from being a descendent of slaves in a country dedicated to freedom, Lewis could not speak the words that he does. He must invent a new way of speaking that comes out of a developing African American sense of what being a free American might mean. So I am making a double argument. On one hand, the tradition of the blues provides a version of the sort of American culture-making that Emerson tried to prepare future generations to recognize; on the other, the blues helps us to rehistoricize Emerson—not to dismiss him but to see him as part of the continuing democratic process of cultural upheaval and transformation.

*III*

For all of the easy declarations that the blues is a truly American art form, it has not been discussed as a mode of experience consonant with American intellectual traditions—a situation perhaps to be expected given that the tradition was carried on by people who in their time would have been called "cornfield niggers."[7] The blues and Emerson share the pragmatist's view that one's perspective is always contingent. Like the pragmatist, the blues artist assumes a fluid universe and makes his perspective out of the world's shifting things, among which he includes himself. To the blues singer, this recognition is often comic. As a familiar blues lines runs (one that Chuck Berry turned into a *Billboard* Top 30 rock-and-roll single, "Reelin' and Rockin'"), "Sometimes I will then again I think I won't / Sometimes I do then again I think I don't." Embedded within experience, both the blues artist and the Emersonian pragmatist realize that there is no transcendent point from which we can make secure judgments, or to which our judgments will ultimately return us. This is a difficult orientation to maintain, because it enforces upon the percipient-maker the insight that the conclusions of whatever critique he is performing will likely undermine its premises. "It is a mischievous notion that we are come late into nature; that the world was finished long ago," Emerson asserts (*Essays* 65); he wanted to loosen the joints of philosophy (or thought) to make it fluid, moving, *active*. Were Emerson a blues singer, or speaking out of the blues tradition, this point would be easier to make. As we shall see, Son House, Muddy Waters, Johnny Shines, and others sang the "Walkin' Blues" in order to express a mode of experiencing—thinking in blues— that followed from making one's identity while one is physically (and hence mentally) in transit. More basically, thinking in blues, a way of acting that makes the best of a bad situation, emerges from earlier forms like the field holler and the work song. Thus where Emerson sees the interpenetration of thinking and acting as a sort of philosophical gambit, a hard-learned lesson of the intellect, the tradition of the blues comes to this way of understanding through the exertion of the body and the language that emerged from this act.

The slaves' singing or even blues singers' recording did not aspire to the cultural or aesthetic permanence of Emerson's writing. Hence we are unaccustomed to attributing to their acts the intellectual labor that they actually involve. We generally identify the blues as a form of cultural history or as a way of understanding how a particular group of people thought about themselves.[8] In so doing, we lose the power of the act that created the expression; instead, we are more likely to see that act as being concluded rather than having precipitated future acts. Blues musician and writer Willie Dixon laments this way of understanding the blues in his autobiography, *I Am the Blues* (1989), where he makes the crucial point that we have "blues books out there that tell a little bit about everybody— his name and what he sang—but they don't have none of the *actual blues experience* involved" (3, emphasis mine). Thus, Dixon says, "the blues have been documented but not written—documented in the minds of various men with these various songs since the first black man set foot on the American shore" (3). Dixon makes a point we will see others making later in this chapter: the power of the blues as a cultural form is bound up in the knowledge that each blues act carries with it the entire history of its creation. "When a person knows what his background is," Dixon observes, "it gives him a chance to be proud" (224).

Dixon knows that the blues belongs to him and other descendants of slaves and that this knowledge is obscured by the history of race relations in this country. He notes that because "the white man has [had] control of everything that the black man has made in America," this control has made him "the owner" of everything, including the legal right to the blues. The Chess Brothers who recorded Dixon, Muddy Waters, Sonny Boy Williamson, and many others owned "the blues" by virtue of their exploitative recording contracts. Dixon is not exactly suggesting that the blues have been taken from him since he knows very well that the blues is the form through which he has invented himself as an American. For Dixon, the meaning of the blues is its invisibility; the blues is a form of American history that remains difficult to hear outside the context of its immediate creation. Dixon makes this point by dedicating his autobiography to the thousands of unknown blues makers whose acts remain unknown because the meaning of their work has not become a part of our collective American consciousness.

> I remember the great blues artists that never had a future, that have made many great songs that blues artists from all over the world have recorded. These were popular as blues artists and no one knows their names. No one knows their picture. They have no history of it. (224)

Though Dixon is speaking mostly of artists who achieved the small fame of being recorded and forgotten, his words might also describe any of the tens of thousands of people whose work—in the fields and with their voices—helped pave the way for the blues. What Dixon wants is more complex than recovering their pictures or the recorded versions of their work. He wants their acts to be understood as thoughts that also invented America. Hence his claim that the true history of the blues has not been written reflects his understanding that Americans have been unable to recognize their own participation in the process that has created them—us—except as a process of exploitation. We cannot piece together a replica of what these makers of blues accomplished to replace what has been lost, but we can reconstruct a version of their making that gives us a better picture of how we came to be who we are.

At this point I should acknowledge that what I am calling the blues tradition is actually a broad one that includes different types of performers, eras, and regions, urban and rural.[9] Because the blues has in a sense crossed over into the consciousness of all Americans, it is tempting to talk about all forms of the blues as if they were the same. They are not. In 1936 Alain Locke was already complaining how the term "blues" had become "a generic name for all sorts of elaborate hybrid Negroid music" (*The Negro and His Music* 33) and that tendency toward mongrelization in the name of the blues has continued unabated to this day. Standard blues histories divide and classify the genre according to style and region: the classic blues of Ma Rainey or Bessie Smith or Alberta Hunter; the urban Kansas City–style big-band blues of Jimmy Rushing or Big Joe Turner; the various country blues of the Mississippi Delta, east Texas, and the eastern seaboard states; the urban country blues of Chicago; the bluesified jazz of Louis Armstrong, Count Basie, and Duke Ellington and others. In terms of style and musicianship, these assorted blues approaches differ in important ways. On the other hand, in a general way, to the extent that the blues has been an expression of African American folk culture, one can say that the blues comprises a coherent tradition. Lyrics that were invented and passed along through the normal process of folk creation became instantly available everywhere with the advent of the radio and the phonograph. In 1941, Muddy Waters, despite living in a sharecropper's shack with no electricity, speaks of teaching himself how to play from the 1928 recording of "How Long Blues" by Leroy Carr and Scrapper Blackwell. This song would then be recorded under different titles by blues artists as diverse as Jimmy Rushing, Otis Rush, Muddy Waters, Big Joe Turner, Alberta Hunter, and T-Bone Walker, exemplifying how particular blues lyrics do cross eras, styles, and regions.

In studying the blues in its various permutations, one is continually reminded that just as the precise origin of the blues cannot be identified, neither is any particular expression of the blues necessarily definitive. Consequently, the history of the blues as a strictly musical form does not make for a linear story. But LeRoi Jones and more recently Angela Y. Davis have argued that the continuity of the blues in its diverse styles derives from its expression of protest against an American society that has tried to exclude the contributions of African Americans from its national story. Prominent white blues scholars such as Samuel Charters and Paul

Oliver, who had much to do with bringing the blues to a white audience, argued quite pointedly that the blues contains little social protest.[10] As Davis recognizes, this argument reflects a very limited understanding of what constitutes social protest and absolutely no awareness of the double-voiced nature of the blues—how the language of the blues communicates on several levels simultaneously. In the Delta blues standard, "Rambling Blues," for instance, Robert Johnson sings "I got rambling, I got rambling on my mind" but adds in another verse "I got mean things on my mind." One cannot be sure if the rambling represents a way of venting his own meanness or a meanness perpetrated on him by others. Compare Johnson's lines with these that Charles Peabody heard from black workers whom he was employing to dig for Indian burial mounds in Mississippi: "I'm so tired I' almost dead / Sitting up there playing mumblely-peg." Here the singers make ironic, witty reference to what Peabody was doing with his friends while waiting for work to be completed.[11] Johnson's lines threaten some kind of immediate (and maybe random) action against an oppressive force, but the workers' song can only obliquely describe an unfair situation. Nor is there any implied compensatory action beyond the singing itself. Davis points out that "the blues absorbed techniques from the music of slavery, in which protest was secretly expressed and understood only by those who held the key to the code" (111).[12] Clearly, Oliver was misguided in asserting that the reason "the number of protest blues is small is in part the result of the Negro's acceptance of the stereotypes that have been cut out for him" (322). On the other hand, to say that the primary function of the blues is to protest African Americans' plight in American society also severely circumscribes its social and aesthetic functions. The power of any performed blues regardless of style is that it is a form of history that seems to include within its performance the actions and gestures of all those who contributed to the form's creation.

To speak of the history of the blues is to speak of an ongoing process of cultural renewal. To speak of the history of the blues is also to speak of a variety of styles. I have taken most of my examples from Mississippi Delta blues tradition primarily because it is the best documented. One can also make a case for its being the most influential given that it moved from the cotton fields of Mississippi and Arkansas to the clubs of London and Paris in little more than a generation.[13] Most important, the style's continuity with earlier African American song forms is obviously discernible.[14] Because this style of blues is so closely tied to the experience of slavery and what we might call the continuation of that experience even after the Civil

War, most Delta blues singers have been men. The "rambling" they sing of often directly reflects the southern black man's attempt to find the means to support himself in a society where such opportunity had been denied to him. As Willie Dixon points out in his autobiography, southern black men had to move to find work, and even so, work was just as likely to find them in the form of forced labor on levee camps and so-called work farms. In *Blues People* Jones points out that the Civil War stripped African American men of their identity within American society (55). As slaves they had a place, whether as economic integers or opportunities for someone else's moral advancement. As free citizens, though, they were denied social sanction. The Delta blues singers named the situation Jones describes the "Walking Blues." Although this phrase signified many possibilities, its genesis derives from the knowledge that walking was their only form of freedom, however limited. As a familiar blues refrain puts it, "There's only one thing I done wrong / I stayed in Mississippi about a day too long."

Strictly speaking, the Mississippi Delta comprises the counties of Coahoma, Humphreys, Leflore, Sunflower, Tunica, and Yazoo. In practice, though, Mississippi Delta–style blues performers come from eastern Arkansas, western Tennessee, northern Louisiana, and of course western Mississippi. Charters helps to explain the singularity of Delta blues when he notes that "Negroes were more heavily concentrated in the delta than they were in many other areas of the South, and because of the violence of the Mississippi caste system they were kept at even further distance from the influence of Southern white music" (27). (The land is well suited for growing cotton because of its rich soil created by a long history of being flooded over by the Yazoo River.) As blacks from the Mississippi Delta migrated to Chicago and Detroit in the 1940s to take advantage of the opportunities in the factories supplying materials for World War II, the music and culture of the blues went too. Although the music became electrified, reflecting its new urban locale, it was nonetheless still being directed at and marketed to sharecropping blacks still in Mississippi.

Delta blues is a coherent tradition through which one can clearly hear the prior forms out of which it was made. Moreover, thanks to the invaluable work of Alan Lomax and other field-workers, it is amply documented. Yet, as Robert Palmer notes, Delta blues is not important because it influenced Bob Dylan or Mick Jagger or because its makers became "successful entertainers," but because it was invented by a "particular people who made particular personal and artistic choices in a particular place at a particular time" (19). Unlike Bessie Smith singing sweetly to Louis Armstrong's trumpet and Fred Longshaw's piano, Delta blues achieves its particularity in part because it comes directly out of the cotton fields and levee camps. For instance, a familiar formal device such as call-and-response, used in the earlier forms of black music, can be heard in all styles of blues. With the Delta blues performers, Charters further points out, one still hears "the dominant strains of older music in the Delta, the gang work song and the field holler," a fact that is reflected in the gruff, almost harsh singing style employed by Delta performers (27). For any blues singer, the meaning of the lyrics is less important than the sounds which can be made out of the lyrics. Certainly, classic blues singers such as Bessie Smith or Alberta Hunter used their voices as instruments to sing against the meaning of the words they pronounced, but it is also true that they were beautiful singers even by conventional European standards.[15] Delta performers Charlie Patton and Bukka White, by contrast, yelled and slurred and growled their words to the point of incomprehension.

Of course incomprehension in this instance is mostly a matter of audience. Willie Dixon says that he first became aware of the power of the blues while serving a stint of forced labor about fifteen miles north of Vicksburg, Mississippi, sometime in the late 1920s. Although familiar with blues music, only when he heard the other prisoners "down there moaning and groaning these really down-to-earth blues" did he begin to inquire about the relationship between the music these men made and the work that they did (25). As Dixon's birth into the blues suggests, the Delta singers learned their art while laboring on levee camps and plantations. When Son House and Muddy Waters sing, one hears the sounds of field hollers and work songs leading all the way back to slavery.[16] In 1965 the already ancient Son House reflected:

> People wonder a lot about where the blues comes from. Well, when I was coming up, people did more singing in the fields than they did anywhere else. Time they got to the field, they'd start singing some kind of old song. Tell his ol' mule, "Giddup There!," and he'd go off behind his mule, start plowing and start a song. Sang to the old mule or anybody. Didn't make any difference. (qtd. in Evans 42–43)

The type of singing House describes is a field holler, a descendant from slavery and quite likely parts of Africa, and its roots remain in the communal singing associated with the work song. For House, the beginning of the plowing and the beginning of the song are the same thing. The song is not merely an accompaniment to work; rather, the work creates the song and the song creates the work. Muddy Waters's reflections on his blues origins reinforces this point while also forcefully suggesting both the communal nature of these spontaneous blues-work performances and the inherent sense of protest that is wedded to the form:

> I was just a boy and they put me to workin' right along side the men. I handled the plough, chopped cotton, did all of them things. Every man would be hollerin' but you don't pay that no mind. Yeah, course I'd holler too. You might call them blues but they was just made-up things. Like a feller be workin' or most likely some gal be workin' near to you and you want to say somethin' to 'em. So you holler it. Sing it. Or maybe to your mule or something or it's gettin' late and you wanna go home. I can't remember much of what I was singin' now 'ceptin' I do remember I was always singin', "I cain't be satisfied, I be all troubled in mind." Seems to me like I was always singin' that, because I was always just singin' the way I felt, and maybe I didn't exactly *know* it, but I jest didn't like the way things were down there—in Mississippi. (qtd. in Levine, *Unpredictable* 95)

When these singers recall their own origins in the blues, plowing day is behind them. They have become professional blues singers singing no-where near the cotton field to audiences who are mostly white. Even when there is no longer any field work for these men to do, the work that they did in the field remains part of the song being sung today. That is, the work that House and Waters describe as being coincident with their coming to blues consciousness remains in the work that they perform in their blues.

House in his example seems to sing for the mule alone, but he really doesn't, of course. As we shall see in the discussion of Frederick Douglass and the slave songs, all blues singers were creating themselves through an established form of communal self-creation. Speaking in 1974, Delta blues singer Johnny Shines traces his manner of blues singing back to how he imagines slaves sang to one another. He notes that while the holler could sound to some ears like a moan or a peculiar form of address to a mule, it was for others a coded message.

> Back in slavery times. Take a young Buck, he have his mind to run off. But he don't wanna go by hisself, see. He wanna carry his girl with him. In the meantime, he can get this message late over in the evening. Leaves was wet. Dew was falling. You see, they [the slaves] sing in a broken language anyway. So they can stand under Old Moster's

feet and sing about him. He didn't know what the heck. He called 'field hollers.' Yeah, man. So this here Buck he would rare back throw his hand upside his head and holler . . .

Mississippi River so deep and wide
Got to talk to my woman on the other side
("Slavery")

Shines goes on to describe how this singer would be heard on the plantation across the river and a meeting would be arranged. Here the blues originates in the slave's need to subvert the master's will in order to communicate with his love.[17] Nearly fifty years earlier, though still more than sixty years after slavery, blues artists such as Tommy Johnson, Arthur "Big Boy" Spires, and Fred McDowell were also speaking in this tradition when they sang, "Don't allow me to holler, I have to murmur low."[18] Though couched as an address to a clandestine lover, the words carry the force of communal knowledge: a tradition of speaking simultaneously to potentially opposed audiences impossible without the experience of slavery.[19] In the voices of these largely anonymous singers we hear what Emerson called the "mysterious process of conversion" by which culture is created. The "holler" becomes a "murmuring low": a secret history of the work that became the blues.

As Shines's example suggests, the tradition of the blues begins in slavery, yet those in slavery could not imagine the tradition of the blues. Recovering an intellectual tradition that comes out of slavery has been understandably easier for musicians than it has been for intellectuals. Indeed, how to appropriate the legacy of the blues—and with it the legacy of slavery—has been a defining issue in African American letters. Frederick Douglass's famous discussion of the slave songs identifies the cultural conflict embedded in African American musical forms. He recalls how the slaves

would make the dense old woods, for miles around, reverberate with their wild songs, revealing at once the highest joy and the deepest sadness. They would compose and sing as they went along, consulting neither time nor tune. The thought that came up, came out—if not in the word, in the sound;—and as frequently in one as in the other.

Created from within the rhythm of slave experience, the songs also provided a means for the slaves to shape that experience. A perfect fit between word and sound, the language Douglass describes is Edenic—prior to what Emerson calls the first fall, into consciousness. Douglass, though, suffers this fall when he abandons slavery.

> I did not, when a slave, understand the deep meaning of those rude and apparently incoherent songs. I was myself within the circle; so that I neither saw nor heard as those without might see and hear. They told a tale of woe which was then altogether beyond my feeble comprehension. . . . To those songs I trace my first glimmering conception of the dehumanizing character of slavery (57–58).

Despite that last sentence, Douglass's account of the songs' meaning is less about a heritage in which he created himself than about one he has had to repress. His example reveals the extraordinary labor required to create a culture different from the one that has been inherited. In Douglass's case, his anguish is that of one who creates his self through one language and then believes that he must exchange this self for a language that belongs to someone else.

Douglass's relationship to the slave songs is complicated because, by the logic of his narrative, they represent a way of life that he is abandoning. As he says, he could not understand slavery until he was no longer a slave. Within a traditional Emersonian frame of self-reliance, the story of how Douglass moves from speaking a slave language to learning standard English makes Emerson's injunction to "trust thyself: every heart vibrates on that iron string" sound quaint (*Essays* 260). How paltry Emerson's words are next to Douglass's achievement. Douglass remembers the slave songs from the perspective of one who has achieved self-reliance: he is a free man and no longer has to speak the language he did as a slave. Adopting a double perspective, Douglass translates these songs' meaning for the white audience that he is implicitly joining. On first hearing, the songs "told a tale of woe" that "breathed the prayer and complaint of souls boiling over with the bitterest anguish." To the outsider, the songs seemed an "unmeaning jargon"; to the slaves, they were "full of meaning to themselves" (57–58). Some generations later Johnny Shines looks to the slaves' songs as the root of his invention, but Douglass sees them as something he has transcended. Douglass's narrative retreats from the central, shocking truth of the slaves' singing: it created an identity outside of the master's knowledge.

To hear and speak the language of the slaves was to be "within the circle." To be free was, necessarily, to be without. As a man writing outside the circle, Douglass hears the slaves' songs as "soul-killing." The river of song that the slaves created becomes the dark undertow to Douglass's narrative. Despite laboring to acquire letters, the tools of self-reliance, he finds himself "regretting my own existence, and wishing myself dead" (58). Learning to read brings Douglass freedom, but at the cost of alienation from his first form of self-consciousness. It is likely that without the sense of self the slave songs gave him he could not have found the means to steal the master's language. Defining his cultural identity along what amounts to political lines obligates Douglass to present "slave" culture and "free" culture as polar opposites. Just as there was no way to imagine the slave as part of American society without changing his political identity, so was there no way to imagine that the culture of slaves was part of the culture of America. Douglass's example reveals how difficult the question of cultural ancestry can be within in a democratic society committed to transformation as an inherent good. Although the slave songs clearly helped to give him a sense of self-consciousness—an identity—he cannot reconcile that prior identity with becoming an American intellectual.

Subsequent generations of African American intellectuals would self-consciously attempt to reclaim what Douglass had surrendered. In the 1920s Alain Locke, Langston Hughes, and Jean Toomer each tried to incorporate vernacular African American expression, in particular the blues, into their literary works. In doing so, they were elaborating upon the seminal example of W. E. B. Du Bois in *The Souls of Black Folk* (1903).[20] Like Douglass, Du Bois hears the songs as "the music of an unhappy people" whose "message was naturally veiled and half articulate" when "the slave spoke to the world" (*Souls* 184–85). But Du Bois is also aware that even though he was never a slave and was in a sense shielded as a child from the legacy of slavery, those slave songs still shape who he is. Du Bois relates how, before learning the slave songs as a scholar, he encountered them as a form of nostalgia. He remembers that as a child growing up in Great Barrington, Massachusetts, far from the sharecropper South that strove to recreate the conditions of slavery, "these songs . . . stirred me strangely. They came from the south unknown to me, one by one, and yet at once I knew them as mine" (180). Ironically, Du Bois's relationship with the slaves' singing is not nearly as intimate as Douglass's, yet he is the one who is able to make the heritage of the slaves' creation a part of his own identity as an American.[21] Yet, in making the argument that the "sorrow songs" constituted the African American's contribution to American culture, Du Bois was not concerned with preserving some essentially true or prior form of African American song so much as transforming it into an intellectual heritage fit for use.

Written on the verge of the Civil Rights Act, LeRoi Jones's *Blues People* (1963) echoed the Emerson-Douglass perspective that the culture of slavery must be abandoned totally. At the same time he revised Du Bois's claims by arguing that the blues is the first truly authentic form of African American expression because it was the first created beyond the shadow of slavery.[22] Though rarely discussed anymore, *Blues People* remains a crucial book for understanding the development of African American music, its relation to African American culture, and its relation to American culture. "When America became important enough to the African to be passed on," Jones asserts, the songs that were formerly about Africa became "*formal* renditions" that "were in some kind of Afro-American language" (xii). On Jones's account, the blues does for the ex-slaves what learning to read did for Douglass. The creation of a language and a form that referred to their experiences on this continent is simultaneous with their creation of an American identity, albeit inflected by Africa. Whereas Douglass distances himself from the experience of the slave song in order to assert an identity that slavery denied him, Jones wants to create a historical tradition in which he can account for his own incarnation as a poet. Ironically, Jones's historical reconstruction bypasses slavery except as something to be transcended and returns to Africa to account for the origins and hence continuity of black identity. Since Jones denies that either the slave songs or the work song are culturally vital forms, his poetic tradition must come from either free-born Africans or free-born blues singers. To Jones, independent, itinerant, free-born twentieth-century blues singers such as Furry Lewis or John Lee Hooker or Robert Johnson are more aesthetically worthy ancestors than the mostly anonymous men and women, these former Africans whose encounter with the experience of American slavery created the verbal context which later spawned the blues.

Jones's example is emblematic of how difficult it is for intellectuals to define themselves by forms that have virtually nothing to do with writing. Bob Dylan's "Blind Willie McTell" and Johnny Shines's "Slavery Time Breakdown" express the continuity of the blues because they speak from within its tradition. To Jones, poetry is a higher form of cultural expression than the blues, which is a higher form than the work song. Although Du Bois brilliantly employs the slave songs in *The Souls of Black Folk*, he does so by transforming them into a metaphor. Each chapter begins with musical notation of a phrase from a slave song juxtaposed with a citation from the European literary tradition. But because the slave songs were created as it were outside of European musical standards, there is no way to capture on the page their authentic form. Implicitly, Du Bois's writing is the form through which the slave songs take on historical meaning. Nonetheless, Du Bois is practicing a form of Emersonian cultural renewal precisely because he is not interested in preserving the slaves' music as an essence. Jones by contrast echoes the soul-killing Douglass by denying that the knowledge gained as a slave is relevant to the culture that the freed slaves created. It may be understandable that the poet Jones would privilege poetry over other forms of intellectual labor, but by taking a conventional intellectual approach to how the slave songs and eventually the blues were made, we miss the chance to explore *how the making of culture* becomes American culture.

Poirier nicely says that "work for Emersonian pragmatists [is] a mode of action by which an inheritance, instead of being preserved or reverentially used in the present, is radically transformed into a bequest for the future" (*Poetry* 123). This description certainly better helps us understand the achievement of the work song—the form that to Jones is to be dismissed because it is intimately tied to physical labor. Indeed, the combination of the words "work" and "song" implies both a song about work and how a song is worked.[23] Robert Palmer points out that for many African peoples, there was no individual word for "music" because music was such a pervasive part of their culture.[24] Lawrence Levine notes that whites were consistently amazed by how the slaves accompanied everything they did with music—and usually dance. "There were songs of in-group and out-group satire, songs of nostalgia, nonsense songs, children's songs lullabies, songs of work and play and love" (*Black* 15). Though all music is a form of expression, the African orientation toward musical expression that the slaves inherited differs from the Western in that the distinction between performer and audience becomes blurred; consequently, there was no central authorizing text.[25] This difference is no doubt one reason why the poet Jones would be uncomfortable claiming the work song as an antecedent. Because African American musical forms were created out of specific shared situations—working the fields or practicing religious rituals—the text was a collective creation of the community. The songs are not only performances but acts, meant to have specific and immediate effects on their community (not just to stimulate applause).

White observers from the North or Europe persistently wondered not only at the fact of the slaves' singing, but at their capacity for spontaneous invention. Did the songs come from a leader or did they grow "by gradual accretion, in an almost unconscious way"? (Levine, *Black* 25). On the other hand, it seemed that these songs so perfectly reflected the slaves' environment that one could imagine they had been created out of the air, as natural as the wind blowing across the marsh. On the other hand, surely some originating mind was responsible for what were after all representations, artifacts distilled from experience. Because music seemed so natural to the slaves, nineteenth-century observers were slow to see that these songs expressed a definite creative will. As I have already observed, beneath the surface of the work songs, chants, and spirituals the slaves created was a protest against the chains that held them. Emerson insisted than an "institution of any kind"—and this would include the institution of slavery—"must stop with some past utterance of genius" (*Essays* 57); slave songs were a form of this genius.

The slaves and their descendants share with the pragmatist a compelling interest in converting the hard facts of their existence into something else. That is, conversion is a good in and of itself. For the slaves, such conversion was a matter of life and death; for pragmatists their interest in conversion has been more theoretical—even if expressed in terms meant to be more practical. William James said that "the pragmatist turns toward concreteness and adequacy, towards *facts*, towards action and towards power" (*Writings* 509, emphasis mine). Emerson observes in *The American Scholar* that "colleges and books only copy the language which the field and the work-yard made" (*Essays* 62), which is precisely where the blues comes from; but the kind of work the blues performs deepens the meaning of the pragmatist fascination with facts. Consider, for example, Robert Frost's "Mowing," which might be seen as a more familiarly intellectualized version of the kind of cultural conversion that the work song accomplishes. Here a speaker describes the joy to be derived from the physical exertion of mowing: "There was never a sound beside the wood but one / And that was my long scythe whispering to the ground" (*Collected* 26). The speaker is trying both to describe the poetry of work and to convert work into poetry. The poem's situation is resolved in this line: "The fact is the sweetest dream that labor knows." The poem moves forward by working backward from William James's assertion that "truths emerge from facts; but they dip forward into facts again and add to them; which facts again create or reveal new truth (the word is indifferent) and so on indefinitely. The 'facts' themselves are not *true*. They simply *are*" (*Writings* 585; qtd. in Poirier, *Renewal* 58). The "truth" of the poem is the evocation of an act: the work of the scythe. The illusion that Frost creates is the sense that fact can supersede truth, as if we can abandon the world of interpretation for one of pure fact—or what James would call pure experience.[26] To a certain extent Frost's poem is an example of copying "the language which the field and the work-yard made." Mostly it proves how hard the intellect has to work to make something the body does fit for intellectual use. For Frost, the point is how hard one must work to achieve the purity of a fact or, really, a fact's purity.

The blues tradition as it comes through the work song, though, presents mind and body, thought and act, as genuine fusion. The singers of the work song understand how "the fact is the sweetest dream that labor knows," yet this insight enables them to transform the drudgery the body is made to perform into something else, an occasion for reflection. Singers of work songs do not generally choose their work; thus the accomplishment is taking possession of an act they have been forced to do. Although the work song is a communal creation, it requires a leader to set the cadence of the song and, along with it, that of the work being performed. The speaker in Frost's "mowing" may contemplate the sweetness of his labor; the work song leader performs so that the other members of his group keep time. Ellington's famous phrase, "it don't mean a thing, if it ain't got that swing," takes on added resonance when the singing provides the accompaniment for four men swinging axes in unison to chop down a tree! Four men with four axes chopping down a tree would have to swing in rhythm. Missing the correct beat, or off beat, could cost a limb or life.

During one of his trips through the state prisons of Louisiana and Mississippi in the 1940s Alan Lomax discussed the aesthetic of the work song with a song leader, Bama. In *The American Scholar* Emerson speaks of culture being created in terms of the strange process out of which "experience is converted into thought, as a mulberry leaf is converted into satin. The manufacture goes on at all hours" (*Essays* 60). In the example of Bama and his companions we hear something of this conversion process. After prompting Bama to confirm that "when you singin', you forgit, you see, and the time just pass on 'way," Lomax asked him what made a good leader, speculating that a "good voice" was probably the essential ingredient. The prisoner's response is revealing. He says that the quality of voice makes no difference; rather, is

> the man with most experience to my understandin' to make the best leader in anything. You see, if you'd bring a new man here, if he had a voice where he could sing just like Peter could preach like Paul, and he didn't know what to sing about, well, he wouldn't do no good, see. But here's a fellow, he, maybe he ain't got no voice for singin', but he's been cooperating with the peoples so long 'til he know exactly how it

should go. And if he can just mostly talk it—why and you understand how to work,—well, it would go good with you. It don't make any difference about the voice. If you take a man with no voice, but plenty of experience, *who knows the time*, then you will have a good leader. (Lomax, *Prison*)

Bama gives a remarkably eloquent discussion that directs our attention to what the work being done requires. From this example, it is easy to pick out the non-Western heritage of blues singing, where the context determines both the song and the song's aesthetic. Hitting the notes called for by the score does not apply in this context, unless the score is a field or a tree, and the musical accompaniment an axe or a pick. Bama is interested not in a voice's so-called purity but in the experience it conveys. It is not just that the voice has done this before, but the doing has somehow become a part of the voice. "Cooperating with the peoples" is perhaps the work song leader's greatest attribute; this is something he has done before with others; their spontaneous act of creation also communicates a shared heritage of hardship *and creation*. The experience of the leader not only translates experience into appropriate work but also enables his work group to "understand how to work." Through the leader they are given the understanding—the thought—that underlies their work.

Though the work provides the occasion for the singing, the singing composes the work. In contrast to Frost's speaker, Bama discovers that the sweetest dream his labor knows is the opportunity to let the mind ramble away from the task at hand to a variety of speculations rendered in verse form that he shares with his fellows. Emerson could be speaking about someone like Bama when he recalls the "old fable" that "implies that individual, to possess himself, must sometimes return from his labor to embrace all of the other laborers" (*Essays* 54). Bama, as well as other singers of the work song, achieve this possession *while laboring*. Thus, their singing recounts, among other subjects, impending tasks such as growing crops or building roads, or how the singers came to be in jail or distances traveled (or not) through trains caught (or missed), the vagaries of the weather, women desired, their prowess with tools (also a metaphor for their prowess as sexual performers)—virtually any vagrant thought or desire that comes to mind and can be raked into song. Most basically, the songs describe the situation the singers occupy and their wish to transform it.

The song "Early in the Mornin'," which accompanies the chopping down of an oak tree, is a representative example. Sung by Little Red,

Tangle Eye, and Hard Hair, with "22" as leader,[27] the men are, according to Lomax, "at work on a live oak, 'double cutting,' that is, standing in a square around the tree, with two men chopping from opposite corners of this square on beat one, the other on the alternate beat" (*Prison*). You hear the chop of an axe before these words sound out: "Well, it's early in the mor—in the mornin' / Baby, when I rise, Lordy, Momma." Addressing someone named Bertha, a name that resounds through documented work songs and early blues, the singer confesses to having "a misery." Through-out, you hear the amazing rhythm between song and labor, the words punctuating the swinging axes, the axes punctuating the words. The singers dramatize their misery through their song, yet they sing them-selves out of their misery too. In the third verse they sing of their situation by analogy, referring to a task they have no doubt also performed, crush-ing the "rocks-a gravel" required "to make a solid road." This image is juxtaposed with one of fantasy and desire: what it takes "to make a good lookin' whore." The fourth verse has an elaborate pun concerning a "peckerwood" (which signifies, among other meanings, both a wood-pecker and a poor white) whose cupidity causes him to "peck so hard, Lordy, Baby / Until his pecker done got sore, Lord, sugar." Lines fre-quently end with a grunt, the "well-a" that will reappear in Mississippi country blues recordings, which keeps the men's singing in time with the axes. The song ends with singers speculating about a better life elsewhere: "Well, hain't been to Georgia, boys, but / Well, it's I been told, sugar." Variations of this refrain are repeated until the singing abruptly ends, as if the reverie of a life beyond the immediate task has become too much to contemplate in light of present circumstances. Thus the singing is re-turned to the labor that prompted it.

Jones suggests that with the work song "America became the reference" for the singing (*Blues* 18). One might conclude that from the point at which the slaves began to sing about the work they were doing on this land their language was no longer African but transitional, medial, American. Jones, though, maintains that the very fact that the work song's per-formance only culminates in more work (though not necessarily in the Jamesian sense) means that the work song is chained to the situation which inspires it and therefore has no art.[28] As we see, however, not only did the work song have concerns other than work, but leaders like Bama bring a recognizably aesthetic orientation to their work. That Bama, in communion with his fellows, self-consciously shapes his songs in response to their shared experience makes him more than a precursor to the blues; he is a creative artist, an American Scholar, if you will.

Bama's example, through his body and in his song, conveys the truth of Emerson's great pragmatist remark, one that may be applied both to the work song and its descendant, the blues: "Art is the path of the creator to his work" (*Essays* 466). The grunting men, the landing axes, the clanking chains: these are the sounds that mark the road these artists of the everyday travel to reach their work. Bama was recorded by Lomax two years after the United States detonated the atom bomb on Japan, seven years before *Brown v. Board of Education*, yet his account of why he was in jail, though admittedly tailored for his audience, reads like something out of Reconstruction: "And sometimes I wouldn't be [doing] nothin', but I'd been doin' so much 'til that when they'd get me, I'd due to been got anyway. An one, two time they 'rest me, an' I told 'um I hadn't done nothin', an' they said, 'Arrest you in egvance [advance]—you gonna do sumpn'' " (qted. in Lomax, *Prison*). Or, as the bitterly comic blues verse runs,

> They 'rested me for murder an' I ain't never harmed a man
> They 'rested me for murder an' I ain't never harmed a man
> They 'rested me for forgery an' I can't even sign my name.

Lomax's presence with a tape recorder enables us to know of Bama's eloquence, which has to stand in for many whose words and acts went unrecorded.[29] Yet Bama's artistry is impossible without the prior form the work song's structure provides. Emerson remarks in "Circles" that "the field can not be seen from within the field" (*Essays* 409). Bama and his companions complicate this remark, though, by making the field the place in which they create their work. That is, the work Bama performs would be impossible without the cultural traditions that other anonymous souls invented in their effort to do something more than copy the language which the field and the work-yard made: their effort to make it s(w)ing.

Art is the path of the creator to his work; the work song is the path of the slaves to the blues. What we hear in the astonishing accounts that Alan Lomax, John Work, and Zora Neale Hurston left of men like Bama is the sound of American culture being broken wide open by people who were legally denied the right to have any kind of true identity. What the work song created out of necessity, the blues stylized into art—that is, one could choose to sing a blues without having to chop down a tree or lay down railroad ties. Most historians have noted that the blues' emphasis on individual creation distinguishes it from prior song forms in the African American tradition. Levine goes so far as to agree with Jones that it is the most "typically American music Afro-Americans had yet created and represented a major degree of acculturation to the individualized world of the larger society" (Black 221). Where slaves or prison gangs invent their songs to make the work they were being forced to perform their own, the blues singer invents his lyrics as a testament to his own creativity. The blues singer is therefore rightly recognized as the master improviser. One can pile up quotes from blues artists testifying to this skill. Mississippi artist Sam Chatmon: "About my blues—man, I can make blues everyday. I can make up a song anytime I wanna make it up, cause I keeps the blues" (qtd. in Lomax, Land 382). Or T-Bone Walker: "I can make up blues faster than I can sing them. I could sing the blues all day for you and never repeat a verse" (qtd. in Levine, Black 206).

Of course the blues musician works from within a form already acculturated in the ways of improvisation. Think of the blues as a process of cultural invention and we can say that it is the form by which African Americans acculturated America to their experience. As early as the 1830s J. Kinnard Jr. recognized this tendency to improvise in black song while being propelled along the St. Johns River in Florida by a boatload of slaves. After noting how the singers altered familiar verses with improvised ones, he described how "they condensed four or five [syllables] into one foot, or stretched out one to occupy the space that should have been filled with four or five; yet they never spoiled the tune. This elasticity of form is peculiar to negro song" (qtd. in Levine, Black 7).[30] Kinnard recognizes that no one song is ever performed the same way. As Robert Palmer notes, the lyrics of the blues tradition comprised "floating verses [which] were the common property of all blues singers" (Deep 5).[31] These floating verses provide an excellent example of the dynamic between individual creation and communal memory that informs the blues tradition. A blues singer is able to invent lines that others have sung before. Within the black song tradition, then, the blues singer becomes the representative figure for performing what the black song form had done all along. He may turn himself into his own band and replace the group of the work song with his own single person, but his verses come from the folk.

Rather than attributing to blues singers the originality that was already a part of the tradition that created them, it is better to think of them as scholars of this tradition—the Man Thinking who make their book out of life and the language they have inherited.[32] Certainly the blues (along with jazz) became the first obviously African American form to be revered, copied, and eventually adapted outside of America. When playing in Europe before rapturous audiences, Louis Armstrong and Duke Ellington were certainly aware that they had transformed the occasion of playing blues into a context that its original or earlier makers never could have imagined. On the other hand, country blues artists such as I have been considering were more likely to understand their blues as the fulfillment of a tradition rather than the extension of one. Describing the tradition of pain that the blues expresses, John Lee Hooker remarks that "it's somewhere down the line that you have been hurt some place. . . . It's not only what happened to you—it's what happened to your foreparents and other people" (qtd. in Evans 17). In this respect, the blues singer very much understands the performance of the blues to be both telling history and making it at the same time.

The fascinating documentary recording, *Blues in the Mississippi Night*, discloses how blues singers view themselves as cultural historians. Recorded in 1946 in the unlikely location of Alan Lomax's Greenwich Village apartment, it intersperses brief snatches of field recordings of chain gangs and church choirs with the music and conversation of three blues singers reflecting on the experience that has made them blues singers. Big Bill Broonzy, Memphis Slim (Peter Chatmon), and Sonny Boy (John Lee) Williamson give an invaluable account of the blues and its cultural background. Their conversation encapsulates the entire history of the blues tradition, from slave song to work song to blues. Listening only to this record, one would hardly know that the blues was already a major American cultural export. Indeed, upon hearing the conversation played back to them, the blues singers were, according to Lomax, "terrified," and asked him to conceal their identities so that their families would not be harmed in retaliation for their telling the truth of the blues (Lomax, *Blues*). Lomax waited thirteen years before releasing a severely edited version of their conversation; not until 1990, well after their deaths, were their names revealed and a more complete version of their conversation released. With good reason, then, did these blues singers understand their art to signify upon the history of African Americans on this continent; it would be incomprehensible to them that anyone outside the circle of the blues could fully understand what they were discussing except, perhaps, as an excuse to silence them.

Nonetheless, *Blues in the Mississippi Night* makes known the almost secret history that was compressed into the blues form. Punctuating their conversation with songs or lines from songs, the bluesmen act out the idea of the blues as an ongoing form of cultural critique. Initially, they define the blues as the condition of unrequited love. This definition of blues is a familiar one as the frequently sung refrains "the blues ain't nothing but a good man feeling bad" or "the blues ain't nothing but a worried old hard disease" suggest. But Son House explained to an English audience in 1970 that the blues describes any form of heart sickness—from love to murder (*Delta Blues*, "Monologue")—and the conversation on *Blues in the Mississippi Night* reveals that the blues comes out of a situation more encompassing than simply a couple's broken relationship. In awed tones the three singers discuss men such as Bama as their precursors. Broonzy says that "those fellows they got down there, on them chain gangs with big balls hangin' on their legs, can't go anyplace, unless there's a guard right over them and all that kind of stuff. Those fellows have the blues, too." When Memphis Slim says that "all the blues originated from such stuff" as the chain gangs, Big Bill adds "that's what I mean about the heart part. You see, you singin' from the heart." At this point, "singin' from the heart" opens up a complicated historical understanding of cultural heartbreak.

Big Bill declares that the blues "didn't start in the North—in Chicago, New York, Philadelphia, Pennsylvania, wha'soever it is—it didn't start in the East—neither in the North—it started in the South, from what I'm thinkin'." Memphis Slim clarifies Big Bill's argument: "Blues started from slavery." As the conversation continues, they elaborate and clarify what they mean to say while underscoring how the blues continues the world that the slaves made. Whether discussing a levee camp holler or a prison work song, one of them will say, "Well, that's what I mean, that's part of the blues," while another concludes, "That's the blues." Not only does their conversation constitute a history of the blues from the slaves' spirituals to the emerging urban blues that they were helping to create in Chicago and New York and Philadelphia, but it suggests how deeply each act of blues creation is concerned with transforming the past into a usable present. Listening to them singing railroad songs, levee camp hollers, prison work songs, rural blues, urban blues, you confront the evidence of cultural continuity and the living evidence of cultural transformation. As we saw with Johnny Shines, who described the origins of the field holler as a kind of prelude to his own blues, these performances convey the knowledge that slavery is somehow present. You hear in their singing what Frederick Douglass in his freedom could no longer bear to hear, the music that made the road that the slaves have built to reach the present America.

As an art form the blues builds the perfectly achieved tension between performer and audience that it inherits from the work song. This almost symbiotic relationship between speaker and listener is something that

Emerson could only imagine in *The American Scholar* because he did not know who his audience would be. The blues singer embodies the past of his audience, yet he also dramatizes the transformation of that past. The work song settled the present to imagine the future; the blues settles the past to make the present. Albert Murray says that wherever a blues performance happens, it takes place in a "temple." Though Murray is speaking of uptown blues performance such as those of Duke Ellington, Count Basie, Jelly Roll Morton, and Bessie Smith, as opposed to the country blues I have been discussing, the performance dynamic is the same at the Savoy Ballroom as it is behind a mule. According to Murray, these performers were "fulfilling a central role in a ceremony that was at once a purification rite and a celebration of the festive earthiness which was tantamount to a fertility ritual" (*Stomping* 17). For Murray, the blues musician is a kind of high priest, one whose "performance is not only to drive the blues away and keep them at bay," but to do so by evoking "an ambience of Dionysian revelry in the process" (17). Though the lyrics are the element of the blues easiest to transfer to the page, Murray rightly suggests that for blues-based musicians the dance is the thing (189).

Murray's remark highlights how the fusion of mind and body that the dance enacts is a highly stylized version of what the work song enacts. The American scholars created within (and by) the blues tradition invent their language, their fossil poetry, through the body. Through the dance the blues singers' art inspires, the group gathers to celebrate the ongoing creation of themselves as a community. Murray says that at a blues performance

> what is at issue is the primordial cultural conditioning of the people for whom the blues music was created in the first place. They are a dance-oriented people. They refine all movement in the direction of dance-beat elegance. *Their work movements become dance movements and so do their play movements;* and so, indeed, do all the movements they use every day, including the way they walk, stand, turn, wave, shake hands, reach, or make any gesture at all. (189, emphasis mine)

In this account, even the most casual gestures have an antecedent in some prior act, yet those gestures represent ways of making over the past into the present. These dance gestures that accompany the blues represent the performance of a performance. Here the blues becomes the medium through which the work song is performed. We may want to say that Emerson's statement that "books are for the scholar's idle times" was merely a figure of speech (*Essays* 58), yet the fact is that a significant part of

American culture has been created by people who were denied access to books. The action that Emerson says is essential to the American scholar achieves its form in the doing, in the work, that Americans perform. Murray's description wonderfully evokes this kind of democratic action: how a dance at the Savoy in the 1930s re-creates previous occasions of communal song and dance, even those occasions such as those work song that had been prompted by outsiders. The story that Murray implies is both more complex and more mysterious than what conventional histories with their commitment to written records can reveal: how layers of culture may be embedded within a single gesture—say, the movement of a hand while dancing.

Murray is right to emphasize how integral the motion of the body is to the playing of the blues, but the body's movements would not be so important to the blues if they were not vestiges of the experience of the fields and the docks. "To possess the full range of Afro-American culture," Ralph Ellison says, one must "know how to dance" (*Going* 208). I underscore this point by way of acknowledging that in focusing more on the lyric content of the blues I am narrowing the full dimension of their expression (but dancing on paper must be done in one's head). Nonetheless, improvisations that transformed physical labor into a cultural inheritance became embedded in the lyric form of the blues. We see this in its flexible lyrics, borrowed rhythms, floating verses, and improvisation. Just as the work movements become dance movements, blues lyrics adapt previous improvisations. Historians of the blues connect its formal flexibility to the great southern black diaspora of the first half of this century. LeRoi Jones is not alone in saying that the blues was created by people who were enjoying for the first time freedom of movement, who were in a way exploring and settling the country at the same time (96). In this respect, that blues lyrics reveal an interest in moving—in rambling—that expands the idea of the dance into larger areas for movement. On the other hand, as lyric, the blues is better able than the dance to comment on the circumstances of its own creation. Douglass can speak of the slave songs as existing within the circle, but the creation of that circle also reflected the fear of being heard by others outside of it. Similarly, the work songs documented by Alan Lomax were sung not only in front of a microphone but before white guards holding guns.

Like the singer of work songs, the blues singer invents his words through an aesthetic of performance, an instance of Emerson's assertion in "The Poet" that "the man is only half himself, the other half is his expression" (*Essays* 448). Big Bill Broonzy's account of his own composition process suggests that he understands his work in precisely these Emersonian terms: "What I mean is you can't put down the music in the blues on no paper" (Lomax, *Land* 453). Broonzy did not even keep copies of his own records—he was not interested in what he had already done, but only what he was doing. For most of the country blues singers only a fragment of their repertoire was ever recorded. Most blues performances were created for a dance or a hayride or whatever would stretch on far beyond the three minutes or so dictated by the recorded performance. As Broonzy's remark attests, blues were conceived and performed as unfinished works—provisional, temporary records of a never-ending process. This tendency reflects the blues' origin within an oral culture, but Broonzy's remarks also suggest that he takes responsibility for the lyrics that he sings—even when borrowed, they are also his.

The blues singer discovers his self in the speaking of his voice: in his blues. Broonzy also told Lomax that "they ain't no blues singer in the world that can sing one three times the same way. He bound to change his blues if he feeling it." Hinging his art on the spontaneity of the creative moment, the blues singer remakes the tradition from which he sings each time he performs. He becomes not only the embodiment of his tradition but a model for how American culture is transformed into something that is within and yet beyond its origins at the same time. Emerson's remark that "everything good is to be found on the highway," which John Dewey took to be emblematic of American thinking, achieves a literal form in the blues. One could adduce hundreds of lines to explore how the blues tradition makes the ideal of movement, of transformation, a goal to be realized, but for my purposes we can concentrate on the song that Muddy Waters referred to as the Delta national anthem, "Walking Blues."[33] At once an individual and a collective creation, "Walking Blues" exists in many versions often with different names. Before considering Son House's epic version, I want first to examine the recently issued version that a then-unknown Muddy Waters made for Alan Lomax in 1941 under the title of "Country Blues."[34]

The song is usually about rambling, but Waters's performance is a harrowing tale of lost love and loneliness, one he would later adapt for his Chess recording "Feel Like Going Home." Waters's account of his composition process extends our understanding of Big Bill Broonzy's definition of what constitutes blues writing. Lomax, who was sure to have heard other versions, asks Waters how he came to compose this song. "I made that blues up in '38," Waters asserts. Somewhat disingenuously, Lomax presses Waters to be more specific, asking him if he remembers where he was, how he was sitting, what he was thinking about, and so forth. Waters says, "I made it up 'bout the eighth of October '38." Then, very precisely, he adds, "I was fixin' a puncture on a car. I had been mistreated by a girl and looked like it ran in my mind to sing this song." On a textual level, this explanation makes sense. Each verse reflects upon the situation Waters describes. Yet as Lomax points out, other performances of the song with identical lyrics and an identical tune also exist. Discerning that Lomax is subtly challenging his authorship of the song, Waters becomes defensive. He acknowledges that "there are some blues that run like this one" and suggests that "this song come from the cotton field." To Lomax's companion, John Work, Waters is more blunt. Referring to "I Be's Troubled," he says with emphasis: "I made that up my own self." In both cases, Waters describes the composition of the song in terms of something that "just came into my mind." Throughout, Waters's seemingly contradictory answers suggest that the process of blues invention is more complicated than assumptions of purity or originality can account for. About "I Be's Troubled," he says, "I was just walkin' along the road and I heard a church song and it kind of 'minded me of that and I just beat off a little song from that." As Waters is well aware, his performances participate in a tradition of creation-by-re-creation.

In "The Poet" Emerson says that "genius is the activity which repairs the decay of things" (*Essays* 457). Above, Waters is repairing the decay of things by transforming something he has inherited into something new. Emerson says that "all symbols are fluxional; all language is vehicular and transitive, and is good, as ferries and horses are, for conveyance, not as farms and houses are, for homestead" (463). The blues that Waters performs are also a kind of conveyance, built out of previous tunes and words, yet they do carry him to a sort of homestead, the refuge he finds in his creation-within-others'-creations. Before admitting that he heard "Country Blues" on a record by Robert Johnson called "Walking Blues," Waters says with authority that "this song come from the cotton field," which is where he knew it even before he heard Johnson's version. Waters knows that the cotton field is the final answer to any question about the blues' origins; on the other hand, Waters also knows that that particular blues he just sang was *his* creation. In the process, Waters reveals how the tradition of the blues partakes of Emerson's central preoccupation in *The American Scholar*: "the sacredness that attaches to the act of creation," the moment at which "the act of thought" is "transferred to the record" (*Essays* 57). The act of creation is sacred because it is transformative. Who knows what future acts will be transform this one?[35] Which is to say, who knows what future at all?

As if to throw the question of origins and authorship up in the air for good, Waters acknowledges that before he heard the tune from Johnson he already knew it from Son House. House's version of that time, recorded for Lomax about a year after Waters's version, is very different from Waters's.[36] This version stands out because Lomax was able to use equipment that allowed him to make a recording longer than the usual three minutes. Ordinarily, a blues performer might sing verses stretching on for quite a bit longer than that—indeed, late in life House would often introduce songs he was to perform "as a piece of old blues" to emphasize that the song he was performing was incomplete.[37] House's 1942 version of "Walking Blues" runs to twelve verses, which, compared with other recorded versions, makes it a mini-epic at six minutes. This longer version enables us to approximate more closely what it was like to hear the blues singer's spontaneous performance of a received tradition in its characteristic environment. Moreover, House recorded with three other musicians (fiddle, mandolin, and second guitar and harmonica), making this a rare document of a Delta blues band that was actually more common than the solo singer accompanying himself on piano or guitar. House's first verse establishes the song's theme with a common blues refrain: "Got up this morning feeling around for my shoes / Know by that I got the old walking blues." I cannot describe the good-feeling, the levity, with which House injects these lines. Before singing this verse, House calls out to his mates something about looking for shoes, and you can almost hear the smiles the musicians exchange. This communal good feeling gets expressed in the shouts of encouragement, amplified by the furious exuberance with which his friends attack their instruments. House calls them out by name as each contributes his voice to the song. On one level, then, the "walking blues" is about the walking the musicians act out with their performance.

House's "Walking Blues" enacts a wide range of observations and philosophies, each of which describes a different experience of having the blues. As this one performance suggests, the blues can encompass many different situations because it is a way of knowing the world. The slipperiness of the term "blues" reflects how each time the singer performs, the singer redefines his or her understanding of whatever situation is being addressed. Memphis Slim says on *Blues in the Mississippi Night*, "Blues is the only thing, you know, that I can consider." Slim does not mean that his life is so oppressive that he cannot escape the blues he feels, but that blues music is his way of interpreting the world. He says that "when I have trouble, the blues is the only thing that helps me. I mean that's the only way to kind of ease my situation." Then more directly: "The blues helps a man out." Memphis Slim here is making the same point Kenneth Burke often made in suggesting that literature is a form of medicine.[38] House also says as much when he avers that "if I don't go crazy I'm sure gonna lose my mind," which is to say that House finds his mind by telling it. That House might have chosen different verses to sing—if Lomax had come back the next week I am sure he would have—underscores how the blues is House's way of thinking through a set of situations. He can ramble, improvise, over a wide field of topics—love, revenge, fidelity, the state of the singer's mind—and never give the sense that he has lost his focus because his form is so closely aligned to the situations it transforms. In describing how Thoreau's thinking derived from his walking, Emerson remarked, "And the relation of body to mind was still finer than we have indicated. He said, he wanted every stride his legs made. The length of his walk uniformly made the length of his writing. If shut up in the house, he did not write at all" (*Portable* 578). What Emerson says of Thoreau is true of the blues singer with the "Walking Blues." Dramatizing the flexibility of the blues form itself, House's performance becomes a perfect example of the continuity between action and thought that the blues singer so often enacts.

"Walking Blues," or walking-the-blues, reflects the hardship that inspires it and provides sustenance and comfort. In a general way, one can say that the blues tradition is created out of the experience of grief, of mourning. "Another man done gone" runs an old spiritual chant, and many blues songs begin with the experience of loss. For instance, in "My Black Mama" Son House sings of receiving a letter informing him that the woman he loves his dead. "I grabbed my suitcase I took on up the road," he sings, and when he arrives she is "laying on the cooling board."[39] The song becomes the singer's tribute to the woman he loved, who is dead. She is immortalized in the lyrics "My black mama's face shines like the sun / Oh, lipstick and powder, well, they sure won't help her none." On the other hand, that House uses these lyrics in other songs that are not necessarily about this particular woman suggests that he is singing for an audience that is both accustomed to mourning and to making something out of that mourning. Rooted in grief, the blues moves its audience toward a new day. Albert Murray says that "the blues as such are synonymous with low spirits" but "blues music is not" (*Stomping* 45).

Thus it makes sense that many blues songs would also begin in morning—the new day that is also an occasion for mourning. "I woke up this morning feeling sick and bad," House sings in another verse of "Walking Blues" (an opening in countless other songs). Johnny Shines somewhat comically laments in "This Morning": "I get up to eat my breakfast I found blues all in my bread." Or Tommy Johnson sings in "Lonesome Home Blues" about waking up with the blues around his bed and thus not being able to raise his head. Usually, this feeling in the blues precedes a leave-taking, and the blues singer often adopts the stance of one who is sorry to leave someone else behind. A familiar verse runs: "I'm leaving in the morning sorry I can't carry you." One might hear in this an echo of slavery and the sort of dilemma that tormented Douglass. The leaving, though, is also a lightening of a burden; he will find company down the road. One hears an answer to this sudden leave-taking in the lines Tommy Johnson uses in his marvelous "Big Road Blues":

> Ain't goin down this big road by myself
> Ain't goin' down this big road by myself
> If I can't carry you I'll carry somebody else.

To mourn of course is to feel that one has been left behind, left alone. These lyrics convey this feeling for both the singer leaving and the one whom he leaves behind. His promise to carry somebody else is also a promise to himself to move despite the grief he experiences. One can hear in his mourning the hope for a future community. Whereas Johnson sings of separation from one person and union with another, Bukka White renders this feeling of separation and potential union in terms of realizing one's individual self. In "Where Can I Change My Clothes," a song about being imprisoned at Parchman Farm, White combines mourning for himself with the hope for his own new morning by singing this devastating line over and over: "I wonder how long till' I can change my clothes." How long, in other words, before his life takes on a new form. Robert Johnson voices another version of this sentiment in "Me and the Devil Blues," singing "You can bury my body down by the highway side / So my old evil spirit can catch a Greyhound bus, and ride." Where that bus will take him is left unclear; it is possibility he seeks. Possibility is precisely what the field holler singer acknowledges at the conclusion of Johnny

Shines's "Slavery Time Breakdown": "I'm going to leave here walking because I can't ride / If you want to go come on by my side."

Waking up to find that one has the walking blues is equivalent to Emerson's question "Where do we find ourselves"? In House's "Walking Blues" the newness of the day prompts the singer to consider his relationship with the world, but not in a "this is the first day of the rest of your life" sense. Rather, "Walking Blues" begins with the singer in flux, recognizing that he is part of a prior situation. He names this situation in the second verse: "The blues ain't nothing but a low-down shaking chill / If you ain't had them I hope you never will." Here the singer faces his situation with courage and bravado. The lines themselves sound fearful, dark, lonelier than Kierkegaard. Yet the playing and singing which accompanies House, with the hollering and ferociously plucked instruments, cry out in joy. One believes that the speaker has known agony, but also understands that he has mastered this feeling. The blues is something that accompanies him wherever he goes, though it is not always a low-down shaking chill. The blues is almost a companion—a medium through which one experiences the world. Robert Johnson and Furry Lewis and Bukka White make this clear when they sing: "Hello blues, blues how you do?" In this line the blues becomes at once a fellow traveler and the inheritance that the singer carries with him and has come to name and thereby shape. "Now I met the Blues this morning walking just like a man," House sings in "Preaching Blues," "I said Good morning, Blues, now give me your right hand." In "Walking Blues" House knows that he cannot escape the blues; this is the knowledge that faces him upon waking each day. The question is: How is he going to live in the face of this recognition? Bluesman Henry Townsend remarks that "most good blues is about telling the truth about things" (quoted in Barlow 326). The blues has a triple meaning: something the singer feels (and may or may not suffer from), something he sings, and the form through which the singing and the feeling are realized. When House proclaims that he hopes "you" will never have the blues, it is at once a boast and a challenge. House expands the meaning of the blues by making them the occasion of his performance, and he also challenges his audience to recognize the extent to which they have been transformed by the blues.

Emerson's version of the "Walking Blues" is his essay "Experience," in which he hopes that a personal recovery from grief might become the basis for a larger cultural renewal. The occasion that prompts the essay is the death of Emerson's son, Waldo. "In the death of my son, now more than two years ago, I seem to have lost a beautiful estate—no more. I cannot get it nearer to me" (*Essays* 473). Although many have read this statement as proof of Emerson's coldness, I think it more likely reflects Emerson's desire to take hold of the grief that has seized him and transform it into something else. He wants to hold on to the grief even as he goes on; he wants to make of his grief a beginning point for some future inheritance, which would make his present act a gesture toward founding. Earlier I discussed how Emerson in this essay described America as "unapproachable" in terms of what had not yet been realized. He writes, "I am ready to die out of nature and be born again into this new yet unapproachable America I have found in the west." By what reasoning or act could Emerson's "death" through his son Waldo become the beginning of an as yet unapproachable America? Cavell says the essay itself stakes "Emerson's claim to something like the inheritance of philosophy, not only for himself, but America, a first inheritance" (*This New* 83). But when understood in the context of the blues, Emerson's gesture sounds wistful, dreamy—just as Emerson sounds so quaintly speculative when placed against the flesh and blood example of Douglass. What America can be imagined and realized that would be built upon the hopes of a single man? The blues, by contrast, embraces Emerson's general commitment to cultural renewal to participate in a truly realized form of America-building. That is, the tradition of the blues helps to make Emerson valid as an American cultural philosopher. The blues grounds Emerson and with him an American culture worthy of building.

Conversely, the blues singer's emphasis on originality makes sense within the context of the American self. "What is the aboriginal Self, on which a universal reliance may be grounded?" Emerson asks in "Self-Reliance" (*Essays* 268). His answer is:

> Power ceases in the instant of repose; it resides in the moment of transition from a past to a new state, in the shooting of the gulf, in the darting to an aim. This one fact the world hates; that the soul *becomes;* for that forever degrades the past, turns all riches to poverty, all reputation to shame, confounds the saint with the rogue, shoves Jesus and Judas equally aside. (271)

The endless circulation of power, of transformation, means there is no aboriginal self to be found. Elsewhere in the essay, Emerson says to "trust thyself," but in practice this means to think of yourself as a "Trustee" (260, 268). Hence, after shoving Judas and Jesus aside, he asks: "Why then do we prate of self-reliance?" Like James, Emerson posits a self that discovers its identity in its actions, so much so that we should "speak rather of that which relies because it works and is" (272). For Emerson the self is both achieved and to be achieved.

The Emersonian self, like the America the blues creates, is not whole unto itself but comprises a series of "nexts." By this reading, it makes little sense to speak of the Emersonian self as one that aspires to transcendence, as we traditionally have, without adding that this putative transcendence is provisional. One's transcendence is the fulfillment of the next self implied by the present one. The series goes on and on, like the steps on which we find ourselves at the outset of "Experience." Or, in another passage from "Circles," "step by step we scale this mysterious ladder; the steps are action; the new prospect is power" (405). It may seem to follow that this account would make the self not responsible for its actions. However, Emerson's hope is that the next self is made possible by the emergence of the present self. Emerson raises this idea in a notorious passage from "Self-Reliance":

> I shun father and mother and wife and brother when my genius calls me. I would write on the lintels of the door-post, *Whim.* I hope it is somewhat better than whim at last, but we cannot spend the day in explanation. Expect me not to show cause why I seek or why I exclude company. Then again, do not tell me, as a good man did today, of my obligation to put all poor men in good situations. Are they *my* poor? I tell thee, thou foolish philanthropist, that I grudge the dollar, the dime, the cent, I give to such men as do not belong to me and to whom I do not belong. There is a class of persons to whom by all spiritual affinity I am bought and sold; for them I will go to prison if need be; but your miscellaneous popular charities; the education at college of fools; the building of meeting-houses to the vain end to which many now stand; alms to sots, and the thousand-fold Relief Societies;—though I confess with shame I sometimes succumb and give the dollar, which by and by I shall have the manhood to with-hold. (*Essays* 262–63).

This passage makes many of Emerson's admirers uncomfortable—including one of his most sympathetic critics, Harold Bloom. After admitting that "Emerson meant by his 'class of persons' men such as Henry Thoreau and Jones Very and William Ellery Channing," Bloom acknowledges that Emerson also sounds dangerously close to Ronald Reagan and Jerry Falwell ("Emerson" 156).

As Cavell suggests, though, the key to this passage is Emerson's use of the word "whim." Emerson chooses this word to suggest his commitment to hold to a desire that might strike others as silly. His commitment is what matters. By writing "whim" on the lintel of his door, he places this act within the context of the "Old Testament command specifically at the time of Passover, as a sign to the angel of death to pass the house and spare its first born" (*Conditions* 136). Emerson aspires to a sacred act—the only kind that would prompt him to leave father and mother and wife and brother when his genius calls. The characteristic stance of the blues singer too is that of conveying a hard-earned lesson that has brought him wisdom which he hopes to pass on. Robert Wilkins sings, "I don't want anybody who don't want me," as if in expectation that his news will be met with suspicion. When he sings in "Fallin' Down Blues" that "I'm tired of standing in this long old lonesome road," he suggests both the loneliness of the position he has adopted and his desire to find others who will join him ("Alabama"). Like Son House attending to the call of the walking blues, Emerson hopes that his course will find others who will join him.

As House is called to sing so that he will not go crazy, so Emerson is called to write. Emerson's commitment to what he calls in "Self-Reliance" his "Intuition," which he also calls "Spontaneity," is so complete that he is willing to commit an act which his audience might judge to be whimsical. Emerson here aspires to the resolve that the Texas blues singer Mance Lipscomb elegantly compresses into one of his favorite statements, "I say me for a parable." Emerson's "whimsical" notion of "self-reliance" risks defying society's expectations only in the hope of founding a better society. Later, Emerson (in)famously lived up to his whimsical nature when he refused to join any of the antislavery societies that recruited him.

> I waked at night, & bemoaned myself, because I had not thrown myself into this deplorable question of Slavery, which seems to want nothing so much as a few assured voices. But then, in hours of sanity, I recover myself, & say, God must govern his own world, & knows his way out of the pit, without any desertion of my post which has none to guard it but me. I have other slaves to free than those negroes, to wit, imprisoned spirits, imprisoned thoughts, far back in the brain of man—far retired in the heaven of invention, &, which, important to the republic of Man, have no watchman, or lover, or defender, but I. (*Emerson in His Journals*, 437)

Guarding his own post enabled Emerson to define the prospect of American culture in such a way that it could include the culture that the slaves created.[40]

Emerson and the blues singer, then, are each painfully aware of the many ways in which American society compromises its ideals; moreover, they both recognize they are complicitous in that compromise. The blues singer, though, actually has a stronger sense of belonging to a community within America than Emerson does. Though the blues singer may be sorry that he cannot carry you, he is more certain than Emerson that he will find companions along the road. In this respect, the blues singer is more confident than Emerson; he knows that his voice is the means by which he and his audience have overcome their loss to inhabit a country that has tried to deny their presence. Rather than choosing the path of an easy cynicism—which can take either the obvious form of removing oneself from society or the more prevalent one of ostentatiously participating in certain cosmetic acts such as the kind Emerson lists above—the blues singer and Emerson both choose to affirm the promises democracy offers regardless that the immediate cost may seem a severe price to pay. Murray says that the main objective of the blues "is to state the facts of life . . . and proceed in spite of, and even in terms of, the ugliness and meanness inherent within the human condition" (*Hero* 36). True enough, but this gesture only has meaning in response to a specific situation, which for the blues singer, as for Emerson, is one of democratic possibility.[41] Both Emerson and the blues singer are looking to perfect the possibilities inherent within their American situation. Describing the motivation behind his somewhat bizarre World War II tribute blues to the U.S. Forces fighting the Japanese, "Junior's a Jap Girl's Christmas for His Santa Claus," the obscure Mississippi Delta blues singer Willie "61" Blackwell defiantly tells archivist Alan Lomax on the album *Walking Blues* that he wrote it because "I'm an American, you know." Part if not all of Blackwell's motivation to create derives from his perception of himself as one worthy of the promises America holds out for its citizens.

Thus Emerson and the blues singer defy expectation ("Don't mind people grinnin' in your face," Son House sings), but they also understand their acts as gestures that can be completed only in a future beyond their knowing. Cavell names this stance "Emersonian Perfectionism," or

> perfection understood not only to be compatible with democracy, but its prize. The idea is that the mode of character formed under the invitation to the next self, entering the next state of society, is one capable of withstanding the inevitable compromise of democracy without cynicism, and it is a way that reaffirms not only consent to a given society but reaffirms the idea of consent as a responsiveness to society, an extension of the consent that founds it. (*Conditions* 28)

The blues singer performing before an audience dramatizes a version of this consent. "Been down so long it look like up to me," a line familiar within the blues tradition, conveys a certain Emersonian whimsy. On the surface it sounds despairing, but shared with a sympathetic audience it becomes a comic-ironic tribute to endurance and hope in the face of much provocation. Performer and audience share the sentiment that despite all, we are here, we abide, we keep moving.

In a memorable remark, John Jay Chapman captured the dark view of Emersonian Perfectionism: "If a soul be taken and crushed by democracy till it utters a cry, that cry shall be Emerson" (202). One is inclined to say that such a cry is also the blues, but to do so would be to say that condition of the African American was one of only despair and would deny the blues a voice beyond protest. Before integration became a genuine possibility, one might have said that lamenting the situation of blacks was the only prerogative for an enlightened white American (someone like Emerson).[42] Chapman's sentence has its roots in Tocqueville's idea of the "tyranny of the majority," the fear that a commitment to equality will breed a mindless conformity in American culture. Emerson's "whimsy" was his defense against such a dreadful possibility. The complementary sentence to Chapman's, though opposite in intent, belongs to Cavell: "To figure that my voice is called for in the social formation is to figure both that I participate in a structure that produces unaccountable misery and that my participation is to be expressed as happiness, even Emersonian joy" (*Conditions* 29). I would say that Cavell's description of Emersonian joy is as perfect a description of the blues as any I know. The call to participate, though, is a call to transform and be transformed.

A work song dating at least back to the end of the nineteenth century gives another version of this call.

> Looked at the sun and the sun was red
> I looked at my partner, he was falling dead,
> But we just kept on moving.
> It was tough. (Lomax, *Land* 67–68)

Certainly the song identifies the social conditions that created it. The day's work is nearly done, the singer's partner will not live to see it end, and the singer has no choice but to go on. Nevertheless, the song must be something more than what it describes, otherwise it could not have been created at all. We can, for instance, jump the song's tracks and ask, what is being moved? In terms of aesthetic form, the song itself is moving—to the blues. But this only raises the issue of the singer's identity. Perhaps the song looks back to slavery, because surely the lines could have been sung then as well. Presumably he moves to another dead-end day on the same dead-end job. On the other hand, if we think of the song as an instance of democratic possibility that includes even the slaves, he might be moving on to something unimaginable, something better. No matter the hardships, they keep on moving, an instance of self-reliance beyond even what Emerson would demand. On a broader level, the song describes the continuity and discontinuity of American experience itself. When the singer confesses that "it was tough," he acknowledges how terrible it is to leave his friend, another version of himself, behind. He has no choice but to move forward to face his future. Likewise, we Americans—all of us—continue to come to terms with the legacy of slavery, acting out our dramas of acceptance and denial. It is tough to admit that slavery defines the American identity as surely as our commitment to equality does. It is tough for all Americans to come to terms with the transformation of identities this contradiction has bred, just as it was tough for Emerson to shun father and mother and wife and brother or for the typical blues singer to leave behind a lover to move down the road toward an unknown future.

Realizing the promises of democracy involves a continual process of habitation that is also a continual leaving. In the previous chapter I discussed homelessness as a condition of American identity. The tradition of the blues, however, creates a home out of the condition of homelessness. From the slaves walking the highways north after the Civil War to the sharecroppers leaving the country for the promises of the big city, "Walkin' Blues" enacts a version of this process as House and his companions walk their blues to claim their share of America's promised equality. In *The American Scholar* Emerson enjoined his audience to hear the ballad in the street; in a certain sense, he urged the makers of American culture to discover themselves on the road. As an instance of American experience, of how democratic culture is created and where our great art comes from, "Walkin' Blues" answers Emerson's call. Now people come from all over the world just to visit Parchman Farm, Mississippi's famous prison which inspired so much of the blues, or Memphis's Beale St. where the sharecroppers and rounders of the Delta came on their way to making the blues an urban experience as well. Will Dockery, the descendant of the man who owned the plantation on which so many of the people mentioned in this essay worked, told Robert Palmer "I sure wish we knew these people were so important" (*Deep* 55). That "we" did not know, and continue not to know, makes us ignorant of working of our own American culture. Emerson assumed that his audience would develop the acuity to perceive and create what it has neither made nor seen; yet his stance also recognized that those who will make this culture are unlike those who presently inhabit it and therefore must remain unknown to us who ask the questions.

I can only assume that Emerson's remark that "everything good is on the highway" (*Essays* 480) was unknown to John Lee Hooker when he sang these lines (known to both Big Bill Broonzy and Eric Clapton): "I got the key to the highway / I'm billed out and bound to go / I'm going to leave here running / Cuz walking is most too slow." I would not say that we Americans are running from our origins, but running to remake them. Certainly John Lee Hooker, in his "Blues for Abraham Lincoln," recorded about a hundred years after Lincoln's assassination, was perfectly aware that the ending of slavery had something to do with his identity as a blues singer, which in turn had something to do with those famous words of Jefferson's that Lincoln used at Gettysburg to justify the Civil War.[43] Eschewing the usual blues verse form, Hooker improvises freely against a familiar blues guitar pattern:

> Abraham Lincoln he got assassinated
> Trying to bring the North and South together
> Although he succeeded, he freed the South and lord don't you know
>     I'm very thankful for what he did
> I'm very thankful people today for the Great President
> You know he died for me
> I have a right to live again
> Oh yeah. ("Blues")

The Declaration of Independence promised equality, and so did Lincoln in the Gettysburg Address. Hooker's reflection on Lincoln occurs three years before the Civil Rights Act, but his song makes a cultural gesture as extraordinary—as visionary—as Lincoln's rewriting of Jefferson at Gettysburg. Not only does Hooker invent a blues for Lincoln, but he includes Lincoln within his own blues tradition by acknowledging Lincoln's act to free his ancestors. I find in Hooker's example the ultimate meaning of Emerson's *American Scholar* and the tradition of the blues: the creations of our culture bring us closer to realizing the promises embedded in our American origins. "So long, so long baby I must say goodbye," Hooker sings as if running toward these promises, "I'm going to run this highway 'til the day I die."

About three paragraphs after Emerson apostrophizes the would-be American poet of my epigraph, he says as in exhortation: "Doubt not, O poet, but persist. Say, 'It is in me, and shall out'" (*Essays* 466). In "Boogie Chillen," Hooker tells the story of his birth as blues poet that also personifies the birth of the blues itself. Hooker raps over a pulsating guitar: "One night I was laying down. I heard papa tell mama 'to let that boy boogie-woogie. *Cuz it's in him and it got to come out*'" (emphasis mine). Hooker answers joyously (singing now), "Well, I felt so good I went on and boogie-woogied just the same!" And the guitar crashes (with a certain action) into a blues beat, making Emerson boogie like you never knew he could.

# 3  Ralph Ellison's Invisible Democracy

■ ■ ■ ■ ■ ■ ■

Whatever else the Civil War was for,
It wasn't just to keep the States together,
Nor just to free the slaves, though it did both.
She wouldn't have believed those ends enough
To have given outright for them all she gave.
Her giving somehow touched the principle
That all men are created free and equal.
And to hear her quaint phrases—so removed
From the world's view of all those things.
That's a hard mystery of Jefferson's.
What did he mean?
—Robert Frost

*I*

At a critical point in *Invisible Man*, the narrator pauses in his account of his own history to wonder what the word "history" means in practice if not in theory. Prior to this moment, the narrator has had an uncomplicated understanding of this term: history is the objective rendering of an agreed-upon set of facts. With the death of his friend Tod Clifton, though, the narrator asks himself if history signifies "only the known, the seen, the heard and those events which the recorder regards as important that are put down, those lies his keepers keep their power by" (432). The narrator had heard Clifton say that "sometimes a man *has* to plunge outside of history," but he could make no sense of Clifton's cryptic comment (370). While pondering the mysteries of history, the narrator hears "a record shop blaring a languid blues" and wonders if this is "the true history of the times, a mood blared by trumpets, trombones, saxophones, and drums, a song with turgid, inadequate words?" (436). The narrator initially misses the connection, but the phrase "inadequate words" reinforces his growing sense that official history never captures the meaning of the event it claims to know while nonetheless suggesting that music composes an alternative form of history. Ellison makes this connection explicit in the Prologue to the novel when Louis Armstrong's "music of invisibility" is transformed by the Epilogue into Ellison's narrative "of infinite possibilities" (13, 567). The narrator hears in Armstrong's trumpet and in his voice a history that goes unrecorded. Thus Ellison begins his meditation on democracy by placing his narrator's thoughts *within the act* of Louis Armstrong playing his trumpet. When the narrator says that Armstrong's "familiar music demanded action," he is acknowledging that he accepts responsibility for converting into words the voiceless history that Armstrong plays through his trumpet.

Albert Murray has said that *Invisible Man* is a twelve-bar blues transcribed to novel form.[1] As enticing as this suggestion is, it is also misleading. Ellison would be the first to point out that an artist is naked without a well-developed sense of form. No mastery of the blues can prepare one to write a novel any more than a mastery of the novel can prepare one to perform the blues. By making Armstrong an aesthetic precursor to his novel's narrator, Ellison intimates that the art of his narrator is superior to Armstrong's. In a sense, Armstrong's message is muted (not like a jazz trumpet is muted) without the narrator's intervention. On the other hand, without Armstrong, the narrator would have no inkling that there might be a medium through which he could explore the ironic vagaries of history's visible invisibilities. Ellison's novel takes shape out of the knowledge that African American culture has been created outside of official versions of American history, and thus that its cultural expressions have often been beyond words.[2] Because African Americans were systematically denied access to democracy's "sacred words," music became the perfect form for articulating the inarticulate—for affirming African American identity. In becoming a form of history, the tradition of the blues is an intellectual inheritance that transcends the occasion of its invention. The blues becomes history in part by protesting its exclusion from history, but it would be of limited cultural value if it did not transform the situation that it protests. The larger significance of the blues tradition, then, is that it *makes history by renaming it.* Ellison's debt to the blues is that it provides his narrator with a model for transforming by aesthetic means someone else's history into a history of his own making.

In American intellectual history *Invisible Man* marks the point where

Emerson and the blues most visibly intersect. Whereas the blues might be described as unconsciously Emersonian in its culture making, Ellison is self-consciously Emersonian. Reading Emerson through the blues historicizes Emerson; we see what happens when his allegedly transcendent cultural-aesthetic theories are put into practice by later artists. To a certain degree, the very existence of Ralph Waldo Ellison, a literate descendant of slaves, is a fulfillment of and challenge to the hopes that Emerson shared in *The American Scholar.* (Ellison admits that he finds it "amusing" that he and many other "Negro youngsters of his generation were named Waldo" [*Going* 314].) Ellison slyly suggests this connection through the figure of Petee Wheatstraw, the "junk man" and "man of vision" who supplies the narrator with "wire and sockets" to light his basement, whom Ellison names after the popular blues musician of the 1930s and 1940s (also known as "the Devil's Son-in-Law"). Wheatstraw is an Emersonian figure in that he furnishes the narrator with the materials to fire the "light [that] confirms my reality, gives birth to my form"; such blues exemplars also provide Ellison with a sensibility through which he can renew and reclaim Emerson (*Invisible* 6).[3] Ellison therefore structures the narrator's experience so that Emerson is reinvented through the blues. In *Invisible Man* Ellison combines the experience of the blues with the pragmatist eloquence of Emerson to imagine an America approachable by all.

Above I intimated that Ellison considered the form of the novel to be superior to that of jazz or the blues. It would be more accurate to say that Ellison's preference for the novel was a reflection of his own choice to be a writer. Certainly, as a failed musician—a trumpet player—Ellison knew very well that one's eloquence as an artist depended on finding the proper form for artistic expression. Though Armstrong's trumpet is lyrical, and though the lyrics of the blues can at times achieve poetry, Ellison knew that the history he wanted to create could only be accomplished through language. Thus, before he could surrender the trumpet for the pen, he had to learn what he elsewhere called "the formal knowledge which is indispensable to the writer" (Cannon, Reed, and Troupe 132). Far from being an expression of cultural elitism, Ellison's nuanced aesthetic of form actually allows him to evoke in as great a detail as possible the innumerable "frequencies"—a key word in the last sentence of the novel—which democratic experience comprises. Just as the narrative of *Invisible Man* searches for the form that will make the narrator visible to himself and his audience, so does Ellison's novel seek to make visible the multiple and always interacting levels of democratic culture.

Although Ellison never identified a specific source for his novel's key concept, it is likely that as an inveterate reader of the James family he adapted it from William James's definition of social invisibility in *Principles of Psychology* (1890). James wrote:

> No more fiendish punishment could be devised, were such a thing physically possible, than that one should be turned loose in society and remain absolutely unnoticed by all the members thereof. If no one turned round when we entered, answered when we spoke, or reminded us of what we did, but if every person we met "cut us dead," and acted as if we were non-existent things, a kind of rage and impotent despair would ere long well up within us, from which the cruellest bodily tortures would be a relief. (281)

James's definition of invisibility underpins pessimistic readings of *Invisible Man* that argue that the narrator's effort to end his hibernation is really only a futile and quixotic attempt to quell his rage and impotent despair. Yet, although the narrator at times suffers the kind of invisibility that James describes, he nonetheless insists that he chooses to affirm his existence despite being cut by others. Trusting the power of his own eloquence, the narrator hopes to show his audience that his invisibility is theirs as well. By James's logic, invisibility is the next-to-last stop on the road to nonexistence; by Ellison's logic, it is the necessary (if paradoxical) self-recognition that precedes any meaningful action. Ellison's understanding of history and culture, though, is consistent with James's idea that experience is always overflowing the boundaries built to contain it. Indeed, *Invisible Man* can be seen as a Jamesian rendering of American experience that is more successfully Jamesian than Horace Kallen's was.[4] Unlike Kallen, Ellison insists that the American commitment to equality insures that no one's presumed cultural identity can remain fixed, which is also his way of suggesting that even moments that remain unrecorded by history nonetheless impinge upon the history that purports to deny them. How else to explain, Ellison asks, the tremendous impact that African Americans have had in shaping American culture while being denied their rightful political place in American society? How else to explain what Ellison calls in an essay on Duke Ellington "the white American's inescapable Negro-ness?" (*Going* 219). How else to explain the narrator who writes the book that we are reading?

Whereas James described invisibility as the nightmare of a single individual, Ellison approaches it in terms of the incompleteness of an entire nation. The narrator comes to understand that his invisibility is the logical consequence of being excluded from the society's official versions of its own birth and being. Against—even in defiance of—the history that has excluded him, he narrates his own coming to consciousness. Like the other figures we have been examining, Ellison insists that the political and cultural consequences of our famous self-evident truth—"all men are created equal"—be examined scrupulously. Ellison's work asks the reader to consider the proposition that American history is but the interpretation, or interpretations, of the ways in which we have struggled to achieve the realization of an ideal.[5] In this respect, not only has the African American's struggle to achieve political and cultural equality clarified the meaning and the practice of democracy, but it has also gradually rendered America's presumption of equality visible. As the narrator asserts near the end of the book, "Our fate is to become one, and yet many—This is not prophecy, but description" (577).

Despite his invisibility, the narrator adopts a stance of democratic optimism. In so doing, he aligns himself with Emerson in *The American Scholar*. Recognizing that his own history—his own existence—testifies to the forbearance and perseverance of others, he seeks to discover the form that will render his knowledge visible. In his 1955 *Paris Review* interview Ellison spoke of "the slave songs, the blues, folk ballads" as cultural expressions that "announced the Negro's willingness to trust his own experience, his own sensibilities as to the definition of reality, rather than allow his masters to define these crucial matters for him" (*Shadow* 172). When Ellison has his narrator wonder if "the true history of the times" might be conveyed "by trumpets, trombones, saxophones, and drums" within "a song with turgid, inadequate words," he is dramatizing a version of the process by which African Americans invented themselves through the blues (436). The narrator's blues, though, is not played through trumpet or trombone, and thus Ellison could not risk writing words that were "turgid" or "inadequate." Like Emerson, Ellison aimed to write in such a way that would incite his audience to action. When the narrator says that Louis Armstrong's trumpet "demanded action," he is drawing on Emerson to recontextualize Armstrong as a kind of American Scholar. On the other hand, neither the tradition of the blues nor of Emerson could help Ellison to write a novel. Seeking to write a novel that conveyed the same sense of democratic action he recognized in the blues and in Emerson, Ellison enlisted the aid of another type of pragmatist, Kenneth Burke.

*II*

In a 1945 letter to Burke, Ellison defined the rhetorical situation of his intended novel with a rather daunting question:

> How will a Negro writer who writes out of his full awareness of the complexity of western personality and who presents the violence of American culture in psychological terms rather than physical ones— how will such a writer be able to break through the stereotype-armored minds of white Americans so that they can receive his message?[6]

Although Ellison's ultimate answer is his own and takes the form of *Invisible Man*, Burke's writing certainly helped him formulate the novel's rhetorical strategy.[7] Ellison's goal was to write what at that time would have been the definitive expression of African American experience and at the same time a representative *American* book. He wrote Burke in the same letter, "I certainly agree that universalism is desirable but I find that I am forced to arrive at that universe through the racial grain of sand." When the narrator asks in the novel's close, "Who knows but that, on the lower frequencies, I speak for you?" he invites his audience to discover their universe within his grain of sand. No question is more vexed in Ellison criticism than how to read the book's seemingly ambiguous ending. The narrator himself appears to criticize his book's ending when he says that "even hibernations can be overdone. Perhaps that's my greatest social crime, I've overstayed my hibernation, since there's a possibility that even an invisible man has a socially responsible role to play" (572). All readers have wondered if the narrator eloquently talked himself into a hole out of which he will never emerge, or whether his promise of future action is a sufficient guarantee that his invisibility has ended, that he will become a visible presence in American culture.

Ellison's critical reception has generally depended on how critics have responded to his repeated insistence that the artist's first obligation is to the work of art and its formal requirements. Because of his stated desire to be considered a canonical author, Ellison has been accused of neglecting the African American folk tradition and being somehow smugly "above" what he depicts.[8] The disagreement over Ellison's literary and cultural sources has been deep and acrimonious, often abetted by Ellison's own critical pronouncements. Ellison sometimes stressed that he had been more influenced by white writers such as Ernest Hemingway and T. S.

Eliot, who seem to have little to do with the African American experience, than by African American writers such as James Weldon Johnson and W. E. B. Du Bois, whose influences so obviously permeate *Invisible Man*.[9] Interestingly, criticism has crossed racial lines, as Ellison has been attacked on these grounds not only by black critics, particularly during the late 1960s and early 1970s, but most famously by the white critic Irving Howe.[10] To those unfamiliar with the pragmatist tradition of Emerson and Burke, in Ellison's famous response to Howe—that his fiction must be "judged as art; if it fails, it fails aesthetically"—it seems as if Ellison is avoiding the issue by pointing to his work (*Shadow* 136–37). Following Emerson and Burke, Ellison understands the novel always to be a social act—one that might inspire future actions.[11]

No less than Jefferson did the Declaration of Independence or Madison the Constitution, Ellison conceived his novel as a founding document of American history. Indeed, he intended it as an answer to all that had come before him. Throughout, Ellison plays upon Kenneth Burke's terms to chart the drift of American history into (and out of) which he would thrust his novel.[12] In reading Ellison through Burke, Charles Scruggs is right to say that *Invisible Man* expresses "the 'revolutionary ideals' of the [American] Republic" and "that for Ellison the key word is always *movement* toward a perfection" (102).[13] But when Scruggs ties the novel's realization of "the revolutionary ideals of the Republic" merely to "a self-reliant individual [who] is continually negotiating his connection to the living polis," he can account for neither the transformative effect the novel intends to have on the meaning of American democracy broadly considered nor the boomeranging shifts that our democratic processes inflict upon its actors. Where we have fallen short in interpreting the novel is in not granting Ellison's vision the scope he aimed for, and this scope has everything to do with the way he creatively reads Burke. Without tracing how self-consciously Ellison adapted Burke, Robert O'Meally recognizes the broader implications of their connection by discussing Ellison's work through Burke's various critical "systems" to show how Ellison depicts "vernacular art and the part it plays in American life" ("On Burke" 245). Displaying an ambition worthy of Tocqueville, Ellison has tried to discover "a true sociology of ideas in this country [which would] have a means of judging the impact of ideas as they came to rest within the diverse groups which make up American society" (*Going* 49–50). Exploring this sociology through his essays as well as his novel, Ellison repeatedly insists that "by ignoring such matters as the sharing of bloodlines and cultural traditions by groups of widely differing ethnic origins, and by overlooking the blending and metamorphosis of cultural forms which is so characteristic of our society, we misconceive our cultural identity" (125). In a sense, the hero of *Invisible Man* is not the nameless protagonist but the restless forces of democracy that he embodies.

Ellison acknowledged in a 1977 *Y'Bird Reader* interview how greatly he was influenced by Burke's 1937 essay "The Rhetoric of Hitler's Battle" (later reprinted in *The Philosophy of Literary Form*), which he had seen Burke give as a lecture. A brilliant exposition of the relationship between literature and politics, Burke's rhetorical analysis of *Mein Kampf* foresaw the likely actions Hitler's words would demand. It also gave Ellison a clear sense of the reciprocal relationship between literature and politics. Interestingly, Ellison says that he learned from Burke "not so much the technique of fiction but the nature of literature and the ways ideas and language operate in literary form" (Cannon, Reed, and Troupe 148). He also took a conception not of what literature is, but of what it can do. In his 1945 letter to Burke, Ellison said that Burke was the only speaker he saw that day who "was concerned with writing *and politics* rather than writing as an *excuse* for politics." Neither Burke nor Ellison is interested in form for its own sake, in bracketing off "the aesthetic" from "life" or "experience" or "reality." What they share, rather, is the belief that our formal renderings, our formal abstractions of reality, are themselves acts that determine the possibilities for others' actions. *Invisible Man* becomes the act by which Ellison will intervene in the construction of American history, and his protagonist cannot be understood except as a part of Ellison's broader vision of the meaning of America.

*Invisible Man* discovers its identity through the realization of its aesthetic form, an aesthetic which is rooted in the mysterious processes of democratic culture itself. Dedicated to the dual notion that not only is our history in our literature, but our literature contains within it the seeds of our history, Ellison offers his novel to his unseen audience as an invitation to democratic action. Burke's notion of form is paramount for Ellison because it enables him to transform his understanding of American history into an aesthetic document. Far from separating art from politics, Ellison employs his art to uncover and highlight what our most meaningful political gestures should be. His act is the sort that Emerson made when he said in "Self-Reliance" that, if need be, he would write "whim" on his doorpost. As we saw in the last chapter, this move is neither whimsical nor irresponsible; rather, it declares Emerson's willingness to risk what others might call fanciful theatrics in the hope that someday the whim will be a founding moment for a truly democratic polis. With the same sense of moral and political purpose, Ellison's narrator declares that "invisible man is responsible for the fate of us all" (14). Ellison's gesture, like Emerson's, will remain merely self-reliant, whimsical, as long as he lacks an audience whose vision of democratic possibility matches his own.

Ellison's essay "The Little Man at Chehaw Station" is his best articulation that the democratic artist's moral responsibility is to develop an aesthetic practice sufficiently supple to convey the unsettling complexity of American experience. "Little Man" explicitly adapts Kenneth Burke's theories of language and form to dramatize Ellison's portrait of how the democratic artist plays upon "the metamorphic character of the general American audience" to reveal "the unrecognized and unassimilated elements of its taste" (*Going* 6). Throughout the essay Ellison expresses how his appreciation for the confusion of American culture, its tendency toward "random accessibility" on all levels, achieves form only when his mastery of technique can intersect with democratic culture in all of its confusion. Henry James once noted that there is such a thing as the clarity of incoherence, and it is this sort of clarity toward which Ellison the democratic artist aspires. Before considering the essay in detail, I will first give an overview of Burke's related notions of language and form.

Burke's theory of "language as symbolic action" centers on the contention that our capacity to be human—that is, the ongoing creation of the human as manifested in language (stories), deeds (action), and tools (technology)—derives from our ability to create, remember, and use language. Burke grants that defining the human as a "symbol-using animal" does seem to be an obvious move, though we have hardly begun to come to terms with what the definition entails. Following Emerson's observation in "The Poet" that "we are symbols and inhabit symbols" (*Essays* 456) and William James's insistence that we see our ideas and interpretations as actions, Burke maintains that our words are activating agents which also encode the range of our subsequent actions. In effect, Burke asks that if we agree that what we mean by " 'reality' has been built up for us through nothing but our symbol systems, what is our reality today but all this clutter of symbols about the past combined with whatever things we know mainly through maps, magazines, newspapers and the like about the present?" (*Language* 5).

Long before that European import poststructuralism became fashionable for American academics to put on, Burke was showing the ways in which we avoid the consequences of this question by "cling[ing] to a kind of verbal realism that refuses to realize the full extent of the role played by symbolicity in [our] notions of reality" (5). This verbal realism betrays itself in a tendency to think of words as being equal to the objects that they name. Naively, "representation" therefore becomes "reality," but not in the dynamic sense that Burke advocates. Understanding words as the sign of things depends upon ignoring the active and creative nature of language. Consider, for example, the word "tree" and the thing it designates. Understood as somehow separate from language (which Burke shows to be impossible), as an object by itself, a tree seems self-sustaining and self-fulfilling, a complete entity. A tree which is also a word, however, can be divided into many possible definitions and subdefinitions, which is another way of saying that in order to define a word we must use words that are different from the one in question. For instance, a tree may be defined as "a piece of wood." And "a piece of wood" may be reconstructed as a paddle, a boat, a sheet of paper, a table, a statue, and so forth. Merely by acting to define an object as a word, we learn to use that word as an object. In this way, definitions, or what Burke calls "entitlements," translate into action; narrowing a definition of a word, as I have done haphazardly with "tree," actually widens the possibilities for action or the uses we may make of a word.

Since language, Burke argues, is symbolic action, our words become more than the mediating agents between our desires and the material objects of the world; in a palpable sense, our words name the limits—and the possibilities—of our material world. In an argument developed most fully in the essay "What Are the Signs of What?" Burke suggests that we not only use words, but that words also use us. Viewing words "dramatistically," or in terms of their potential for action, Burke insists that instead of seeing words as the signs of things, we should see how "things would be the signs of words" (*Language* 379). Burke acknowledges the deceptively easy way in which language comes to seem prior to nature in this example: "If I say 'table,' and you don't understand me, there is at least the possibility of my using the physical object as the source of communication between us" (375). Burke grants that this example hardly covers such words as "democracy" or "dictatorship" or "rights," but the point behind the "table" example drives his argument. Precisely because these words "do not enjoy the kind of extraverbal reality we find in the common sense vocabulary of the natural realm," Burke presses us to see how our creation of language continually builds us away, so to speak, from our so-called natural state, or the extraverbal realm, and places us in ever more complicated structures of symbols (375). Hence Burke claims that "words communicate to things the spirit that the society imposes upon the words which have come to be the 'names' for them. The things are in effect the visible tangible material embodiments of the spirit that infuses them through the medium of words" (362).

Although following Emerson's example, Burke, like Saussure or Jacques Derrida, stresses that our "overall 'picture' is but a construct of our symbol systems" (*Language* 5). Burke's notion of "but a construct," however, differs crucially from most contemporary uses of the idea and underscores the pragmatist assumptions of his work. As well as Derrida or Paul de Man, Burke recognizes how language undermines epistemological claims of representation. Burke never lets one forget, however, that language is not merely deconstructive but *constructive* as well. If language reveals the shifting ground upon which our cherished concepts try to stand, then it nevertheless coalesces into the systems which we would later deconstruct. Insofar as the nature of language "is such that it can be used as a tool," it becomes the instrument through which we create and manipulate power, or, more concretely, for example, technology.[14] Through language we create a concept such as "democracy," which, in turn, exists as a living attitude, determining the ways in which we order our actions. Certainly concepts such as "democracy" and "technology" can precipitate actions which we would like to see undone, or deconstructed. We might employ our "technology," say the automatic rifle or the small-pox-infested blanket or the atomic bomb, in the name of "democracy" to destroy some other presumably hostile symbol, say the "other Americans" or "savages" or "the yellow peril." Conversely, also in the name of "democracy," we might come to view our prior action as wrong and seek to undo its pernicious consequences. The Civil Rights movement is our most glorious example of this democratic undoing in the name of democratic doing.

This Burkean process whereby "doing" becomes its own "undoing" in the name of a revised "doing" is what fascinates Ellison. Frank Lentricchia says of Burke what we can also say of Ellison: "Aestheticist theory is for Burke as much social theory as it is art theory" (*Criticism* 89).[15] Ellison's "Little Man at Chehaw Station" employs Burke's theory of language as symbolic action to suggest that the history of American politics and culture has been the search for the embodiment of the "sacred principles" of "the Declaration of Independence, the Constitution, and the Bill of Rights" and to make that very search the artist's goal for his art (*Going* 17).

Our democratic culture "dances out" the meanings and promises embedded in these, our sacred texts, to become in Burke's words "visible tangible material embodiments of the spirit that infuses them" (*Language* 362). As if he had just come fresh from one of Burke's lectures, Ellison writes:

> [We Americans] are dedicated to principles that are abstract, ideal, spiritual: principles that were conceived linguistically and committed to paper during that contention over political ideals and economic interests which was released and given focus during our revolutionary break with traditional forms of society. . . . [This] property of linguistic forms of *symbolic action*, these principles—democracy, equality, individual freedom, and universal justic—now move us as articles of faith. Holding them sacred, we *act* (or *fail* to act) in their name. . . . *They interrogate* us endlessly as to who and what we are; *they demand* that we keep the democratic faith. (*Going* 17–18; except for "fail," emphasis mine)

Ellison uses Burke's terminology to explain how American culture is produced as a consequence of our belief in our sacred words. Ellison insists that we should understand our democratic culture's relationship to its sacred texts in the same way that Burke teaches us to understand how "the nature of our terms affect the nature of our observations" (*Language* 46). That is, our "observations [or actions] are but implications of the particular terminology in terms of which the observations are made." In Burke's words, our political and cultural actions, therefore, are "but the spinning out of possibilities implicit in our particular choice of terms" (46). Americans act on the assumption of a universally shared relationship to our nation's sacred promises. Our triumphs, our failures, even our acts of secession, all flow from this knowledge, which includes the despair and guilt we share over the rift that separates democratic ideal from democratic practice. Those who would claim that Ellison's work is apolitical must address this stunning pronouncement: "We [Americans] have been reluctant [to pay the cost of desiring identity] since we first suspected that we are fated to live up to our sacred commitments or die, and the Civil War was the form of this fateful knowledge" (*Going* 253). Ellison's protagonist's search for identity—for an equality visible to all—cannot be separated from our national destiny. As the embodiment of the democratic principle, he shows how our cultural actions strive to realize what Burke calls that "principle of perfection implicit in the nature of symbol-systems," even if this means destroying ourselves in the name of democracy, as we nearly did with the Civil War (*Language* 17).[16]

The word "democracy," insofar as it evokes the principles of our sacred texts, is Ellison's term for "transcendent order," or what Burke calls in his *Rhetoric of Religion* (as Ellison notes) a "god-term" (*Going* 18). This is Ellison's enabling point: without it his novel would have no hope of registering on the lower frequencies which our culture also comprises. Ellison's belief in democratic action is rooted in his *linguistic understanding* of our national promises. By discovering the possibilities of democratic culture within the promises of democratic language, Ellison insists that there is a wholeness to democratic culture. Paradoxically, this wholeness expresses itself in the heterogeneity of parts which can never be entirely self-contained. If democracy is always active, working out the endless possibilities of its own undoing, for Ellison the chaotic meaning of democratic action becomes visible through the democratic artist's manipulation of form.

In his first critical work, *Counter-Statement*, Burke defined the term "form" in relation to a literary work without assuming a necessary distinction between art and politics. According to Burke, form is "an arousing and fulfillment of desires. A work has form insofar as one part of it leads a reader to anticipate another part, to be gratified by the sequence" (124). Burke's notion here involves what Ellison calls an "antagonistic cooperation" between artist and audience. By Burke's logic, the artist's successful manipulation of form addresses and transforms whatever objections the audience may have to the work during the act of encountering it. Form thereby becomes a mutual creation through which artist and audience meet one another. For Ellison, artistic rendering of democratic form reveals the antagonistic cooperation that takes place through the many conflicts our shared diversity uncovers, and the form is bounded, as it were, by our shared commitment to equality. The dialectic of this antagonistic cooperation is complex: if we view democracy as a form waiting to be uncovered, then precisely who—or what—is the shaping force behind the eventual realization of its cherished principles? Does the democratic artist somehow exist above, or prior to, the form he helps uncover?

On the surface, Ellison's reading of Burke encourages the understanding that the artist would be at least equivalent to the god-term itself, "democracy," and that the meaning of "democracy" would then be worked out through the artist's form. But Burke's theory of language as symbolic action, which was really his working out of the problems associated with literary form that he raised in *Counter-Statement*, obliterates an easy distinction between artist and audience. Since words have meaning only because they translate into action, the sacred text that composes the democratic artist's form can only be expressed in the artist's interaction with his audience. Gestures committed in the name of democracy, as all American gestures are, can be frustratingly contradictory. Emerson's admonishment to all Americans "to go alone" in the pursuit of "self-reliance" is a perfect example of our democratic waywardness. For his words can be taken to justify Thoreau's uncompromising moral and spiritual stands against gestures of national-self-aggrandizement, such as our war against Mexico, as well as gestures of personal self-aggrandizement, such as those embodied by Horatio Alger. "In the beginning was not only the word," Ellison writes, "but the contradiction of the word; sometimes we approach life out of a tragic sense of necessity, and again with its denial" (*Going* 243). For Ellison, democratic word becomes flesh through the contentious acts created by a diverse culture's effort to realize itself in the form of an ideal democracy; in other words, in the "formal" battle that takes place between artist and audience over the meaning of our democratic self-representations. Ellison defines the nature of this battle: "By playing artfully upon the audience's sense of experience and form, the artist seeks to shape its emotions and perceptions to his vision; while it, in turn, simultaneously cooperates and resists, says yes and no in an it-takes-two-to-tango binary response to his effort" (7).

Given that Ellison's "duty," as he calls it, as a democratic artist is to depict the unexpected ways in which our democratic cultural action expresses itself, his form is nothing but the expression of action. Yet the mere depiction of action seems a curious characterization for an artist's form, as if the form wishes to surrender to the drama it presumably conveys. In this regard, the distinction Burke draws between action and motion is suggestive. Where action characterizes what results in and from our symbolic gestures, motion connotes "sheer physicality" and describes the type of world which would remain if "all symbol-using animals and their symbols [were] to be erased from the face of the earth" (*Philosophy* xv). In Ellison's Burkean reading of democratic culture, there is a sense in which the sheer unexpectedness of democratic cultural action verges on being motion as Burke defines it. That is, because the American is often unaware of his own identity, his symbolic gestures, even when made in the name of democracy, carry multiple meanings to sometimes unknown audiences. For Ellison, democratic actions are always motivated by the desire to make democratic practice equivalent with democratic ideal. For the democratic artist, the goal is to help his audience learn to distinguish between democratic action and motion so that each can learn how the other's symbolic gestures partake of the same ideal. Ellison's representative figure for dramatizing the possibility of this mutual recognition rendered through artistic form is "the little man at Chehaw station."

Ellison's first glimpse of the little man occurred after he had suffered through a frustrating recital while studying the trumpet at Tuskegee Institute. He relates having "outraged" his teachers "by substituting a certain skill of lips and fingers for the intelligent and artistic structuring of emotion that was demanded in performing the music assigned to me" (*Going* 3). Ellison hints that the mere mastery of form is inadequate to convey the complexity of the artist's subject matter. With "ears burning" from the faculty's criticism he sought the comfort of his teacher, Hazel Harrison. Rather than merely admonishing her student to practice harder, Miss Harrison explained that "in this country" an artist's form is incomplete without a thorough appreciation for his audience's diversity, which often transforms the artist's sense of what is required of him.

Acknowledging that Ellison "must be prepared to play the very best wherever" he finds himself, she adds that this includes even "the waiting room at Chehaw Station, because in this country there'll always be a little man hiding behind the stove. [There'll] always be the little man whom you don't expect, and he'll know the music, the tradition, and the standards of musicianship required for whatever you set out to perform!" (4). As the young Ellison reflects on the dismal isolation of Chehaw Station, which was only an oft-passed-over outpost on the way to bigger and better places, he finds himself rendered speechless by Miss Harrison's advice and wonders if she wasn't joking with him (4). The absurdity of Ellison playing the classics on his trumpet at an isolated whistle-stop is compounded by the incongruity of playing them there for an informed audience. Only his respect for Miss Harrison prevents him from expressing his incomprehension over her riddle of the little man (5). But a healthy sense of confusion over the meaning of being an artist in America is precisely what this expert teacher wanted to convey to her student. She tells him that by the time he becomes an artist he will be familiar with the little man. In effect, Miss Harrison has challenged the young Ellison to unsettle his sterile conception of form for an appreciation of a fluidity of form required to reach his diverse audience that will both admire his art and, by their participation in his art, create it.

Ellison conjures a version of the little man and the complicated relationship that pertains among artist, audience, and form in his marvelous description of the democratic cultural incoherence he witnessed one day "on New York's Riverside Drive near 151st Street" (*Going* 22). There Ellison encounters a figure who requires no less than six hyphens to be described adequately: "a light-skinned, blue-eyed, Afro-American featured individual who could have been taken for anything from a sun-tinged white Anglo-Saxon, an Egyptian, or a mixed-breed American Indian to a strayed member of certain tribes of Jew" (22). Driving an incongruous "new blue Volkswagen Beetle decked out with a gleaming Rolls-Royce radiator," he was

> clad in handsome black riding boots and fawn-colored riding breeches of English tailoring [with] a leather riding crop. A dashy dashiki (as bright and as many-colored as the coat that initiated poor Joseph's troubles in biblical times) flowed from his broad shoulders down to the arrogant, military flare of his breech-tops, while six feet six inches or so above his heels, a black Homburg hat, tilted at a jaunty angle, floated majestically on the crest of his huge Afro-coiffed head. (22)

As if his outfit were not enough, this "elegant gentleman" placed a "Japanese single-lens reflex camera . . . upon the hood of his Volkswagen and took a . . . series of self-shots in which, manipulating a lengthy ebony cigarette holder, he posed in various fanciful attitudes against the not-too-distant background of the George Washington bridge" (23).

The scene recalls a moment from *The American Scene* (1907) when Henry James, another noted stroller of the streets of New York, worried that the babel of languages that surrounded him would someday coalesce into an English language so different from his own that he would have to invent a word to convey its new identity: "abracadabrant" (122). James's "abracadabrant" is fully realized in Ellison's example as stylistic boundaries are crossed and recrossed so flagrantly that here the typical expression of democratic culture figures as a perpetual flaunting of its own manifold tendencies. As Ellison admits, one cannot say with certainty what this person had in mind by his display; on the other hand, there is no doubt that he wished to convey "his complex sense of cultural identity" (23). The man's photo session also appeals as a kind of theater. There is no doubt he relishes the audience he draws, that he performs for the sake of his unknown audience, just as he unquestionably collects elements of various styles to edify and challenge the assumptions of his impromptu audience. The interest the man draws elicits from his audience an "antagonistic cooperation" which is at once democratic action and Burkean form personified. His body incarnates that sacred text, the living word "democracy," in the simultaneous moment of doing and undoing. Burke writes in *Counter-Statement* that "any reader surrounds each word and each act in a work of art with a *unique* set of his previous experiences (and therefore a unique set of imponderable emotional reactions), communication existing in 'the margin of overlap' between the writer's experience and the reader's" (78). Likewise, in taking his own picture, this embodied hyphenate is at once performer (writer) *and* audience; he too is caught up in his display of democratic possibility and affect. When later he views his pictures, or perhaps arranges them among pictures of previously adopted styles, he will no doubt have moved on to a different combination of possibilities.

Of all the possible interpretations one might tease from this example, Ellison highlights "the *improvised form*, the willful juxtaposition of modes" (*Going* 24, emphasis mine). That is, the "man of parts" makes an aesthetic gesture, but its formal rendering connects him to his audience (and vice versa) in a way that involves their collective transformation; it is a picture of democracy at work. Ellison's formal point is that "whatever sheerly ethnic identity was communicated by his costume depended upon the observer's ability to see order in an apparent cultural chaos" (23). The master of form must also be a master of improvisation. Otherwise, his form will not be alive to the fluidity of his subject. The artistry of the "man of parts" is described in Ellison's famous "jazz moment":

> Each true jazz moment springs from a contest in which each artist challenges all the rest; each solo flight, or improvisation, represents (like the successive canvases of a painter) a definition of his identity: As individual, as member of the collectivity and as a link in the chain of tradition. Thus, because jazz finds its very life in an endless improvisation upon traditional materials, the jazzman must lose his identity even as he finds it. (*Shadow* 234)

As with the man of parts, one is struck by the fluidity of the situation, both for the soloist and the group. Yet the flight of the artist's solo is not wholly indeterminate; it is a reaction to what the group has been playing, just as their playing reacts to his. A process of persistent accommodation and challenge, the jazz player's solo expresses his own rich sense of individual possibility, yet that expression depends on the possibilities latent within the group. Though the jazzman must lose his identity to find it, the discovery of his identity will constitute a loss—and not merely the shedding of an old skin for a new one. Just as he emerges from the collectivity of the group to articulate his voice, the end of his flight carries him to a different shore and a new identity, where he returns to the relative anonymity of his group, who have been transported along with him.[17] For Ellison, the perpetual transformation that the jazz moment enacts evokes the ceaseless changes of American identity that ensure that mainstream culture never remains equivalent to itself.

According to the *American Heritage Dictionary*, "improvise" means "to invent, compose, or recite without preparation." In Ellison's context, however, a more accurate rendering of the word would be "the *preparation to invent, compose, or recite without preparation*." The jazz or democratic artist's improvisation is the precisely appropriate response to the setting in which he finds himself, as well as a transformation of that context. Understanding the consummate taste of the artist's performance depends upon recognizing how the performance gives form to the fluidity of the setting. This artist's form distinguishes action from motion, the majestic arc of the solo flight from the random flapping of wings, the chaotic splattering of sounds that a beginner might play. A different situation on a different date will inspire a different flight, and, in a limited sense, a different form. Yet though the form may change according to circumstance, the function and the necessity of the form remain the same: the evocation of chaos through its hesitant ordering, a performance akin to Frost's "momentary stay against confusion." Moreover, the artist brings to the moment of cultural transmission the experience of prior transformations. Be it through Ellison's man of parts or his jazz soloist, artistic perspective is created and re-created in these moments of cultural incongruity.

If this sense of cultural fluidity makes for liberating possibilities of individual and aesthetic expression, as Ellison's examples seem to indicate, then a culture comprising rapid transformations and assertions of incongruity can just as easily inspire feelings of anxiety, uneasiness, and ultimately, betrayal.[18] One can imagine any of the variety of ethnic groups evoked by Ellison's man of parts insisting that he is not the expression of an identity but either its confusion or its betrayal. Michael Rogin, in a brilliant reading of the film *The Jazz Singer*, articulates this point of view. Rogin maintains that the film addresses the cultural insecurity brought on by the preceding forty-year period of Jewish immigration from Europe. The power of *The Jazz Singer*, like that of its predecessor *Birth of a Nation*, was "to make African Americans stand for something besides themselves" (417). Thus, according to Rogin, when Al Jolson donned blackface to sing to his mother the song "Mammy," he appropriated black culture in order to efface his own Jewish culture and thereby assimilate into the white world. "Blackface," Rogin writes, "liberates the performer from the fixed, 'racial' identities of African Americans and Jew" (440). From Rogin, we can derive the strongest case to be made against Ellison's man of parts. Instead of a celebratory cultural fluidity, Rogin finds "a sinister paradox": "Assimilation is achieved through the mask of the most segregated; the blackface that offers Jews mobility keeps the blacks fixed in place" (447). Rogin's point is that celebrations of cultural fluidity often mask an essentialized social inequality based on color.

True enough, Ellison might respond, but it is precisely our American need to undermine this social inequality that creates the fluidity conveyed by our inevitably multiethnic cultural gestures. In "Twentieth Century Fiction and the Black Mask of Humanity," Ellison observed that "the Negro stereotype" is "a key figure in the magic rite by which the white American seeks to resolve the dilemma arising between his democratic beliefs and certain antidemocratic practices" (*Shadow* 28). Ellison would see in this dilemma ironic confirmation of his point that whatever else the American is, he is also black—as the "Optic White" paint in *Invisible Man* requires one black drop to achieve its pristine white color. On the other hand, no amount of hoodoo whitewashing by blackface could obliterate the distinctive ethnic quality of Jolson's voice and appearance. Thus one might question whether Rogin's argument is at the mercy of the very "racial and cultural purity" he would seem to want to critique. Has Jolson lost his Jewish identity, however we might define that, simply by donning blackface and doing an impersonation of a jazz singer that no one who knows anything about jazz could take seriously? Does acceptance—or distortion—by mainstream American culture necessarily mean the loss of ethnic culture? Must "ethnic/mainstream" be a static binary entity? Or might Jolson also be read as another man of parts who combines recognizably the feature of at least three American cultures into one incongruous figure? If it is true that part of his representation partakes of an unfortunate stereotype, it is also true that by acting out his identity through his understanding of African American culture, he is, however unconsciously and awkwardly, acknowledging the function that African Americans *already* play in the creation of mainstream American culture.

At this point in the discussion one must observe that there are no blacks speaking for themselves on the screen, and what is on the screen grossly misrepresents black experience. Ellison's retort might be: look at the situation. Here we have a Jewish man dressed up like a darky, who, without embarrassment, sings a hopelessly sentimental song, which, as most African Americans who saw the movie would know, has nothing to do with jazz as it was performed by Paul Whiteman, let alone Duke Ellington, hoping to win over his white audience, who, as the film's popularity suggests, are indeed moved to tears and approval. Who is the joke on in that convoluted cultural contraption? Interestingly, Ellison and Rogin both adapt their ideas from Constance Rourke, whom Ellison invokes when he asserts that "when American life is most American it is apt to be most theatrical" (*Shadow* 54–55). Hence, a founding American gesture occurred when several white men asserted their American cultural independence by dressing up like Indians and dropping tea, that prime symbol of Britain, into a harbor. In a multiethnic nation dedicated to a notion of equality, figures such as Al Jolson portray our complicated, groping attempts to work out the multiple identities that our commitment to equality requires of us. The Al Jolson of "Mammy," like the man of parts, might be seen as a likely American artist because of his ability to invest incongruity with form, form with incongruity.

Ellison invokes Burke's famous notion of "perspective by incongruity" to describe his first self-conscious meeting with Miss Harrison's little man. Burke's term is meant to describe the way in which new orders of perception emerge from unexpected encounters.[19] Ellison explains how in the early 1940s he discovered the little man in the flesh while canvassing New York ghetto tenements to find signers for a petition he was carrying. To his surprise and wonder, he heard four "foul-mouthed black working-men" arguing in quite sophisticated terms the merits of the divas who performed for the New York Metropolitan Opera (*Going* 34). Closer inspection revealed that these men had worked at the Met for years as extras and thus had ample opportunity to refine their philosophies of opera. Ellison enjoys imagining a director outfitting these men in the painted masks of the primitive Egyptians, never realizing that these "primitives" from the ghetto were as sophisticated opera critics as he. Ellison admits the "shock of recognition" that causes him to enjoy this "hilarious joke that centered on the incongruities of race, economic status, and culture," which enables him to see for the first time the little man behind the stove (37–38). Along with the man of parts, the little man behind the stove realizes the democratic ideal translated to the realm of culture. Ellison is explicit on this point. If as a citizen the little man endures with grace certain restrictions of social mobility, then as a reader, a participant in the production of democratic culture, he "senses that the American experience is of a whole, and he wants the interconnections revealed." Among these interconnections is his equality (14).

Though this example may seem to privilege opera over vernacular American culture, Ellison is actually suggesting the ways in which even so-called high culture is transformed in America's cultural chaos. He puts lofty thoughts concerning opera into the highly idiosyncratic language of uneducated African Americans. Yet Ellison's plea for the transformative power of vernacular American culture is written in a "high" style for the pages of the mostly conservative *American Scholar*. These examples suggest that we communicate through masks of race, class, religion, and gender, but each of us wants to claim that the mask we wear today is the mask we have always worn. In this respect, we are invisible to each other and to ourselves, and it is this invisibility that Ellison the democratic artist seeks to illuminate. If invisibility is the perpetual condition of being American, it can also be a source of power. The little man's appearance signals an act of self-illumination on the part of his interlocutor that can only occur in moments of incongruous social interaction. His sudden visibility does not uncover the face behind the mask so much as cast a light upon the ongoing drama of American identity in which every masked American plays a part. The little man provides what Burke calls the "comic frame" which "enable[s] people to be observers of themselves, while acting." The comic frame's ultimate perspective is, Burke notes, "not passiveness, but maximum consciousness" (*Attitudes* 171). In Ellison's example, the little man represents maximum consciousness in the sense that he appears when mere invisible democratic motion becomes democratic action, and artist and audience recognize their mutual involvement and creation of each other's American self. With this typically American confrontation of identities, the little man, a consummate trickster, takes on a new shape, his chaotic identity known only by the fluidity of his form. For Ellison, this form is ultimately that of *Invisible Man*.

In situating the events of this essay during the years before he became a writer, Ellison makes his birth as an artist coincident with his discovery of the many meanings and problems defined by the little man at Chehaw Station. Behind his vision of the little man lies his remark that for the artist "his form is his greatest freedom and his insights are where he finds them" (*Shadow* 59). That is, form is what enables the democratic artist to render the chaotic motion of American culture visible. The discovery of the little man clarified for Ellison what it meant to be invisible in America and helped him to understand that invisibility transcended race and was a condition common to all Americans, written, so to speak, in the relation of each American to his country's unfulfilled ideals. Invisibility therefore is as much due to the percipient as to the unseen object: African American culture has always affected mainstream culture whether anyone has wanted to see this or not. Unexpectedly, when Ellison grew into an artist capable of mastering the form required of him, he no longer found himself playing the trumpet but writing a novel. Still, his purpose would be the same as if he were playing the classics for the little man behind the stove at Tuskegee station, that crossroads of American culture. His art and form would seek those "perspectives by incongruity" wherein democratic artist and audience become visible to each other, possibly for the first time.

## III

Searching for the little man at Chehaw station, *Invisible Man* takes shape as a great release of democratic energy that is also an ordering of that energy. As with other momentous and chaotic democratic forces—the Declaration of Independence, Emerson's essays and speeches, Elvis Presley's appearances on the Ed Sullivan Show—readers have had difficulty trying to contain the potent charge of Ellison's novel rather than plugging into the surges of its transformative energy.[20] Returning *Invisible Man* to the risky ground upon which it was written requires that we understand the novel both as an examination into and embodiment of the pragmatic orientation toward action.[21] This aim requires not only that we understand Ellison's use of Burke to structure his novel as a kind of pragmatist move, but that we recognize how Ellison's use of Emerson is also pragmatist. In the Prologue the narrator announces the underlying credo of his democratic vision in terms that evoke Emerson's declaration in *The American Scholar* that "the one thing in the world of value, is the active soul" (*Essays* 56). Likewise, Ellison's narrator asserts: "I believe in nothing if not action" (13). Emerson's ideal scholar is of course "Man Thinking." As the gerund suggests, Emerson assumes an active mind that discovers its insights while in transition. *Invisible Man*'s narrator's belief in action is also a defiant expression of self asserted despite the many obstacles to insight he must confront. That is, in the face of the complete denial of his identity, his commitment to action is his only tangible evidence that he exists. In what is the central paradox of the novel, were he not aware of his transformation into an invisible man, he would not be aware of himself at all. The narrator recognizes that no matter where one is, even in a forgotten basement on the border of Harlem, democratic energies buzz on. Thus his belief in action is a principle to be valued in and of itself, since it provides the hope of some future transformation which will once again make him visible not only to the world but to himself. In a sense, the protagonist dissolves his self into the action of his narrative, and the self that emerges will be the form the narrative takes.

The narrator's relationship with Monopolated Light & Power suggests that he longs to become one with the pure transmission of energy. The narrator confides, "I use their service and pay them nothing at all," and "they suspect that power is being drained off but they don't know where" (5). Having spent the better part of life up to this moment seeking to insinuate himself into the conduits of power, the narrator uses this electricity as a form of self-empowerment. Yet the narrator's sabotage is both passive and active. That he lines the room with 1,369 lights in order to illumine for himself his invisibility indicates the degree to which his use of the siphoned power is a form of self-expression. However, the more profound discovery is that the power is not self-generated, and that he is a function of its energy.[22] Surrendering his compulsion to believe in himself as the orgination of power, he learns the power of adaptation. As his narrative will show again and again, the narrator's failures and misadventures stem from a naive search for the origin of power. Thus, Norton, Bledsoe, Brother Jack, and the mysterious and vague northern white men from whom he hoped to gain influence become godlike figures to him mostly because he saw in them some originating force which he could neither find nor copy, though he tries to do both.

The point is significant because it suggests how traditional Emersonian readings of the novel commit the same fallacy concerning the origin and dissemination of power that the narrator enacts repeatedly until he lands, blind, in the basement. Norton of course advises the narrator to read Emerson's "Self-Reliance." Forgetting that Norton is hardly a figure of enlightenment in the novel, most readers have taken his advice and the essay he admires literally. Certainly the narrator does since it is his unquestioning commitment to the idea that he can transcend his circumstances continually that gets him into trouble. Blind to the world in which both black and white "keep this nigger boy running," the narrator has no one but himself upon which to rely. Yet this self-reliance, which is pitted against the ways in which others see him, cannot by itself sustain the narrator. He becomes an invisible man not because of any failure of self-reliance but because of a naive insistence upon the transcendent value of self-reliance. As it turns out, pure self-reliance leads to a denial of his existence as a social being.

Consequently, Ellison has stressed that "the hero's invisibility is not a matter of being seen, but a refusal to run the risk of his own humanity, which involves guilt" (*Shadow* 179). John Callahan aptly notes that the narrator "ends up committed to self-reliance as an optimist as well as an ironist" (59). Ellison's choice of the word "risk" indicates that in order to be seen the narrator will have to be willing to place his self in jeopardy—he cannot control, except perhaps through his narrative, how others see him. Ellison notes in a letter to Alan Nadel that "rather than go after Emerson's oracular stance, I went after some of the bombast that has been made of his pronouncements" (159n. 7). Ironically, a true fulfillment of a naive, bombastic Emersonian self-reliance would make any social gesture, responsible or otherwise, impossible, since such a gesture would depend on a mutual recognition between at least two parties. Just as an improvising jazz musician may quote a familiar refrain in order to estrange his audience from what has become, through overfamiliarity, a hackneyed phrase, so does Ellison's novel ring the changes upon Emerson's self-reliance in order to revivify it. From a pragmatist and Emersonian perspective, the most damning criticism Ellison makes of the conventional Emersonian tradition is that an unexamined self-reliance inhibits the possibility of further action. In a very funny joke on the traditional ending to the canonical American novel where the hero flees a corrupt and constraining civilization, Ellison ends his book with the narrator making his moral gesture by running in search of society.

The brunt of the narrative, though, is about failed communication. In his 1955 *Paris Review* interview, Ellison said that *Invisible Man* was "not an important novel" because in it he "had failed of eloquence" (*Shadow* 175). I think that what he meant was that his work had failed to inspire its audience to adopt the same stance of democratic optimism that Ellison's narrator adopted. Thus it is possible that Ellison's sense of failure was as much a comment on his audience as it was on his work. In his 1981 introduction to *Invisible Man* he noted that "one of the ever present challenges facing the American novelist was that of endowing his inarticulate characters, scenes and social processes with eloquence" (xviii). For Ellison, though, endowing inarticulate characters and social processes with eloquence includes dramatizing those moments where eloquence fails to materialize. Otherwise, he would have to admit that the status quo cannot be changed and that there is no basis for democratic optimism.

Though Ellison dramatizes the failure of eloquence throughout the novel, he establishes the pattern he wishes to break in the "battle royal" scene. A brutal satire of Jim Crow cultural conventions, the scene is also the narrator's chance to dramatize himself confronting an audience concerning the subject of democratic possibility. Only here the text is Booker T. Washington's Atlanta address—a masterpiece of Jim Crow rhetoric long outdated by the time the narrator employs it. Although the speech is thoroughly appropriate to the context in which it is delivered, the depressing question the novel confronts is by what or whose language could the context ever be transformed?

The narrator believes that he has been invited to make this speech as a reward for his intelligence, but he is actually there to learn a basic lesson in conformity. Prior to being invited to give the speech before "the town's leading white citizens," the narrator had delivered "an oration in which I showed that humiliation was the secret, indeed, the very essence of progress" (17). The origin of the invitation is left intentionally ambiguous. Is it a gesture of appeasement offered from the black community to the white community? Is it the black community's way of knocking a gifted but obviously naive young man down a peg or two? Or is it just routine brutality from the whites who rule the Jim Crow world? Whoever invited him was certainly aware that the theme of his speech was probably the only permissible topic a talented black boy could present to a southern white audience. Even before he gives his speech, it is already redundant—in a sense, invisible.

Readers have of course been struck by the incongruity of the narrator's persistent concentration upon the speech at the same time that he is being beaten to a bloody blind pulp for the amusement of his white audience. As probably all readers have noticed, the blindfold is a rather blatant symbol of the narrator's inability to perceive his true relation to the scene. Not only does the blindfold reveal the protagonist's lack of insight, though, it also reflects his audience's view of him. (An additional irony lies in the recognition that the narrator's eventual optimism depends on the naivete he exhibits in this scene.) The social processes of this scene dictate that black and white be separated from each other and that the basic absurdity of this dictum be denied at all costs. So predictable have the gestures between white and black become that neither side realizes these gestures would not exist were it not for each other's presence. Invisibility blankets everyone in this scene, black and white, and, if we are not careful, readers too.

The narrator's speech makes this farce of communication visible. Though the speaker does not achieve eloquence, the narrator in depicting the scene's failed communication does. Speaking "automatically" to an audience "as though deaf with cotton in dirty ears," he gives a speech that is at once hilariously appropriate and inappropriate. He intones Booker T. Washington to his "neighbor," the "Southern white man": " 'Cast down your bucket where you are' " (30). The audience does not have to listen to him because they know already what he is going to say. When he employs the phrase "social responsibility," he momentarily focuses his audience's attention, but only so that they may jeer at whatever those words might mean. The point of the exercise after all, is to deny the responsibility each side has toward the other. When he "makes a mistake" and replaces the phrase "social responsibility" with "social equality," however, the Jim Crow assumptions which have governed both parties' reactions momentarily disappear (31). Pulsing with the incongruity of one of Louis Armstrong's breaks in tempo, this slip injects a moment of spontaneity into the gathering that startles the speaker and his audience into a mutual recognition of each other. The narrator's unwitting improvisation dramatizes that essential Ellisonian moment when our sacred democratic principles emerge to haunt the meaning of our cultural gestures. In the sudden glare of his slip, both sides risk the possibility of seeing across what Ellison elsewhere has described as "our barriers of race and religion, class, color, region—barriers which consist of the many strategies of division which were designed . . . to prevent what otherwise would have been a more or less natural recognition of black and white fraternity" (*Invisible* xxvi). In this scene, the unexpected appearance of the word "equality" threatens to overcome those barriers; ironically, black and white find fraternity in burying the potential insight the word encourages.

Some remarks Kenneth Burke makes in *Counter-Statement* clarify the principle of democratic action dramatized here. Burke notes that "subject-matter is categorically 'charged,' in that each word relies for its meaning upon a social context" (164). Thus " 'meaning' [depends] upon the reader's previous experience with the object or situation which the word suggests" (180). Here the previous experience being referred to is the ideal one created by the words "all men are created equal." The word "equality," like the meaning it suggests, is something shared theoretically by both parties. The unlikely appearance of this word not only chastises both sides for their mutual failure to live up to the word's meaning, but it demands that they acknowledge their failure. Furthermore, the appearance of this word, even as a reproach, highlights the fact that our symbolic gestures of disaffiliation and disassociation cannot completely displace the democratic principles they seek to hide.

One could hardly ask for a better example of Burke's theory of language as symbolic action. When the narrator's speech conforms to the assumptions of his audience, his words essentially duplicate the experience and the social context of his humiliation, as if the occasion itself had placed the words in his mouth. But when his slip of the tongue announces a potential "equality" between speaker and audience, the word acts with the force of a gunshot. The speaker and the audience are forced to confront the potential world the symbolic action of this word envisions. We are told "that the [white men's] laughter hung smokelike in the sudden stillness" (31). One feels that in this moment of mutual visibility anything might happen. Perhaps speaker and audience will use this moment to begin to perceive one another as equals and thereby change their world. Predictably, though, each turns away from the responsibility and the social vision the word "equality" demands, and the narrator chooses to bury the potential of this lost moment, exploring instead the aftermath of mutual invisibility it brings.

This scene marks the narrator's baptism into invisibility. Not until he falls into his hole and burns his accumulated papers, beginning with the diploma given to him to mark this occasion, will he break the pattern that this ritual establishes. The failed communication that this scene represents cannot suppress the hidden and potential actions that are safeguarded, in effect, by the suspicion that "equality" might be acknowledged as a worthwhile value. The narrator's primary concern will be with what Burke defines as "eloquence," a definition that Ellison likely had in mind when discussing his novel in the *Paris Review* interview. According to Burke, "eloquence" pressures obvious instances of plot "until those elements of surprise and suspense are subtilized, carried down into the writing of a line or sentence, until in all its smallest details the work bristles with disclosures, contrasts, restatements . . . which in their line for line aspect we call style and in their broader outlines we call form" (*Counter* 37). Ultimately the novel provides the context that enables us to interpret the word "equality" in a way that the scene in which it was uttered will not allow, thereby conferring it with "eloquence." In great art, Burke further notes, "our sense of certain forces gathering to produce a certain result" will be "snapped" by the artist's skill, but our satisfaction arises from our participation in the process" (145). Our participation in the pursuit of the meaning of this word creates, in effect, the ideal democratic process to which Ellison's art aspires. On the level of the novel itself, though, the battle royal scene dramatizes the broader and more sustaining relationship the narrator wishes to uncover with his audience. In this respect, Ellison dramatizes both the plight of an aspiring democratic artist and ours as ideal democratic audience. That is, as an aspiring democratic artist, he seeks an "antagonistic cooperation" with his audience in the hope that from this collaboration will emerge the true meaning of democracy's sacred word, "equality."

If in the battle royal scene the meaning of "equality" is buried, it resurfaces later through Rinehart, the riot, and ultimately, in its most fully realized form, in the narrative voice that controls novel. The failed communication that the speech enacts will be replayed in speech after speech, yet with each speech the narrator learns more about the kind of artist he wants to be and the kind of audience who might heart him. John Callahan has brilliantly analyzed the narrator's speeches to show how Ellison transforms this ranter into a writer. What has not been recognized, though, is how integral to the narrative is the sense of rising discord that each speech releases. Beginning with the eviction speech, the narrator becomes increasingly aware that each time he meets his audience there is an unspoken context—a buried history—that governs what possible action may result from the occasion. When the narrator addresses a spontaneous gathering over the scattered belongings of the evicted old couples, he begins to realize that this buried history might be unearthed to transform the present. The various mementos that the narrator finds—"portrait of the old couple when young," the " 'knocking bones,' used to accompany music at country dances, used in black-faced minstrels," the "nuggets of High John the Conqueror," "the tintype of Abraham Lincoln," and, perhaps most important, "the 'FREE PAPERS' of Primus Primo" (265–66) all indicate a cultural identity that has persisted despite attempts to eradicate it. These objects of history fail to give the gathering audience an identity; instead, they become a mob. The narrator tries to channel the crowd's energy into an appropriate response, but cannot. Unlike the battle royal speech, here he has a potentially receptive audience but together they cannot imagine an appropriate action. Ultimately the energy takes the form of a disturbance that will be contained by the police. Ironically, the narrator's failure to incite effective action earns him the attention of Jack, who will employ him to perform a similar role for the Brotherhood as their speaker on racial issues.

Burke said that "form is a way of experiencing" which also is an act eliciting its own "unintended by-products" (*Counter-Statement* 143). *Invisible Man* achieves its art by drawing these "unintended by-products," such as those thrown out into the street during the eviction, to the surface. As I suggested at the outset of this chapter, Clifton's death forces the narrator to confront how he himself is an unintended by-product of history and to imagine how he might complicate that history which would exclude his voice. By their involvement with the Brotherhood, Clifton and the narrator had hoped to be active participants in the shaping of their community's history and, by extension, their nation's. The Brotherhood, no less than the southern gentlemen of the battle royal scene, believe that the unintended by-products of history can be controlled and therefore erased. In considering the possibility that one sometimes has to plunge outside history, Clifton was implicitly questioning the Brotherhood and their rigidly formal version of history. He was also discovering that, according to Brotherhood's logic, he did not exist. Unfortunately, Clifton's plunge becomes for him a death sentence; selling Sambo dolls on the street until he is senselessly killed by the police, he acts out a version of William James's definition of invisibility in *Principles of Psychology*.[23] The narrator by contrast wants to enact a history that would have allowed Clifton not to disappear. He takes hope from the fact that history's "recorder" cannot suppress "an accident, like [Frederick] Douglass," which "by all historical logic [should] have disappeared around the first part of the nineteenth century, rationalized out of existence" (435). Like the free papers of Primus Primo, the example of Douglass suggests to the narrator that beneath official history lies a more turbulent history that may erupt into the flow of official history.

The example of Douglass also allows the narrator to recognize other less obvious but perhaps more telling examples of how invisible Americans might leave an image of themselves that others later will see. Thus, in one of the novel's key passages, the narrator notices a group of hipsters, others "outside history" with whom Clifton had occasionally consorted. These young black men express their identity in a style noticed neither by the Brotherhood nor, until now, the narrator.

> What about those of us who shoot up from the South into the busy city like wild jacks-in-the-box broken loose from our springs—so sudden that our gait becomes like that of deep-sea divers suffering from the bends? What about those fellows waiting still and silent on the platform, so still and silent that they clash with the crowd in their

very immobility; standing noisy in their very silence; harsh as a cry of
terror in their quietness? What about those three boys, coming now
along the platform, tall and slender, walking stiffly with swinging
shoulders in their well-pressed, too-hot-for-summer suits, their col-
lars high and tight about their necks, their identical hats of cheap
black felt set upon the crown of their heads with a severe formality
above their hard conked hair? (433)

This lyrical passage evokes beautifully the sense of untapped possibility
which has been surging through the narrative. By any definition of history, these young men have been forgotten, yet here they are. They represent the detritus of democracy filtering throughout the book's pages.
However, even in their exclusion they vivify democratic principles in the
proud assertion of their style. Their "too-hot-for-summer suits" and
"swinging shoulders" and "severe formality" betray a desire to assert their
identity within and upon their community regardless of who is not watching or listening or recording. They embody what Ellison elsewhere calls
the "American style" which "*is* that of the vernacular," which he defines
as a "dynamic process in which the most refined styles from the past
are continually merged with the play-it-by-eye-and-by-ear improvisations which we invent in order to control our environment and entertain
ourselves" (*Going* 139). Like Louis Armstrong, these young men have
improvised a style which does not merely voice their voicelessness but
projects a sense of identity *through* invisibility. Wearing their coats of
many colors, these young men flaunt their invisibility. For this reason
their immobility can still manage to clash with the scene around them.

The experience of these men who moved "outside the groove of history" profoundly affects the narrator, making him in a sense the by-
product of their experience. The narrator worries that these men will be
forgotten unless he can "get them in" history, but the larger point is that
they are already in it. Ellison notes elsewhere, "History has no vacuum.
There are transformations, there are lesions, there are metamorphoses,
and there are mysteries that cloak the clashing of individual wills" (*Going*
205). Reading the novel in a time well past the events depicted, we know
that the hipsters he describes are products of the jazz culture, which
animated Harlem during the vague time period of the novel. As I suggested at the beginning of this chapter, it is appropriate that the narrator's
reflections about history should be prompted by "a record shop blaring a
languid blues" and that the narrator should wonder if this is "the true
history of the times, a mood blared by trumpets, trombones, saxophones,

and drums, a song with turgid, inadequate words?" (436). "The inadequate words" has two distinct but related meanings. First, the words are
inadequate because they are inherited rather than invented, a floating
verse likely, that has been sung many times before. Yet a master such as
Ellison's friend Jimmy Rushing charges seemingly "banal lines with the
mysterious potentiality of meaning which haunts the blues" (*Shadow* 245).
The narrator's situation mirrors Rushing's in that he too must work with
words and promises that have become perhaps lifeless from misuse and
overuse. Just as Rushing charges those lyrics with hidden meanings, so
does the narrator seek to find a language commensurate with the style he
recognized in those three hep-cats.

The riot that leads to the narrator's disappearance is a kind of blues
explosion, but without the order—the elegance—imported by either of
these anonymous men or Jimmy Rushing. A direct response to the narrator's funeral oration for Clifton—his final speech—the riot represents
democratic possibility unleashed to the point of terror and as a result
contrasts directly with the failed communication of the battle royal scene.
Although the riot too is a kind of failed communication in that it results in
the destruction of the Harlem community and the reorganization of the
Brotherhood, it is also the medium through which the narrator discovers
Rinehart, and the key to understanding his own invisibility. Through the
related experiences of Rinehart and the riot the narrator begins to realize
both that there might be an audience capable of hearing him and that he
might have the eloquence to speak. The riot also provides confirmation
that others besides himself are lost to history and are angry enough to take
action, however misguided. Still, without this action the narrator would
remain ignorant of the democratic force that awaits his formal rendering.

In terms of energy, one might say that the riot is a verbal representation
of what the narrator wants us to experience should we ever hear Louis
Armstrong's "What Did I Do to Be So Black and Blue" playing full-blast
on five phonographs at once. When the invisible rise, as Dupre does by
lifting his Dobbs hat or burning down the building in which he lives, it is
with unrestrained fury, the sort of collective craziness that surfaced with
John Brown or Nat Turner or the Whisky Rebellion. At one point a man's
wife begs him to return to the "the hill" with the "respectable peoples," a
mocking allusion to America's mythical "city on the hill." Her husband's
response suggests that if that hill has only respectable people for its denizens, then its founding principles have been lost. Lighting out for the
territory within, he shouts: "Hill hell! We stay right here. This thing's just
starting. If it become a sho' 'nough race riot I want to be there when

they'll be some fighting back" (543). And Dupre says, "Damn *who* started it. All I want is for it to last a while" (531). Martin Luther King Jr. once remarked that the riot is the voice of the unheard, and certainly for Ellison's narrator this fact constitutes the riot's appeal. Just as the riot is re-created through the narrator's rendering of his consciousness, the riot's celebration of the fluidity of cultural lines is re-channeled into the form of this book. Thus it is significant that the narrator never tells us how the riot ends, since in the Burkean sense of symbolic action it cannot end except through the narrator's formal intervention.

One sees the narrator learning how to accomplish this difficult feat through his discovery of Rinehart—a trickster figure whose many forms may even include the riot itself. Ellison emphasizes this connection when he remarks that Rinehart "is my name for the personification of chaos" (*Shadow* 181). Nearly all critics have seen Rinehart as a cynical character, a crass con man. The narrator seems to confirm this view when he says in the Epilogue that though he wants freedom, it is "certainly not the freedom of a Rinehart" (566). Likewise, most critics have seen Rinehart as a foil to the narrator's own hard-won self-reliance. If the narrator allegedly discovers his self, Rinehart literally has no self. A version of Melville's confidence man, democracy's bad guy, Rinehart takes advantage of America's cultural fluidity to dupe others. Kimberly W. Benston, Rinehart's sharpest critic, notes that he is the "Emersonian Orphic Poet" who also represents "the central Melvillean critique of Emersonian fluidity, the distaste for the social parasite who benefits from, yet undermines, cultural forms." Thus Rinehart "is a mode of being," but what he "gains in energy [he] loses in affiliation, for the pure self can have no social existence whatever" (161–62).[24]

This criticism of Rinehart, ironically, depends on the traditional Emersonian view that the novel is merely an individual's story and not one about our collective invisibility. But if we see Emersonian "fluidity" as endemic to our democratic culture as a whole, then Rinehart becomes a more sympathetic character. He embodies, however loosely, the very democratic energy that the narrator is counting on to obliterate the distance between him and his audience. As an individual he may be merely cynical (I will debate this in a moment); as a symbol of our invisible democracy Rinehart represents the turbulent force of our suppressed, but nonetheless active, commitment to equality. We should recall that Ellison said he "intended Rinehart to represent America and change," the representative figure for a "country with no solid past or stable class lines"

(*Shadow* 181–82). Combine this remark with Ellison's additional clue that B. P. Rinehart's full name is "Bliss Proteus" and we see that Rinehart avoids any static characterization (56). Like electricity, he runs positive and negative.

Not merely a series of transformations, Rinehart is transformation itself: the fury of the American underground, its blues, its jazz, its vernacular grace and turbulence, unleashed.[25] Appropriately, the narrator discovers Rinehart in the act of donning a disguise. Rinehart enables him to act out the hidden history he heard in that "languid blues" and saw in the style of those proto-bebop hipsters on the subway platform. Copying the style of "three men in natty cream-colored summer suits," donning the pose and power of the jazzman, the narrator races into a drugstore to snatch up as many artifacts of their style as he can. The language he uses to describe the adoption of his new identity underscores the meaning of his gesture: "I put [the glasses] on immediately, plunging into blackness and moving outside" (474). He hardly needs to add the word "history."

Becoming Rinehart, he moves thrillingly among the many conduits of American style, slipping into the breaks and looking around. He discovers where the blocked political principle of equality achieves its cultural form in the rapid exchange of styles and identities. Our protean protagonist is taken for a pimp, a zoot-suiter, someone's lover, a runner, a reverend, a gambler, and who knows what else. Through the guise of Rinehart he sees that "the world in which we lived [is] without boundaries," "a vast seething, hot world of fluidity" in which "freedom was not only the recognition of necessity, it was the recognition of possibility" (490). When he was nearly lobotomized after the explosion at the paint factor, a doctor had asked him "WHO . . . ARE . . . YOU?" (236). Now, as Rinehart, the narrator asks his most searching question, which characterizes his invisible audience as well: "If dark glasses and a white hat could blot out my identity so quickly, who actually was who?" (485). For Ellison the fear is not that one's identity can be so easily transformed, but that his audience will not recognize this fact as a necessary consequence of democratic optimism.

Though ultimately the narrator seems to turn away from Rinehart, I would say rather that he out-Rineharts Rinehart, just as we can say that Ellison in this novel wishes to out-Emerson Emerson. Without referring specifically to Rinehart, Alan Nadel clarifies the connection between Rinehart and Emerson by placing the narrator's actions in the context of that thoroughly Rinehartian Emerson essay, "Circles." Nadel's key point is that only when the narrator realizes he has been sent on a fool's errand, which a man named "Emerson" helps him to see, can he reject the circular pattern of his life, in effect transcend the circles. Thus, according to Nadel, "he learns this Emersonian principle [of self-reliance] only through a rejection of Emerson" (119).[26] Nadel's reading, though, overlooks how Emersonian this putative rejection of Emerson is. Emerson's essay emphasizes the way we move *through* these various circles only to encounter a different circle. "The life of man," Emerson says, "is a self-evolving circle, which, from a ring imperceptibly small, rushes on all sides outwards to new and larger circles, and that without end" (*Essays* 404). Since "nothing is secure but life, transition, the energizing spirit," it follows that "the way of life is wonderful" for "it is by abandonment" (413, 414). Achieving Emerson's democratic wisdom, the narrator must learn through Rinehart that power resides in the act of transformation, or what Emerson identifies as the "energizing spirit" (413).

Ellison reinforces the idea that his narrator discovers this Emersonian-Rinehartian wisdom in two scenes where the word "circles" prominently appears. The first scene occurs when the narrator ventures to see the Brotherhood's chief theorist on African American matters, Brother Hambro. In yet another scene of failed communication—failed eloquence— the narrator is unable to convince Hambro that "the Negro problem" merits special attention. While talking with Hambro, the narrator "describes a circle in the air," wondering what his "circle" has to do with Rinehart, all the while holding the circular chain link that Tarp carried with him from his days on the chain gang. When the Brotherhood's chief theorist tells him he will have to be patient and follow the lines of history, he retorts, "You mean . . . the old wheel of history. Or is it the little wheels within the wheel?" (495–96). The image conveys his Emersonian desire to draw a circle around the circle in which he is currently running and take sustenance in the knowledge that "the universe is fluid and volatile, . . . permanence but a word of degrees" (403). This feeling is reinforced when he abandons the circles he has been running to fall through the saving but not final circle of the manhole: "I stumbled about in circles, blindly swinging the briefcase," he says as he disappears, only to reappear later as the circular "I" or eye (a classically Emersonian pun) who traces the histories of his many circles (552).

Again, cultural fluidity is an enabling notion for this narrator. This fluidity is not embraced for its own sake, however, for the sheer "fascination of donning a role," as the narrator puts it later, *but for the possibility that it will have a social outcome.* In our astonishment at Rinehart's mercurial force we overlook the fact that he leaves something in his wake. Strictly speaking, the character does not exist in the novel except as another character's projection, but neither did the narrator exist in the eyes of his audience at the battle royal. Rinehart's absence, as the saying goes, is also a presence. The many people with whom he is involved may regret his absence or they may revel in it; from the examples we are given most seem solicitous for his welfare. In either case they accept him, however brief his stay, as an informing presence in their lives. In this sense, Benston is wrong to say that Rinehart "can have no social self whatsoever" (162). With a style that Ellison surely envies, Rinehart magically adapts to the conflicting demands created by our nation's fluid lines of culture and communication. As the embodiment of the ideal form for democratic expression, Rinehart enacts the principle of democratic energy simultaneously released and contained that the narrator has been seeking ever since he plugged into the Monopolated Power line. Ellison clings to "Rinehart methods" even if his narrator will not; after all, Elison, like Rinehart, makes his art by trading in "perspective by incongruity."

The fluidity of experience that Rinehart represents involves the narrator in a paradox endemic to American culture. Though the narrator may distance himself from Rinehart, he cannot escape the fact that he is implicated in the same network of forces as "Rine the Rascal." The narrator turns away from Rinehart because he sees in this slippery figure a nightmare version of himself; that is, he sees his own invisibility. The deceptive assumption that Rinehart's presence dredges up and forces us to confront is the illusion that one can identify one's American essence. A society which can create a Rinehart has possibilities that even Rinehart cannot realize. Rinehart is a circle that will ultimately be abandoned, as the narrator does. Without realizing it, he has become one of Rinehart's untapped possibilities, the medium of expression for this mathematically improbable beast, Rinehart (or infinity) plus one. Borrowing again from Kenneth Burke, we can say that through Rinehart the narrator has increased the strategic possibilities of his artistic situation. Burke notes of the artist, "*He contains* [these possibilities], *but encompasses them within a wider frame—and as so encompassed, they act entirely differently than they would if 'efficiently' isolated in their 'purity'*" (*Philosophy* 49). On the verge of finishing his memoir, the narrator says, "The old fascination with playing a role returns and I'm drawn upward again" (570). Adding a role to the many he has already played, he brings with him out of his hole every possibility

Rinehart has suggested and more. Moreover, as a creative artist seeking to deflect the democratic energy he has discovered through the recognition of his invisibility, he faces the same challenge as Rinehart: to make visible the widest possible variety of our democratic hodgepodge.

At this point the allegedly ambiguous ending of *Invisible Man* begins to take form as well. Burke wrote in *Counter-Statement* that "a form is a way of experiencing," but one that is worked out between artist and audience (143). In a sense the artist's form is the path he creates to his audience. Thus Burke writes that "it is the audience which dreams, while the artist oversees the conditions which determine this dream" (36). For Ellison, the dreams of the artist and the audience are conditioned by a shared sense of democratic possibility. His role as democratic artist is to wake his audience up to their shared dream, to remind us that the very conditions of their dream of equality must imbue all of our present and future actions. Ellison's novel is necessarily prospective; it believes in the future. For this reason the narrator can discover in his grandfather, a man born into slavery, the same commitment to equality and progress that Thomas Jefferson voiced: "Did he [his grandfather] mean that we had to take responsibility for all of it, for the men as well as the principle, because we were the heirs who must use the principle because no other fitted our needs?" (565).

That slaves and the sons and daughters of slaves shall inherit the world that Jefferson dreamed suggests an astonishing capacity for hope. This hopefulness may strike some as naive. I think that is why Ellison interprets the grandfather's words in the form of a question, as if he were deferring the realization of this interpretation to some later date. Just as Frederick Douglass used to quote the Declaration of Independence for the edification of his slave-obsessed audiences, so does Ellison demand that we see the democratic principle as a heritage that continually gains momentum, gathering all within its force, black and white, past, present, and future. The crucial point, so often missed, is that *his audience, alas, is invisible as well*; we are all underground. This is the great irony of those readings which want to see Ellison as the high modernist god paring his fingernails somewhere above the political fray. Alone in his basement, writing the narrative in which he uncovers his own invisibility, the narrator understands that he cannot be seen because others cannot see him in the light in which he sees himself.

The narrative act that is *Invisible Man* is not a gesture of withdrawal or uppity Emersonianism. For the sake of argument, grant that Ellison has achieved a perfectly realized aesthetic universe, a world complete unto itself. What meaning does this aesthetic achievement have without an audience who will meet him on the ground of his vision? The answer the novel gives to this question is that his ground is *your* ground. The narrator recognizes his invisibility in relation to the democratic principles that would include him *on paper* but not in real life. His only choice is to follow the Burkean notion that language is a form of symbolic action to its logical end: to show that his paper identity is real. The best way of doing that is to write a novel that will demand action of his readers. What else can an artist do? As he writes in his Prologue: "I believe in nothing if not action" (13). We do not have to place the word "symbolic" before the word "action" in order to see that action implies a reciprocal gesture on the part of his reader. With exactly the same logic that we saw Ellison applying earlier to the Civil War, as if prophesying how he himself will be misread, his narrator declares in his Epilogue: "You won't believe in my invisibility and you will fail to see how any principle that applies to you could apply to me. You'll fail to see us even if death waits for both of us if you don't" (571).

Having made this difficult and risky gesture of communication, his "completion of personality," the narrator requires a reciprocal gesture on the part of his audience. The book ends with that tantalizing question with which we began: "Who knows but that, on the lower frequencies, I speak for you?" (572). The last word of the novel, "you," invites a response. Burke notes "that the poem is designed to 'do something' for the poet and the readers" so that we should consider "the poem as the embodiment of this act" (89). Or, as he says most forcefully in *Counter-Statement*, "The formal aspects of art appeal in that they exercise formal *potentialities* in the reader" (142, emphasis mine). The narrator's gesture for recognition constitutes his artistic act; the "something" his act does is to create the form that makes artist and audience potentially visible to each other. What that something does further is up to us, but, as Ellison notes, "Once introduced into society the work of art begins to pulsate with those meanings, emotions, ideas brought to it by its audience and over which the artist has but limited control" (*Shadow* 38).

The ending therefore remains ambiguous, but in two distinct ways. In the first place, our condition as Americans hides our identity as a culture from ourselves. Committed to cultural transformation in the name of social equality, American identity will never be static. Democratic action ensures the continual transformation of our character, as with Al Jolson or the man of parts. This ambiguity we must accept and embrace, painful as it may be sometimes, as tribute to our belief in equality. This second ambiguity dramatizes the mutual invisibility that pertains, in the case of *Invisible Man,* between artist and audience, but also for every American as a consequence of our failure to live by the ideals we profess and, despite our gestures sometimes, continue to place our faith in. This ambiguity, ironically, Ellison the artist illuminates, but only in the hope that together artist and audience may make it disappear. Thus the ending is ambiguous by necessity, for Ellison knows that without the mutual recognition between artist and audience that his novel hopes for, his democratic vision cannot be realized.

It was Ellison's nature, as I said earlier of Emerson, to risk a whimsical novel in the hope that something lasting would arise from it. But he knew all too well that Americans can be not only blind, but deaf too, that a promise, though embedded in language—hence ensuring that its principles will be either worked out or will vanish—contains within it the possibility not only of its eventual realization but its betrayal as well. Ellison wrote *Invisible Man* not only as the ideal incarnation of the little man behind the stove, but in search of him as well. At his most hopeful, he could say with Burke that the artist creates his audience; perhaps because this particular artist descended from slaves, however, he could only hope that his audience would discover their way to him too. Just as the narrative of *Invisible Man* searches for the form that will make the narrator visible to himself and his audience, so does the form of Ellison's novel seek to make visible the multiple and always interacting levels of democratic culture. A few moments before his final gesture the narrator observes that "a mind that has conceived a plan of living must never lose sight of the chaos against which that pattern was conceived" (571). Echoing William James's "Stream of Thought" chapter in *Principles of Psychology,* Ellison conveys the fundamentally American truth that our surest thoughts and our most secure identity wash away the limits by which we claim to know them. With his death, Ellison is part of history now, but his words have joined themselves in Burkean fashion to our other sacred democratic words, working out their perfection, symbolically acting, inviting us to recognize and realize their form.

# 4    Philip Roth: The Jew That Got Away

■ ■ ■ ■ ■ ■

Talking about Jewishness hardly interests me at all.
—Philip Roth

*I*

At the conclusion of *The Counterlife* (1986), Philip Roth's alter ego, Nathan Zuckerman, decides that if there is such a thing as "an irreducible self, it is rather small, and may even be the root of all impersonation—the natural being may be the skill itself, the innate capacity to impersonate" (320). As with Ellison's Rinehart, Roth's heroes delight in the provisional, contingent status of their self-making and role-playing. The crucial difference between them is that whereas Ellison's confidence in his African American identity prompted him to challenge received notions of American identity, Roth's confidence in his American identity has prompted him to challenge inherited notions of ethnic identity. Because Roth's characters are inclined to believe that American society, despite its many inequities, offers the best opportunity for self-realization anyone is likely to find, they are unconcerned with how they are perceived as Americans. Instead of challenging Roth's audience to live up to the promises contained within the Declaration of Independence, his characters take them for granted. They explore their American selves through the identity conflicts they experience as a result of their comfortable Americanness. In Roth's early story "The Conversion of the Jews" the fully assimilated Ozzie challenges his Jewish elders by wondering "how Rabbi Binder could call the Jews 'the Chosen People' if the Declaration of Independence claimed that all men are created equal" (*Goodbye* 153). Couched as a kid's joke, Ozzie's question suggests that Roth's art emerges from the same circumstances that animated Mary Antin and Horace Kallen: the tensions that emerge from being of the Chosen People in a nation that already considers its citizens to be chosen, if not necessarily Jewish.

Like Ellison, Roth explores the contingency of identity; his protagonists test their self-making capacity as a kind of performance. More than Ellison, though, Roth has emphasized the almost irreducible ethnic aspect of these performing selves. Although early in his career Roth explicitly linked his view of the aesthetic representation of ethnic identity with that of Ellison, his later fiction has moved away from Ellisonian humanism and more toward the aggressive ethnic stance of Horace Kallen. Though Roth will never quite allow that one's Jewishness is prior to all other forms of self-making, he nonetheless makes this possibility the given of his fiction. His recent Pulitzer Prize–winning novel, *American Pastoral* (1997), underscores how Kallenesque his approach to the evolution of Jewish identity in American culture has become. In this novel Roth employs Nathan Zuckerman to tell the story of the rise and fall of Swede Levov, "the blue-eyed blonde born into our *tribe*," a man cursed with an "unconscious oneness with America" (3, 20). Swede's ascension into an assimilated American identity is destroyed when his daughter protests the Viet Nam War by blowing up the local post office. The narrative frames Swede's fall from grace as the inevitable result of having married outside the tribe. Had Swede followed his father's advice and chosen to marry a Jew rather than a Catholic, then none of the terror that afflicts him would have occurred.

In *American Pastoral* Swede cannot transcend his ethnic identity; it is his only constant in a world of shifting possibilities. At one point Zukerman imagines Swede reflecting that "what was astonishing to him was how people seemed to run out of their own being, run out of whatever the stuff was that made them who they were" (329). Swede's thought is surprising since in Roth's fiction—and especially in his Zuckerman fiction—the self runs out only because it is undergoing a process of renewal, one that willingly risks in Emersonian fashion the misperception and even the anger of friends and family. By the end of the novel, though, Swede's self has run out of being to reveal the Jew who remains. It may be that Roth tells Swede's story as a warning about what happens to those who cannot transform their origins into something else.

No American writer, not even Ralph Ellison, has outraged his audience as effectively as Philip Roth has outraged sections of his. The "stuff" that has kept Roth going and has resulted in an *oeuvre* as impressive as that of any American writer since Henry James has been the conflict he perceives to exist between others' demands that he conform to Jewish communal expectation and his own will to aesthetic experimentation. In *American Pastoral*, though, Roth subsumes the voice of artist Nathan Zuckerman within the story of Levov, heroic high-school athlete and ultimately failed avatar of an assimilationist American dream. Swede's meditation upon the inevitable exhaustion of self becomes in this novel Roth's way of exploring the cost of cultural transformation in the name of self-renewal. Zuckerman's narrative of Levov's failed transformation from descendant of immigrant Jews to assimilated American is framed as the answer to the question that has driven Roth's fiction. "Where," Zuckerman asks of Swede, "was the Jew in him?" (20). Zuckerman's answer in *American Pastoral* is that the Jew is that element of his identity that cannot be abandoned.

Where is the Jew in one is the question that Kallen made constitutive of American identity. To Kallen you achieve the fullness of your American identity by asserting your ethnic identity. You make an almost magical journey from the present to the past, back to the land of your ancestors, only to arrive at last an American. Ellison would have considered this argument to be absurd since it would require that he deny his American identity for an African origin that he could not have embraced even as a mythical fantasy. The past of *Invisible Man* goes no further back than the end of slavery. Yet this idea of Kallen's has come to life with a vengeance in postmodern America as writers from all ethnicities have been redefining their American identities by visiting the past of their ancestors.[1] Philip Roth is an exemplary instance of the kind of American identity making that Kallen described. He initiated his career in the 1950s by writing comic stories about recent immigrant Jews and their descendants living in Newark, New Jersey. By the 1970s and 1980s his imagination had journeyed back to the Europe from which those immigrants had migrated. Speaking of Roth's Zuckerman trilogy, Hanna Wirth-Nesher suggests that "Philip Roth's long odyssey from Newark to Prague is also a turning point in the Jewish-American literary tradition, for it marks the passage from a literature of immigration and assimilation into a literature of retrieval, of the desire to be a part of Jewish literary legacy alongside the European and American literary traditions" (31). Roth's work is part of a larger turning point in which contemporary American writers are reinventing their literary and cultural heritages through fictive reconstructions of ethnic and often racialized pasts.[2]

What we see happening in the work of Roth, as in the works of these other writers, is exactly what Kallen said would happen to Americans who nourished their ethnic identity as the fulfillment of their American identity: they would move forward as Americans by looking backward to their ethnic past in order to create their American selves. No contemporary writer including Toni Morrison, Gloria Naylor, Charles Johnson, James Welch, Leslie Marmon Silko, Sandra Cisneros, Christine Garcia, and Maxine Hong-Kingston, to name just a few, has explored as thoroughly this kind of thinking as Philip Roth. Although critics of Roth—indeed Roth himself—have always discussed him as a *Jewish* American writer, it is important to recognize that Roth is more than just the representative of a particular ethnic group. Along with faithfully recounting the range of intellectual positions implicit within American identity politics, he constructs his fictions to explore how these ethnic conflicts are invariably American ones. Roth's characters accept their ethnic identity as a given, but it is also true that their understanding of their own ethnic identity is never consistent. The essential ethnic identity that Kallen assumed becomes in Roth's formulation something that is always shifting—even if the word "Jew" always accompanies these shifts.

Roth is not a cultural theorist in the way that Emerson, Kallen, and Ellison were, yet implicit in his work is a pragmatist practice of American identity consonant with theirs. Roth is the pragmatist as fictionist, which may make him, as Richard Rorty has suggested of those who write fiction, more fully pragmatist than any philosopher, since the theories that Roth explores are to be inferred from the acts that he depicts. Drawing on the work of Milan Kundera (a writer whom Roth also admires), Rorty has suggested that the "art of the novel" betrays a pragmatist sensibility in that the masters of the novel did not structure their works "around transcultural notions of validity" ("Truth" 638). Kundera writes that

> Don Quixote set forth from his house into a world he could no longer recognize. In the absence of the Supreme Judge, the world suddenly appeared in its fearsome ambiguity; the single divine Truth decomposed into myriad relative truths parceled out by men. Thus was born the world of the Modern era, and with it the novel, the image and model of that world. (*Art* 6)

Likewise, Roth's work obsessively constructs, deconstructs, and reconstructs provisional and usually contradictory answers to questions that allow the characters no opportunity for closure. Rorty's description of the novel's function applies quite well to Roth's fiction: "The realm of possibility is not something with fixed limits; rather, it expands continually, as ingenious new redescriptions suggest even more ingenious reredescriptions" ("Truth" 639).

Roth's fiction takes shape as a relentless exploration of the contingent nature of history, self, and identity. If William James fought to abolish the gap that is presumed to exist between abstract thinking and acting, Roth has used the gap that is presumed to exist between life and art in order to show how his characters' self-inventions transform both the selves they would invent and the fictions they make of those selves. Roth himself makes this point in his so-called autobiography, *The Facts* (1988). In the guise of explaining his theory of autobiography, Roth justifies his orientation toward fiction by emphasizing the contingency of all narrative. As he explains, the relation between his so-called real self and his narrative self stems from the shared assumption that both are inventions: "It isn't that you subordinate your ideas to the force of facts in autobiography but that you construct a sequence of stories to bind up the facts with a persuasive *hypothesis* that unravels your history's meaning" (8). Roth defines his philosophy of composition in terms virtually identical in intent to William James's own understanding of the pragmatic method. A self is invented through narrative form; conversely, narrative forms create possibilities for different self-inventions. For Roth, *the self is fiction*; hence he understands narrative form and personal identity to be in reciprocal relation.

Roth's formal experimentation is intimately bound up in the cultural issues he depicts. Over and over Roth's characters assume "authentic" identities only to find that experience causes them to revise what they once took for granted. Most Roth critics (including Roth himself) have seen how his career has been constructed out of his creative and cultural conflict with his Jewish audience. Against charges that his fiction has compromised an essential Jewish identity, Roth has repeatedly and flagrantly violated Jewish cultural taboos in order to assert his primacy as an artist—a power that he associates with the freedom to invent himself as an American. Instead of championing an essential Jewish identity against an oppressive, monolithic American society, his novels examine how American culture enables his characters to radically transform their sense of themselves as Jews. Although nearly all of Roth's protagonists confront the consequences of having a strong sense of ethnic identity, Roth's subject is not, as he suggests in this chapter's epigraph, Jewishness per se. Rather, he exploits the form of the novel to explore what we might call Roth's comedy of identity: the compelling but ultimately futile desire to achieve an authentic Jewish identity.

In *The Facts* Roth relates how his birth as a "Jewish" novelist occurred in 1962 at the Yeshiva University Symposium, "The Crisis of Conscience in Minority Writers of Fiction." On this memorable night Roth was publicly and permanently "branded"—the word is Roth's—a Jew. Witnesses to this ceremony were fellow "minority" writers Pietro di Donato and Ralph Ellison, the latter inspiring in Roth a feeling of "awe." Wary of attending an event that was likely to be hostile toward him, Roth considered it his "duty to respond to the pronounced Jewish interest my book continued to evoke" (125).[3] Invoking Kafka, Roth characterizes the experience as "the trial," and the moderator and audience become his unforgiving judges. "Mr. Roth," the moderator intones, "would you write the same stories you've written if you were living in Nazi Germany?" (127).[4] Still being "grilled" thirty minutes later, Roth says his "combative instinct" abandoned him. By the end of the evening he is staring into "the faces of my jury" confronting "the final verdict against me, as harsh a judgment as I hope to hear in this or any other world." Roth leaves Yeshiva vowing that "I'll never write about Jews again" (129).[5]

Prior to this incident, Roth saw his identity as a Jew and his identity as an American as seamlessly bound in the same person. "Not only did growing up Jewish in Newark in the thirties and forties, Hebrew School and all, feel like a perfectly legitimate way of growing up American, but, what's more, growing up Jewish the way I did and growing up American seemed to me indistinguishable" (122). After the Yeshiva incident, Roth's sense of wholeness is severed. He tries to make light of the situation by suggesting that the incident offered him "the luckiest break I could have"; in other words, it gave him his subject. But his next sentence, which ends the chapter, is perhaps more telling: "I was *branded*" (130, emphasis mine). No longer an unselfconscious American Jew, Roth instead becomes aware of himself as "other." His recognition mirrors the one Nathan Zuckerman experiences in *The Counterlife* when a British woman intimates that there is "a terrible smell" in the restaurant and that the smell emanates from Zuckerman. Roth leaves room to interpret the scene as Zuckerman's paranoid fantasy, but the underlying motivation is the same for Zuckerman as it is for Roth in *The Facts*. Both have been branded—"*Jew*." The difference is that with Roth it was the Jews who did the branding.

Branded a Jew by his Jewish audience, Roth becomes divided—hyphenated—into Jewish-American. In a general sense he embodies Kallen's ideal that one becomes a good American by realizing the potentialities inherent in one's ethnic identity, but not in any way that would accommodate what Kallen understood his argument to mean. For Kallen, as for Roth's antagonists, the expression of one's ethnic identity finally becomes an expression of one's authentic self; for Roth, the expression of his Jewish identity is merely one performance among many possible ones. The crucial difference is that where as Kallen assumed that the individual could choose to resurrect his ethnic heritage, Roth finds that his ethnic identity is enforced upon him by others. Roth clarifies his understanding of Jewish identity in this sentence: "To me being a Jew had to do with a real historical predicament into which you were born" (126). That is, Roth understands his (or anyone else's) Jewish identity to be contingent, historically situated, provisional; it is a practice. Obviously, had he been born in Nazi Germany and had the chance to write, his stories would have been very different, perhaps more along the lines of Bruno Schulz, a writer killed in the Holocaust and whose work Roth helped to bring into print. Instead, as the grandson of Jewish immigrants who had left Europe because "life was awful," he encountered a "willful amnesia" that he "came up against whenever I tried as a child to establish the details of our pre-American existence" (123). Aware of his ancestors only as avatars of his present, Roth, unlike Kallen and more like Antin, does not look back fondly on some idealized Jewish past or self. Whereas Roth's antagonists posit an essential Jewish identity to which one is either loyal or disloyal, Roth sees identity to be in perpetual transition and contingent upon, among other factors, his identity as an American.

In *Portnoy's Complaint* (1969) Roth assumes his antagonists' assumptions in order to turn them inside out. There he uses his protagonist to project to the most outrageous degree every conceivable stereotype of American Jews. The violent critical reaction to Portnoy exacerbated the uneasiness—or the betrayal—that Jewish readers had already felt with Roth's previous work.[6] Irving Howe's reaction was the most virulent. He suggested that "the cruelest thing anyone can do with *Portnoy's Complaint* is to read it twice" and that Roth wrote out of a "thin personal culture" ("Philip Roth" 82). Aside from trying to skewer Roth, Howe was pointing out that Roth's fiction had strayed from the rich heritage of Jewish immigrant culture that Howe admired and from which Howe thought *Goodbye Columbus* had emerged. To Howe, *Portnoy's Complaint* celebrated a rootless, transitory, assimilated American culture over a backwards, provincial immigrant tradition. Roth would later take his revenge on Howe in *The Anatomy Lesson* (1983) through the character of Milton Appel, but Mark Krupnick is correct to observe that Howe's critique is "challenging" in that "Roth's admirers must find it hard not to agree that his writing shows few traces of the immigrant sensibility that Howe defines as *the* Jewish tradition" (102). In fact, Roth has updated the immigrant sensibility that

Howe championed by showing its inevitable transformation through the ways that the immigrants' descendants interact with American culture.

In his own essays on this subject, Roth has emphasized how his interest in Jews necessarily differs from and augments the tradition that Howe protects. Comparing himself with Malamud, an obvious inheritor of Howe's tradition, Roth writes:

> Malamud, as a writer of fiction, has not shown specific interest in the anxieties and dilemmas and corruptions of the modern American Jew, the Jew we think of as characteristic to our times; rather, his people live in a timeless depression and a placeless Lower East Side; their society is not affluent, their predicament not cultural. (*Reading* 183)

Roth's characters struggle to define themselves against the immigrant experience of their forbears. As Aharon Appelfeld observes, Roth's sense of himself as a Jew is specific to his situation as an American. Ironically, Roth's Americanness also means that he has rejected many of the elements of identity that have historically made one Jewish. Of Roth's characters Appelfeld writes: "They are the descendants of the Eastern European Jewish tribe who in the beginning of the century were threatened by evil forces, both from within and without, that dispersed them to the four corners of the world. Some came to America" (14). With its eloquent terseness, the sentence "Some came to America" acknowledges that Roth writes about Jews from within an American sensibility. Appelfeld maintains that Roth is unquestionably "a Jewish writer," even if "Roth's Jews are Jews without Judaism." Thus "Roth's works have no Talmud, no Jewish philosophy, no mysticism, no religion" (14). Roth does not so much write about European Jews, Israeli Jews, or even immigrant Jews. He writes about the descendants of those immigrants who have found in America something they never imagined in Europe: the opportunity to define how they perceive or do not perceive themselves to be Jews.[7]

Though Roth's Jewish fictions are never about the shtetl or the shtetl's modern analogue, the ghetto, they consistently depict Jews who continue to experience their lives as if they are immigrants. That is, Roth's characters experience their selves as transitive entities. Of all Roth critics, Donald Kartiganer has made this point better than anyone: "At the centre of virtually all of Roth's fiction is an action of character transformation: a bizarre metamorphosis in which a new self emerges to stand in striking opposition to the old" ("Fictions" 82). Rothian characters such as Alexander Portnoy, David Kepesh, Peter Tarnopol, Nathan Zuckerman, and, in *Operation Shylock*, Philip Roth are joined in the shared fear that some-how their self-transformations will come to an end and that they will become, in Tarnopol's words, "this me who is me being me and none other" (*My Life* 330). If at times Roth's characters seem to value transfor-mation for its own sake, they also never quite escape the occasion of their transforming. Kartiganer perceptively adds that Roth's characters seek "not so much an escape from a personal and cultural past as an oddly courageous discovery and enactment of the conflicts embedded within it" (82). Roth accepts and even embraces his historical fate to be a Jew. None-theless, as a writer committed to a sense of his own chosen American identity, he also asserts his power to reinvent the meaning of that histor-ical fate in order to claim authorship of the process by which he came to be the Jew that he now portrays himself to be.

Roth's characters at times exert a weird mixture of a will to freedom combined with ethnic determinism. Rebelling against the ways in which they are constructed as Jews, his protagonists never refuse to be known as Jewish. If they are American in the way that they conceive the fluidity of their cultural identity, they are also American in their insistence that without a prior cultural identity with which to invent themselves they would have no identity at all. Thus the thrust of Roth's writing has been against both the longing for an essential Jewish self and the desire to conceive of one's self as free from social and cultural constraints. In negotiating this tension, Roth habitually defends his depictions of Jews by claiming the right to artistic integrity. At times Roth's artistic self-justifications sound almost Nabokovian, as if his only interest were the achievement of aesthetic bliss. But Roth's claim to pure aesthetic bliss is the set-up to the joke that he always plays on his characters: invent your self as you will, you cannot escape the history of your self-invention. In *The Counterlife* and *Operation Shylock* Roth's fiction voyages to Israel not to find a true point of ethnic cultural origin but to explore how American identity is invented from the desire to find an origin which no longer exists. Israel provides Roth's characters with the perfect setting for enact-ing a persistent American question: What would it mean to be authen-tically yourself?

## II

The structure of *The Counterlife* is ingeniously designed to refuse narra-tive or interpretative closure; it comprises a series of beginnings with no endings. In the section entitled "Judea," when Zuckerman's sister-in-law,

Carol, asks Nathan how he and his brother Henry know one another, he replies: "How they know each other, in my experience, is as a kind of deformation of themselves" (80). Nathan Zuckerman, famous novelist of Jewish life, and Henry Zuckerman, anonymous dentist and brother of famous novelist of Jewish life, continually trade identities and fictional contexts until the reader is unsure of what really happened to whom when. As the title suggests, Roth's premise in this book is that for every life there is a counterlife; more exactly, every self contains within it a counterself. In the novel's opening section, "Basel," brother Henry dies during the elective open heart surgery he has undergone in order to regain his sexual potency and continue his affair with his dental hygienist. In the next chapter, "Judea," the reader learns that Henry has survived his operation, abandoned his happy assimilated bourgeois existence in New Jersey, and moved without his family to Israel to find fuller meaning as a Jew. "Basel" begins almost as a version of the Tin Man's story in *The Wizard of Oz:* by getting a new heart, Henry can become a new person. Seen in the context of "Judea," however, Henry's American dream of self-transformation is actually the death of his Jewish heart. Henry dies of murder by assimilation. Hence when Henry surrenders not just the dental hygienist but the wife and two kids who are also part of his assimilation, he is able to go to Israel and make his heart beat again.

Based on the "Judea" section alone, *The Counterlife* seems to suggest that American identity and ethnic identity are mutually exclusive. But Roth complicates his drama of ethnic identity in the next section, "Gloucestershire," where he reveals that it was not Henry who died from heart surgery but Nathan. Upon discovering that the manuscripts of the chapters we have been reading are among his brother's papers, Henry, horrified by the use Nathan has made of his private confessions, burns them. That there is no way to square these contradictory versions corresponds with Roth-Zuckerman's ideal of the novelist as a performing self. Zuckerman observes in the text he writes for his own eulogy:

> What people envy in the novelist aren't the things that novelists think are so enviable but the performing selves that the author indulges, the slipping irresponsibly in and out of his skin, the reveling not in "I" but in escaping "I," even if it involves—*especially* if it involves— piling imaginary afflictions upon himself. (210)

Whereas for many writers these kinds of conflicting stories would highlight the indeterminacy of narrative, Roth suggests that everyone uses conflicting stories to define identity—his narrative merely reflects this tendency. Thus once Roth challenges the reader's knowledge of who has died, Henry or Nathan, *The Counterlife* is no longer simply about being Jewish or American in the context of ethnic identity. Rather, it is American in the sense that it explores how being Jewish allows one to invent one's identity. For Roth, racial heritage does not determine who you are; the stories you tell about your heritage do.

Thus Roth's fictions are not, as they are often said to be, narcissistic ventures into the fun house of fiction making.[8] Of *The Counterlife* Roth forcefully states: "There is nothing " 'modernist,' 'postmodernist,' or the least bit avant-garde about the technique. We are all writing fictitious versions of our lives all the time, contradictory but mutually entangling stories that, however subtly or grossly falsified, constitute our hold on reality and are the closest things we have to truth" (*Conversations* 11–12). Roth is not only interested in the performances his characters undertake but also *the roles they adopt*, the stories that are told about their self-transformation and self-incarnations. Nathan identifies what is at stake in his characterization of Henry's decision to abandon his comfortable life as an assimilated Jew in New Jersey: "Henry appears to have left his wife, his kids, and his mistress to come to Israel to become an *authentic* Jew" (*Counterlife* 74, emphasis mine). As crazy as this seems to Henry's wife, Carol, and perhaps many readers, Henry's decision can be seen as a logical extension of Horace Kallen's argument. If one's true identity is determined by one's ethnic or racial ancestry, then Henry's ethnic identity conflict can be resolved only by returning permanently to the land of his grandfather. The name of the opening chapter, "Basel," confirms this reading by referring to the city in which the Zionist movement began. Indeed, reading Roth's Israel novels, one often has the sense that modern-day Israel owes its invention not to Theodore Herzl, the international Zionist movement, centuries of European Jewish history, or even Moses, but to Americans, dreaming Americans. In *The Counterlife* Basel is the home of Henry's first shiksa girlfriend, Maria, for whom Henry contemplates leaving his comfortable life. Nathan speculates that Henry cannot join her "because Maria observed Christmas and we do not" (41). Henry's identity as a Jew, however attenuated, prevents him from setting out for a new life. From this perspective, the chapter title takes on added significance since Basel was where Herzl's Zionist movement originated. Instead of following Maria to Basel, Henry dies and wakes up in the modern Jewish Land of Zion, Israel.

Henry describes to Nathan the transformation into his true self as a conversion experience. Sitting "on the stone still of this brokendown cheder," Henry is struck by the sound of children chanting their lessons.

> And when I heard them, there was a surge inside me, a realization—at the root of my life, at the very *root* of it, I *was them*. I always *had* been them. Children chanting away in Hebrew, I couldn't understand a word of it, couldn't recognize a single sound, and yet I was listening as though something I didn't even know I'd been searching for was suddenly reaching out to me. . . . And that's when I began to realize that of all that I am, I am nothing. I have never been *anything*, the way I am this Jew. . . . Can you understand? I may not be expressing this right, but I actually don't care how it sounds to you or anyone. I am not *just* a Jew, I'm not *also* a Jew—*I'm a Jew as deep as those Jews*. (60–61)

Though I have condensed what is actually a long, haltingly eloquent speech, the quoted section still reveals the quality of Henry's yearning for cultural authenticity. On one level, Henry's desire to be "a Jew as deep as those Jews" suggests a feeling of cultural inadequacy. His Jewishness is deracinated and hence inauthentic. Henry's speech also betrays a deep dissatisfaction with a life that most Americans are encouraged to see as the embodiment of the American dream; his desire for cultural authenticity is also a condemnation of American materialism and acquisitiveness. His condemnation of American life is reflected in the self-revulsion he feels as a consequence of risking his life in order to continue his affair with his office assistant. Speaking of those "hellenized—hedonized—egomaniaized" American Jews—"galut Jews, bereft of any sort of context in which to actually be Jewish," Henry is describing himself (111). He sees his betrayal of family and self as emblematic of the liberal and pluralistic American social context in which he was raised. Earlier we saw that Roth defined being Jewish as being part of a historical situation, one that for him could not be separated from a history of being American. For Henry, however, American identity and Jewish identity are incompatible. This means that he cannot be a Jew in Newark, New Jersey—surrounded by Jews though he was—because, according to Henry, these people have surrendered their claim to being Jewish.

Though Henry suggests that to become fully and truly Jewish he must live among other authentic Jews, the truth is that even this is not enough. Rather, Henry can reclaim his Jewish self only through the recovery of the

Hebrew language. Ironically, this desire probably has its roots in his American childhood when he attended Hebrew school so he could become familiar with Hebrew as a vestigial reminder of his cultural heritage. That his childhood introduction to Hebrew was a reflection of an *American* longing to hold on to a vanishing past is an irony lost on Henry. In the passage quoted above, Henry cannot understand the words' meaning, but this does not matter because what he hears in them is beyond language and even, perhaps, beyond irony: he thinks their sound names his essential self; by the magic of the Hebrew language, he would speak his Hebrew identity, "Hanoch," and abolish the American "Henry" from existence. For Nathan, however, the recovery of this prior identity marks not a return of the self but the extinction of selfhood entirely. The longing for an essential identity masks a desire for self-obliteration. Henry himself makes this argument to Nathan: "You still don't get it. The hell with *me*, forget *me*. Me is somebody *I* have forgotten. *Me* no longer exists out here. There isn't time for *me*, there isn't need for *me*—here Judea counts, not *me*" (105). Henry says "the hell with me" but what his statement really means is the hell that is me. Where Nathan revels in "escaping 'I'" as an act to be repeated, Henry wants to lose his "I" once and for all.[9]

Henry's action puts Nathan on the defensive because it threatens his own identity on every conceivable level: as a Jew, as an American, and as a writer. His confrontation with Henry is one of a series in which the authenticity of Nathan's position is put under scrutiny by Jews who have rejected Zuckerman's American pluralism. The most spectacular confrontation occurs when Nathan visits the school/camp that Henry has joined. The scene is clearly a rewriting of the "trial" that Philip Roth faced at Yeshiva University in 1962, only this time his alter ego is facing an audience of American Jews who have chosen to remain in Israel. Zuckerman is presented as an expert on American Jews, but these emigrant American Jews want only to attack his claim to be a Jew at all. First, he is accosted for not knowing his own "native" tongue: "Do you speak Hebrew?" an American-accented boy asks. Next, he is accosted for not wanting to leave America: "Were you a Zionist when you were growing up?" Whereas Roth at Yeshiva tried to win over his audience through polite reasoning, Zuckerman in Israel responds in kind with an ad hominem counterattack. Zuckerman's answer turns the tables on his accusers: "I never had enough Hebrew, Yiddish, or anti-Semitism to make me a Zionist when I was young" (101). By hinting that these American Jews are transforming their individual psychoses into a collective cultural self-aggrandizement, Nathan insinuates that perhaps they are the self-hating Jews, not him. Along with suggesting that Roth never got over the Yeshiva experience, Zuckerman's response suggests that the older Roth has determined that there is no answer to these questions that can please both sides.

The implication is lost on Zuckerman's immediate audience, though, precisely because they have eliminated from their thinking the idea that the self desires its own transformation. After Zuckerman suggests that the desire to eliminate the self is itself fanatical, a student stands up and shouts: "Excuse *me!* What is *fanatical?* To put egotism before Zionism is what is fanatical! To put personal gain and personal pleasure before the survival of the Jewish people! *Who* is fanatical? The Diaspora Jew" (102). Ever the comic, Roth reduces these modern-day Zionists' position to a one-liner way beyond what Henny Youngman might come up with. If Roth was asked during his branding at Yeshiva if he would write the same stories were he living in Nazi Germany, Zuckerman is accused of helping to complete Hitler's Final Solution. The teacher, Ronit, another American expatriate, states: "What Hitler could not achieve with Auschwitz, American Jews are doing to themselves in their bedroom" (103).

Roth structures this as a bitter joke, but as he well knows, it is appropriate only when spoken by an American Jew to other American Jews, since, in terms of Jewish history and specifically the Holocaust, the repatriation of Israel has a convincing logic. From an American perspective, Ronit's comparison breaks down as soon as one realizes that the societies in which European Jews of the Holocaust lived did not allow for intermarriage on the massive scale allowed in America. Jews who choose to marry non-Jews, as Zuckerman does—four times—can do so only because, as Zuckerman elsewhere observes, they live in a society "that had placed pluralism smack at the publicly advertised dream of itself" (54). Ronit's fear of intermarriage does not so much salvage a true and proper history, as she implicitly suggests, as deny history's unexpected possibilities and entanglements. With an eye toward his American audience, Roth suggests that arguments based on appeals to cultural authenticity fail to come to terms with the possibilities that a pluralist society allows. Despite insisting that the preservation of a pure Jewish identity is a logical response to nightmares of Jewish history, Ronit's conception of cultural identity is essentially static. Though a pluralist society does not require its citizens to intermarry, the fact that they can confirms the society's ethic of toleration. At the root of Ronit's argument is an inherent racism that underlies her claims to cultural "authenticity." The ultimate logic of her position, then, is that to fulfill herself she must escape American society. The American irony is that while a pluralist society can tolerate her position, she cannot tolerate American society's toleration of her.

A measure of Roth's complexity in portraying this issue is that instead of attributing to Nathan an easy intellectual and moral superiority, Roth shows him to be vulnerable to the logic of identity that Ronit and her students employ. In Israel Zuckerman can view these sorts of debates as all part of the living Jewish theater that follows him wherever he goes, but when his English wife, Maria, raises these issues he becomes as defensive as any of his Israeli interlocutors. After chastising Nathan for sometimes "finding things horribly anti-Semitic, or even mildly so even when they aren't," Maria admits that she gets tired of attracting the glances of Jewish men, what she calls being subject to "shiksa-fancying." She suggests that "there are enough politics in sex without racial politics coming into it" (70–71). Nathan fires back that "we are not a race," but she insists that it is a racial matter and besides Caucasian is classified as a different race from Semitic (71). Nathan informs her that according to the U.S. Census he is Caucasian. Even though their exchange reveals the absolute futility of arguing over what constitutes a racial identity, the fact is that once the category is admitted as worth contesting, arguments (and even wars) are inevitable. This conversation takes place in Manhattan where Nathan feels relatively secure; when it is replayed in England—where Nathan himself feels like an alien—after his trip to Judea, Nathan reverses positions to argue for an enlightened racist antiracism.

This reversal occurs during the scene in the restaurant in which Nathan is convinced that a woman is talking about him and his Jewishness when she demands a window be opened "before we are overcome" by an un-named smell. This demand, which may or may not have been directed at Nathan, prompts him first to ask the woman directly if she "finds Jews repellant" and second to threaten having her thrown out of the restaurant (292). When Maria informs Nathan that he "went quite crazy," he becomes so angry that Maria asks if his rage is the result of his trip to Judea (293, 297). Henry's counterlife resurfaces to haunt Nathan: the very desire that Nathan discovered and doubted in Henry in "Judea" now becomes, by Maria's view, Nathan's own desire in the chapter called "Christendom." As the conversation escalates, Nathan finds himself, despite Maria's tolerant point of view, defending himself not as a writer or as an American but *as a Jew*. The scene reads straight out of the Horace Kallen textbook on the meaning of minority identity in a pluralistic society. Maria, as if taking the side of Kallen critics David Hollinger or John Higham on this question, objects "to people clinging to an identity just for the sake of it," because they "simply make life more difficult in society where we're just trying to live amicably, like London." Nathan, as if taking the side of Kallen responding to E. A. Ross, says that she may "talk about *Jewish* tribalism," but really "this insistence on homogeneity is a very subtle form of *English* tribalism" (301). Arguing as a Jew, Zuckerman identifies the hypocrisy that often accompanies gestures toward unity that are really appeals for someone else to forego his racial thinking. By the time the conversation ends with Maria accusing Zuckerman of having reversed fields from his earlier claim in New York that Jews are not a race, the reader is not sure who is right. Is Maria right to suggest that Zuckerman's sensitivity to others' prejudice causes him to insist on an essential Jewishness that withstands all gestures of rationality, toleration, and intellectual sympathy from an outsider? Or is Zuckerman right to suggest that Maria is merely displacing her tribalism onto him and that his putative essentialism is really hers?

Perhaps the most stunning remark Nathan makes in the whole novel regarding his cultural identity is the one he makes to Maria's openly anti-Semitic sister: "I don't have to act like a Jew—I am one" (279). This assertion, like the conversations he has with Maria, seems to undercut his novelist's ethic of the performing self and certainly contradicts the position he takes with Henry in "Judea." But as I have suggested, the structure of the book discourages us form viewing any intellectual position, and especially one of Nathan's, as final. Certainly in "Judea" Nathan portrays himself as deeply disturbed by his brother's choice. He writes draft after draft (including, à la Bellow's Herzog, imaginary letters) trying to put Henry's startling action in some perspective. He vacillates between dismissing it as mere family drama, a belated revolt against an oppressive father, and rationalizing it (though in a somewhat condescending way) as poor straightlaced Henry's attempt at injecting his life with the same sense of theater by which Nathan presumes that he lives his. As compelling as each of these explanations is, though, Nathan is likely using his invented quarrel with Henry to argue himself out of his own Jewish essentialism. By this reading, his remark to Maria's sister Sarah suggests how strongly he identifies with Henry's return to Jewishness and how inadequate his own role-playing sometimes seems to him against the primal desire to return to the womb of authentic self.

In order for Roth's antiessentialism to be compelling—to have interesting fictive consequences—he must portray how seductive the longing for an essential Jewish identity can be. To Roth's American Jews, the re-creation of Israel in the twentieth century is a vestige of this longing. Its historic monuments—the Wailing Wall and the Ark of the Torah—come to represent tangible evidence of a permanent Jewish identity. In this context, the scene in "Christendom" where Zuckerman asserts his in-controvertible Jewish identity should be read against his visit to the Wail-ing Wall where he encounters a personification of a pull toward an essen-tial Jewish identity in the figure of a young Chasid who approaches him. Yet another role available in this "enormous outdoor theater," the Chasid offers the creepiest overture that Zuckerman receives while in Israel, one that anticipates the scene in *Operation Shylock* where the character Philip Roth contemplates, however briefly, sleeping with his double. The en-counter is framed as a seduction narrative: "The elongated fingers with which he was tapping my shoulder suggested something erotically creepy at one extreme and excruciatingly delicate at the other, the hand of the helpless maiden *and* of the lurid ghoul" (88). Roth employs eroticized language to emphasize the sexual desire latent in the longing for union with the essential self. If achieved, this merger would, for the American Jew, eradicate his own sense of being "other." This is what is at stake for Henry, whose surgery began in "Basel" with his desire to regain his sexual potency. The recovery of his Jewish identity in "Judea" does not mean that Henry has sublimated his sexual desire but instead has consummated it through Israel. Whether intentional or not, Nathan's encounter evokes a scene from Hawthorne's *The Marble Faun* where Miriam encounters the "dead Capuchin" whom she associates "with the evil spirit which blasted her sweet youth and compelled her . . . to stain her womanhood with crime" (*Novels* 1011). The necrophilia that Hawthorne finds implicit within the rites of ancient Catholicism Zuckerman experiences also in this ghostly return to the rites of ancient Judaism.

If Zuckerman is subjected to a creepy seduction ritual by the vestige of a dead past, it is also true that he visits the Wailing Wall as a kind of aesthetic voyeur. Roth's basically pragmatist orientation toward the issues that his novel raises is best displayed at the wall, where Nathan is "curious to see if anything like what happened to my brother in Mea She'arim would surprise and overtake me while standing at this, the most hallowed of all Jewish places." Acting on the advice of the clerk at his hotel, who said that "every Jew should go at night" because "you'll remember it for the rest of your life," Zuckerman finds that "it *was* more impressive" than he had expected (84). Alone before the wall, he thinks of "the massive weight of the ancient stones" as the "illumination" of history's endurance. Though he stops short of saying that this wall and he are part of the same bedrock self, he nonetheless treats it with a kind of reverence.

His attitude changes, however, when his experience merges with others' experiences before the wall. Then these massive ancient stones provide the scenery to "an enormous outdoor theater, the stage for some lavish, epic, operatic production" (84). Although his descriptions of women "who'd come to pray piously" and even of the Orthodox seeking charity from him have an almost lyrical quality, Nathan's comic irony breaks out at the sight of "seventeen of the world's twelve million Jews communing with the King of the universe" (86). Instead of thinking of them as participating in a ritual that binds the past to the present, Zuckerman sees them as "communing solely with the stones."

> I thought (as I am predisposed to think), "If there is a God who plays a role in our world, I will eat every hat in this town"—nonetheless I couldn't help but to be gripped by the sight of this rock-worship, exemplifying as it did to me the most awesomely retarded aspect of the human mind. Rock is just right, I thought: what on earth could be less responsive? (86)

This scene underscores Appelfeld's remark that Roth's characters are Jews without Judaism. If being Jewish has an essential component, it presumably derives from neither a shared language nor a history of oppression but from the practice of the ancient religious rites. (On this score, Henry's conversion is less to a religious ideal than a cultural one.) If elsewhere Zuckerman mocks the literal-mindedness of Jewish fundamentalism (as with Lippman at Henry's school), here he literalizes a religious rite. He drains the wall of the sacredness that is imputed to it and turns it into a purely physical object, mere rock, no longer even the harbinger of history. It may seem absurd that Zuckerman should transform the Wailing Wall into mere rock and then lament its lack of responsiveness, but he does so because he requires theater and because the worship that surrounds this rock denies everything he values. To these worshiping people, there is no acting, there is no drama, there is even no self: there is only their sacred shared bond with the King of the Universe.

Confronting this powerful vestige of an ancient, enduring Jewish heritage, Zuckerman decides that he "would have felt less detached from seventeen Jews who imagined themselves telexing the Creator directly;

had I known for sure it was rock and rock alone that I was kissing I might have joined in" (86). Though he very tentatively and only for the sake of argument holds open the possibility that there may be more to this rock worship than mere rock, he can only strike up a relationship with the scene as another participant in a form of bizarre theater. He will not be converted. He is willing to recognize the seductive appeal that the old rituals have for these modern-day Jews, but he will not grant that they confer an authentic identity—an Absolute Truth—upon their practitioners. He sees in their gestures what Henry cannot see in his own: the *performance* of a rite ostensibly rooted in ancient tradition. The ritual does not establish a true continuity with the past, whatever that would mean. Instead, it can only be understood as *a reinvention of the past.* Placed in the context of the present, their affirmation of themselves as Jews before God is merely a choice they are making, which is as valid in some essential sense as Zuckerman's choice to practice rock worship. By this view, Zuckerman, with his shiksa wives and his alienated Jewish family and audience, is "as Jewish" as these worshipers because he too has chosen to accept his identity as a Jew, however provisional.

Zuckerman finally redeems himself from essentialist thinking through a paradoxical redefinition of what the act of circumcision means. Instead of insisting that circumcision marks an essential Jewish self, he argues that circumcision is the symbolic mark by which one's identity is stamped as contingent, provisional, historical. He makes this argument to Maria when he discovers that she is pregnant and they must decide if the child should raised Catholic or Jewish or some combination thereof. Zuckerman argues that circumcision marks not one's essential self but one's self as contingent in a way that is perhaps essential.

> Circumcision makes it as clear as can be that you are here and not there, that you are out and not in—also that you are mine and not theirs. There is no way around it: you enter history through my history and me. Circumcision is everything that the pastoral is not and, to my mind, reinforces what the world is about, which is not strifeless unity. (323)

You can choose, perhaps, to become theirs and not yours, but doing so is a reaction against the mark that defined you in the first place. You cannot find some prior origin separate from the historical-social-psychological context in which you find yourself. Hence Roth, through Zuckerman, can endlessly reinvent his Jewish identity without ever abandoning it. As he said in *The Facts*, he was branded a Jew. Here he transforms the mark of essential Jewish identity into a symbol for the irredeemable contingency of all identity.

Nathan's circumcision argument in "Christendom" clarifies his earlier exchange with Henry in "Judea." Henry asserts that the appeal of Judea is that "this is where the Jews *began*, not in Tel Aviv but here." "*This* is Judaism, *this* is Zionism, right here where we are eating our lunch!" (109). Nathan suggests, in turn, that Henry's obsession with his Jewish origin is more likely a reflection of his own circumcised origin in Newark, New Jersey. What Henry sees as a tribal journey spanning the centuries Nathan sees as a manifestation of the familiar (if hard to understand) circumstance of being born American to the children of recent immigrants. Nathan suggests that in finding Lippmann Henry has merely traded one demanding Jewish father for another. Henry responds by noting that "there's a world outside the Oedipal Swamp." Henry does correctly identify the psychological motivation for many of his brother's actions, but Nathan's point is more than psychological. He writes to Henry in the "Aloft" section:

> It may be that flourishing mundanely in the civility and security of South Orange [New Jersey], more or less forgetful from one day to the next of your Jewish origins but remaining identifiably (and voluntarily) a Jew, you were making Jewish history no less astonishing that theirs [the American Zionists at Agor], though without quite knowing it every moment, and without having to say it. (146)

Over fifty years earlier Horace Kallen and Randolph Bourne had argued that realizing one's "minority" identity could be a way of fulfilling one's American identity. Kallen saw the expression of a Jewish (or minority) self as an end in itself, while Bourne felt that the inevitable consequence would be an invigorated American identity, a genuine realization of the promises inherent in our cultural diversity. Zuckerman sounds closer to Bourne here as he points out that to "say Jew and goy about America is to miss the point, because America is simply not that, except in Agor's mythology." In America, identities are traded so easily and often—"a country full of Chicanos who want to look like Texans, and Texans who want to look like New Yorkers, and any number of Middle Western Wasps who, believe it or not, want to talk and act and think like Jews"—that to see one's desire for an authentic identity as anything other than a response to the fluidity of American identity is naive (146). The branding that Roth came to embrace is transformed into Zuckerman's act of symbolic self-circumcision. Through Zuckerman, Roth has named the condition which enables him to pass on his Jewish heritage for his heirs to accept or reject as they will: his American will to renew the past by transforming it into something else.

### III

In *Operation Shylock* Philip Roth continues the journey that Zuckerman undertakes in *The Counterlife* by subjecting his own persona to the same identity conflicts that menaced his alter ego. The defensiveness that Zuckerman experienced when Maria confronted him about his own militant Jewishness Roth experiences in this novel as a threat to his identity as an author and as a Jew. Roth's previous three books—the slight bedroom novel *Deception* (1990) and the two memoirs, *The Facts* and *Patrimony* (1991)—leading up to *Shylock* had each featured "Philip Roth" as their focal point. Combine this with the fact that Roth had purposely constructed Zuckerman's career to parallel his own and it should be no surprise that Roth would place himself at the center of his magnum opus. Whereas the previous works were sly and even defensive in their use of the autobiographical device, *Operation Shylock* is both aggressive and outrageous in its attempt to present itself as the "true" story of Philip Roth's career and art. Thus the book begins with Roth's account of how the appearance of his double—whom, after Roth's example, I will call Pipik—threatened Roth to the core of his being. In *The Counterlife* Zuckerman argued that if any "irreducible self" exists it must be "the root of all impersonation"; Pipik in *Operation Shylock* threatens to abscond with Roth's self by usurping his capacity for impersonation. As "Philip Roth," Pipik becomes Roth's most outrageous impersonation yet.

*Operation Shylock* implicitly contains within it both everything that Roth ever wrote and every critical attack his work has engendered. By using his own name as that of his protagonist, Roth pursues to the end of logic and identity the consequences of having written novel after novel that featured a character, Nathan Zuckerman, whose experiences mirrored his own.[10] Roth underscores this point in "A Bit of Jewish Mischief," a brief essay he published in the *New York Times Book Review*. Presenting the events of the book as if they did indeed happen, Roth suggests that the appearance of his double caused him to confront "an impertinence as galling, enraging and, yes, personally menacing as my own impertinence could ever have seemed to [my own readers]" (20).[11]

Several years before *Operation Shylock* Roth had spoken of his admiration for writers such as Konwicki and Gombrowicz, who used their own names as those of their protagonists (*Reading* 146). Though Roth offers a plausible reason for the appearance of his double by describing the nervous breakdown (to which he refers in *The Facts*) that ensued from his dependence on the subsequently banned sleeping pill, Halcion, this explanation is irrelevant because Roth is not interested in "the truth," whatever that is.[12] Rather, he wants to exploit the friction that occurs when the presumed authenticity of autobiography, or self, rubs up against the unreality of fiction, or self-making. Robert Alter suggests that Roth "construes the double not as the embodiment of a hidden self, but rather as that other kind of doubling, much less threatening, which is the re-invention of the self for the purpose of a fiction" (32). Actually, Roth does portray Pipik as a threat to his identity because, for Roth, the act of making fiction always threatens and transforms identity. Insisting that this is an authentic narrative of a true story is Roth's way of raising the critical and authorial stakes as well as making the cultural identity issues seem more real by imagining "true," if still fictional, consequences. Harold Bloom's discussion of this point is excellent: "Roth has succeeded in inventing a new kind of disciplined bewilderment for the reader, since it becomes difficult to hold in one's head at every moment all of the permutations of the Rothian persona" ("Operation" 45). By pretending to write a book that is "really" about himself, Roth actually demonstrates how fictive reality is.

Without forgetting that the book takes shape as Roth's response to his own American Jewish predicament, we should note that it incorporates virtually all of twentieth-century Jewish history from the European Diaspora into America to the Holocaust to the creation and consolidation of the state of Israel. The novel's expansive historical and cultural context is an extension of a remark that Roth once made concerning the composition of *The Ghost Writer*: "The difficulties of telling a Jewish story was to become *The Ghost Writer*'s theme" (*Reading* 166). The difficulty of telling a Jewish story is further complicated by the Jewish imperative not to tell stories against the Jews—a point that Roth brings out in the hilariously comical interpretation he gives to the Talmudic concept of *loshon hora*, or evil speech, through Smilesberger's reading of Rabbi Chofetz Chaim.[13] *Operation Shylock* reveals how this conflict between telling Jewish stories and telling stories on Jews defines Roth's career. In this novel Roth at last acknowledges the force of those critics who have suggested that his work is anti-Semitic. First through the character of David Supposnik, and then later through the spy mission that Roth undertakes for the Mossad, Roth questions the ability of any Jewish writer—himself included—to write free of the fear of reinscribing potentially anti-Semitic stories. As we shall see, Supposnik's reading of *The Merchant of Venice* exists in obverse relation to those Jewish critics who have attacked Roth's work. Supposnik claims that the image of the Jew in Western literature begins and ends "with the savage, repellent, and villainous" Shylock who "entered as our doppelganger into the consciousness of the enlightened West" (*Shylock* 274). Thus not only does the character Philip Roth have to confront both his double, Pipik, and the implications of being an American in the twentieth century, but the author Philip Roth must confront the ingrained anti-Semitism of the Euro-American literary tradition. In offering a justification of his work up to this point, Roth also hopes that his readers will recognize how he has in this work found the form that allows him to absorb his many literary influences and complete the story he has been trying to tell for his entire career. "Operation Shylock" therefore designates both the spy mission that the character Philip Roth undertakes for the Mossad as well as the author's own literary spy mission. With *Operation Shylock* Roth surmounts "the difficulties of telling a Jewish story" by seizing control of his own oeuvre, as if this novel, in overturning the critical misreadings he has himself suffered and which have influenced his work, can also overturn Shakespeare's invention of Shylock in *The Merchant of Venice*.

Pipik's appearance in Israel articulating a strange theory called Diasporism, which he passes off as the invention of the "real" Philip Roth, initiates Roth into the critical-fictional drama that he has been performing since the beginning of his career. Once Diasporism becomes public property by being reported in newspapers and broadcast over the radio, the real Philip Roth decides "the disease espoused" is "mine now and would likely endure as mine in the recollection of those who'd read the retraction tomorrow" (*Operation* 35). The issue in this novel is possession. Roth himself has noted that "what I want is to possess my readers while they are reading my book" (*Reading* 170). In *Operation Shylock* his ideal writer-reader situation is reversed: Roth imagines what would happen were he to be possessed by a reader who was also himself. In this case, the creation creates, or recreates, his creator. A classic instance of what Girard calls the "triangulation of desire," Roth's desire to possess himself in this novel expresses itself through his desire to possess the one who has already possessed him.

This scenario of mimetic desire is complicated by the fact that the other

Philip Roth, Pipik, in effect has not only stolen the real Philip Roth's work, but also his sense of his own Jewish identity. Pipik is an inspired misreader of Roth's work, but more formidable than even Milton Appel was to Nathan Zuckerman in *The Anatomy Lesson* because Roth suspects that Pipik's ludicrous idea may really represent Roth in some undeniable way. In offering comically simplified versions of ideas implicit in Roth's fictions, Pipik causes Roth to double back on his own understanding of himself as a Jew. This becomes a pivotal moment in the context of Roth's career since he has always acted as if the ability to construct his identity as a Jew is something that he takes for granted. Pipik says:

> Forget about just you and me—there would have been another fifty little Jewish boys of our age growing up to look like us if it hadn't been for certain tragic events that occurred in Europe between 1939 and 1945. And is it impossible that half a dozen of them might have been Roths? Is our family name that rare? Is it impossible that a couple of those little Roths might not have been called after a grand-father Fayvel, like you, Philip, and like me? You, from your career perspective, may think it's horrible that there are two of us and that you are not unique. From my Jewish perspective, I have to say that I think it is horrible that only two are left. (79–80)

The "other" Philip Roth, though, is not one of those lost potential Roths. He is not a Holocaust survivor but an American who, in a nice comic twist, was a private investigator specializing in missing persons cases before he undertook to be Roth's double. As becomes clear, the other Philip Roth is less interested in confronting the losses of the Holocaust than in denying its significance. In this scene, the one obsessed with the meaning of these lost identities is the author Philip Roth, who may or may not share his characters' points of view. As Debra Shostak points out, Roth's rejection of essentialism does not mean a rejection of Jewish identity. Yet this rejection, certainly one the "real" Philip Roth endorses, also serves to undermine the real Roth's sense of himself. The other Roth's existence suggests that in being concerned with the authenticity of his identity, the real Roth depends on the same sort of essentialized self that underpins the cultural theories of his fiercest Jewish critics. To combat the views put forward by his double (which are a distorted reflection of his own), the real Roth is very nearly forced into the position of defending Israel because it pre-serves an essential Jewish self that he has abandoned in America.[14]

As defined by the imposter Roth, Diasporism is the recognition that as a response to European Jewish history that culminated in the Holocaust, Israel has been a terrible mistake. Diasporism recognizes that the true meaning of Jewish identity resides in its European history: Europe is where Jewish culture, as Americans know it, was created. Roth, impersonating Pipik, says Diasporism envisions "the Jew for whom *authenticity* as a Jew means living in the Diaspora" (170)—a position, ironically, that Roth himself has frequently presented as his own. In their obsession to make sure that a second Holocaust does not occur, the Jews have assumed the worst tendencies of their historical oppressors. Roth allows Pipik to imply a thought that is almost unthinkable (to Jews): what the Germans did to Jews, the Jews are now prepared to do to Arabs. The ironical and, to Pipik, morally just consequence to this aggressive military stance would be Israel's self-annihilation: "The destruction of Israel in a nuclear exchange is a possibility much less farfetched today than was the Holocaust fifty years ago" (43). Thus Pipik advocates returning the Ashkenazi Jews to Europe (the Sephardic Jews may remain in the Middle East that is their home) in order to save them from the destruction that will be brought down on them as a result of their own fanatical militarism. Not only will returning to Europe save the Jews from themselves, but the Europeans will welcome them back as their long-lost family members. "You know what will happen when the first trainload of Jews returns? There will be crowds to welcome them. People will be jubilant. People will be in tears. They will be shouting, 'Our Jews are back! Our Jews are back!' " (45).

The author Philip Roth had adumbrated these ideas in *The Counterlife* through the character of Jimmy, author of "The Five Books of Jimmy." Jimmy also is a double figure who knows Zuckerman's work inside out— indeed, he sees himself as a possibility of Zuckerman's fiction. "It's really you," he shouts when he meets Zuckerman at the Wailing Wall. "I've read all your books! You wrote about my family!" (*Counterlife* 91). Jimmy is a student at "the Diaspora Yeshiva." His basic idea, outlined in a treatise called "Forget Remembering," which he pointedly says he gleaned from reading Zuckerman's novels (167), is that Yad Vashem, Jerusalem's museum devoted to the memory of the Holocaust, should be closed down permanently. For the American Jews touring the museum, Yad Vashem preserves Jewish identity in a mythology of the victim that prevents Jews from facing the future. Moreover, Jimmy tells Zuckerman, the fetishizing of the Holocaust so affronts the Gentiles that they will obliterate Israel to rid themselves of the monstrous "*Jewish conscience*" (166). Insofar as Israel's identity depends on the fact of the Holocaust, the logic of Jimmy's argument, when extended, demands the dismantling of Israel—exactly the case that Pipik makes in *Operation Shylock.*

Unlike Pipik, Jimmy is presented as one capable of doing real harm to others. He is eventually captured by the Israeli secret police for threatening to blow up the plane he and Zuckerman are traveling on. Pipik, however, cannot be so easily disposed of because his pronouncements achieve a kind of authority—to Roth—by being recirculated through the media. Pipik threatens not just Israel but Roth's identity as an author. The affronted Roth chooses not to take any kind of concrete action, legal or otherwise, that might stop this imposter from misrepresenting him because, finally, he wants to see if the imposter might not truly be Roth after all. Thus Roth goes from trying to prove to Pipik how absurd his ideas are to trying them on for size: he becomes an interpretation of someone else's interpretation of him. As such, Roth is even more convincing as his double than his double is in becoming, in Mrs. Ziad's derisive words, "the anti-Moses leading them [the Jews] out of Israel" (*Operation* 160). Roth draws the conclusions to Pipik's premises with more flair and urgency than even Pipik could bring. In one scene, Roth, as Pipik, explains to the delight of his Arab friend, George Ziad, how he "got the idea" for Diasporism while listening to Irving Berlin's "White Christmas" on the radio.

> God gave Moses the Ten Commandments and then He gave to Irving Berlin "Easter Parade" and "White Christmas." The two holidays that celebrate the divinity of Christ—the divinity that's the very heart of the Jewish rejection of Christianity—and what does Irving Berlin brilliantly do? He de-Christs them both! Easter he turns into a fashion show and Christmas into a holiday about snow. Gone is the gore and murder of Christ—down with the crucifix and up with the bonnet! *He turns their religion into schlock.* (157)

Roth-as-Pipik draws the conclusion that "if schlockified Christianity is Christianity cleansed of Jewish hatred, then three cheers for schlock" (157). The irony is that here Roth-as-Pipik is presenting an antiessentialist argument as if it were obviously absurd. Zuckerman's sarcastic rock worship is not too far removed from this ode to the genius of substituting snow and Bing Crosby for Christ. To many Jews, it is the essentialism of Christ-worship that has justified pogroms, Holocausts, and, finally, the security that a fully militarized Israel allows. Of course Irving Berlin is an *Americanized* Russian Jew. Hence the more subversive point is that through Irving Berlin the Christian holiday of Christmas has been transformed into a Jewish fantasy. In the Roth-Pipik version of "White Christ-mas," a complicated reciprocal cultural process is being acted out. Instead of only Irving Berlin being assimilated to American culture, Roth suggests that Berlin's Jewish dream of an American Christmas has become one that American Christians choose to dream too.

In terms of the character Philip Roth, the Irving Berlin fantasy doubles back on itself as well. Philip Roth the American might see "White Christ-mas" as a plausible example of the kind of cultural cross-dressing that American culture encourages. But Philip Roth the Jew is aware that Israel is very much the response to the historical condition of being a Jew, especially the stubborn fact that Jews have been persecuted for being Jews. Certainly, he does not object to Israel as a state or even, in a limited way, as an ideal. This, I think, is why Aharon Appelfeld is in the novel and pre-sented straightforwardly as Roth's counterself.

> Aharon and I each embody the reverse of each other's experience; because each recognizes in the other the Jewish man he is not; be-cause of the all but incompatible orientations that shape our very different lives and very different books and that result from antitheti-cal twentieth century Jewish biographies; because we are the heir jointly of a drastically *bifurcated* legacy—because of the sum of all these Jewish *antinomies*, yes, we have much to talk about and are intimate friends. (201, emphasis mine)

In part, Roth's affinity for Appelfeld, which is revealed in the interviews that he published in the *New York Times* and which are included in the novel's text, is for the Jewish self—the Jewish historical possibility—that did not include him. Appelfeld is Jewish in a way that Henry Zuckerman could not be precisely because Appelfeld's Jewishness is not realized as a consequence of an American longing. Both Appelfeld's and Zuckerman's ancestors come from Europe; nonetheless, the two men are living out different versions of Jewish history and hence have different Jewish identi-ties. Thus Roth underscores that he and Appelfeld are *Jewish* opposites because they are living out opposed Jewish—as opposed to American—stories. Nor is this the same thing as saying that they are doubles. As the words "reverse," "not," "antithetical," "bifurcated," and "antinomies" suggest, Roth sees the two of them as complementary halves of a whole Jewish self. Appelfeld is a Holocaust survivor, an Israeli citizen, whose fiction is rooted in the experience of the Holocaust. Roth is a Jew of the American Diaspora, free to reinvent his relationship to questions of Jewish identity as he chooses. (It is no small coincidence that in Roth's fiction the only characters capable of cracking jokes about the Holocaust are American Jews.) European Jewry, broken in half first by mass immigration to America and then the Holocaust, is recombined into one body whenever Roth and Appelfeld meet—be it in Jerusalem or New York.

Roth trusts Appelfeld, whom he sees as comfortably "other." Roth confides in him about Pipik because Appelfeld does not threaten his identity. Pipik, however, forces Roth not only to confront himself as a Jew but to see his Jewishness from the point of view of one outside a determining American cultural context. Pipik's usurpation of Roth's identity, or Roth's denial of Pipik's identity, becomes dangerous for Roth because it seems to demand that either he defend his identity as a Jew by proclaiming himself to be aligned with an essential Jewish identity or surrender to Pipik and renounce his Jewish identity altogether. These positions mark the poles of fictional possibilities that Roth first explored in "Eli the Fanatic." By imagining himself as a continuation of Henry Zuckerman's story in *The Counterlife*, Roth places his own identity and his oeuvre at risk.

Pipik, however, represents a form of Jewish identity that is almost exactly identical with Roth's, that of Diasporan assimilation. Moreover, because he claims to have conceived his doctrine of Diasporism due to his reading of Roth, the threat he represents to Roth's identity is compounded. Throughout his entire career, Roth has continually reinvented himself and his fiction through the reconstruction of Jewish identity. Pipik, emerging as if he were a real-life character out of Roth's oeuvre, represents the most extreme form imaginable of this tendency. He is Roth's most monstrous misreader and one very different from previous misreaders. The Jewish readers who have most objected to Roth have typically been Orthodox and nationalistic in their condemnation of what they have seen as Roth's Jewish self-hatred. Pipik, by contrast, is what might be termed an extreme antiessentialist. Pipik's appearance therefore places Roth in a doubly ironic situation. If Pipik's creative misreading of Roth is correct and the state of Israel as it currently exists should be discontinued, then he forces Roth to confront the idea that doing away with a belief in a core Jewish identity would, in effect, do away with the motivating force of Roth's fiction. Where would Roth's fiction go without the existence of militant, essentialistic Jews as foils? Adopting Pipik's logic, Roth can only counter by defending the existence of Israel as a safeguard to the preservation of Jewish identity, which is exactly the sort of position that his fiction, particularly *The Counterlife*, has always ironized. Second, insofar as Roth grants to Pipik the status of being his own double, he cannot do away with the threat that Pipik represents except through a form of self-hatred. Thus Pipik at once articulates a form, distorted to be sure, of Roth's own thinking about identity while also confirming the worst accusations that Roth's most antagonistic readers have leveled at him. For the moment, Roth obscures the insight that Pipik's own position is essentialistic since he would disband Israel in order to preserve the Jewish self. Instead, Roth explores the possibility that Roth himself will at last be fixed to an essential position.

Roth portrays how threatening Pipik's usurpation of his identity is during the hysterical encounter that occurs between the two in Roth's hotel room. In this scene Roth tails Pipik only to find that his double has already occupied his—Roth's—room. Roth intends to chase Pipik out, but he is nearly paralyzed by his recognition that Pipik's occupation of his room makes manifest Pipik's prior occupation of his self. His dominant thought is "now I was locked up with him" (192). Philip Roth the author, though, recognizes what Philip Roth the character cannot: this meeting of doubles provides Philip Roth, the alleged all-time champion of literary self-indulgence, with an opportunity he is not going to pass up. Roth highlights the idea that this scene represents the culmination of a lifetime of writing stories about self-obsession: "Philip Roth fucking Philip Roth! . . . is a form of masturbation too fancy even for me" (191). This joke feebly tries to conceal the possibility that the scene demands be confronted: that, speaking vulgarly, Philip Roth might at last realize the implications of his novelist's ideal of the performing self by disappearing up his own asshole. After allowing that "there is more than a grain of truth in recognizing and acknowledging the Eurocentrism of Judaism," Roth pleads, "tell me, please, what *is* this really all about? Identity theft? It's got to be the stupidest con going. You've got to get caught. Who are you?" (191). He wants Pipik to leave but he cannot stand the idea of his leaving—how does he know "he" will not disappear with "him"? Roth is at the very edge of his Jewish theater here. Pipik's ultimate desire—to eradicate Israel—coincides with his desire to usurp and hence extinguish the author known as Philip Roth. To be or not to be Jewish, Roth seems to ask in this scene, as if answering either question affirmatively will consummate his end. The terrifying irony is that in Pipik he has at last found a role that might actually abolish all others: becoming his double will extinguish him.

Does this confrontation suggest that Roth accuses himself of Jewish self-hatred just as his critics have done? He answers this question first by projecting the question onto Pipik. The irony—and risk for Roth since Pipik is but a version of himself—of Pipik's position is that in the name of saving Israel he really wants to destroy that part of himself that identifies with Israel which, in Pipik's case, means his own Jewish identity. Applying Roth's definition of a Jew as one who embraces his historical position, Pipik wants to murder the Jew in himself. In this respect, Pipik is the ultimate assimilationist. Like Henry Zuckerman, Pipik wants to solve his identity crisis by removing himself from his historical moment. From this perspective, he wants less to return to Europe than to abolish Jewish identity and history altogether. Unable to resolve his Jewish identity crisis, Pipik wants to be a Jew without experiencing the cultural difference of being Jewish. Achieving this paradoxical state would resolve the identity crisis he experienced because of the Jonathan Pollard case, which he says was the inspiration for Diasporism in the first place. "I am haunted by Jonathan Pollard," he tells Roth. "An American Jew paid by Israeli intelligence to spy against his own country's military establishment" (81). Pipik holds Israel, not Pollard, responsible for his treason to the United States—he intimates he would have done the same thing. What authentic Jew would not? Pipik's Diasporism becomes Roth's depiction of the awful schizophrenia that ensues both when one's authentic identity puts one at odds with one's country and when one's country cannot accommodate multiple identities within its mythology. Whichever answer pertains, for Pipik the lesson of the Pollard case is that the existence of Israel engenders a potentially unbearable cultural identity conflict for American Jews.

Roth contrasts the Pollard case with what I guess we should call the Roth case, for Roth too agrees to spy for Israel. "Operation Shylock" names not only the novel but the mission that Roth performs as an agent of the Mossad.[15] The code for the mission is "three thousand ducats," a reference to Shylock's entrance in *The Merchant of Venice*. In a nice twist, Roth agrees to complete the task that Pipik had previously arranged: a meeting with Yassir Arafat. Roth slyly invites us to think that here is proof at last that his loyalty is first and foremost to Israel. (One can almost hear him asking, Do you think Irving Howe or Norman Podhoretz had the guile to be recruited by the Mossad to spy for Israel? Let's have a special issue of *Commentary* on this twist of fate!) Roth reinforces this view by agreeing to withhold the chapter of his book which was to detail the events of his mission. We do not know whether he does this in deference to Smilesburger's special plea to uphold Israeli security or on account of the undisclosed amount of money—the "three thousand ducats"—that Smilesburger offers him. We can extend this reading to say that withdrawing the chapter becomes Roth's version of refusing to practice *loshon hora*, or evil speech. If so, then Roth has followed the advice of Smilesburger, a disciple of Rabbi Chofetz Chaim who taught against the dangers of *loshon hora*, perhaps because he has chosen to abide by a principle that has never seemed to guide him before: "You shall not go about as a tale bearer among your people" (333).

The key to the mission is not in what Roth chooses to keep from the reader but in what he keeps from the Mossad. Earlier in the novel, while traveling in a taxi back to Jerusalem after visiting George Ziad in Ramallah, Roth is asked six times by his driver: "Are you a Zionist?" (167–68). Roth's refusal to answer causes the driver to abandon him, whereupon Roth, unbeknownst to him, is picked up by the Mossad, who have been running the entire game. Smilesburger later puts a different version of this question to Roth when he tries to convince Roth to perform the spy mission, except that he frames it as the logical conclusion to an imaginary Arab inquisition. According to Smilesberger, when the Arabs finally capture Israel they will ask one question of their captives to determine if they should live or die: " 'Did you approve of Israel and the existence of Israel?" (351). In this scenario, this will be the last question that Roth hears before the Arabs kill him—unless he is confused with Pipik. Answering the question requires that Roth confess what his position on Jewish identity is, which only sets up an irreconcilable contradiction. Either he undergoes the mission because he is a loyal Jew, or he does so because he is willing to be perceived as conspirator against Israel in order to save his skin when Pipik's direst prophecies come true.

I submit, however, that Roth enacts the mission for neither of these reasons; rather, his refusal to reveal whether he is a Zionist signifies his refusal to identify himself with the notion of an essential Jewishness. This response touches on at least three levels of Jewish self-representation: that of English and American literature, of Roth's own fiction, and of Philip Roth himself—whoever he may be. By refusing to affirm or deny that he "approves of Israel," he tries to evade the legacy of *loshon hora*, inaugurated in Shakespeare's representation of Shylock. That his fiction has been obsessed with negative and even stereotypical representations of Jewish identity only reinforces the stunning audacity of Roth's move. In a sense, Roth's mission—as enacted in the novel—becomes a reclaiming and renaming of those three thousand ducats. Conversely, Roth could be admitting that he cannot subvert the image of the Jew in English and American literature that he has inherited from Shakespeare. In "A Bit of Jewish Mischief," he suggests this interpretation himself by acknowledging that the experience of confronting Pipik has given him "more than a faint idea of why [my critics] have wanted to kill me and what, rightly and wrongly, they have been through" (20).

Roth's self-laceration is given literary-historical perspective by the antiquarian bookseller and sometime agent for Shin Bet, David Supposnik. Along with telling Roth he talks too much, Supposnik suggests that Shakespeare's original Jew—as a literary creation—is incontrovertible. He describes the phrase "three thousand ducats" as "three words encompassing all that is hateful in the Jew, three words that have stigmatized the Jew through two Christian millennia and that determine Jewish fate until this very day, and that only the greatest English writer of them all could have had the prescience to isolate and dramatize as he did" (274). Recognizing how powerful this goyische literary tradition has been, Roth can only hope to follow Smilesberger's comical interpretation of Rabbi Chaim after all. By promising to suppress information about his mission, Roth hints that he is perhaps preserving an authentic Jewish identity by keeping this identity a secret—the story of which he either cannot or refuses to tell. Of course his novel is still a tale, a story, but, if read correctly, it refuses to tell tales against the Jews. That the missing episode depicting his spy mission becomes the title for the book suggests that *Operation Shylock* is not so much about the stories that Roth has told, as critics have always complained, but about the story he has not told.[16] The silence that has traditionally surrounded the Holocaust here becomes a source of Jewish storytelling power.[17]

In terms of his own fiction, what matters is that Roth has possessed Pipik, who began by possessing Roth. Thus he has both accepted and subsumed within himself all the possible permutations that his fiction allows—especially the ones over which he would seem to have no control. This possession occurs in the way that writers usually control experience: through the act of naming. By naming the other Philip Roth "Moishe Pipik" (Moses Bellybutton), Roth assimilates Pipik into his own family history. As Roth relates, Moishe Pipik, a figure out of Yiddish folklore, was also the most treasured figure in Roth family folklore when he was a kid. Pipik would make his appearance in the Roth household every weekend after a visit to Meema Gitcha's in Danbury, Connecticut. In order to assure Meema that the Roths had returned to Newark safely, Roth's mother would place a collect phone call to Meema under the name of "Moishe Pipik." Much of the fun, according to Roth, was in listening to "the goyisch operator" mispronounce the name. The event had the aura of ritual; it provided the Roths an opportunity to confirm themselves as Jews by using a language that the goyisch operator could not understand, while at the same time allowing them to trick the phone company out of a charge and reassure Meema of their safety. More precisely, they employ Yiddish instead of English to create of Yiddish a language that expresses their own complex American Jewish identity. Through this weekly family ritual, Yiddish is transformed into a kind of American language, a language of Americanization.

Naming his double Pipik, however, does not initially enable Roth to extricate himself from Pipik's power. When Roth explains to his double why he has named him Pipik, he is excited to find that it had "anesthetized him," that he "had put my sonny boy to sleep" (186). Staring at the sleeping Pipik, Roth imagines him dead. Part wish, this reaction is another reminder that Roth cannot suppress the fear that his double's appearance will require his own death. Pipik is an absence, a blank space capable of absorbing Roth's identity into its own nullity. On the other hand, what he told his double about the meaning of Pipik is also true: this blank can be turned into anything; it is "protean, a hundred different things" (185). From this perspective, the name's associations with Moses and the bellybutton are significant. Once the umbilical cord is cut, one's self must find its way among other selves. The name's association with Moses at once evokes the origin of Jewish identity and its loss. Pipik therefore represents to Roth the necessary cutting of the cable that enables the invention—and perpetuation—of his own identity. By this view, Moses is transformed from a figure of austere purpose and Godly mission into a trickster whose natural habitat has become the phone line between Newark, New Jersey, and Danbury, Connecticut. If this myth can be interpreted to explain how Jews managed to move from Egypt to Europe to America, it also becomes Roth's myth of how he ventures to Israel to repossess himself as a Jewish American author.

The moment of repossession occurs later in the novel, while Roth is sitting in an Israeli classroom. Kidnapped and in utter confusion about his own identity because of the appearance of his double, Roth sees nine Hebrew words written on a chalkboard and suspects "that these markings might provide the clue to exactly where I'd been held captive and by whom" (315). In the context of the novel the word "captive" is doubly suggestive because Roth could be the prisoner of his double, the Mossad, the Arabs, or the sense that his own identity is fracturing. The writing prompts him to recall afternoons as a child spent in Hebrew school learning Hebrew.[18] The experience of this school had unconsciously taught him to lead a doubled existence: America and Israel colliding for a moment before "we escaped back into our cozy American world" (310). Roth reflects that Hebrew school was less for his generation than "the deal that our parents had cut with *their* parents" who had "wanted the grandchildren to be Jews the way that they were Jews." Roth recalls this as "the leash" meant "to restrain the breakaway young" who wanted "to be Jews in a way no one had ever dared to be a Jew in our three thousand year history: speaking and thinking American English, only American English." This new American-Jewish identity is what Pipik threatens by luring Roth to Israel. Roth realizes that the "cryptography whose signification I could no longer decode had marked me indelibly four decades ago." Regarding his attempt to repossess himself, this scene may mark Roth's lowest moment in the novel. He feels as helpless before these ancient words as he does before the presence of Pipik. If Henry felt that the Israeli children singing in Hebrew were marked Jewish by the language that they sang, then Roth fears that these strangely familiar letters mark him as an essential Jew in a way that he cannot name and hence cannot control. Yet, as I have suggested, the absence that Pipik's name denotes represents the possibility for Roth's self-renewal. If he can embrace Pipik's evocation of possibility, of endless self-invention, then he can cut the cord that threatens to tie him to a permanent Jewish self.

Ironically, the fact that Roth cannot understand the words is what enables him to cut the cord to his double. Robert Alter, clearly frustrated with this scene, asks "how, really, can the key to Roth's own work be an unintelligible language?" (34). The answer for Roth is that the letters' mark on him *becomes his own invention*. Certainly, Alter is right to suggest that Roth's ignorance of Hebrew is a cultural impoverishment—Roth himself would no doubt agree. But in this scene the protagonist Philip Roth uses his ignorance of the words' meaning to transport himself back to what becomes his mythical originary moment as an American Jew, a Jew who need not know Hebrew to know his Jewishness. In any case, the author who constructed this scene, while not fluent in Hebrew, obviously knows what these words mean as they contain an important gloss on the story at hand and compose one of the book's two epigraphs. These words from Genesis do not finally show either his origin or his "capture" by that moment of

origin. The fact that these words offer an important gloss on the story
should not be taken to mean that Roth really "knows" Hebrew after all or
has learned the Hebrew school cultural inheritance of his youth. As the
story about uttering "Moishe Pipik" to the telephone operator suggests,
Roth's cultural inheritance as a Jew and as an American is embedded in the
way that his family was able to transform Yiddish into an American language. The appearance of these Hebrew letters at the decisive point in
Roth's search for self-repossession similarly obligates him to confront the
impossibility of recovering his original Jewish tongue. Rather, almost
triumphantly, the link between the unreadable text on the blackboard and
Roth's story demonstrates precisely that his identity remains Jewish in the
absence of that essentializing linguistic cultural inheritance.

Though not translated by Roth except as an epigraph to the novel, the
Hebrew words are of course significant. They come from Genesis 32:24:
"So Jacob was left alone, and a man wrestled with him until dawn." The
story in Genesis concerning the strange encounter between Jacob and the
mysterious presence seems to refuse interpretation. We can say with certainty only that Jacob has driven away his pursuer and in the process has
been touched with holiness. By invoking this story in its ancient Hebrew
language at this moment, Roth implies that Pipik was as much angel as
tormentor. Just as Jacob wrestled the angel until it mysteriously disappeared, so does Roth wrestle with Pipik until he is gone and Roth finds
some measure of tranquillity. He relinquishes his obsession with differen-
tiating between his authentic self and Pipik's impersonation of him. The
holiness Roth finds in embracing Pipik as he departs is purely secular—
his unironic version of the rock worship that Zuckerman mocked at the
Wailing Wall. In embracing his contingent, secular identity, Roth nonetheless seems to ask if the recovery and reinvention of self can occur
without some vestige of holiness or at least mystery.

Unable to decode the Hebrew letters, Roth speaks the word "Pipik."
Having copied down words whose meaning he cannot understand, Roth is
"startled" to find himself "speaking out loud"—as if somehow the writing
of the strange words prompted him to speech. Roth calls to his double
assuming that Pipik is present. Though his double does not answer and is
likely not there, this moment becomes the point at which Roth possesses
himself. He asks Pipik to forgive him for "trespassing against you as I
have" (319)—as if to acknowledge that his fault was in transgressing
against his own ethic of impersonation. Forgiveness, though, can only
come with true recognition: "Only when I spoke my name as though I

believed it was his name as well" would his nightmare be over. By saying "Philip" aloud he embraces Pipik as his own self, the genie, as it were, that composes his genius. He accepts, as it were, his bellybutton as his own, though it is also the mark of his connection in birth to someone else. The scene takes on added poignancy given the fact that by this point in the novel both the reader and the protagonist know that Pipik is riddled with cancer and will eventually die. Indeed, Roth invokes a potentially grisly image of his own death by portraying himself standing over the dead Pipik's body. For Roth, though, the point is that though the "other" Philip Roth is dead, Pipik lives on in the Roth who survives. The death of the double becomes a moment of authorial resurrection. Where the dying Philip Roth was reduced by his cancer to using a penile implant in order to simulate sexual potency, the victorious Philip Roth assumes Pipik into his own identity in order to assert his regained creative potency. Thus at the moment when Roth at last speaks Pipik's name, his double vanishes. Roth's voice is at last triumphantly his own.

Significantly, the moment in which Pipik vanishes coincides with Roth's initiation into the spy mission that gives the novel its title; Smilesburger enters the classroom almost at the instant that Pipik—metaphorically—disappears. Roth's stance as a spy addresses the contradiction that Pipik (and perhaps previously Roth) could not resolve. Pipik, though not affiliated with the Mossad, is truly a "double" agent in the sense that he is working out his Pollard complex by allowing his obsession with Israel to lead him into betraying Israel. Once we realize that Pipik is a trickster figure, though, we see that Pipik's identification with Pollard is really Roth's. Roth may think he is making "Jewish Mischief" when he chooses to elaborate upon Pipik's ideas, but the difference is that where Pipik is only play-acting, Roth finds himself taking his role seriously. Thus Roth's refusal to answer the question about his loyalty to Israel partakes of the same canniness that enables him to escape the identity trap that his obsession with Pipik sets for him. If Roth's absorption of Pipik's Pollard argument breaks down because the lesson of the Pollard case is that Israel requires an unbearable loyalty, then Roth's trump is that he has found a way to negotiate this double identity, this double consciousness. His problem with Israel is rooted in an American dilemma that Philip Roth, in his fiction anyway, has managed to solve: the conflict of identites that being a Jew who is also an American imposes upon him. Roth's advice to Pipik, a version of William James's imperative to dive into the flux, becomes advice for himself. "Surrender to reality, Pipik. There's nothing quite like it"

(204). Once Roth reconciles himself to Pipik's meaning, we can see this advice is actually in keeping with Pipik's trickster spirit. Thus Roth's self-recovery is not the recovery of some essential Jewish identity, though the narrative flirts with that interpretation. Rather, Roth discovers that what drove Pollard to spy against his country and Pipik to advocate the extinction of Israel need not divide or destroy him. Roth may or may not be first and foremost a Jew, but he—not the outraged Yeshiva students and faculty, Pipik, Smilesburger, or even William Shakespeare—is the one who is doing the branding. In accepting the chaos—the flux—that Pipik offers while rejecting his desire to erase Jewish identity in the name of preserving it, Roth has mastered his double American identity.

To reinforce the point that the solution to his Jewish-American dilemma is not, as many of his critics often claim, that of transcending history, Roth allows Smilesberger to voice his critics' argument:

> You are that marvelous, unlikely, most magnificent phenomenon, the truly liberated Jew. The Jew who is not accountable. The Jew who finds the world perfectly to his liking. The comfortable Jew. The happy Jew. Go. Choose. Take. Have. You are the blessed Jew condemned to nothing, least of all our historical struggle. (352)

Roth rightly objects that this is not true since it contradicts his assertion, borne out by his fiction, that being Jewish involves understanding one's identity as made of a complicated and mostly inescapable historical situation. In *The Counterlife* Henry wishes to escape his history as an American Jew when he travels to Judea to find his "true" identity. In *Operation Shylock* Philip Roth ventures to Israel not to abandon his Jewish self, like Henry or Pipik, but to embrace it more fully. The emphasis is important because it suggests that Roth is never fully himself, even if he is always in some sense both a Jew and an American. Indeed, as Kallen might have suggested, it is through his Jewishness that he expresses his American and his authorial self. The drama of this novel for the reader has been to witness the amazing, demanding spectacle of a major American author attempting to confront the implications of his entire oeuvre and then repossess them as *something or someone else*. The scope of this effort is unrivaled in American fiction—with the exception perhaps of Henry James's famed New York edition for which he revised the works most important to him and wrote prefaces that he aggressively presented as a *re*-vision, a reworking of his work and self.

We should not see Smilesburger as only a stand-in for Roth's Jewish audience, though. As his name suggests, he too is a trickster figure. In a sense, he sets Roth's self-confrontation in motion when in their first meeting he apparently mistakes the real Philip Roth for his double and gives him a check for a million dollars. This check is a crucial plot mechanism that pushes the story along. Roth even suspects that Pipik's appearance in Israel was Smilesburger's invention, which might suggest that what Roth suppressed was his admission that Operation Shylock was really Operation Pipik (389).[19] Smilesburger, like Pipik, has been an instigator of the sort of Jewish mischief that has led Roth to repossess himself. In other words, he did not suppress anything at all. It is fitting, then, that Smilesberger should be present at the conclusion of the novel, which, crucially, takes place not in Israel but in a Jewish deli on Amsterdam Avenue in New York. By removing Smilesberger from Israel to New York in order to give Roth his final lesson about identity, the author reinforces the point that his Israel novel takes its fullest meaning in an American context.

As a place of memory and communion, the deli that they visit embodies in its very atmosphere the provisional truth of Roth's novel. Under the store's influence, Roth recalls the store he frequented as a boy where his family purchased "silky slices of precious lox, shining fat little chubs, chunks of pale, meaty carp and paprikaed sable, all double wrapped in heavy wax paper" (378). Roth's description of this deli and the associative memories it conjures come together in one of his best pieces of writing, one that may fairly compare with Proust's more famous passage about the madeleine.

> The tiled floor sprinkled with sawdust, the shelves stacked with fish canned in sauces and oils, up by the cash register a prodigious loaf of halvah soon to be sawed into crumbly slavs, and, wafting up from behind the showcase running the length of the serving counter, the bitter fragrance of vinegar, of onions, of whitefish and red herring, of everything pickled, peppered, salted, smoked, soaked, stewed, marinated, and dried, smells with a lineage that, like these stores themselves, more than likely led straight back to the shtetl to the medieval ghetto and the nutrients of those who lived frugally and could not afford to dine a la mode, the diet of sailors and common folk, for whom the flavor of the ancient preservatives was life. (378–79)

An account of how everyday details are transformed into personal and cultural mythology, this passage is a beautiful evocation of a timeless Jewish history fixed to a specific spot. The layers of memory summoned here seem if only for a moment to connect the present seamlessly with the past. Yet Roth observes that by 1993 "the ordinary fare of the Jewish masses had become an exotic stimulant for Upper West Siders two and three generations removed from the great immigration" (379). For Roth the American Jew, one's Jewish homeland may not be Israel or Europe but a New York restaurant where Yiddish is still spoken. This provisional home is redolent with the smells of Galicia but involves none of its torments. Among those Upper West Siders are, presumably, non-Jews who have no authentic connection to the "bitter fragrance" that somehow makes the current smell so savory. The aroma of a Jewish past—sharp and full of difference remembered and preserved—now permeates a present that includes diners who come from different pasts, ones who may or may not visit Israel as many of these Jews do. Certainly this Jewish deli does not exist in Israel, nor did it in Europe; it exists only in a New York not too far removed from the Newark classroom in which Roth as a boy was not learning Hebrew.

From this perspective, one could argue that the deli is less an image of Jewish assimilation than a reflection on the process of how the assimilation of the Jews in America has assimilated non-Jews too. The experience of the deli perhaps communicates to those non-Jews who also recognize it as a home a nostalgia that has become their own, though it emerges out of somebody else's past. Here, where cultural memory is consumed with lox and bagels, Roth is at last in his element. The joke that Roth gives to Smilesberger to tell defines this element perfectly:

> A man comes into a Jewish restaurant like this one. He sits at a table and picks up a menu and he looks it over and decides what he's going to eat and when he looks up again there is the waiter and he's Chinese. The waiter says, *"Vos vilt ihr essen?"* In perfect Yiddish, the Chinese waiter asks him, "What do you want to eat?" The customer is astonished but goes ahead and orders and, with each course that arrives, the Chinese waiter says here is your this and I hope you enjoyed that, all of it in perfect Yiddish. When the meal's over, the customer picks up the check and goes to the cash register, where the owner is sitting. . . . In a funny accent much like my own, the owner says to the customer, "Everything was all right? Everything was okay?" And the customer is ecstatic. "It was perfect," he tells him, "everything was great. And the waiter—this is the most amazing thing—the waiter is Chinese and yet he speaks *absolutely perfect Yiddish.*" *"Shah*, shhh," says the owner, "not so loud—he thinks he's learning English." (385)

This is not an instance of assimilation as it is usually understood, where the new immigrant is expected to conform to an already existing and basically static conception of national identity. As when the Roth family giggled "Moishe Pipik" to the uncomprehending phone operator, the point of the joke is not that Yiddish has been assimilated into American culture, but that Yiddish has become a means for becoming American. In suggesting that Yiddish has developed into an American possibility, the Chinese waiter joke undermines the logic that there is such a thing as an authentic ethnic identity not implicated within a broader system of identity acquisition. The joke intimates two interrelated ideas: first, that immigrants are never fully absorbed into a prior, stable national norm; second, that prior immigrants help to establish and therefore change the context in which future immigrants will know themselves as Americans. The Chinese waiter realizes his identity as an American through an ethnic identity that is not truly his. Likewise, this American restaurant, redolent with the odors of food that Jews have eaten for centuries, is home to Jews who speak only American English, or, in some cases, Americans who have no Jews for ancestors. You visit this place when in the mood—to pick up a snippet of Yiddish here and there, to breathe air that carries the aroma of your ancestors, to soak up the atmosphere as if it were your very own. Perhaps it is.

## 5   Don't Be Cruel: Elvis Invents America Again

■ ■ ■ ■ ■ ■ ■

If I could find a white boy who sang like a nigger, I could make a billion dollars.
—Sam Phillips, Elvis Presley's first producer, as quoted in Albert Goldman's *Elvis*

Everyone who writes about popular music knows that before Sam Phillips, the proprietor of Sun Records, recorded Elvis Presley in 1954, he used to go around saying "If I could find a white boy who sang like a nigger . . . "
—Louis Menand, in the *New Republic*

Elvis was a hero to most / But that's beside the point / A Black man taught him how to sing / And then they crowned him king.
—Living Colour, "Elvis Is Dead"

## I

No one knows exactly where or when the blues originated. Son House is probably closest to the truth when he says the blues began with a sharecropper singing to the back of a mule.[1] What we do know is that the blues was invented by post-slavery blacks in an ongoing response to the demands of becoming American. Throughout the history of the blues the conditions of performance have undergone constant change. When and where you hear the blues determines what kinds of cultural claims you can make about it. Looking for an already dead Robert Johnson, Alan Lomax, the anthropologist of American blues, recorded Muddy Waters for the Library of Congress in 1941; listen to the recordings and you can imagine that slavery is only recently over but the news has not yet reached the man singing. Two years earlier John Hammond had also tried to track down Robert Johnson—this time so that he could perform in the 1938 "From Spirituals to Swing" concert Hammond was organizing at Carnegie Hall.[2] From Dockery's plantation near Clarksdale, Mississippi, to Carnegie Hall is a long journey indeed, but the tail to the tale is the timing of these two searches for Robert Johnson. While Lomax was looking for the "authentic" blues of the cotton fields, Hammond had already moved the cotton field uptown. By the time House offered his history of the blues that I allude to above, he had long since left Mississippi, lived through a twenty-year period of not playing the blues, and had only recently been "rediscovered." Instead of playing to the back of a mule or to a young, awestruck Muddy Waters at a country dance near Clarksdale, Mississippi, in the 1930s, House was now playing before largely white, college-educated audiences of the 1960s who were not born when he was mastering his form.[3] In other words, House was playing for money.

Once the blues left the cotton field its meaning changed, simply because as folk expression becomes accepted as art its audiences and their expectations change. Country blues singers of the 1920s and 1930s such as Son House created music that came out of the cotton field but was sung into a microphone. As a result, those recordings exist on a historical divide—in an important way the dividing line between the nineteenth and twentieth centuries. While Alan Lomax was wandering the South trying to preserve rural folk culture, those such as record industry talent scout Ralph Peer were discovering that rural folk culture was marketable. In less than fifty years the blues went from being incomprehensible outside the original circle of its creation to being a musical form that theoretically anyone from any country could learn to play. The Mississippi-born blues piano player Sunnyland Slim, who lived through the blues' migration from country to city, notes that those who first created the blues "weren't doing it for no money or nothin' like that. No, they was doin' it 'cause it just sound so good to them, you know, it allowed for them to express themselves" (qted. in Barlow 27). Phil and Leonard Chess, the Jewish brothers who ran Chicago's Chess Records, which catered exclusively to black audiences, had a saying: if it won't sell in Mississippi, it won't sell in Chicago. Louis Jordan, Roy Brown, and T-Bone Walker, whose blues were certainly more urbane than most of what the Chess brothers were recording, still addressed the situation of their black audiences.

If an early blues artist lived long enough, he or she was likely to end his or her career playing before white audiences—as Son House and Memphis Slim and Big Joe Turner, among many, many others—all did. Certainly, "forgotten" country blues artists such as Son House or Bukka White or Mississippi John Hurt were grateful and surprised to find themselves sought out decades after their slight fame by people who had only heard their music on scratched 78s. They also understood that the music they made during their second, more lucrative career did not mean the same thing to this audience that it had meant to the audiences before which they had learned their art. What they presented at the Newport Village Jazz Festival was an art form that had come undone from the cultural conditions of its creation. A film record exists of Son House playing in the 1960s.[4] Before performing each song, he describes—mumbles, actually, as if he does not expect to be heard or understood—to the audience the rhetorical situation, the social context, that made this song significant to him when he first created it. Son House recognizes that the blues as art, as cultural expression, involves not just certain notes or phrasings but an integration between song and situation, act and thought. In trying to recreate the context of his initial blues he is not so much creating the blues as glossing an already finished artifact.

Though a poor southerner raised not too far from Son House and at times among the company of poor blacks, Elvis Presley has not been seen as part of the cultural situation that includes Son House. The recurring charge that Elvis merely imitated or mimicked black styles is not meant merely to denigrate Elvis's artistic talent but to reinforce the understanding that he had no right to practice the form in the first place. Son House singing to college kids is an artist finally receiving his due; Elvis singing "from the waist up" on the Ed Sullivan Show is making booty by shaking his. Only from this perspective can Son House be excused for making money by playing his form to an audience who was not, so to speak, raised to it, while Elvis is denigrated for copying a style that could never be his. The unquestioned fact that Elvis's style had something to do with black culture prompts uncomfortable critical positions. We can label him an imitator or a usurper or an aberration; he is usually discussed as a cultural phenomenon—someone who liked fried peanut butter and banana sandwiches, loved his mother too much, and, when he was not giving away cars or shooting guns at television sets, somehow found the time to steal the blues from African Americans. Alice Walker's short story "1955" relates how an Elvis figure rises to fame and fortune singing, in this case, a black woman's song. The female singer is obviously modeled on Big Mama Thornton, the "original" singer of "Hound Dog," one of the handful of songs most often associated with Elvis. Near the end of the story the Elvis figure asks the Thornton figure to explain the meaning of her song that he has been singing all of these years. He dies fat, alone, confused. Walker's story plays with the fact that the song's refrain, "You ain't nothing but a hound dog," makes more sense coming out of a woman's mouth—or Big Mama Thornton's—than a man's.[5] We would rather reinvent Elvis as a cultural sight gag than confront his true legacy: one who self-consciously attempted to remake how we conceive ourselves as Americans. An inheritor of the blues no less than Son House or Muddy Waters, Elvis is one of those rare figures in American culture whose presence seems to render our diverse American culture whole. Far from stealing the blues and selling off its legacy to ignorant buyers, Elvis is a version of Ellison's "man of parts," who links America simultaneously to both slavery and the promises written into our utopian American beginning.

Making this argument involves reassessing a statement that has been influential in defining the critical and cultural context in which Elvis has been normally discussed. Sam Phillips, his first producer, is alleged to have said: "If I could find a white man who sings like a nigger, I could make a million dollars"—or a billion dollars, depending on who is telling the story.[6] Because this statement is attributed to Phillips, The-Man-Who-Discovered-Elvis-Presley, it has acquired the status of a myth of origin. Given that Phillips established Sun Records exclusively to record black musicians, it is extremely unlikely that he said any such thing. Greil Marcus points out that he was mocked by fellow Memphians for spending so much time with blacks: "Hey, Sam, you smell okay today—must not have been with those niggers!" was to him a familiar greeting (*Dead* 52). Probably, he said something like "If I could find a white man who had the Negro sound and the Negro feel, I could make a million dollars." As things turned out, he sold Elvis's contract to RCA for $35,000. This story is repeated endlessly, though, because it recognizes a cardinal truth about Elvis at the same time that it turns away from confronting this truth: Elvis's power did derive in part from his affinity with black culture. The irony of understanding Elvis as a mere imitator is that this view replicates and reverses the pattern, identified by the eminent African Americanist Henry Louis Gates, by which white America has traditionally dismissed the cultural accomplishments of blacks. Thomas Jefferson drew on a prevalent cultural stereotype in *Notes on the State of Virginia* (1787) to argue that blacks were "imitative" rather than "creative," and Albert Goldman's presumption that Elvis stole the blues dresses up that stereotype in modern garb (Gates, *Signifying* 66). Such arguments obscure not only the fact that Elvis was a maker but how a tradition such as the blues, an instance of descendants of Africa remaking themselves into Americans, can become a tradition that defines all Americans.

Understanding the blues as a tradition that can be exploited for the pleasure of outsiders violates its purity as a form of cultural creation and memory; yet no less of an authentic blues figure than W. C. Handy, the self-
proclaimed "Father of the Blues," understood his relationship to the blues
in precisely this way. Ironically, Handy's story of the origin of the blues
reveals how the kinds of cultural-aesthetic issues associated with Elvis
were implict from the moment the blues crossed over from the cotton
fields. In 1903 Handy was sitting on a train platform when he took notice
of a

> lean, loose-jointed man [who] had commenced plunking a guitar
> beside me while I slept. His clothes were in rags; his feet were out of
> his shoes. His face had on it some of the sadness of the ages. As he
> played, he pressed a knife on the strings of the guitar popularized by
> Hawaiian guitarists who used steel bars. The effect was unforgetta-
> ble. His song, too, struck me instantly.
> Goin' where the Southern cross the Dog.
> The singer repeated the line three times, accompanying himself with
> *the weirdest music I had ever heard.* The tune stayed in my mind. When
> the singer paused, I leaned over and asked him what the words meant.
> He rolled his eyes, showing mild amusement. Perhaps I should have
> known, but he didn't mind explaining. (74, emphasis mine)

In this story about cultural authenticity, Handy is the one who comes
across as counterfeit.[7] A musician who depends on formal musical notation to guide his playing, Handy hears this "weird" music as primitive—as
strange to him as the singing of the slaves was to white observers such as
Frances Kemble or Thomas Wentworth Higginson during slavery times.
His musical background gives him no way to account for what he hears.
Handy might not have remembered this encounter so vividly were it not
for the engagement he and his orchestra had a few days later in Cleveland,
Mississippi. When someone in the audience asks Handy's orchestra to
play "our native music," Handy is both "baffled" and worried by the
request (76). His response is to copy whites copying blacks: he does a
minstrel version. Dissatisfied with Handy's "blues," the audience calls out
for a local band who obliges them. Handy declares their music to be an
endless "monotony," a "thump-thump-thump" sound that he associates—with evident distaste—with "cane rows and levee camps" (77). Nor
does he admire the enthusiastic dancing the music elicits.

Handy's perspective changes dramatically, though, when he sees the audience's reaction. In the idiom of the blues, Handy dreams lucky and wakes up in a place where his money will stay green—or, in his case, silver.

> A rain of silver dollars began to fall around the outlandish, stomping feet. Dollars, quarters, halves—the shower grew heavier and continued so long I strained my neck to get a better look. There before the boys lay more money than my nine musicians were being paid for the entire engagement. *Then I saw the beauty of primitive music.* They had the stuff that people wanted. It touched the spot. Their music wanted polishing, but it contained the essence. Folks would pay money for it. (77, emphasis mine)

In this passage the "Father of the Blues" brings new meaning to the term "essentialism." "The beauty of primitive music," as Handy describes it, is not an aesthetic quality but a financial one. "My idea of what constitutes music," Handy confesses, "was changed by the sight of that silver money cascading around the splay feet of a Mississippi string band." On that night, against all training, Handy discovered himself to be an authentic blues scholar. His career and fame were the result of his polishing that untutored music into numbers that could be published as sheet music and sold to orchestras to play. As we have seen, Big Bill Broonzy would not recognize this style of composition as having anything to do with the blues, since to Broonzy "you can't put down the music in the blues on no paper" (Lomax, *Land* 453). Perhaps because Handy by this definition was not a blues composer, he instead became, in his phrase, "an *American* composer" (77).

Handy's presentation of himself as the father of the blues needs not so much to be contested as to be set against his own account of his relationship to the blues. As we saw in chapter 2, Muddy Waters can claim a song as his own composition even though it consists of borrowed lyrics and a borrowed tune. Handy, too, of course works with borrowed material, though he "jazzes" them up in a more obvious way than Waters does. Handy's fame as a blues composer derives from his ability to transcribe, arrange, and set songs to written scores. Handy's relationship to the music he hears in Mississippi is analogous to Czech classical composer Anton Dvorak's relationship to the spirituals he adapted for his "New World Symphony." By a strict definition, Waters is inside the blues tradition and Handy is outside it. Even though his blues begins in imitation of House (who himself learned by imitating someone else and so on back into folk obscurity), Waters earns the right to claim "Country Blues #2," a song that he learned from Son House, by virtue of the experience that inspired him to transform already existing words and tune into an expression of his personal situation. For Muddy Waters music is the expression of his personal experience: feeling, act, and performance are integrally related. In a sense, this way of making music cannot be stolen. For Handy, songs are the expressions of an individual's ideas: they are conceptual innovations that can be copyrighted.

It is only in the musical tradition represented by Handy that the story about Elvis stealing blacks' music makes sense since Handy's relationship with the musical form associated with his name is not nearly as intimate as Elvis's was. Elvis's way of creating shares common ground with Muddy Waters rather than with Handy. To be sure, both the "Father of the Blues" and the "King of Rock and Roll" played the blues for outside audiences—as did House and Waters and Big Bill Broonzy. Although Elvis's primary audience was never predominantly black, his music makes little sense outside the tradition of the blues that he inherited from artists like House and Waters—even if he never performed one of their songs.[8] He tried to explain this to a reporter in Charlotte, North Carolina, in June 1956 after his fame had already begun to explode. The immediate context for these remarks is the furor being stirred up over way he moves his body while he sings.[9]

> The colored folks have been singing it and playing it just like I'm doin' now, man, for more years than I know. They played it like that in their shanties and in their juke joints, and nobody paid it no mind 'til I goosed it up. Down in Tupelo, Mississippi, I used to hear old Arthur Crudup bang his box the way I do now, and I said if I ever got to the place where I could feel all old Arthur felt, I'd be a music man like nobody ever saw. (qted. in Guralnick, *Last* 289).

Looking for justification of his style, Elvis immediately turns to the blues and its emphasis on rhythm and dance. At the outset of his career we see how intimate is Elvis's affinity with the blues. He does not think to justify his association; he leaps to it as his only possible explanation. In so doing, Elvis's account of his musical heritage, respectful and discerning, underscores his own connection to a blues tradition. Even as Elvis suggests the difference that separates him from Arthur "Big Boy" Crudup, he also demonstrates, in his emphasis on the way Crudup's technique incorporates personal life experience, a full understanding of what makes the blues. Elvis does not claim to share the same experience with those who performed in the shanties and the juke joints, but his familiarity with the music that came out of that experience is not that of an outsider either. In identifying his music with Crudup's, Elvis is not exactly claiming to be a blues singer; rather, he wants his music to project the same assertion of identity that he heard in Crudup and in the blues.[10] According to Sam Phillips, Elvis identified with the mixture of insecurity and confidence projected by the great blues singers of his youth (Guralnick, *Last* 133). Phillips linked what he called "the lack of prejudice on the part of Elvis Presley" with something "subversive, sneaking around through the music." What is subversive about Elvis Presley? Phillips provides a revealing response: *"He didn't draw any lines"* (Guralnick, *Last* 135). Stated differently, Elvis Presley remains subversive because he drew lines between places that Americans have never wanted to see connected. If the tradition of the blues allows us to examine how Emerson's ballad in the street was transformed into a holler from the cane field, then the example of Elvis allows us to see how the tradition of the blues has transformed mainstream America culture. Even so, despite Elvis, American culture remains, as Ralph Ellison says, an undiscovered country.

"Elvis was a hero to most / But that's beside the point / A Black man taught him how to sing / And then they crowned him king." These lyrics from Living Colour's 1990 "Elvis Is Dead" rewrite Public Enemy's 1989 "Fight the Power" to invoke the image of Elvis as the boy who stole the blues. For Public Enemy, fighting "the power" means fighting the racist constructions of identity that define power relations in American society. Noting that most of his heroes do not appear on any national postage stamps, Public Enemy's Chuck D. summons the image of Elvis as the stamp by which the United States sanctions its own racist culture. Rather than dismissing Elvis as a simple bumpkin, a cracker, Living Colour complicates Public Enemy's image of Elvis by pointing out that Elvis's power as an icon derives from his intimacy with African American culture. Greil Marcus, Elvis's most discerning critic, intimates what this view might mean when he avers that Elvis comprises our "cultural epistemology," in that he holds the "skeleton key to a lock we've yet to find" (*Dead* xvi). Peter Guralnick, at the end of his magisterial biography of Elvis, suggests that through "the cacophony of voices" that have tried to bury Elvis's meaning we continue to hear "the voice that the world first heard" in 1954, which remained consistent in its ability to convey Elvis's "belie[f] in a democratic ideal of redemptive transformation" (*Careless* 660–61). If Elvis remains our cultural reference point, our skeleton key, a question left over from his life remains: What will we find when we unlock his mystery? Perhaps surprisingly, lead singer Corey Glover answers: "A black man." Glover recognizes that such a response suggests both how difficult and desirable the final burial of Elvis would be. Given the history of black and white in America, its slavery and Jim Crow, what could be less simple than looking at a white man and calling him black?

Such a question conjures forth images of the white minstrel tradition, apotheosized in the image of Al Jolson singing "Mammy." Mary when confronted with such an unlikely spectacle will respond with a rueful clucking of tongues, maybe a sharp, short whistle that says how awful it is that white people are always appropriating the black folks' culture in their never-ending desire to contain the inventiveness of black culture. As is usual in these sorts of discussions, black culture is seen as a passive object to be done unto by whites. Any recognition that culture, whether we define it as "white" or "black" or "mixed," changes under the stress of competing influences is denied. Elvis is no Al Jolson, but we continue to discuss him as if he were; thus we wilfully segregate American identities even where they might be said to merge. Against this view of a segregated American culture, Albert Murray has argued that "American culture, even in its most rigidly segregated precincts, is patently and irrevocably composite. It is, regardless, of all the hysterical protestations of those who would have it otherwise, incontestably mulatto" (*Omni-Americans* 22). Murray here may as well be describing Elvis—as even the stereotypical view of Elvis confirms. The fear that Elvis stole black music is not just an issue of cultural theft, but one of cultural mixing. Thus one can argue that Elvis "mixed" (to use a word that recalls the 1950s' fear of miscegenation) his music with black music to achieve on a cultural level what *Brown v. Board of Education* decreed on a legal one.

Despite its title, "Elvis Is Dead" gives no indication that Elvis has passed from the cultural scene. Living Colour takes a more ironical stance that betrays less cultural and perhaps aesthetic anxiety toward Elvis than Public Enemy projects. Because "Elvis Is Dead" relies so heavily on quotation and parody, it is sometimes difficult to determine exactly toward what end its irony is being deployed. "Fight the Power," for instance, quotes James Brown as a foil to their Elvis. Not only is Brown's music relentlessly sampled throughout the song, but his best-known political statement, "Say it loud—I'm black and I'm proud," is quoted verbatim by Chuck D. as a period to the discussion of Elvis. The Godfather of Soul is thus summoned as an authentic black presence meant to scare away the phony white one that Elvis represents. As we shall see, Living Colour also structures their presentation of Elvis around James Brown (as well as Little Richard), and it may be that they are merely following Public Enemy's lead. Living Colour also parodies another white performer with a somewhat controversial relationship to black music. "I got a reason to believe / We all won't be received in Graceland," Corey Glover asserts in a clever parody of the refrain of Paul Simon's song "Graceland."[11] Though Simon envisioned an Elvis who could accommodate us all, Living Colour worries that Elvis's so-called appropriation of black identity is but another way of denying blacks their cultural power. On the other hand, Living Colour is perfectly aware that their authority to make such a claim is possible only through their extension of the blues tradition that Elvis himself employed. That is, just as blues singers might repeat others' identical lyrics and riffs in songs that they legitimately consider theirs, so does Living Colour's sampling technique integrate previous performances into their original critique of Elvis. Moreover, prior to Elvis the cultural popularity of Public Enemy and Living Colour—both of whom sell to predominantly white audiences—would have been inconceivable.

In exploring the meaning of Elvis's cultural legacy, "Elvis Is Dead" offers an amazing blend of musical sources and cultural criticism, and about the only voice omitted belongs to Elvis himself. Copyright issues aside, the decision not to sample Elvis underscores how difficult it is to hear Elvis through the cultural noise that engulfs his art. Except for his performances, most of the comments Elvis made about how he himself understood his relationship to black music are obscure and far-flung, outside the realm of the Elvis myth. Guralnick reminds us, though, that his scattered interviews collectively reveal his bewilderment and pride at causing the disturbance that he did (*Last*). Unfortunately, the context in which he was understood—as a hillbilly singing sensation—did not allow his relation to black music to be considered in any serious way. Elvis told the *Waco Tribune News* in 1956 that "I'm no hillbilly singer," but part of the tragedy that was Elvis's life derived from his inability, except in his concerts and records, to define the context of his own critical reception (Guralnick, *Last* 269). Assigned to do a piece on Elvis, wire reporter Fred Danzig recalls Elvis describing the many blues singers he admired. "I was very surprised to hear him talk about the black performers down there," Danzig told Guralnick, "and about how he tried to carry on their music" (248).

Calvin Newborn, a Memphis guitar legend, tells Stanley Booth a less well-known "Hound Dog" story. This one takes place in 1952 at the Flamingo, an all-black club in Memphis when Elvis

> came in there, didn't have on any shoes, barefooted, and asked me if he could play my guitar. I didn't want to let him, I don't usually—I don't know him from Adam. I'd never seen him before. In fact, he was the only white somebody in the club. He made sure he won that one. He sang "You Ain't Nothin' but a Hound Dog" and shook his hair—see, at the time I had my hair processed, and I'd shake it down in my face—he tore the house up. And tore the strings off of my guitar so I couldn't follow him. (Booth 202)

Although Elvis could not play the guitar as well as Newborn, as this account subtly indicates, the story is nonetheless emblematic of how inimitable Elvis was. His success on that night comes from his ability to adapt Newborn's physical mannerisms. His "victory" over Newborn, though, derives from his extraordinary effrontery in tearing off the strings from Newborn's guitar. The gesture acknowledges Newborn's superior musical skill while nonetheless asserting the power of Elvis's performative talent. It is hard to imagine this Elvis Presley asking Big Mama Thornton to explain to him the song that he has been singing. Rather, Newborn's story strongly suggests that Elvis was perhaps more comfortable within a blues tradition than within mainstream American culture. No Ed Sullivan lurks in this scene to proclaim Elvis's movements obscene and demand that he be filmed from the waist up to protect the innocence of the audience. Newborn's story stands against Alice Walker's, but so do the remarks about Elvis that legendary blues singer Howlin' Wolf made to Peter Guralnick. Asked to identify a white blues singer he liked, Wolf pointed to "what's his name? Somewhere out in California, that 'Hound Dog' number." Admitting that Elvis was not purely a blues singer like himself, Wolf nonetheless asserted that "he started from the blues. If he stopped, he stopped. It's nothing to laugh at. *He made his pull from the blues*" (Guralnick, "Elvis Sings the Blues"). What if stories like Newborn's or Wolf's had been as widely circulated as Sam Phillip's misunderstood quote? Would we understand Elvis differently? Would we understand the practice of American identity differently? Why is it that we would rather misread Phillips than listen to those who tell a different, more accurate version of Elvis's identity?

An exemplar of the unpredictability of American culture, Elvis brings us face to face with William James's idea that once one's hypotheses are set within the "stream of your experience," the discoveries that one makes "appear less as a solution than a program for more work."[12] Elvis helps us to reinterpret what we mean when we employ the term "American"—not by saying what it means to be an American but by enacting the cultural possibilities inherent in his American identity. The examination of the cultural possibilities to be realized from the American ideal of equality, which Ellison and Emerson and Kallen and the blues singers found crucial to their work, is crucial to Elvis's as well. The story of Elvis is more than that of a poor boy becoming rich—he never realized the cultural privilege and power that comes with wealth. Even at his most successful, Elvis remained for most the incarnation of the poor white southerner. Without the tradition of the blues Elvis Presley as an icon of American cultural possibility would not exist. Though there are obviously other perspectives from which to consider Elvis, the pragmatist view of truth and experience underscores how Elvis's actions are themselves redefinitions of what is said to constitute American culture. Not only is Elvis, along with the blues singers discussed, the exemplary pragmatist theorist of this study, but his example leaves most of us still trying to come to terms with what he both theorized and practiced.

## II

Above I suggested that when the blues transcended its rural folk audience and moved uptown it opened a fissure between memory and money. If the blues is an art form, like watercolor painting or marble sculpting, then anyone possessing enough skill can learn how to master it. If the blues expresses the soul of a people, then only those who are of that people can claim its soul. In *Our America* (1995), the neopragmatist Walter Benn Michaels argues that contemporary constructions of "race" and "culture" confuse the meaning of these two terms.[13] In our pluralistic society, according to Michaels, "cultural practices are yours even if you don't practice them . . . and [those] cultural practices are attractive to you insofar *as they are yours*" (emphasis mine). In America's culture of cultures "authenticity becomes a crucial aesthetic concept" because it points to some essence by which culture—and art—may be defined ("Race" 682). Michaels argues that all assertions of cultural pluralism from the 1920s to today are based on "race." When we are asked to respect someone's culture, Michaels claims, usually we are really being asked to respect their race. A consequence of this logic is that, for example, one white person can be thought of as speaking for all white people, regardless of all the differences in social circumstances. Thus "culture" becomes an entity that can be possessed—and hence stolen. This is the perspective of those who claim that Elvis stole black culture.

Michaels shrewdly points out that defining who one is by what one does has gone against the grain of most assertions of American identity. Michaels's argument runs counter to Kallen's aphorism that men can change many things but "they cannot change their grandfathers" (*Culture* 122). In a land where fluidity of identity prompts many to rediscover a stable identity in some heritage of their grandfathers or grandmothers, today's multiculturalism, like Kallen's cultural pluralism, depends on understanding and tolerance. That is, we have come to value difference for its own sake. Michaels explains: "The pluralist gesture toward tolerance requires an essentialist assertion of identity; instead of who we are being constituted by what we do, what we do is justified by who we are" ("Race" 683). Stressing doing over being is a likely pragmatist move that opens the possibility of eliminating race as a category for analysis. But if this move allows one to ask why does it matter what we do, it also raises the question of who the "we" is. The fact is that cultural practices also become cultural heritages. Otherwise, the example of Elvis would not be so divisive. Even if we manage to replace race as a category of authentification, we still require some way of talking about what different groups of people happen to do.

An understanding of culture that stresses doing over being, for instance, may have difficulty distinguishing between what a group of people do and how they are perceived by those outside the group. Consider "Blue Yodel #9," a record that paired the "Father of Country Music," Jimmie Rodgers, with America's ambassador of jazz, Louis Armstrong. On the face of it, the differences between these two forms are as clear as, well, black and white. Especially if we consider the social context in which these men came to fame, the 1920s and 1930s, it is hard to imagine a public performance where the audience of one performer could or would want to attend the performance of the other. Jimmie Rodgers was a hero to mostly poor southern whites of the Depression era who admired the devil-may-care attitude with which he faced, first, overwhelming social despair and then his eventual death from tuberculosis at the age of thirty-five. Louis Armstrong learned his art in the Storyville section of New Orleans. While jazz was becoming, as J. A. Rogers pointed out in *The New Negro* (1925), "a transplanted exotic" making its way to Europe as a kind of export of

American modernism, it was, like the blues, the creation of the slaves' descendants ("Jazz" 216–24). As great as Armstrong's fame would become, we are hard-pressed to place him and his magnificent trumpet in an after-hours rural white southern honky-tonk.

Nevertheless, on July 16, 1930, Louis Armstrong and his piano player, Lil Hardin, found themselves with Jimmie Rodgers in Hollywood, cutting one of the most treasured and sought-after performances in the history of the recording industry.[14] The record is valued in part because their performance is sublime. Against Rodgers's trademark yodels sound Armstrong's legendary piercing wails. Rodgers' yodel, known for conveying a sense of freedom and possibility, he learned from the black railroad workmen he knew as a child in Meridian, Mississippi. This record makes sense of the claim made by the great blues singer Howlin' Wolf that his moan was patterned after Rodgers's yodel.[15] Given that Wolf's moan, which was more of a growl, is perhaps the apotheosis of the great Mississippi blues tradition of Charlie Patton, Son House, Tommy Johnson, Robert Johnson, and a handful of others, we see how logical the pairing of Armstrong and Rodgers is. Indeed Wolf's remark confirms what "Blue Yodel #9" enacts: Armstrong and Rodgers, jazz and country, shared a common cultural lineage known as the blues.

This record is a crucial cultural crossroads of sorts, and a good starting place for anyone who wants to investigate the fluidity of American cultures, who wants to see where "doing" upsets "being." On the other hand, part of the appeal of the recording is the unexpected coupling of diverse sounds, no matter how common their origin. As country blues singer Robert Johnson suggests, though, a cultural crossroads can as unsettling as it is exhilarating. His song, "Crossroad Blues," relates the fear the singer experiences while standing at a crossroads and hoping to flag down a ride from someone. Instead of being picked up and carried to safety, the singer, with increasing horror, confronts the possibility that he will be left to find his way through the darkness, in unfriendly territory, alone. The singer experiences the idea of cultural crossing as a threat, inescapable, verging on nightmare. Greil Marcus points out that the horror the singer experiences is of being "caught by whites after dark" with no safe way to run (*Mystery* 25). And if the lyrics do not make this reading clear, Johnson's swooping, magical slide guitar runs combined with his ferocious plucking of the strings leave no doubt that doom draws nigh. As wonderful as is the crossroads where Armstrong and Rodgers meet, the fact is that their audiences would most likely interpret "crossroads" in Johnson's sense and not be inclined to meet there. Thus Chet Flippo, in his biography of Hank Williams, notes that the only demand that a country music fan makes of his hero is that the hero remain exactly like the fan. Respect becomes resentment when the hero "quit being just a singing representative of [his] peers and started putting on airs" (qted. in Marsh, *Elvis* 126). As congruent as "Blue Yodel #9" shows the music of Armstrong and Rodgers to be, cultural identification with the recording requires the sort of transgression of boundaries that Flippo's definition excludes. We might argue that this contradiction proves what I claimed in chapter 1, that American culture is more progressive than American social and political institutions, and a proof that in the future such collaborations will not be surprising. A less positive interpretation would be that this contradiction reveals the social discrepancies that go hand-in-hand with our most cherished democratic assumptions.[16]

In this latter context, the term "blues" signifies something more than "doing"; it reflects a way of life that excludes Jimmie Rodgers—he does not have to be worried about being caught at the crossroads. Keeping in mind Robert Johnson's reading of "crossroads," consider Ralph Ellison's justly famous definition of the blues:

> The blues is an impulse to keep the painful details and episodes of a brutal experience alive in one's aching consciousness, to finger its jagged grain, and to transcend it, not by the consolation of philosophy but by squeezing from it a near-tragic, near-comic lyricism. As a form, the blues is an autobiographical chronicle of a personal catastrophe expressed lyrically. (*Shadow* 78–79)

In his essays and interviews, Ellison has emphasized that the blues is a technique, and as such is available to anyone who can master its formal demands. Moreover, as an art form, the blues can express any human emotion, ranging from despair to happiness, and it is a mistake to see it only in terms of the unhappiness its name suggests. In Ellison's old-fashioned humanistic sense, the blues is universal. Nevertheless, in its characterization of the blues as keeping "the painful details and episodes of a brutal experience alive," Ellison's definition is clearly rooted in the same cultural context which produced Robert Johnson's "Crossroad Blues." As a form of cultural memory, the blues is rooted in a particular experience of shared oppression. As an art form the blues may transcend this oppression, but the audience for which the blues is originally performed and who in a certain sense have created the blues for their own enjoyment will necessarily be suspicious of anyone who masters that form without having shared the experience that created it.

Given that cultural forms in America such as the blues have found their form, expression, and audience in the context of racial inequality, the notion of crossing over, as Elvis Presley did in 1954, will remain a problematic one in discussions of American culture.[17] Nelson George's study, *The Death of Rhythm and Blues* (1988), helps explain why crossing over is not necessarily met with enthusiasm. George connects it with the death of a cultural tradition: "Unhappily, while the drive behind the movement for social change was the greatest inspiration for [rhythm and blues], the very success of the movement spelled the end of the R&B world" (xii). George explores the ways in which record executives, black and white, worked to make African American music cross over, to the detriment of the quality of African American music. George argues that by the 1980s crossover was accomplished (Michael Jackson is an example), and the result has been a fatal watering-down of African American culture.[18] Though acknowledging that "the interactions between blacks and mainstream culture are too intimate for a separatist philosophy to work in the United States," George, somewhat histrionically, finds the African American's "assimilationist obsession" to have been an act of "cultural suicide" (199–200). In the end, George's study laments the loss of segregation less than the loss of the style that the sense of African American cultural unity created. Crossing over for George is painful because it means the loss of an African American identity; it means the loss of history and self.

American popular culture is a realm in which the conflicts resulting from our Edenic democratic promises are acted out. In asserting that "a Black man taught [Elvis] how to sing," Living Colour wishes to rehistoricize how we understand African American music and culture. By repeating the line "Elvis is dead" (I count forty-four times), the song both plays out a drama of burying Elvis and acknowledges how Elvis's cultural remains resist burial. Though the song toys with the possibility of laying claim once and for all to the musical and cultural heritage that Elvis Presley is perceived to have usurped, the story it tells is too tangled to achieve this end. Calling on the voices of Little Richard and James Brown to help tell their story is of course a possible way to authenticate Living Colour's claim. Little Richard raps about the vultures who pick over Elvis's cultural body, James Brown appears via Corey Glover's own impersonation—he sings Brown's favorite declamation, "Hit me," over and over for rhetorical emphasis—and Maceo Parker performs a dead-on-the-one sax solo that is a perfect imitation of the ones he used to perform for Brown.[19] Thematically, Brown's presence makes sense since Glover's appropriation of the "Godfather of Soul" serves to legitimate Living Colour's claim for an authentic African American identity that contrasts with what they depict as the usurpations of Elvis. In Living Colour's theater of American music, James Brown comes on as a heroic figure capable of rescuing black identity from the kinds of incursions depicted by Nelson George and, in the eyes of many, exemplified by Elvis Presley.

As his stage shows emphasized Brown is a man who should need no introduction, and his music has never been confused with any aspect of Caucasian culture. Rapper Africa Bambaata captures his cultural cachet: "James helped to show us he was black. Then people wanted to get away from blackness. Today they still arguing over whether this is Negro color, black American, African-American—all that stuff. Well, before anything else, you was BLACK" (qted. in Rose 148).

In his prime, Brown represented the African American transcendent. He arranged his own tours, produced his own music, owned the rights to his songs as well as several radio stations and even an airplane, and by most accounts, he owned his band as well. Nelson George characterizes Brown "as a businessman with a long and lucrative career based on astute self-management, . . . a sterling example, and advocate, of black self-sufficiency" (*Death* 104). "Open the door, I'll get it myself," he sang in one of his greatest songs. Even Brown's recent bouts with the law have reinforced his image of the bad black man who will not compromise his identity to please white expectations; his 1989 arrest under uncertain circumstances was likely a case of a black man's being caught at the crossroads after the sun had gone down.[20] Confirming his defiance, Brown remarked of his imprisonment, "If America can stand to have James Brown in prison, James Brown can stand it" (xxviii).

Complicating the image of James Brown as the embodiment of an uncompromised black self, though, is the image of James Brown, long-time friend to Elvis Presley. The phrase "Elvis is dead" has a completely different meaning to Brown than to Living Colour, since it is unlikely that they know of what we might call the secret friendship between Elvis and James Brown. It is said by those who are close to Brown that there were only two times that he broke down emotionally. The first was at the funeral of his son, Teddy. The second was when Elvis died.

> There was one time, Fred Daviss remembers, when the Godfather nearly lost his cool, and that was over the open casket of his friend of twenty years, Elvis Presley. The night after Elvis died, James char-

tered a jet and flew to Memphis, where a special unmarked police car sped him through the hysterical crush to Graceland, Presley's mansion. Eyes filled, he stood staring down at the bloated face, stroking the King's arm.

"Elvis," Daviss heard him say, "how could you let it happen? How could you let it go?" (Hirshey 248)

To my knowledge neither Brown nor Elvis ever recorded a song of one another's. Still, it is clear that their friendship came from something more than the fact that both were famous musicians and cultural icons. Each was born dirt-poor in the South. As a child Brown was more than once sent home for "insufficient clothes" (Brown, 45); Elvis's family struggled for respectability and had to overcome, among other things, the stigma of his father's being sent to prison for forgery. Coming from humble beginnings, neither surrendered his sense of the place that had shaped him. Elvis wore and was made to wear his improbable success in the flash of glitter on his wide sequined sleeves and was championed for rising above the very circumstances he would not let anyone forget. On the other hand, Elvis's southern heritage became stultifying. Of Elvis's long run of fame, and the solitude it enforced, Brown tersely remarks, "The way they had him livin', they never turned on no air condition.' Took away all that good air. You get sick from that" (Hirshey 57).

Perhaps for this reason Brown has periodically been grateful to deny his fame and fortune, as if to avoid Elvis's fate. Thus Brown proudly tells Gerri Hirshey of a "100 degree day in 1977" on his South Carolina ranch when he walked outside to see his father on his knees pulling up clumps of chickweed. "Daddy, what you doin' there?" Brown asks. "I'm diggin' this grass up," Browns father answers, "'cause we ain't able to hire nobody." Hirshey writes, "James dropped to his knees alongside his father [and] worked until the sweat came. . . . He says it was handling the dirt that made him feel clean—baptized" (269). If Brown recognized Elvis as a peer in his own ambition and drive to escape his humble beginnings, he also saw in Elvis the cost of straying from those beginnings. By this view, Brown would recognize Elvis's crossing of cultures as a potentially dangerous act—not just for the audience but for the one doing the crossing. In a sense, Brown sees Elvis as African American because it was his refusal to abide by others' definitions of him that brought about his downfall. Discussing the case of Elvis with Hirshey, Brown remarked, "Look how they done him," as if to say that Elvis's refusal to hide his vitality necessarily brought him down (287).[21]

Their secret friendship was also reflected in their politics and, in particular, their mutual admiration for Richard Nixon. To a certain extent, their politics conflicted with the cultural upheaval each seemed to represent. Elvis's affiliation with Nixon makes it easier for some to associate him with the element of the Republican party that is aggressively uninterested in squaring a history that has tried to deny African Americans full citizenship and Brown's relationship with Nixon might be seen to undercut his perceived African American militancy. Presley contacted Nixon in 1972 to offer his help in the government's never-ending war on drugs. Nixon apparently was cool to the offer until his staff informed him that rejecting Elvis out of hand might upset millions of voters. Nixon relented and made Elvis an unofficial law enforcement agent, and their meeting was memorialized with the now legendary picture of Nixon and an obviously stoned Presley shaking hands. The image becomes part of the cultural record that is Elvis Presley and, in effect, blots out the less famous but perhaps more revealing pictures of Elvis at home with the black rhythm-and-blues singer Bobby Blue Bland, B. B. King, Junior Parker, and Jackie Wilson. Brown's admiration for Nixon, of a slightly different order, shows how Brown the musician contrasted with Brown the cultural figure. Wishing to live up to his moniker as "the hardest workingman in show business," Brown understood his success in twentieth-century Republican terms: he had pulled himself up by his own bootstraps. Thus, he enjoined others to work hard and do the same: "I don't want nobody to give me nothin' / Open the door, I'll get it myself," he sang over and over in one of his greatest songs.

If Elvis was always very careful to avoid commenting on the youth culture of the sixties and in particular Vietnam, Brown's politics do not sound out of place on the same op-ed page with George Will or William F. Buckley. Hearing Brown's music through his political commentary one might think of him as a kind of latter-day Booker T. Washington preaching black self-sufficiency over the risks of relying too much on the favor of white people. Brown's endorsement of Nixon—after switching over from Hubert Humphrey in 1972—confirms this reading. Brown explains with Benjamin Franklin–like shrewdness:

> I could see that Mr. Nixon was going to win in a landslide. Everybody could. A situation like that puts somebody's who's sort of a spokesman in a dilemma: You can either try to get inside and have some influence, or you can stay outside and be pure and powerless. Either way you're going to get criticized, especially if you're a black spokesman. (229)

From a perspective in which blackness is seen to be antithetical to established political authority, Brown's response to the choice that Nixon represented might trouble those who identify him with a "pure" blackness. Yet, as his own different use of the term "pure" suggests, Brown recognizes that in America the meanings of cultural gestures and political gestures do not always coincide. This discrepancy is what makes figures such as Brown and Elvis so confusing. Without such an understanding Brown probably would not have acted as he did in 1968 on the night of Martin Luther King Jr.'s assassination. At the request of Boston mayor Kevin White, Brown, then the biggest draw in rhythm and blues, played a free concert on WGBH, the local public television station, to encourage people to stay off the street and not riot. And as Brown proudly points out, Boston was the least afflicted of the Eastern seaboard cities (188). Brown's friend and critic Cliff White tells a different story of Brown's political astuteness. According to White, Brown's landmark single, "Say It Loud— I'm Black and I'm Proud," one of the capstones to the Civil Rights movement, was written as a "direct result of James being threatened by submachine toting Black Panthers."[22] Brown well knew that the politics of race cuts both ways.

Brown was made uncomfortable by the notion that his music could be turned into a specific cultural or political argument. Although he is always willing to assert his identity as a black man, he is less willing to see his music as being specifically black—even if Michaels says the "doing" of Brown's music must be described as *African* American. "It's a funny thing about me and African music," Brown reveals. "I didn't even know it existed. My roots may be imbedded in me and I don't know it, but when I went to Africa I didn't recognize anything that I had gotten from there" (221). Brown's lack of interest in his African roots reveals his commitment to his work as an expression of his own American perspective—which may help to explain why he distances himself from the blues as well. He sees the blues as outdated, something to be overcome. The blues is his father's music. "I still don't like the blues," he says at the outset of his own story (6). Brown's understanding of himself as an artist requires him to see his art moving beyond that of his predecessors. Interestingly, he applies a similar logic to Elvis's debt to the blues. Brown remarks that if Elvis began by copying blues singers, he advanced to the point where "they didn't have enough fire for him." Brown continues: "Elvis was great. People said he was still copying, but he found his own style. He was a hillbilly who learned to play the blues" (165–66). Brown reverses the conventional view of their musical heritage; Elvis, not Brown, derives from blues roots.

Judging by their work, though, one would not say that Brown and Elvis are obviously similar in their achieved forms of musical expression. When Elvis was singing Frank Sinatra's "My Way," James Brown was dropping funk bombs such as "Hot Pants." James Brown completely reinvented rhythm and blues into funk and paved the way to rap. Elvis reinvented the blues and hillbilly music, transforming virtually every genre of American vernacular music except jazz. In terms of influence on audience and other performers, Brown and Elvis are the giants of the second half of the twentieth century in American popular music. Despite their obvious differences, the fact is that they both came out of the tradition of rhythm and blues.[23] Each began his career singing a kind of rhythm and blues associated with the Drifters or the Five Royales or Hank Ballard and the Midnighters. In the 1950s it was Brown, not Elvis, who came across as the Little Richard imitator.[24] Elvis never stopped performing the songs of Clyde McPhatter and Little Willie John, and Brown produced recordings by Hank Ballard twenty years after Ballard's prime. Elvis certainly was aware of their common musical origins. According to Brown, when Brown was at his peak in the 1960s and Elvis was at his nadir, Elvis wanted to employ Brown's band to back him on a album with Brown producing. Though this possibility boggles the mind (imagine Elvis doing "Sex Machine"), it does reflect that these two performers, so different and yet so similar, met at the intersection of doing and being. Certainly Brown views Elvis as his peer, and insists that others see them as peers too.

I bring Brown into the discussion not to make the disingenuous argument that Elvis did not steal black culture because James Brown, a black man who claims to be Elvis's friend, says so. Rather, a fully historicized understanding of the friendship between Elvis and James Brown suggests an affinity between them that further complicates the sorts of stereotypes that Living Colour plays with. Indeed, even imagining a scenario by which a pure African American musical heritage could be recuperated through any single act or recording is impossible. Of course there are scores of instances of whites exploiting the musical talent of blacks to make money—though this history does not obviously include Living Colour. James Brown is a case in point. Harassed by the law from the beginning—for the first few years of his career James Brown was on parole for a fairly harmless stolen car conviction and was required to report back to his parole officer before *every* show—Brown nonetheless seized control of every aspect of his career. The question, though, is not solely who cashed whose check—how easy these questions would be if money were all that mattered. Saying that a black man taught Elvis to sing and then they crowned him king is a potentially subversive act since it defines the source of Elvis's power as African American at the same time that it jeopardizes the categories by which we know something or someone is African American.

As hattie gosset's moving essay "billie lives! billie lives!" suggests, this latter possibility is threatening because it may challenge what is for many the authority of black music. Would the form of the blues exist without slavery? How would African American identity be defined outside of the racism it fights? gosset raises these kinds of questions by transforming Billie Holiday's version of "Gloomy Sunday" into a pop drama of racial revenge and redemption. gosset portrays intense identification a marginalized person may conceive for one who represents her status as cultural outsider, an identification so strong that gosset cannot imagine that this relationship might be appropriated by someone or something outside, as Living Colour imagines Elvis to have done. gosset's story hinges on the bitterness which she presumes Holiday to have felt because others, particularly white men, chose her songs for her and tried to use her to express their vision of the tragic mulatto woman.[25] For gosset, "Gloomy Sunday" accords perfectly with this image as her white producers—she calls them "bigtime daddies"—project through Holiday the figure of the tortured black artist suffering for the sins of her racist white audience. The song's lyrics dramatize such a stereotype with its evocation of a woman happy to commit suicide among gloomy Sunday shadows she will be glad to leave.

gosset protests white constructions of black identity by derisively labeling "Gloomy Sunday" one of those "funereally [sic] dirge numbers (tragic mulatress division) that [the bigtime daddies] used to mash on billie" (110). Instead of these bigtime daddies being tearfully moved by the spectacle of an oppressed woman whom they had helped to oppress, gosset imagines a Holiday who creates an identity distinctively other than the bigtime daddies' construction of her, an identity that is distinctively hers. Holiday's ironic interpretation "had those bigtime daddies jumping outta windows and otherwise offing theyselves that time" (109). The crucial turn of the story is that "Gloomy Sunday" was not a blues, but "some of their shit and billie said okay watch this and she took the tune and turned it around on them" (110). Holiday's interpretation revenges itself on a white culture that has both marginalized and profited from black culture, and reaffirms the value of a distinctively black culture in spite of its marginalization. Though we cannot overlook the feminist way in which gosset's Holiday upsets the expectations of those bigtime daddies, for our purposes we need only observe that she signifies upon "Gloomy Sunday" to reclaim Holiday's African American language and identity.[26] There is a further irony, however. Though gosset's essay redresses a cultural wrong, or theft, and suggests that "we have other ways [of subversion] now," the fact that the story has to be told forty years later indicates that African American culture continues to see itself as the product and celebration of its alleged marginalized status. The essay requires an either/or logic: instead of Billie Holiday in effect killing herself through the abusive life-style which the misunderstanding of others forced upon her, her art forces the white male establishment to kill itself in recognition of its own moral horror.

On the other hand, regardless of how we draw the lines of the power relationships, as an artifact Holiday's "Gloomy Sunday" is a culturally mixed product. Nearly all of her marvelous catalogue is the product of collaboration with whites. John Hammond, who may be the prototype of gosset's bigtime daddy, was responsible for making sure that Holiday was paired with the best jazz musicians of the era during her stint at Columbia. Like Alan Lomax, Hammond spent his life trying to make sure that the music invented by African Americans, blues and jazz, received the appreciation it deserved. Hammond, moreover, wanted white Americans not only to applaud the music; he wanted it to change their conception of who they were as Americans. Like any benefactors, both Hammond and Lomax could be patronizing, and at times insisted upon their own definitions of authentic blues or jazz.

What distinguishes Elvis from Hammond and Lomax, by contrast, is that he heard African American music not just as a critical listener but as a performer. Elvis was not limited by commitment to some prior definition of musical or cultural authenticity, and thus he was freer to experiment with the cultural possibilities that Hammond and Lomax recognized.[27] For gosset, however, the pattern of her parable is black shaping white shaping black to become, triumphantly, black; still, this triumphant end is also the product of cultural interaction and, really, confusion. Perhaps the true dream of gosset's essay and Public Enemy's "Fight the Power" is an American culture separate but equal, where neither black culture nor white culture appropriates the other but both remain effectively closed off from one another. The fact that Holiday's bigtime daddies are *moved* to jump and therefore capable of transformation matters less than the fact that they are now controlled by what they tried to control. In this context, one might conclude that the friendship between James Brown and Elvis has never become a part of the public discourse about either figure because it challenges the fear that there is a context in which blacks and whites can be truly equal.

As Living Colour recognizes, even black hip-hop artists depend more on a white audience than Billie Holiday did precisely because of the multicultural Pandora's box that Elvis helped to open. Consequently, it has become much harder to communicate the kind of coded cultural messages which gosset's essay, however appealingly, transmits. As Elvis knew, so-called black and so-called white culture are the perpetual productions of their own veiled interaction. Ralph Ellison has remarked that "most American whites are culturally part Negro American without even realizing it" (*Going* 108). Miles Davis, though a bitter critic of white intrusions upon what he sees as the black art form jazz, acknowledges that his unique trumpet phrasing was influenced by Frank Sinatra and Orson Welles! (*Miles* 70).[28] W. E. B. Du Bois famously captured this contradiction of identities with his notion of "double consciousness," which he defined as at once the curse and the gift of the African American who has the "sense of always looking at one's self through the eyes of others" and "ever feels his two-ness—an American, a Negro" (*Souls* 8). Living Colour's "Elvis Is Dead" expresses this "double consciousness" in the sense that the group's identity is inextricably mixed with a version of African American culture as it has been shaped through Elvis.

If Du Bois sought reconciliation between these two warring ideals of being American and black, I see Living Colour seeking to understand its position in a culture in which double consciousness may be common to all Americans. By this view, the assertion that "Elvis is dead" can be read as an admonishment to put away the sterile definitions of race and culture that collided in his name, a recognition that we all live in a post-Elvis America where questions of cultural authenticity and racial purity should no longer matter. I say "post-Elvis" even though Elvis found the meaning of his art in the fluidity of American culture and the slipperiness of his own American identity. His life cast light on the form that this fluidity was already taking; his death made our blindness to his meaning no longer tenable. In this respect, Elvis's most fanatical fans are right. He died for our (cultural) sins, and his shade haunts us because we cannot escape his wisdom. Without Elvis, a black rock-and-roll band such as Living Colour, for better or worse, would not have been possible. Like the protagonist of Delmore Schwartz's "In Dreams Begin Responsibilities," who recognizes his origin in the meeting of his parents on the movie screen he is daydreaming,

Living Colour stares at another never-distant screen where Elvis can be found performing his magic, watching him in disbelief, transfixed, crying out with joy and terror at the recognition of their eventual—and inescapable—birth.

## III

Try as we might, there is no turning back from the cultural confusion Elvis Presley's appearance has generated. Living Colour can no less return to some mythical "pure" African American past than the cultural critic Alan Bloom could return to a world where every citizen reads only the "Great Books" of Western civilization. The difficulty with this sort of cultural nostalgia—be it Bloom's or Public Enemy's—is that by asking us to ignore the phenomenon of Elvis Presley, it asks us to conceive of culture as a static entity. Even if we are careful to acknowledge the pervasive influence that race has in our definitions of American culture, ultimately doing takes precedence over being. Rather than defining our culture in terms of "people we happen to be," perhaps we can think in terms of "people democracy hopes to make possible." Figures such as Elvis Presley and James Brown suggest that if we cannot write away the instances of racist exploitation in our history, we can embrace cultural practices—as opposed to mere laws—that have worked to resist racist paradigms.

Any number of his recordings can be adduced to see how Elvis challenged the paradigms of racial thinking in American culture, but a recent posthumous release helps to clarify the issues I have been examining—and it lets Elvis speak for himself. *The Million Dollar Sessions* (1990), released more than ten years after Elvis's death, contains not only his most sustained commentary on the cultural confusion he generated as a performer, but shows how he worked out his attitudes *through performance*. The music included on this release was never meant to be heard, though portions of it had been bootlegged for years. Before we convict Elvis of stealing the blues, then, we need to listen to his own account. If we attend carefully to Elvis's testimony, we can hear another version, one that reminds us that with any "theft" the issues of circumstance and alibi mean everything.

Elvis's testimony occurs on December 4, 1956, when he had returned as budding star to his old haunt, Sun Studios in Memphis, where he recorded before signing with RCA the previous year. The famous question asked by Dewey Phillips, the first DJ to play Elvis on the radio, had by now exploded into a national sensation.[29] Elvis was there as the guest of Carl Perkins, who was still recording for the tiny label. He and Perkins's Sun label mates, Jerry Lee Lewis and Johnny Cash—essential figures in the so-called birth of so-called rock and roll—sing informally, mostly gospel songs, some old-time country and bluegrass, and a handful of current hits, ranging from Pat Boone ("junk," Elvis calls "Don't Forbid Me") to Chuck Berry. Singing with Lewis and Perkins (Cash had left by the time the recorder was turned on), far from the demands of stardom and national scrutiny, Elvis is naturally himself. The songs move quickly and rarely is one completed, as each singer is anxious to recall a particular favorite to share with the others. The session is spontaneous. At one point a member of the impromptu audience, apparently friends and acquaintances of the singers, asks "if this Rover Boy trio can sing 'Farther Along,'" a gospel song frequently recorded by both black and white artists. The performers acquiesce with Jerry Lee Lewis shouting out "Soul Stirrers," the black gospel group who had recently released a version of the song. The young men and the handful of listeners sound joyful; the bonds of a shared community are distinctively evident. The feel is of a gospel jubilee; the listener is aware that he is eavesdropping.

In the middle of this jam session, Elvis recounts for his audience a curious incident from his recent trip to Las Vegas. To the wonder of his peers, Elvis tells of seeing Billy Ward's Dominoes, a seminal African American rhythm-and-blues group. Elvis probably went to that show hoping to see one of his heroes, Clyde McPhatter, whose songs Elvis had covered. Indeed, in McPhatter Elvis must have recognized that blend of gospel and blues that Elvis himself identified as being "basically" rock-and-roll music during his 1968 television special.[30] McPhatter had left the group shortly before Elvis's stint in Las Vegas, though; thus Elvis had to settle for McPhatter's replacement, an unbilled Jackie Wilson. Wilson had just joined the group, so Elvis was witnessing one of his first public performances with the Dominoes. Instead of seeing a prior version of himself in McPhatter, an astonished Elvis confronted what might be called his destiny as Jackie Wilson did a takeoff on him.

Speaking with an awe that has not faded away, Elvis describes watching Wilson imitate himself, Elvis, singing "'Hound Dog,' 'Don't Be Cruel,' and a couple of others." After dismissing Wilson's first attempts, Elvis relates that Wilson got the better of him with "Don't Be Cruel": "He tried so hard until he got much better, boy, much better than that version of mine. That boy hit it. Man, he was cutting me all over the place. I was under the table when he got through singing. I went back four straight times to hear him sing that song." Interspersed in Elvis's story is his impersonation—and explication—of Jackie Wilson impersonating (and cutting) Elvis, or Elvis Presley impersonating and cutting himself. (It is axiomatic that from the very beginning Elvis was the best Elvis impersonator.) Elvis, like Wilson learning Elvis on stage before his very eyes, tries to match Wilson matching Elvis. In the impersonation of an impersonation, Elvis sings "Don't Be Cruel" in a way almost unrecognizable when compared to the hit version. Elvis, while imitating Wilson's dance steps, which one assumes were partially predicated on Elvis's own steps, which in turn were learned by going to the all-night rhythm-and-blues "cutting contests" on Beale St. in Memphis, tries again and again to match Wilson, or more precisely, to understand what he has wrought and what has been wrought in him. What remains unclear, despite Elvis's description of his reaction in Las Vegas, is whether he considers himself to have been "beaten" by Wilson; certainly, he does not see Wilson's initial impersonations as a threat, and does not seem threatened by the "other" Elvis that Wilson improvises. As a participant in a culture in which he obviously considers himself a member, Elvis is interested only in what Wilson performs, just as Wilson seems to have been intrigued by what Elvis has performed. Ultimately, Elvis experiences a supremely American moment: standing amazed before the spectacle of his own self-transformation.

Elvis becomes obsessed with this self-transformation, obsessively retracing its mysterious contours. He turns futilely to his audience for clarification and confirmation. As if to find a coherent frame for a story which belies coherence, Elvis presents his impersonation by and of a "colored boy" who is also a "Yankee." Elvis speaks the words "colored boy" softly and quickly, perhaps because he seems to be saying it for the benefit of his audience, to make them fully understand what he saw occurring in Wilson's performance. If so, this moment reflects Elvis's awareness that cultural boundaries are being transgressed. That Elvis identifies Wilson as a Yankee more clearly and effectively establishes Wilson as an outsider to the scene in which Elvis is currently performing than identifying him as colored does. By engaging so intimately with the "other," an "other" that was already latent in the variety of songs being sung, Elvis, more than his companions, realizes the extent to which his art is transforming how others perceive the creation of American culture.[31] Elvis's subsequent career became, in a sense, the playing out of this moment. What he dramatized to his friends he would also try to convey in his art to that vast out there, America. After Elvis had observed that Wilson had "cut" him, someone, probably Perkins, said "that'll never happen." But Elvis ignores this comment, not really interested in who is better. The mystery of the encounter, the odd spontaneity of the competing impersonations, the confusion of identity, pursues Elvis. Elvis knows, even if his companions do not, that their community has been altered as well. To put the matter too strongly, they have been African-Americanized, too strongly because these white country boys were, in Carl Perkins's phrase, boppin' the blues before Elvis ever went to Las Vegas.

When later in the session Carl Perkins asks Elvis to sing "Paralyzed," a song Elvis had just recorded for RCA, Elvis initially puts him off, relentless in his exploration of the encounter with Wilson. At last he accedes, but only after wondering if he shouldn't rerecord "Paralyzed" in the same manner that Wilson reinterpreted "Don't Be Cruel." As an instance of cultural symbolism, Elvis's question is asked even to this day, though Elvis spent his life answering it. One may want to suggest that Elvis would not have been Elvis without Jackie Wilson, but such a reading would misunderstand what is going on in this collaboration. On Elvis's first recordings he performed, among others, songs associated with blues singers (Arthur Crudup and Roy Brown), pop singers (Dean Martin), and western singers (Gene Autry and Slim Whitman); on his last recordings he performed, among others, songs associated with rhythm-and-blues singer Johnny Ace and country master George Jones. Elvis's approach to his art never wavered: it came out of his daring involvement with traditions thought to be separate from one another. To answer the question Elvis asked Perkins, one has to hear all of Elvis's influences, pin down where one stopped and the other began. Not everyone of course could match Elvis in the way that Wilson did—Frank Sinatra knew enough not to trade styles with Elvis in their only joint appearance together.[32] How excited Elvis must have been that evening to see that his style had inspired someone who also knew some—though certainly not all—of Elvis's sources to answer back. In this encounter, one imagines Elvis influencing Wilson, who in turn influences Elvis. By contrast, when Elvis and Sinatra performed versions of each other's songs (Sinatra did "Love Me Tender" and Elvis did "Witchcraft") on Sinatra's television show in 1960, there was none of the explosive synergy one hears here with Perkins et al. Even though each performer had learned from the blues, Elvis and Sinatra did not overlap except as pop-culture stars. Sinatra had adapted the vocal techniques of Louis

Armstrong and Billie Holiday, but his style did not seem to come directly out of African American culture.

Elvis, obviously, is a different story. A casual listing of Elvis's influences may make one think that he is merely a dilettante. His collaboration with Jackie Wilson, though, proves how misleading this characterization of Elvis is. What Elvis was doing with Jackie Wilson was not such an extraordinary occurrence since it reflected his usual approach to making music. Elvis never sought to imitate a song so much as to make it over in his own image. Remember, Elvis was a singer who wanted to sound not only like Roy Brown or Wynonie Harris, but like Dean Martin, Mario Lanza, Bill Monroe, and perhaps most of all, Jake Hess.[33] Certainly, his thirty-eight-second fragment of Monroe's "Little Cabin Home on the Hill" on the Sun jam session proves how well Elvis could distort his voice to make it sound like his influences. A wonderful impersonation of Monroe, it sounds nothing like Elvis. The truer gauge of Elvis's relationship with Monroe is his 1954–55 version of Monroe's "Blue Moon of Kentucky" (*Complete Sun Sessions*). In Elvis's hands, a mournful, disconsolate song of love lost becomes an exuberant boast brimming with confidence and possibility. One could say that perhaps Elvis did not understand the original (as Alice Walker said he did not understand "Hound Dog"), but I would suggest that Elvis's confidence has less to do with the words he is singing than with what he is doing with Monroe's song. Elvis knows that he is "goosing up" Monroe, just as he would later say he had goosed up the blues.[34] Certainly, Bill Monroe recognized Elvis's inventiveness. Known for being jealous of his rivals and protective of his own musical purity, Monroe nonetheless paid tribute to Elvis by altering his version of "Blue Moon of Kentucky" and performing it at Elvis's accelerated tempo for the rest of his career.

Elvis's method for choosing which songs to record further shows that he was a maker and not an imitator. Indeed, the version of "Don't Be Cruel" that Jackie Wilson first heard was itself already the product of an elaborate reworking process. Hopkins and Guralnick both document the fact that when Elvis chose to record a song for a given album, he began by listening to the demo of that song, usually sung by the songwriter. Often, but not always, Elvis used the demo version as a starting point for his own version, whether the model was Eddy Arnold or Little Richard or an anonymous songwriter. Generally, Elvis would try to match the feel of the original—even if no one else would hear it—before creating his own version. In the case of "Don't Be Cruel," the anonymous songwriter and demo singer was an African American man named Otis Blackwell, one of the great "unknown" writers of early rhythm-and-blues songs, who composed "Fever" for Little Willie John and Peggy Lee and "Great Balls of Fire" and "Breathless" for Jerry Lee Lewis. Beginning with Blackwell's demo, Elvis reworked the song first on his guitar and then sketched out an arrangement on piano. According to Guralnick, Elvis's lead guitar player, Scotty Moore, "tried out a couple of openings," but "Elvis suggested that he leave a little more space" (*Last* 300). He also instructed the drummer, D. J. Fontana, to slow the tempo down. Once the backup vocal group, the Jordanaires, had worked out their arrangement, the nominal producer, Steve Scholes, was ready to cut the record. But Elvis was the one truly in charge and he did not declare the song finished until they had run through several recorded takes. The end result, as Guralnick points out, sounds casual, almost offhand, but the history of the session shows how hard Elvis had to work to achieve that sound. As with his collaboration with Jackie Wilson, Elvis was still not finished with the song.

The other side to the "Don't Be Cruel" story begins with another collaboration—the phantom one between Elvis and Otis Blackwell. Though listed with Blackwell as a cowriter of the song, Elvis did not write "Don't Be Cruel" in any traditional sense related to copyright. In order to get Elvis to record the song, Blackwell admitted that he "was told I had to make a deal" (Guralnick, *Last* 299). The deal he made with Elvis was the same one that all songwriters had to make in order to have Elvis record their songs. Hill and Range, a song publishing company, had through Colonel Tom Parker worked out a contract whereby any songwriter who wanted to have a song recorded by Elvis was required to surrender one-third royalty, which went straight to Hill and Range. This 33 percent was then split between Elvis and the songwriter. The performance royalties, Peter Guralnick explains, "were calculated on the basis of live performance and jukebox and air play were not affected." Elvis himself was upset that his name would appear on the songs since, as he told anyone who asked, "I've never written a song in my life . . . it's all a big hoax" (387). The advantage for Elvis and his manager to this arrangement was that they could circumvent RCA and receive royalties that ordinarily would have gone to the record company. The shadiness of the arrangement should not obscure the fact that songwriters were going to make more money this way than without the arrangement and without Elvis singing their songs.[35] This side of the "Don't Be Cruel" story returns us to the question of what happens to the tradition of the blues when memory can be turned into money.

In 1986 Otis Blackwell appeared on *Late Night with David Letterman* to sing his version of "Don't Be Cruel."[36] After some prodding from Letterman, Otis admits that Elvis "took" "Don't Be Cruel" from him. How Blackwell truly feels is unclear since he is playing the role scripted for him: an authentic black performer. Letterman's hook is that after thirty years of anonymity we finally get to hear the "real" singer, the singer to whom the song "belongs." What is striking about Blackwell's performance, who after all was a writer rather than a performer, is how little resemblance his version bears to Elvis's "Jackie Wilson" version. Blackwell's version of his "own" song strikes one as a competent but unequal impersonation of Elvis. The real point, though, is that regardless of whose version is "better," there is no longer an origin to the song that Blackwell performs. He and Elvis are members of the same rhythm-and-blues community, in the same way that Wilson and Elvis are.

Despite charges that Elvis merely mimicked, say, Otis Blackwell, his way of creating is similar to Muddy Waters's adaptation of Son House. Elvis is taking already existing words and tune and making them into an expression of his own personal situation. Unlike Waters, however, Elvis does not claim to have written the song. If Waters had been familiar with copyright laws and known that House was too, he might have answered differently. Whereas Waters was creating out of a folk tradition in which everyone understood the rules of creation, Elvis was creating for outsiders who did not understand his work, but appreciated that it made money. His desire to expose the hoax of record labels that identified him as the songwriter reflects his desire to make sure that everyone did receive proper credit—Elvis's way of saying, yes, Son House did this before me. Though Elvis was always confident when performing and knew in his own mind that he was exploiting no one in his music, he did not know how to interpret his work to an outside audience who did not share his understanding of what he did. In a way, Elvis constituted his own tradition. Granting that whites and blacks had been exchanging musical styles since before the Civil War, Elvis was the first to present himself and be perceived by his audience in terms of that cultural exchange. Consequently, he had neither the confidence that creating before one's folk audience brings nor the intellectual perspective to justify his art on the basis of its ability to transform received material. Had Elvis seen his own work as most see the work of John Coltrane or Sonny Rollins when they remake a Rodgers and Hammerstein standard, he would not have had a problem justifying the songs he "coauthored" as being his creations. Rollins's version of "All the Things You Are" definitely belongs to Sonny Rollins, though he shares the royalties with Jerome Kern and Oscar Hammerstein (and whoever else is in on the deal).[37] Likewise, Elvis's transformations of already existing songs are extensions of Big Bill Broonzy's understanding of what constitutes blues writing. Just as Broonzy said that "you can't put down the music in the blues on no paper," neither can we understand Elvis if we think of his creations as things that can be written down.

The moment Presley shared with Wilson might be understood in terms of Ellison's definition of a jazz moment that we first encountered in chapter 3:

> Each true jazz moment (as distinct from the uninspired commercial performance) springs from a contest in which each artist challenges all the rest; each solo flight or improvisation represents (like the successive canvasses of a painter) a definition of his identity: as individual, as member of the collectivity and a link in the chain of tradition. Thus, because jazz finds its very life in an endless improvisation upon traditional materials, the jazzman must lose his identity even as he finds it. (*Shadow* 234)

The mutual signifying that Elvis and Jackie Wilson perform upon each other creates a shared culture, even if one is singing in Vegas and the other is in Memphis. Of course we do not know what Wilson's intentions were in imitating Elvis, just as we do not have a record of those performances. Perhaps Wilson knew that Elvis was attending the show, and saw it as an opportunity to knock him down a peg. Perhaps Wilson's performance was parody. Perhaps it was a sincere attempt to put Elvis in his place by showing Elvis how it was really done. Possibilities, but I doubt they tell the story.[38] Given that Elvis and Wilson were both singing rhythm and blues, it is likely that Wilson was having about as much success in Vegas as Elvis was, which was little. (The only real setback Elvis faced before going into the army in 1958 was during his stint in Vegas. The elderly audience preferred the song stylings of Mel Torme to Elvis's controlled anarchy.) If so, then Wilson might have seen Elvis as a peer rather than a usurper. Certainly the fact that Wilson later in life carried two photographs of himself and Elvis everywhere he went—one autographed by Elvis with the inscription "Jackie, you have a friend forever"—suggests that Wilson saw Elvis as an equal and likely even cherished Elvis's admiration of him.

Then again, from Elvis's perspective, it was Wilson's version of "Don't Be Cruel" that made Wilson his peer and caused Elvis to keep up with

Wilson's career even after Wilson's fame had been eclipsed (Guralnick, *Careless* 687). Otherwise, Elvis might have seen this black man *as just another imitator of him*. Besides, even if Elvis's first encounter with Wilson had never taken place, Elvis had already been shaped by the blues. What makes this exchange so tantalizing is that it makes visible the interaction between black and white cultures that culminated in Elvis Presley. Their collaboration blurs not only the line between white and black, but it transforms the tradition of the blues into a history—a form of cultural memory—that can include Elvis Presley. Whereas the usual plotting of American history shows blacks trying to prove how they have acculturated themselves to the American ideal as defined by whites (Frederick Douglass or Martin Luther King Jr.), the example of Elvis Presley shows a white man trying to acculturate himself to a tradition defined and created by African Americans.

This is not to say that Elvis's goal was to pass as black, though it is what many whites feared; they even attributed that power to him. (If Elvis was not white, were they?) At the time of his rise to fame, though, Elvis was not seen as a threat by the black community. Nat D. Williams, a high school teacher who was known as the "unofficial mayor of Beale Street" (the first black disc jockey for the first radio station in America to provide an all-black program format (WDIA in Memphis) and emcee for the Palace Amateur Nights on Beale Street in the early 1950s, describes the impression Elvis made in the African American community.

> Elvis Presley on Beale Street when he first started out was a favorite young man. When they saw him coming out, the audience always gave him as much recognition as they gave any musician—black. He had a way of singing the blues that was distinctive. He could sing'em not necessarily like a Negro, but he didn't sing'em altogether like a typical white musician. He had something in between that made the blues sort of different. . . . Always he had that certain humaneness about him that Negroes like to put in their songs. So when we had a show down there at the Palace, everybody got ready for something good. Yeah. They were crazy about Presley. (qtd. in McKee and Chisenhall 95)

In December 1956 Elvis was coaxed into appearing at the annual fundraiser put on by WDIA for impoverished black children. Though he did not sing that night, Elvis was thrilled to see many of his own heroes perform—Ray Charles, B. B. King, Phineas Newborn Sr. (brother of the aforementioned Calvin), and the local Memphis legend Rufus Thomas. Thomas remembers telling the show's organizers:

> If you put Elvis into the front of the show, the show is over, so they took me at my word and put Elvis on near the end. I took Elvis on stage by the hand, . . . and when I took Elvis out there and he did that wiggle that they wouldn't let him do on television, the crowd just went crazy. They stormed all backstage, beating on the doors and everything. (qtd. in Guralnick, *Last* 369)

These stories reveal both an Elvis comfortable within the African American community of Memphis and an African American community appreciative of his talents. According to Guralnick, a newspaper the next day reported hearing Elvis tell B. B. King "Thanks, man, for the early lessons you gave me." Guralnick adds, "various reports pointed out that Elvis freely acknowledged his debt not only to B. B. King but, implicitly, to black music in general," and *The Memphis World* cited an account of six months earlier that had Elvis "crack[ing] Memphis segregation laws by attending the Fairgrounds Memphis amusement park on East Parkway, during what is designated 'colored night'" (*Last* 369–70).[39] Films that exist from his performance during the 1956 Mississippi State fair in Tupelo show Elvis bringing his segregated audience (blacks were made to sit in the balcony) to its collective feet.

Ultimately, Elvis challenged not only the Memphis segregation laws but the unwritten ones that continue to define how American culture is understood. Elvis did it in Memphis and he did it on Ed Sullivan's show and he did it in every performance he ever gave. His performance of "Don't Be Cruel" on January 6, 1957, on Ed Sullivan's *Toast of the Town* is a case in point, and it completes the circle around the song that he and Jackie Wilson traced together. This was his first appearance on Sullivan's show after his December visit with his old mates; it was also the show on which Ed Sullivan declared Elvis to be "a fine, decent boy" who was "thoroughly all right." Colonel Parker, Elvis's manager, had threatened to remove Elvis from the show if Sullivan did not apologize for telling the press that Elvis's "gyrations" were immoral. Before singing the song, Elvis, with a wry grin, introduces it to the live audience and the television audience with the familiar show-business patter: "I'd like to do our version of one of my biggest records—it goes something like this."[40] Elvis is double-voiced here. His showbiz jive conceals how he is actually playing with the audience, for he then proceeds to perform a version of the song that is nothing like the original version: he does the modified Jackie

Wilson version. Most of the trademark moments he pointed out to Jerry Lee Lewis and Carl Perkins are there. Barely able to contain a laugh, he pronounces the word "tellyphone" as he said Wilson did. Before one of the instrumental breaks, he injects an over-the-top self-conscious moan (again a takeoff on Wilson) that sends the live audience into a frenzy. Then, with a strange intensity, he concludes the song with the big finish he had told Perkins and Lewis he wanted to perform. He does not drop to his knees as he said Wilson did, but instead pivots side to side on his heels, flings his arm back and forth, and nails the song's ending as if he were doing the most serious thing in his career. Perhaps he was—bringing something like the Palace Amateur Night to mainstream America. The gesture and the moment of which it is a part is emblematic of Elvis's career because its meaning is invisible to Elvis's audience, if not to Elvis himself. No one could know what Elvis was doing—except maybe Lewis and Perkins and Wilson, and they were not talking. Ed Sullivan could hardly have suspected that he was giving the stamp of approval not only to Elvis but to the night that Elvis-the-Pelvis made American pass for black without ever knowing it. As for the audience, they go wild, wilder than usual.[41]

## IV

*If I could find a white man with the Negro feel I could make a million dollars.* Why Elvis? Answering this question means acknowledging that white Americans have always been fascinated with black culture—even love black culture—but their racism prevents them from seeing how intertwined are white and black. Part of Elvis's appeal lies in the fact that he was a white boy singing the blues who was perceived as "other" by mainstream America. As we have seen, James Brown identified with Elvis largely because he considered Elvis to have been treated as he himself was—as a black man. Not everyone would make this particular connection, though. Some preferred to see him as extraterrestrial. The southern writer Stanley Booth recalls walking down Beale St. "with two men who had written books about Elvis Presley." Stopping at the window of Lansky Brothers, a men's clothing store, before a picture of Elvis "looking characteristically greasy," one of the writers said 'Like a creature from another planet'" (46).[42] Booth is taken initially aback by the reaction of this "writer from Berkeley," but then realizes that he too would appear to be from another planet if he were to land in Berkeley. The point is that if Elvis was "other" to many, he was not so to southerners.

Yet Elvis was never welcome, even with his success, in well-to-do southern society.[43] Nor, to this day, has he been elected to the Country Music Hall of Fame. This sense of being an outsider without obviously being what Emerson would call a nonconformist is reflected in his initial musical ambitions. Before achieving stardom on his own, Elvis dreamed of being a singer in the all-white Blackwood Brothers or Statesmen quartets. Yet even the pastor of the church Elvis and the Blackwood Brothers attended did not approve of gospel singing for money because "good Christian people didn't seek out that sort of adulation" (Guralnick, *Last* 78). Elvis persevered and auditioned for the Songfellows, a sort of junior version of those groups, but was turned down (*Last* 78). It may well be true that had Elvis passed that audition, he might have never become the Elvis of legendary fame and cultural contradiction and instead remained a gospel singer. He could have settled down to be truly what he often pretended to be: a mama-lovin', authority-respectin', Godfearin' nice country boy next door. His musical identity would have taken shape along the lines of Gene Autry or Bob Wills or the Carter family—legendary white country-and-western performers whose work was impossible without the blues, but whose involvement with the blues did not compromise their identity (or their audience's identity) as white Americans.[44] Without this cultural confusion Elvis would have remained anonymous and no one would have thought anything about him at all. In this light, Ira Louvin, an achingly pure country-and-western singer who, along with brother Charlie, composed half of the legendary Louvin Brothers, tells the other side of the Elvis-stole-black-music story. Upon hearing Elvis practicing some gospel songs between shows, Charlie Louvin summed up the country music establishment's view of him: "Why, you white nigger, if that's your favorite music, why don't you do that out yonder [on stage]? Why do you do that nigger trash out there?"[45]

Elvis's iconic fame conceals an important point: his talent and ambition were what made him special. If all that was required to become "Elvis" were white skin and the willingness to sing music associated with blacks, then Pat Boone or Fabian would have achieved the lasting fame that Elvis represents. The example of Boone is instructive on this point. Boone's recordings of Little Richard and Fats Domino songs can only be described as hilarious—like watching a small child trying to wear the clothes belonging to his or her mother or father. Boone himself was embarrassed both by his immediate success and—one can only hope—his performances. In interviews, Boone freely admitted that he did not know what Little Richard's phrase, "wopmopalubopalopbamboom," meant.[46] The ultimate company man, Boone was merely following orders from record executives trying to cash in on the Elvis craze. Boone was quite happy to suggest that he was singing nonsense and that the kids buying his records made no sense to him at all. Interestingly, when Elvis sang Little Richard's "Tutti Frutti" on the Dorsey Brothers show in February 1956—one of his first national television appearances—he, too, expressed self-consciousness. There he distances himself from the song's lyrics by saying "it really tells a story" when of course the song has no true narrative. Elvis's apprehension, however, reflects not his own failure to understand what he is doing but concern that his audience will not understand it. (I doubt, though, that he was as anxious as W. C. Handy was when trying to pass off an old-hat "old time Southern melody" to a country black audience as blues.) On the Dorsey shows, Elvis is singing to an audience that has virtually no acquaintance with his music. When over six months later he gives an extraordinary performance of Little Richard's "Ready Teddy" on the *Ed Sullivan Show* of September 9, 1956, he betrays none of this anxiety because his intervening success had given him the confidence to think that he could transform his audience's apprehension into an appreciation of what he wants them to hear.[47]

That Elvis must have believed himself to be misunderstood when described as a usurper of black music can be inferred from his private dismissal of Boone. On the same recording session where he performs the Jackie Wilson version of "Don't Be Cruel," he does a funny, vicious parody of Boone. Elvis tells his companions to throw Boone's record out since "it's just junk." He never asked anyone to see him either as an imitator or an innovator. When given the chance, he always paid respect to his mentors—black or white.[48] As the Wilson example suggests, Elvis's performances have nothing in common with Boone since Elvis understood his music to exist within an aesthetic and cultural tradition. Singing Arthur Crudup's "My Baby Left Me" in 1956, Elvis hollers out to his band mates to "play those blues, boys" (*Reconsider Baby*). Although Scotty Moore, Bill Black, and D. J. Fontana will never be confused with Jimmy Rogers, Baby Face Leroy, and Little Walter Jacobs (Muddy Water's great electric blues band), Elvis means what he says. He knows that in some way they are playing the blues. Twelve years later, when John Fogerty yells out the same phrase in Credence Clearwater Revival's version of the song, he is only copying Elvis (*Cosmo's Factory*). Elvis's exhortation, by contrast, conveys his exaltation at making the music he has grown up with. Not only is he realizing his version of the music man that he dreamed of being as a boy, but he is increasing the possibilities of American culture by marking the crossroads where Muddy Waters and W. C. Handy and thousands of others meet.

Sam Phillips's desire to find a white man who could sing like a black man did not merely reflect his dream of becoming rich. (He became rich by investing in a small Memphis hotel chain named after a Bing Crosby movie, Holiday Inn.) I agree with Stanley Booth's revision of Phillips's famous statement: "If Phillips could find a white man who could sing with a *black man's individuality and conviction,* he could make a billion dollars" (49). In other words, Phillips was not looking to exploit black culture so much as wondering if white Americans had the critical ingenuity and cultural flexibility to identify with the creativity and resiliency of black culture. Equating this talent with a billion dollars only suggests the value that Phillips himself attributed to the achievement that is the blues. Seen this way, Phillips is merely offering another version of what W. E. B. Du Bois tried to argue in 1903 when he said that without the song of African Americans, America would not be America. If African Americans had not woven themselves "into the very warp and woof of this nation" (*Souls* 189), Elvis Presley could not exist. Our refusal to recognize Elvis's achievement reflects also our discomfort with accepting the validity of Du Bois's claim that African Americans have remade American culture into a genuine consequence of Jefferson's famous words from the Declaration of Independence.

As for Phillips's famous remark, we should remember that it was Phillips who said he wanted to make a billion dollars, not Elvis. Elvis understood his success in terms of the music he was making, not an audience he was duping. One suspects that in Elvis's mind he never became the music man that he understood Arthur Crudup to be. Certainly he never claimed to have surpassed any of his masters—black or white. Nonetheless, Elvis's conception of himself as one who had crossed racial and cultural barriers never wavered. Late in his career the guaranteed show-stopper of his concerns was his rendering of "American Trilogy." Written by Mickey Newbury, "American Trilogy" seeks to bring together irreconcilable aspects of American history—slavery, the Old South, and the abolitionist North—by combining into one song verses from the slave song "All My Trials," "Dixie," and the "Battle Hymn of the Republic." Elvis made this song the centerpoint of the shows he gave during his last five years. According to Guralnick, Elvis's rendering of "American Trilogy" "never failed to bring down the house" (*Careless* 455). Noting that its popularity proved that Americans of all regions identified with the song, Linda Pratt says that Elvis's rendering of "American Trilogy" has special meaning for Southerners.

> The trilogy seems to capture Southern history through the changes of the civil rights movement and the awareness of black suffering which had hitherto been largely excluded from popular white images of Southern history. The piece could not have emerged before the seventies because only then had the 'marching' brought a glimmer of hope. Elvis could not have sung this song in Madison Square Garden before there was some reason for pride and hope in the South. (99)

I agree with Pratt, but I also think that Elvis's vision is broader than she suggests. When Elvis sang "American Trilogy" at Madison Square Garden in 1972 before an audience that included Bob Dylan and John Lennon, he was not merely presenting to northerners his redeemed vision of the South. Rather, this song was Elvis's way of proclaiming his accomplishment. After performing this number, Elvis would generally turn the house lights on the audience, as if to emphasize that his vision is mere show business unless it includes everyone. Certainly, one could not offer such a fusion of black and white, North and South, as flamboyant pageantry in the 1950s. "American Trilogy" was as close as Elvis ever came to saying, Here is my legacy: the nation's contradictions written into our history with the Declaration of Independence have been fused in me. His audience's consistently frenzied response suggests that, for the moment anyway, his claim had been answered.

On the other hand, Elvis's art was about the cultural processes that make "American Trilogy" true. Anyone can perform "American Trilogy," but Elvis creates it as our truth. He does this not by proclaiming America's unity in the spectacle of magnificent bombast that is "American Trilogy," but through the work that led up to the declaration that is "American Trilogy." He was doing the same thing on the *Ed Sullivan Show* in 1956, though few could see it. Like Ellison's narrator in *Invisible Man*, Elvis renders visible the invisible cultural connections that make the term "American" mean something more than an ideological excuse to go to war. Elvis forges these connections more convincingly when he trades performances with Jackie Wilson than when he forces them with "American Trilogy." In the latter example, Elvis offers his accomplishment—his terminal point; in the earlier performance, he acts out the cultural processes that make his claims in "American Trilogy" provisionally true.

The real question that the example of Elvis raises may turn out to be not whether he stole the blues, but whether anyone will care to see otherwise; too many edifices are constructed on the belief that American culture is not mulatto. Confronted with a pure expression of democratic culture such as Elvis Presley, most of us flee to the security of our fragmented cultural enclaves in the hope that we can shelter ourselves from the multiple identifications that Presley seems to demand from each of us, regardless of which hole we are shacked up in. As each of the figures discussed idn this chapter shows, "crossing over" in a secular context is freighted with ambiguity and loss. Like Robert Johnson we are frightened by the fate we seem to divine at the crossroads—but without his excuse. To see Elvis Presley performing a version of some undefinable something that you thought represented solely "your" or "their" culture is to understand that the meaning of your American identity has been transformed. This certainly is a painful recognition given that, for many, American identity was formed as a consequence of social oppression committed by people who looked and talked a lot like Elvis did. If Elvis Presley can do what was once only mine to define, then does his doing mean my undoing? The example of Elvis, which also happens to be pragmatist, yields an ambiguous "no." The exhilarating and painful truth is that in our turbulent, fluid, heterogenous culture, your American self is already being undone.[49]

I close with an American tableau, one which Living Colour's "Elvis Is Dead" helps to uncover for us. Longtime friends, Brown and Elvis usually met in secret. Brown says Elvis would come disguised to his shows, always leaving before the encore (165). From a public perspective, their friendship was as segregated as their musical styles are supposed to be.[50] For a moment, let us try to imagine them together. There's Elvis: forever being played on a tape loop, pictures of black artists such as Arthur "Big Boy" Crudup, Sister Rosetta Tharpe, Roy Brown, Big Mama Thornton, Chuck Berry, Jackie Wilson, Otis Blackwell, and others interspersed between shots of Elvis performing "their" songs on Ed Sullivan, or perhaps at the 1956 Mississippi State Fair where the audience was "mixed" but segregated; there he is again performing the songs of white artists such as Eddy Arnold, Bill Monroe, Hank Snow, Hank Williams, Frank Sinatra, filling the spaces between these performances with his performance of Jackie Wilson performing him . . . In other words, picture Elvis as he was—beyond boundaries. Now imagine James Brown when the mayor of Boston begged him to broadcast a concert on public television to stay the "race riot" that was threatening to erupt as a result of Martin Luther

King's assassination. Imagine Brown singing "Say It Loud, I Am Black and I Am Proud." Imagine the very incarnation of a self-defined black identity, free from white-imposed versions except as those white versions may come crawling to him. Imagine Brown, the African American self transcendent, versus Elvis, American music man such as even Handy could not have dreamed.

Yet somewhere between and among these competing images remain Elvis and James themselves, isolate, ignored, nearly mute in their separate peace. With no one but themselves to attend to their conversation, what can this friendship mean, this friendship forged in difference and sameness? In today's fragmented cultural and critical context, James Brown's words will strike many as hardly creditable and almost certainly nostalgic. Democracy, with its city on the hill, whispers amid them, calling from the crossroads where "doing" and "being" intersect. The Godfather of Soul and the King of Rock and Roll are together on their knees. Can I get a witness?

> It was late, real late at night. Elvis had thrown this big party, all kinds of big stars, the Rollin' Stones, all of them. But you could tell he wanted to be somewhere else. And I was tired, and so did I. So me and Elvis sat together in that room and sang jubilee. Yeah, we sung gospel, and Elvis, he could sing it pretty. "Old Blind Barnabas," I remember, we sang. He knew the harmony. Me and Elvis never talked much about bein' superstars or nothin'. Never did discuss it. But when you sing together, real close, jubilee now, like I told you . . . well now, *that* is communication, yes ma'am. What else you think gospel harmony is? (Hirshey 58)

# NOTES

■■■■■■■

## Introduction

1 What frightened Adams (and discouraged him in his democratic idealism) emboldened Du Bois to hope that democracy was at last coming to America.

2 See Jay, "The End," and Spengemann, *Mirror.*

3 Along with his influential *The Puritan Origins of the American Self* (1975) and *The American Jeremiad* (1978), see Bercovitch's "Afterword" to *Ideology and Classic American Literature* (1986) for his discussions of what he alternately calls "the myth of America" and "the idea of America."

4 Sacvan Bercovitch argues for Emerson's "capacity to absorb the radical communitarian visions it renounces, and its capacity to be nourished by the liberal structures it resists" (*Rites* 348).

5 West and Poirier both see Emerson as the first pragmatist. Whereas West's *American Evasion of Philosophy* (1989) identifies a pragmatist lineage of cultural criticism running through Emerson, James, Dewey, Mills, Trilling, Rorty, and Quine, among others, Poirier traces "an Emersonian linguistic skepticism that significantly shapes" a literary pragmatist heritage that runs through Thoreau, William James, Gertrude Stein, T. S. Eliot, Robert Frost, and Kenneth Burke (*Poetry* 5). Posnock also has expanded our understanding of the pragmatist tradition by persuasively arguing in *The Trial of Curiosity* (1991) for Henry James's status as a pragmatist novelist and cultural critic. In *Color and Culture* (1998) Posnock identifies an African American pragmatist tradition that includes W. E. B. Du Bois, Zora Neale Hurston, Alain Locke, Ralph Ellison, and Samuel Delaney, among others.

6 For relatively recent histories of pragmatism that precede Rorty, see Kuklick and Thayer.

7 Citing the work of Carolyn Porter, Gloria Anzaldúa, Arnold Krupat, and José David Saldívar, among others, Jay has advocated a "border studies" as an alternative to the pragmatist work of Rorty, Gunn, and Poirier (169).

8 Following a line of thought that goes back to Bertrand Russell, F. H. Bradley, and A. O. Lovejoy and on up through Lewis Mumford and Mortimer J. Adler, John Diggins uses Bourne's critique of Dewey to identify "the central deficiency of

pragmatism," which is "its lack of a 'poetic vision,' a sense of the true and right as opposed to the efficient and expedient" (*Promise* 254).

9 For full discussions of this exchange and how Dewey co-opted Bourne's critique into his subsequent work, see Westbrook and Posnock, "Bourne."

10 Where Rorty's arguments become problematic, it seems to me, is not in his explanations of how antifoundational thinking works but in his attempts to apply pragmatism to cultural issues. His arguments that culture be conceived of as a "conversation" among a plurality of voices and cultures, or that ethnocentrism is the only defense of liberal Western values, have met with criticism even from other pragmatists because they seem to ignore how one's position in society often dictates what one can or cannot say. On these issues Rorty sometimes shows the same blind spot that Dewey did, which has prompted Cornel West to suggest that Rorty's "historicist sense remains too broad, too thin, devoid of the realities of power" (207). Likewise, Rorty's justification of ethnocentrism has also been criticized for its unproblematic endorsement of a kind of "us versus them" mentality that at its most stringent seems to preclude the possibility that one's ideas can be changed by alternative points of view. For a critique of Rorty on these issues, see Gunn, *Thinking* 107–10. For a discussion of Rorty's ethnocentrism and how he has backed off some of his earlier stances, see Hollinger, *Postethnic* 75–76.

11 In *The Promise of Pragmatism* (1994) John Diggins argues that a kind of pragmatism informed the founding of the nation.

## 1 *What Difference Does the Difference Make?*

1 Ironically, Kallen had the last say on this matter. Kallen's professor, Barret Wendell, wrote Kallen that with Locke's social acceptance "the kind of American which unmixed nationhood has made me must only be a memory." Kallen then included in *Culture and Democracy* a similar remark by Wendell to clinch his point about how "typical Americans" were having to rethink the meaning of their American identity! See Sollors, "Critique" 271 and Kallen, *Culture* 93.

2 Orlando Patterson recognizes this point as well (168).

3 Most influential critics of Kallen have hardly concerned themselves with how his later work addresses and revises the shortcomings of his earlier work. In this essay Kallen retreats from the "racist" and "separatist" implications of his earlier argument. "The concept of 'race,'" he notes, should not apply to the question of cultural "differences since any species whose members can breed together may be said to belong to the same race" ("Alain Locke" 125). Race is only a factor insofar as racism exists—and Kallen was never naive enough to ignore the existence of racism. He argues that "cultural pluralism signifies" a "voluntary and cooperative relationship where each, in living on, also helps, and is helped by, the others in living" (126–27). See William Toll for an excellent discussion of how critics have ignored Kallen's later work and how that work revises the limitations of his earlier essays.

4 Locke's response anticipated his future argument that "to be 'Negro' in the cul-

tural sense, then, is not to be radically different, but only to be distinctly composite and idiomatic, though basically American" (Locke, "Who" 213). Kallen pointed out later that this perspective accords with his own understanding of cultural pluralism (Kallen, "Alain Locke" 119–27).

5   Kallen's father, Jacob David Kallen (altered from Kalonymus), wanted his son to be a rabbi as well. Kallen did not begin public school in the United States until he was obliged to by the truant officers of Boston. His father had been instructing him at home and continued to require Horace to attend cheder. According to Milton Konvitz, Kallen frequently ran away from home during this period in his life. Milton Konvitz notes that "when he received his B.A. degree [1903], all the essential components of his philosophy of cultural pluralism were already parts of his intellectual, moral, and spiritual equipment" (65). For another excellent biographical reading of Kallen's cultural pluralism as a response to his father's influence, see Schmidt.

6   Konvitz, who has written the most thorough and fair-minded evaluation of Kallen's thought, suggests that Kallen's double consciousness derives from his acceptance of the Hebraic faith. "Thus to be a creative American the Jew must be a Jew; and to be a Jew, he must be creative both as a Jew and as a human being, one who has inherent and inalienable rights, who has the freedom and the right to be different, and therefore the right to be a Jew: to express the human essence as a Jew, to belong to the family of man as one who belongs to the family of Jews" (80).

7   As I argue throughout, Kallen had no interest in dismissing "American" as a useful term; rather, he wanted to strip the term of its racial (Anglo-Saxon) implications.

8   For a discussion of how many Mexicans remain, in effect, residents of Mexico even while living in the United States, see Rodriguez, 48–79.

9   Along with Gordon and Glazer and Moynihan, see Steinberg. Unlike most critics of Kallen, Steinberg recognizes that the key issue for Kallen is social equality, or, as Steinberg puts it, "social inequality." See 253–62.

10  See Berkson 81; Sollors and his essay on Kallen and the birth of cultural pluralism ("Critique" 262–63); see also Posnock (*Color* 191–92), and Gordon.

11  Milton Konvitz suggests that Kallen's thinking on these issues evolved through the years, so that eventually Kallen "tended to think that, without exception, all associations were, or ought to be, voluntary; for a person has the liberty to reject the fact that he is a Jew or a Pole or an Anglo-Saxon; a man cannot change, but he can reject the fact that he is a Jew or a Pole or an Anglo-Saxon; a man cannot change, but he can reject his grandfather, as indeed many have done. In a free society, membership in a group is effected not by status but by contract" (66). For another critic who recognizes Kallen's evolution of thought on this issue, see Toll.

12  I take up Michaels's argument more fully in chapter 5.

13  Indeed, Hollinger suggests that Kallen himself transcended his own argument when he "married the daughter of a Methodist minister" and "lost interest in these issues," as if the former act determined the latter (*Postethnic* 96). John Higham likewise suggests that Kallen "argued for the indestructibility of ethnic cultures in order to resist the disintegration of hiw own" (*Send* 205). The irony here is rich—

and thoroughly American. After arguing that Kallen's cultural pluralism depends on a notion of cultural authenticity, critics then attack him because he himself is culturally inauthentic!

14  Rather than accept the idea that various Americans will wish to define themselves in terms of ancestry, the universalist finds ways to challenge the authenticity of their ethnic assertion. Drawing on the work of sociologist Herbert Gans, Hollinger argues that many people are only "symbolically" ethnic because "they take pleasure in a subjective feeling of ethnic identity, but shy away from a more substantive ethnicity that demands involvement in a concrete community with organizations, mutual commitments, and some elements of constraint" (*Postethnic* 40). My argument is that this distinction is irrelevant on its own terms since it implies that there is such a thing as an authentic identity.

15  Toll's analysis of Kallen's relationship to the pragmatist philosopher focuses primarily on James's *Varieties of Religious Experience*. He does not deal with James's explicitly pragmatist works, *Pragmatism* and *The Meaning of Truth*, nor does he consider James's radical empiricist work, *A Pluralistic Universe*, which had perhaps the greatest influence on Kallen.

16  For a discussion of James's influence on twentieth-century ethnic thought, including the work of Robert Park and W. E. B. Du Bois, see L. Miller.

17  This sort of logic is what Rorty uses when he says that James and Dewey helped to inaugurate the general postmodern—Rorty would say post-Nietzschean—project of "junking" the notion of epistemology altogether. I agree with Rorty's assertion that "James's point . . . was that there is nothing deeper to be said: truth is not the sort of thing which has an essence." "As long as we see James or Dewey as having 'theories of truth' or 'theories of knowledge' or 'theories of morality,'" Rorty writes, "we shall get them wrong." He adds, "They had things to say about truth, knowledge and morality, even though they did not have *theories* of them, in the sense of set answers to textbook problems" (*Consequences* 160–62).

18  The usual critique of James is that his ardent individualism prevented him from thinking in social terms. Certainly it is true that James's thought was formed as a response to a personal crisis; he also understood ideas as important only insofar as they made a practical difference in society. James T. Kloppenberg is right to suggest that James's concept of immediate experience did assume that "social relations are a fundamental part of individual life," and that this philosophy derived from the individual's experience, which nevertheless "altered the meaning of individuality by excluding the possibility of presocial or nonsocial experience" (412).

19  See James, *Writings* 652 and Kallen, *Culture* 61.

20  Orlando Patterson makes a similar case (167–69).

21  There were even attempts to prevent immigrants from southern and eastern Europe from entering the United States, as these "swarthier" types were thought to be less assimilable. See Higham, *Send* 39–43.

22  For accounts of the many tides of immigration and the U.S. government's attempts to hold them off, see Howe, *World* 53–57 and Higham, *Send* 29–70.

23  For a discussion of the cultural displacement associated with the Revolution, see Pease, *Visionary*.

24 According to Werner Sollors, it was not until "World War II and in the Supreme Court decisions and civil rights bills of the 1950s and 1960s that the term 'American' actually became intertwined with ethnicity and was flexible enough to include—in widely accepted public usage—such groups as immigrants, African Americans, and American Indians" ("National" 115).

25 I can only give a capsule summary here. Along with Gleason's essay, the essential works on this subject are Higham, *Strangers* and *Send*.

26 Kallen notes that it was this atmosphere of fear and ignorance of the "other" which reinvigorated institutions such as the Ku Klux Klan and the exclusive men's social clubs depicted in works such as Sinclair Lewis's *Babbit* (1922). See his "Culture and the Klan" in *Culture* 9–43.

27 For another discussion of how Kallen, in effect, re-Americanized 100% Americans, see Priscilla Wald's illuminating discussion (243–45). Wald also connects Kallen's ideas to the work of another student of William James, Gertrude Stein.

28 Higham notes that much of the immigration to the United States in the 1860s and 1870s was the result of legislation that either "authorized employers to pay the passage and bind the services of prospective migrants" or allowed the western and southern states to employ "promotional agents and other forms of inducements" to entice immigrants to come over (*Send* 33).

29 John Patrick Diggins, Hartz's best critic, remarks "that Hartz expected to be dismissed as a scholar who could neither please nor be pleased, but I do not think he expected to be classified as a defender and promoter of the 'consensus' school of thought" ("Knowledge" 370). Carolyn Porter has also tried to resuscitate Hartz, arguing that "if American history is, as Hartz argues, distinguished by the dominance of liberalism, perhaps we would do well to explore in our literature the complexities generated from within a liberal, capitalist society ("Are" 18). For accounts critical of Hartz as a consensus historian, see Pells 182 and Hofstatder 446–68, 456–57.

30 Here is a representative sentence from Boorstin's *The Genius of American Politics*: "It is my belief that the circumstances which have stunted our interest in political philosophy have also nourished our refusal to make our society into the graven image of any man's political philosophy. In other ages this refusal might have seemed less significant; in ours it is a hallmark of a decent, free, and God-fearing society" (3–4).

31 Bernard Bailyn has argued that the fear of a contaminating power as represented by the British crown was the animating force behind the American Revolution, thus reinforcing Hartz's thesis. John Diggins observes that "Bailyn demonstrated how the decisive influence of dissent ideas of English origin mediated the colonists' perceptions of their mother country, impelling them to see a deliberate 'conspiracy' against their liberties" (*Lost* 22).

32 George Santayana makes a similar point throughout *Character and Opinion in the United States*. For example: "If there are immense differences between individual Americans—for some Americans are black—yet there is a great uniformity in their environment, customs, temper, and thoughts. They have all been uprooted from their several soils and ancestries and plunged together into one vortex, whirl-

ing irresistibly in a space otherwise quite empty" (104). Santayana remarks that if somehow someone is not drawn into the vortex of "work, growth, enterprise, reform and prosperity," he finds that "he either folds up his heart and withers in a corner—in remote places you sometimes find such a gaunt solitary idealist—or else flies to Oxford or Florence or Montmarte to save his soul—or perhaps not to save it" (105). As we shall see, a version of this lonely American is Henry James in *The American Scene* (1907).

33  Discussing Hartz's analysis, Richard Hofstadter aptly if somewhat acerbically said, "One may differ whether to call the impassioned arguments of the North and South ideological differences—but if this was not an ideological conflict (and I think it was), we can only conclude that Americans do not need ideological conflict to shed blood on a large scale" (461). In my view, Hofstadter's remark does not refute Hartz but extends his argument since it recognizes that American struggles over cultural self-definition are fought over racial rather than ideological difference.

34  This is basically the stance that Lawrence Levine (*Black*) and Eugene Genovese have taken in their works on how the slaves invented a culture separate from the one their masters tried to inflict upon them.

35  If Locke won Kallen over, it can be argued that Kallen won Locke over as well. Locke contributed "Pluralism and Ideological Peace" (63–69) to Hook and Konvitz's *Freedom and Experience: Essays Contributed to Horace M. Kallen*. In his introduction to the anthology *The New Negro* (1925), Locke called Harlem "the home of the Negro's 'Zionism' " (14).

36  See Handlin vi–vii.

37  Stephen J. Rubin says that Antin's work was "the classic story of assimilation, of transformation, and of hope" (36). Louis Harap implies that Antin's story was calculated to appeal to an audience otherwise unlikely to accept her as a cultural equal when he labels her "the ideal Jewish immigrant for the era of Americanization" (18). More forcefully, Sara Blacher Cohen charges that Antin was eager to "cast off the albatross of Judaism" to become an "assimilated American" (qted. in Rubin 41). Richard Tuerk has noted that the narrative of her life parallels "the story of the Exodus from Egypt," and her "Americanization" represents her deliverance from bondage (30). James Craig Holte has compared *The Promised Land* to Franklin's *Autobiography*, the ultimate American success story (33–34), while Sam B. Girgus has borrowed Sacvan Bercovitch's influential paradigm of the jeremiad to suggest that Antin "offers one of the strongest expressions of the myth of America as an ideal and vision" (*New Covenant* 14).

38  Antin is viewed as being too grateful for being given the chance to sacrifice her Jewish heritage in favor of the WASP majority, an instance of what Melvin Tumlin has called the "cult of gratitude" (69–82). Sollors recognizes that she "took a position of apparent self-effacement only to proclaim loudly her sense of equal entitlement" (*Beyond* 45).

39  Perhaps Kallen here was following his mentor, Barret Wendell, who complained of Antin's "irritating habit of describing herself and her people as Americans." In

spite of this remark, Wendell had met Antin years before and had even given her "a reader's ticket at the Athenaeum, our chief private library." That is, Wendell had helped her to help herself to one of the chief democratic agencies in her Americanization. See Wendell 281–82.

40 Interestingly, in this article for the *Atlantic Monthly*, Bourne, without irony, praised Antin as a "patriot" and remarked that "Antin is right when she looks upon our foreign born as the people who missed the *Mayflower* and came over on the first boat they could find." Bourne criticizes Antin for failing to recognize that the immigrants "bring with them national and racial characteristics, thus complicating the American identity Antin celebrates." See Bourne, *Radical* 248–50. As we shall see, I argue that Antin actually dramatizes Bourne's point.

41 Handlin notes that Antin was writing in response to the Dillingham Commission's report to Congress, which argued that immigrants from southern and eastern Europe were inferior to immigrants from northern Europe and mongrelized American identity (vi–vii).

42 William Boelhower likewise notes that Antin employs her Jewish, Russian, and American names (Maryashe, Mashke, Mary), thus continually unsettling any claim to having a persistent identity: "Her various identities co-exist; she both is and is not 'Mary' Antin" ("Making" 136).

43 This is another similarity she shared with Kallen: the tendency to substitute the sacred stories of American history for the icons of her discarded Jewish religion. In the Foreword to his *Individualism—An American Way of Life* (1933) Kallen described how as a boy he escaped the influence of his rabbi father to visit Bunker Hill and Lexington and Concord. As we have seen, Kallen found that the "Declaration of Independence came upon me, nurtured upon the deliverance from Egypt and the bondage in exile, like the clangor of trumpets, like a sudden light." He employs the language of the sacred to describe his discovery of the Declaration as if to emphasize that he was trading one religion for another.

44 Elsewhere, Antin extends this argument: "If I ask an American what is the fundamental American law, and he does not answer me promptly, 'That which is contained in the Declaration of Independence,' I put him down for a poor citizen." She further observes, "What the Mosaic Law is to the Jews, the Declaration is to the American people. It affords us a starting-point in history and defines our mission among nations" (*They* 3–4).

45 Eight years before her death in 1949, Antin was still returning to the meaning of her ethnic heritage. Responding to Nazi Germany, she writes:

> I can no more return to the Jewish fold than I can to my mother's womb; neither can I in decency continue to enjoy an accidental personal immunity from the penalties of being a Jew in a time of virulent anti-semitism. The least I can do, in my need to share the sufferings of my people, is to declare that *I am as one of them.* ("House" 37, emphasis mine)

Thirty years later she still cannot disassociate herself from the Pale.

46 He wanted to call his book *Return of the Native* but that title was already taken (Edel 317).

47  For an excellent analysis of Henry James as a pragmatist thinker, see Hocks.

48  Edel's remark is reflected in a quick survey of other critics. John Carlos Rowe notes that "the 'vanished . . . birthplace,' that Washington Place house where Henry was born in 1843, sets the tone for all the other historical absences he encounters in *The American Scene*" (*Theoretical* 214). The interpretative problem has been what to make of this tone. Rowe, I think, misses the mark by arguing that James seeks "detachment" from his subject (202). Actually, he seeks to establish a relation with how his past has been changed. Rowe's notion of James's detachment reflects a persistent view of *The American Scene* that Richard Lyons has fairly recently reiterated: "What is at stake [in *The American Scene*] is the continuity of James's own identity as well as that of the larger community" (523). That is, James fears his potential discontinuity and flees it. For critics who argue that James uses his discontinuity with his subject to produce an analysis that is both subtle and intriguingly engaged, see Posnock, *Trial*, and Gervais.

49  F. O. Matthiessen said that James "drifted dangerously close to a doctrine of racism" (*Henry* 110). The indefatigable James-baiter, Maxwell Geismar, described these sections as "purely" and "thoughtlessly" and "crudely" the "nightmarish fantasies of prejudice and doom" (347–48). Alan Trachtenberg argues that James's visit to Ellis Island "reveals a set of snobbish biases" which indicate his "martial spirit against the barbaric German hordes of World War One" (293). See Posnock, *Trial*, and Boelhower, *Through*, for views that dissent from the main line of James critics.

50  Posnock's *Trial of Curiosity* (1991) is a work of impressive ambition and erudition. Indeed, I could not make this criticism of his work if he did not convincingly connect James to so many issues and figures—intellectual, historical, and cultural. Posnock and I both see "democracy" as somehow always exceeding its own cultural boundaries. James's fascination with the alien is a case in point. Coequal with democracy's desire to exceed itself, however, is its need to contain and to assure conformity. I see James as depicting these two great and contradictory forces at once, essentially willing the former to prevail. But he knows and fears that this will not necessarily happen.

51  The similarities between Hartz's critique and James's are uncanny. Hartz: "How can we know the uniqueness of anything except by contrasting it with what is not unique? The rationale for a separate American study, once you begin to think about it, explodes the study itself" (*Liberal* 4). James: "We lost ourselves in the intensity of the truth that to compare a simplified social order with a social order in which feudalism had once struck deep was the right way to measure the presence of feudalism" (*American* 24).

52  Sharon Cameron and Mark Seltzer present opposing views. Cameron sees James's complicated response to his native land as "embracing [his] embattlement" in order "to banish it, and to substitute for what is there what is wanted to be there (3)." Seltzer finds in James's response a "disavowal of the actualities of history (109)."

53  Stuart Johnson has likewise argued that James "tries explicitly to maintain the position of insider and outsider." Johnson astutely describes the complexity of

James's critical position in terms similar to my own: "A point of origin . . . would provide a center, a point of reference for the returning exile. He would be able to gauge his nearness and his remoteness from a centered, present entity. But the center is lost, on the personal scale as well as the national" (84, 88).

54 Mark Seltzer has pointed out the organic quality of the hotel world probably appealed to James the artist. Seltzer interprets James's account of the hotel world in a spirit of Blackmurian organicism, seeing it as "reiterat[ing] and reenact[ing] his own policies of aesthetic form. Incorporating the normative and the organic, the hotel is a triumph of form, of the Jamesian imperative of organic relation" (113). Perhaps because James himself seems to be absorbed by the hotel world, Seltzer fails to notice that the form of production it validates has little to do with where James finds his creative energy. Actually, James laments the equilibrium of this mutual creation since it means "reduction of everything to an average" with no room for the "overflow and by-play," the excess that James's risky openness to experience enjoins upon him.

55 Cynthia Ozick offers a different conclusion on this point. She focuses on James's obsession with changing American speech, and especially on the essay-lecture he gave at Bryn Mawr College on June 8, 1905, "The Question of Our Speech." Ozick also sees that James was ambivalent about the effect immigrants were having on the national culture, but says that he did not realize in his uneasiness how the "common schools and the newspapers" were helping to bring about "the idea that a national literature can create a national speech." She sees her mother, an immigrant at roughly that time, as an example of democratic education in its best sense, producing someone who had mastered English through sustained encounter with the classic literature schools then required. Ozick argues that James was indifferent to the very important issues of class in America and did not see that his own speech was the product of his own lifelong dedication to literature. Ultimately, Ozick laments what she sees as the decline of the public school system as it was constituted in James's day, in terms very similar to what we might expect James himself to use if he had had a more thorough knowledge of what was actually going on then in the public schools. See Ozick 155, 161.

## 2  Thinking in Blues

1 West is more inspired by the idea of the pragmatist evasion of epistemology because of pragmatism's concomitant emphasis on philosophy as a mode of continuous inquiry than he is by the practice of pragmatism. He finds much of the pragmist tradition to be naively individualistic, unconsciously racist, and regrettably class-bound. I think that West's argument suffers from his wanting his intellectual heroes to have said in the past what he would have them say in his present.

2 I want to acknowledge how crucial Poirier's work has been to my own. Though Poirier is interested in Emerson's literary inheritance, his arguments about Emerson can be put to other, broader uses. Along with Stanley Cavell, there is no more instructive or creative contemporary reader of Emerson than Poirier.

3 Cavell is interested in finding for Emerson a place within the history of philoso-

phy. In connecting Emerson to Heidegger and Wittgenstein, Cavell finds an intellectual inheritance that we have been late to discover. Although Cavell will not surrender his attachment to the word and discipline "philosophy," I think his project is similar to Rorty's. Acknowledging that Rorty remarked that he is "engaged in a process of recanonization" and that he need not worry if "the texts I promote are philosophy or are something else (say literature)," Cavell says of himself that he "muttered something about there being different ways of raising the worry and about my caring in principle not at all which texts get on a list but rather how a text is to be discovered and taken up—taken up, of course, with my interests" (*This New* 4). What Cavell does for Emerson in this respect is similar to what Rorty has done for James and Dewey. Like Emerson, Cavell is whimsical enough to think that others too might take up his interests. Certainly, I understand my work to be doing just that.

4 Reynolds does not make a direct connection, but places Emerson's oratory in the context of the "larger change in the style of popular religious discourse" that had been taking place since the Great Awakening. Reynolds says that it was not until the Second Great Awakening (1798–1815), when "an indigenous speaking style" rooted in "the daring pulpit storytelling" of southern blacks "who at first addressed only their fellow slaves but who were destined to attract increasing attention among white mainstream Protestants," that black oratory began to influence white oratory (17). Most prominent among the white preachers was Virginia-born Edward Thompson Taylor, minister of Seamen's Bethel Church in Boston and a crucial model for both Emerson and Melville, who based *Moby Dick*'s Father Mapple on him. Reynolds shows that Taylor was decisive in inspiring Emerson's "brash assertions of self-reliance," which was reflected in "a new *stylistic* self-reliance whereby the emphasis in religious discussion shifted from dogmatic content to creative image"—a style rooted in vernacular expression (20–21). Reynolds's study explores the kinds of subtle cross-cultural influences that our Jim Crow cultural and critical heritage has prevented us from seeing.

5 During Clinton's impeachment trial, Toni Morrison argued in the *New Yorker* that "white skin notwithstanding, this is our first black President" ("Talk" 32).

6 That Emerson has been seen as an originary figure in American letters is useful, but not essential, to my argument. What matters is that my understanding of Emerson is filtered through my understanding of the blues. Without knowing the blues, I could not know Emerson as I do.

7 Robert Palmer reminds us, "Blues was so disreputable that even its staunchest devotees frequently found it prudent to disown it. If you asked a black preacher, schoolteacher, small landowner, or faithful churchgoer what kind of people played and listened to blues, they would tell you, 'cornfield niggers'" (*Deep* 17).

8 Even a champion of indigenous African American forms such as Alain Locke saw the blues as but a small step toward some truly distinguished African American creation. "Neither American nor the Negro," he wrote, can rest content so long as it can be said: 'Jazz is America's outstanding contribution, so far, to world music.'" He called for a black Dvorak to do for "Negro music" what Dvorak did for Czech music (*The Negro and His Music* 130).

9  One can go to any number of fine studies that define either the blues or, more generally, African American folk song. Those that have been most useful to me include: David Evans's *Big Road Blues* (1982), Ralph Ellison's various essays in *Shadow and Act* (1964), Peter Guralnick's *Feel Like Going Home* (1970) and *Lost Highway* (1981), Zora Neale Hurston's *Mules and Men* (1935), LeRoi Jones's *Blues People* (1982), Lawrence Levine's *Black Culture and Black Consciousness* (1977), Alan Lomax's *The Land Where the Blues Began* (1993), Greil Marcus's chapter on Robert Johnson in *Mystery Train* (1975), Albert Murray's *The Hero and the Blues* (1973) and *Stomping the Blues* (1976), and Robert Palmer's *Deep Blues* (1980). See also William Barlow's *Looking Up at Down* (1989), Samuel Charters' *The Legacy of the Blues* (1977), Angela Y. Davis's *Blues Legacies and Black Feminism* (1998), Willie Dixon's *I Am the Blues* (1989), William Ferris's *Blues from the Delta* (1978), Mance Lipscomb's fascinating oral autobiography *I Say Me for a Parable* (1993), Paul Oliver's *Blues Fell This Morning* (1990), and Jeff Todd Titon's *Early Downhome Blues* (1977). Though not obviously about music, Eugene Genovese's *Roll, Jordan, Roll* (1974) certainly helped me to think about how the experience of slavery was both preserved and transformed through the blues. Most important, though, has been the work of blues artists themselves as it has been preserved on tape and record and compact disc (see selected Discography).

10  In 1963 Charters wrote: "There is little social protest in the blues" (*Poetry* 152; qtd. in Davis 92).

11  Both Palmer (*Deep* 3) and Levine (*Black* 206) recount Peabody's story. Howard Odum reported hearing a black road gang singing,

> White man settin' on a wall
> White man settin' on a wall
> White man settin' on a wall all day long
> Wastin' his time wastin' his time. (qtd. in Levine 205)

The white man in question was Odum.

12  Concentrating on the classic blues period of the 1920s, Davis nonetheless is largely interested in exploring how "Gertrude [Ma] Rainey's and Bessie Smith's songs constituted historical preparation for social protest" (42). Although this claim is likely true and gives to these singers' work a necessary social dimension that is often overlooked, it also implies that the primary function of these singers was to clear a path to the future—to "create the emotional conditions for protest" (113). Certainly, Bessie Smith or Gertrude Rainey issued "direct and audacious challenges to a male dominance," just as early blues challenged white dominance, but as valuable as this perspective is, it overlooks another important consideration: they were great singers. However defined, their expressions of protest were mixed with the joy of performing. Finally, it is the joy of expression that makes possible the cultural renewal that is enacted through the blues. Having said that, I think Davis's study does an excellent and thorough job establishing how Bessie Smith, Gertrude Rainey, and Billie Holiday "openly challenged the gender politics implicit in traditional cultural representations of marriage and heterosexual love relationships" (41). Arguing that these women articulated "an important elaboration of black working-class social consciousness" that was also pro-

tofeminist, Davis suggests just how radical and far-seeing the classic blues singers were (42).

13  The classic study of Delta blues is Robert Palmer's *Deep Blues* (1980).

14  David Evans and Robert Palmer have both shown how the Mississippi Delta blues remained closely tied to its pre-blues roots. The verses and tunes of the most well-known figures—Charlie Patton, Son House, Robert Johnson, Tommy Johnson, Son House, and the early Muddy Waters—float from song to song and performer to performer. See Evans 167–264 and Palmer, *Deep* 23–132.

15  Part of the reason for the obscurity of the blues' origin is that its expression was invented before it was recorded. Mamie Smith was the first recorded blues singer, but her 1920 "Crazy Blues" is blues mostly in name rather than in practice. She was identified on the record sleeve as "Mamie Smith, contralto" (Palmer, *Deep* 106). The country blues recorded by performers such as Charlie Patton, Son House, and Bukka White, though recorded after classic blues singers, is actually an earlier form.

16  As one would expect of a folk creation, the precise point at which the blues began is a matter of debate. Based on the accounts of performers such as W. C. Handy, Gertrude "Ma" Rainey (Work 32–33), and Ferdinand "Jelly Roll" Morton (Lomax, *Mister* 51–60, 269–73), the blues falls into history during the 1890s—in Alabama, Missouri, and New Orleans, respectively. Archaeologist Charles Peabody left an account of the music his black laborers made while digging up Indian burial mounds in Stovall, Mississippi, in 1902, which is probably blues. Folklorist Howard Odum documented the blues as early as 1911 in his article "Folk-Song and Folk-Poetry as Found in the Secular Songs of the Southern Negroes." See Evans 32–48 for a good summary of the scholarship in this area. From my perspective, the moment of origin is much less significant than the fact that the blues is an ongoing process of culture creation that continues to absorb and transform American experience.

17  Evans notes that most blues historians agree that the field holler "served as a major source for the creation of the blues" (41).

18  Spires's version comes from a song entitled "Murmur Low" from the collection *Drop Down Mama;* Johnson's version is from a song entitled "Big Fat Mama Blues"; McDowell's version ends a song entitled "You Gonna Be Sorry."

19  Du Bois famously spoke of the African American's feeling of "double-consciousness" that results from always perceiving one's identity through the mediating perspective of an unfriendly other; most likely this form of double-voiced speech is a rhetorical strategy for adjusting to the conflicts such a situation entails.

20  Du Bois's example was taken up by other African American intellectuals in the 1920s and 1930s. In 1930 James Weldon Johnson argued that the blues was a form of folk poetry (*Black Manhattan* 228). A reexamination of blues and jazz was a central component of Alain Locke's influential anthology, *The New Negro* (1924). Locke anticipated the work of Albert Murray in emphasizing the crucial component that dance played in the blues (*The Negro and His Music*, 1969).

21  In an effort to blend the intellectual with the vernacular, Du Bois begins each

chapter of *The Souls of Black Folk* by juxtaposing a citation from the European literary tradition with the European musical notation of a black "sorrow song." Though some scholars find this to be a masterful blending of two different traditions, it seems contrived to me, especially compared with the work of Ralph Ellison. The slaves and their descendants did not invent music that could be accommodated by European musical notation. To so notate it is to distort it. For a full discussion of Du Bois, the heritage of the slaves, and the difficulty of translating vernacular expression into literary art, see Sundquist, *To Wake*.

22   In an act of Emersonian renewal, the author of *Blues People* subsequently changed his name to Amiri Baraka. But I use "LeRoi Jones" whenever referring to the author of *Blues People*.

23   For anthologies of work songs see Gellert, *Negro* and *Me*; see also Greenway.

24   See Palmer's excellent discussion of the African dimension to the blues (*Deep* 25–39).

25   William Ferris has shown how what he calls the "blues house party," or a typical blues performance performed in a juke joint, functions in the same way (101–5).

26   See Poirier's discussions of "Mowing" and its relation to James (*Renewal* 58; *Poetry* 85–89, 111–12).

27   These names are their prison aliases.

28   Jones's stance is not an isolated one in African American letters. Toni Morrison's *Beloved* reiterates Jones's view when Paul D reflects that you cannot enjoy the birds' singing when you know you are the property of someone else, for the sounds that birds make are not yours to enjoy. The birds' freedom mocks your slavery.

29   Any student of Emerson knows there is no such thing as a perfect transcription of experience. Of course Lomax's presence makes a difference in how the men perform, though maybe not so much because he was white; Zora Neale Hurston encountered difficulty from suspicious subjects in her fieldwork, too. Lomax's recordings are the best documentation we have of these types of music making.

30   Kinnard's essay, entitled "Who Are Our National Poets," was published only seven years after Emerson's *The American Scholar*. Observing his black soldiers during the Civil War, Thomas Wentworth Higginson was also amazed at "how 'easily' a new song took root among them" based on the singers' ability to improvise (qtd. in Levine, *Black* 25).

31   Palmer further notes that the *aab* rhyme scheme of the conventional blues lyric clearly echoes the traditional call-and-response pattern of spirituals or slave songs. By sliding a knife or bottle along the guitar strings, the blues singer can make the guitar literally talk in response to his singing, another inheritance from earlier forms. Palmer and Evans trace this technique back to Africa. Palmer adds that blues instrumentation probably derives more from African traditions than blues singing, which has more obviously been tempered by American experience (*Deep* 18–19).

32   It was not hyperbole that caused New Orleans–based piano player, Roy Byrd, aka Professor Longhair, to name one of his bands "The Blues Scholars."

33   Muddy Waters told Robert Palmer that "Walkin' Blues" defined Mississippi Delta

blues. "That was the theme in Mississippi. Most every guitar player played that." The sound of "Walkin' Blues" is, for Waters, the Delta sound. He observes that "there's so many musicians. They can sing and play the guitar so good, but they can't get that sound to save their life. They didn't learn that way. That's the problem. They learned another way, and they just can't get it" (*Deep* 104).

34 See Waters. The recently released compact disc contains four different conversations with Waters along with numerous performances. Besides performing solo blues with guitar only, Waters also performs various "breakdowns" with a string band. The compact disc provides a rare glimpse of the full musical spectrum of what came to be known as Delta blues.

35 Certainly Waters was surprised by the future that this act for Lomax set in motion. Hearing himself on record gave him the confidence to go to Chicago and become a truly professional performer. He told Paul Oliver that "I really HEARD myself for the first time. I'd never heard my voice. I used to sing; used to sing just how I felt, 'cause that's the way we always sang in Mississippi. But when Mr. Lomax played me the record I thought, man, this boy can sing the blues. And I was surprised because I didn't know I could sings like that." See the liner notes to Waters.

36 Waters frequently told a story of being asked to fill in for Son House in the late sixties at a blues festival when "the old man" could not make it. The song Waters chose to perform was "Walking Blues."

37 In 1915 the young Walter Prescott Webb left an account of a song called "Dallas Blues," performed by Floyd Canada in a Beeville, Texas, pool hall, that ran to eighty stanzas. Because the song seemed to Webb to encapsulate the African American experience from slavery to the present moment, he called it "The African Iliad" (Evans 38). Although Webb is clearly romanticizing both the song he heard and African American experience, he is right to suspect that with any blues performance one is hearing only a fragment of an entire tradition.

38 In "Literature as Equipment for Living" Burke suggests that there is no "pure" literature but that "everything is 'medicine'" (*Philosophy* 295).

39 Another example is the lyrics that House sings in "Levee Camp Blues" (which appear in many other songs too):

> I'm going away and not coming back no more
> I'm going away and not coming back no more
> I'm going away to hang crepe on your door [track 2]

40 Recent scholarship has shown that Emerson, despite his misgivings, was actually very involved in the political fight against slavery. See Gougeon, and Emerson, *Emerson's Antislavery*.

41 Murray tries to elevate the blues to the condition of epic and tragedy and in so doing risks essentializing the blues. He forgets (as Kenneth Burke would not) that its power derives in part from its being a response to a particular situation, which is what makes it American.

42 One should also add that this was Jones's perspective in *Blues People*.

43 I am referring to the argument that Garry Wills makes in *Lincoln at Gettysburg*

(1992). Wills argues that in his Gettysburg Address Lincoln reinterpreted Jefferson's Declaration of Independence so that its assertion of "equality" included slaves. The Civil War was fought to realize this reinterpretation.

## 3  Ralph Ellison's Invisible Democracy

1   The importance of jazz and blues to *Invisible Man* has inspired many perceptive studies. Robert O'Meally's *The Craft of Ralph Ellison* was the first extended treatment of the many ways in which Ellison employs African American folk culture in the novel, including jazz and blues. Other fine discussions of Ellison and musical form include Bone, Kent, Ostendorf, Wright, Savery, and Baker, *Blues* 172–99.

2   Henry Louis Gates Jr.'s *The Signifying Monkey* (1988) is the most often-cited study of the way in which displaced Africans have adapted a foreign language, English, to their own cultural ends. Ellison would expand Gates's argument to suggest that "signifying" is a practice and skill shared by all Americans, just as "Americanizing" the English language has been an ongoing national project since the Puritans encountered the Indians.

3   The Real Wheatstraw was a boogie-woogie piano player. Ellison, too, aimed to make Emerson boogie.

4   Ross Posnock connects Ellison to William James through "a pragmatist lineage which aims not to make identity merely more fluid but to abolish its status as a grounding term" (*Color* 186). Posnock reads Ellison in light of William James's injunction in *A Pluralistic Universe* that his audience join him in abandoning "the logic of identity." Rather than saying that Ellison wants to do away with the logic of identity, I would say that Ellison wants to explore the unlikely and unperceived ways in which American identity is expressed. His narrator is one such unlikely expression.

5   Jamex Cox makes nearly the same point in an acute analysis of Jefferson's Declaration of Independence. Cox notes how Jefferson insisted that regardless of what his contemporaries believed, the ultimate fate of the slave was to go free, yet at the same time he could not imagine the slaves' being free as their masters were free. Rather than branding Jefferson a bigot or proclaiming him to be "tolerant" for his time, Cox argues that "Jefferson was fully recognizing the violent history that the Declaration of Independence has inaugurated and was himself realizing the inevitability and irresistibility of the force that had been unleashed. [W]hen he says that he does not believe that the two races can live in the same government, we have to know that we are still contending that they can; that contention is nothing less than the violent course of our history" (139).

6   This letter is included in the collection of Burke correspondence at the Pennsylvania State University Library. All subsequent references to the Ellison-Burke correspondence will be from this letter, unless otherwise noted.

7   For Burke's retrospective answer, see "Ralph" 349–59.

8   Ellison's novel could be used as a sort of litmus test for the status of African American studies. With the novel's arrival in 1952, two years before *Brown v. Board*

*of Education*, African American language and literature could no longer be denied a place in the canon of American literature, which was Ellison's avowed integrationist aim. When the Black Aesthetic movement emerged in the late 1960s and early 1970s, however, Ellison's triumphant integration was seen as a cop-out, a surrender of black culture to white cultural agendas. *The Black Aesthetic* (1971), edited by Addison Gayle Jr., is a representative account of this period of Ellison studies. More recently, Houston A. Baker Jr. in *Blues, Ideology, and American Literature* (1984) and Henry Louis Gates Jr. in *The Signifying Monkey* (1988) have sought to return Ellison's work to a distinctively African American tradition of language and attitude. Baker's book also gives an overview of the "paradigm shifts" that have occurred in the study of African American culture (64–113), which is useful for understanding how views of Ellison's work have changed through the years. The best discussion of the shifting relationship between Ellison and his black critics is Larry Neal's 1970 personal essay "Ellison's Zoot Suit," collected in his *Visions of a Liberated Future* (30–56). Robert Stepto's *From Behind the Veil* (1979) contains a probing discussion of Ellison's place in the canon of African American literature (163–94). See also C. Davis 272–82.

9  For an in-depth discussion of Ellison's debt to Du Bois and Johnson, see Stepto 163–94.

10  So pervasive is the seductive appeal of race for describing complexities of culture that this argument often crosses the very lines of identity its premises deny. Howe, anticipating the strident critiques of the Black Aesthetic movement, accused Ellison of avoiding the social obligation required of a black writer. Along with Kenneth Burke's essay "The Status of Art" (*Counter-Statement*), Ellison's response to Howe, "The World and the Jug," is an excellent analysis of the relationship between art and politics in American letters. See Howe, "Black." For Ellison's response, see *Shadow* 107–14. More recently, Jerry Watts has tried to rescue Howe's argument from Ellison's characterization of it. But in rescuing Howe he trivializes Ellison's position. For instance, in his eagerness to expose Ellison for his "social and political disengagement," Watts champions the example of Langston Hughes, even though, as Watts admits, "Hughes was too busy to write well" (116, 113). If an artist's work is measured only in terms of the political causes he supports, then why bother arguing about art at all? For an argument that places Ellison within a Cold War context of the valorization of ambiguity as an aesthetic good, see Schaub.

11  Many critics of course have stressed this side of Ellison. Most notably, John F. Callahan's excellent essay, "Frequencies of Eloquence," itself a fine example of democratic eloquence, argues for an understanding of the novel which includes its call for social action, recognizing the extent to which Ellison elucidates "the rights and responsibilities" of "citizenship" (91). Callahan speaks of "the symbolic action possible through literary form," tracing the phrase to Burke but without discussing in detail Ellison's relationship to Burke. As a result, he underplays how Ellison's Burkean sense of the reciprocal relationship between symbolic action and audience permeates the *entire* novel and not just the Epilogue.

12 For a long time most critical commentary regarding Ellison's connection to Burke was brief, tangential, usually thrown off in passing. Robert O'Meally notes that Burke's "comic perspective" informs Ellison's novel (*New Essays* 18). In the same volume, Berndt Ostendorf makes this same point as well as connecting *Shadow and Act* with Burke's *Philosophy of Literary Form* (98, 119 n). John Wright discusses the influence of Burke's "language as symbolic action" upon Ellison's understanding of African American forms of ritual (Benston, *Speaking* 67–68). Thomas Whitaker suggests that Burke's discussion of the "I" as being mediated through social interaction influenced Ellison's conception of identity as presented in *Invisible Man* (*Speaking* 394–95). In the past five years, fuller critical treatments have appeared. See Adell, Albrecht, O'Meally ("On Burke"), and Parrish ("Ralph").

13 For Scruggs, the city becomes the potential repository of our national ideals.

14 This point has caused Burke much despair. Along with Henry Adams and Thomas Pynchon, Burke is the great prophet of the disasters which technology can bring, decrying the potential doom which is also encoded in man's capacity for symbol manipulation. As the years passed, Burke became increasingly concerned with technology's power, as the many Afterwords to his books have shown. In a published letter to Ellison, Burke comments "that the human animal's great prowess with the resources of symbolic action has carried us so extensively far in the astoundingly ingenious invention of technology that we are all a part of the same threat to our destiny" (Benston 358).

15 Lentriccia's *Criticism and Social Change* (1983) is an excellent introduction to Burke's work. But as strong as the book is, it still does not do justice to Burke's achievement, for, if anything, it narrows Burke to only a Marxist perspective, when his interests are more catholic than that. Also see Rueckert.

16 Henry Louis Gates Jr. sees "Little Man" as a "salient example of Signifyin(g)" because Ellison's "dilemma was solved through allegory" (*Signifying* 65). Though Gates is right, he misses how Ellison places "signifyin(g)" in a national context, not only an African American one. Houston A. Baker Jr., however, notes that the essay intends "to advocate a traditional 'melting pot' ideal in American 'high art' " but that Ellison's "injunctions" actually "comprise the *All* of American culture" (*Blues* 13). Cushing Strout (80) and John M. Reilly ("Discovering" 42) both notice the crucial importance of the sacred democratic texts and words to Ellison. Robert Bone stresses the sense of personal responsibility Ellison and his narrator each feel for the realization of democracy's ideals (103).

17 Consider this example Ellison gives of dancing among slaves: "A slave could be in the yard looking in at the whites dancing and come out and imitate that dance, and put his own riffs to it, and you've got something else. That's how American choreography developed" (qted. in Benston 41).

18 D. H. Lawrence memorably observed of America that a nation seeking a "spirit of place" has no true identity, and its movement, or action, while allegedly claiming freedom, is only "a rattling of chains" (*Studies* 6). Lawrence's study of American literature, alternatively hostile and affectionate, sought to identify for America a nourishing sense of tradition out of which a spirit of place could grow. And except

for his admiration of Whitman's mystical, divine soul which could absorb all of our democratic souls into one, Lawrence knew that the American's search for a sense of place was doomed. He may as well have been describing Ellison's "man of parts" or even Ralph Emerson when he defined the "the true myth of America": "She starts old, wrinkled and writhing in an old skin. And there is a gradual sloughing of the old skin, toward a new youth. It is the myth of America" (54).

19  See Burke's 1953 Prologue to *Permanence* for a discussion of this concept.

20  Reflecting a basic assumption of Ellison criticism, most of the book jackets for the novel have told us that the narrator is on a search for self. Usually, this "good" but hidden self is seen dualistically, in opposition with "bad" society which will not let this self be itself. As Cushing Strout puts the matter, "Instead of asserting his own independent judgment, he internalizes the expectations of others" ("An American" 81). Elizabeth Lyons argues that the narrator strives to be "an uncompromised individual" who "will seek the Emersonian independence that would free him from self-imposed bondage" ("Ellison" 95, 100). See also Lyons, "Ellison's Narrator" 75–78. From different perspectives, Nadel, Albrecht, and Kun Jong Lee argue that Ellison is critiquing Emerson. Whereas Lee says that Ellison critiques Emerson's inability to deal with racism, Albrecht argues that Ellison transformed his philosophical affinity with Emerson into a political critique. I discuss Nadel in detail later in the chapter. For other readings that connect Ellison to Emerson, see Deutsch, Nichols, and Rovit.

21  For two other discussions of Ellison's pragmatism, see Posnock, *Color;* and Albrecht. In passing, Berndt Ostendorf calls Ellison "a radical American pragmatist" without actually explaining how he fits into the pragmatist tradition (105).

22  Tanner provides an excellent discussion of the narrator's use of electricity (80–94), as does Stepto (163–94, esp. 192–94).

23  Nadel, *Invisible*, gives the most thorough examination of Clifton. Nadel focuses on the Sambo doll Clifton is selling before he dies, especially the puppet's "black string" which he interprets as "an emblematic lesson about the possibilities of black power: Clifton could make the image do anything he wanted it to, but, having gotten control of the invisible black string, he could not discover what to do with it because every choice was subject to the interpretation by a world with different assumptions" (81).

24  Elizabeth A. Schultz compares Rinehart to Melville's Pip, saying both come "to mirror formless chaos, and in doing so, are annihilated" (191). Elizabeth Lyons adds tht he "is the individual who in Emersonian terms has so thoroughly violated the integrity of his being that he assumes the contours of his situation" ("Ellison's" 76). On the other hand, Tony Tanner notes that Rinehart is less a man than "a strategy to made aware of" (86).

25  Robert O'Meally correctly notes that Rinehart is meant to evoke "the strutting bad-man of many blues" (*Craft* 90). As such, he evokes the myth of Stagger-Lee, who acted out the violent fantasies of African American culture, a figure so "bad" that his power transcended racial lines, which may have been a part of his mythic power. See Marcus, *Mystery* 65–68, 223–25.

26  See Nadel 111–23. He acknowledges that Ellison's final position on Emerson is ambivalent.

## 4  *Philip Roth: The Jew That Got Away*

1  The explosion of ethnic writers has been reflected in the way American literature is taught. For at least the past decade all over the country English departments have been hiring "Americanist" professors on the basis of their ability to teach certain kinds of ethnic literatures.

2  In her valuable study *A Measure of Memory* (1996), which discusses "the evolution of American Jewish literature from its immigrant origins to the present," Victoria Aarons argues that "while one would expect that a preoccupation with the past would fade as the immigrant's marginalized status in America became less distinct," actually "we find a growing preoccupation with an even more vigorously imagined past" (170).

3  A typical response to his early work, according to Roth, was that of "an eminent New York rabbi who wrote a letter of protest to the Anti-Defamation League of B'Nai Brith" to ask: " 'What is being done to silence this man?' " (*Reading* 133).

4  As Roth points out, this question was to turn up twenty years later in *The Ghost Writer*, asked of Nathan Zuckerman by Judge Leopold Wapter (127).

5  It is interesting that when Roth can no longer stand up to the grilling, Ellison takes over for him. "Ralph Ellison must have noticed my tenacity fading because all at once I heard him defending me with an eloquent authority that I could never have hoped to muster from halfway out to oblivion. His intellectual position was virtually identical to mine, but he was presenting it as a black American, instructing through examples drawn from *Invisible Man* and the ambiguous relationship that novel had established with some vocal members of his own race" (128). A crucial difference between Ellison and Roth, though, is that Ellison was never interested in exacerbating the conflict he experienced between his work and his audience so much as reconciling it.

6  Reading the reactions to Roth's earliest work thirty years later, one is struck by the enormous critical importance placed on Roth's subject matter, that is, the fact that he was writing about Jews. Prominent Jewish intellectuals exerted considerable critical energy in assessing the work of an unestablished young writer. In part, they meant to defend Roth from the accusations of readers whose sense of literature had not been refined by a healthy dose of modernism. Leslie Fielder, Alfred Kazin, Irving Howe, and Saul Bellow each weighed in on Roth and in the process gave to Roth's work an early stamp of seriousness that it likely would not have received had he not been writing about Jews. Indeed, Jeremy Larner, writing in the *Partisan Review*, took it upon himself to defend those who had attacked Roth for cultural insensitivity. Larner took issue with Bellow's, Howe's, and Kazin's assessments of Roth on the grounds that Roth's account of suburban Jewishness is "incorrect." Roth himself seemed uncomfortable that he could excite so much critical attention writing about Jewish characters, and his next two works, *Letting Go* and *When She*

*Was Good*, in different ways veered considerably from the cultural milieu of *Good-bye, Columbus* and the early stories. Roth's return to an aggressively Jewish subject matter with *Portnoy's Complaint* again touched off a critical firestorm among his Jewish audience. Yet after this reaction, which included Howe's famous critique, it was Roth, not his critics, who continued to make an issue of how American Jews read his work. In addition to Fiedler, "Image," Kazin (written after *Portnoy*), Howe, "Philip Roth," and Bellow, "Swamp," see Guttman, "Philip Roth," and Solotaroff for essays that try to place the reaction to Roth in a cultural-historical perspective.

7  Mark Schechner suggests that "Roth's Jews are not a *people*, a *culture, nation, tradition,* or any other noun of rabbinical piety. They are a *tribe*, which, after its own primitive fashion, observes arbitrary taboos and performs strange sundown rituals that look like obsessional symptoms" (122–23). This claim made more sense in 1974 when Schechner wrote it than it does now. Prior to *The Ghost Writer* (1979), Roth's Jews existed primarily to persecute his protagonists. Though Zuckerman and later Roth certainly have their problems with other Jews, their actions are placed in the broader context that Appelfeld describes.

8  David Monoghan wrote in 1975 that criticism of Roth "has tended to be over-preoccupied with Jewish cultural issues to the exclusion of discussion of the novel as literature" (68). Since *The Ghost Writer*, though, many readers have been more likely to go the other way and say with Jonathan Brent that in Roth "the self is always a literary construction" (181–82). Brent, though, needlessly isolates Roth's narrative experimentation by arguing that "in Zuckerman we do not find the portrait of the artist brought up to date since Stephen Dedalus, but that portrait of the imagination severed from any world except that contained in the artist's mind" (183). To the contrary, Zuckerman's portraits of the artist are always being com-promised by their interactions with the world outside of the artist's mind. Roth does not hold up the artist severed from any world but that of his own making as a desirable dream since both his fiction and Zuckerman's assumes an audience that will challenge the claims of his fiction making. I would argue that Roth's work since *The Ghost Writer* has tended to blur the distinction between these two cate-gories so that one cannot discuss self-making, Jewish or otherwise, in Roth with-out discussing his experimentation with narrative and form (Pinsker 113–20).

9  In this scene Roth is likely playing with the mystery that surrounds the four-lettered Hebrew word ("Yahweh") that stands for an inscrutable, ineffable God whose name cannot be spoken. As a writer, Roth too sees language as constitutive of identity and therefore, in a way, holy. Thus Roth's deepest anxieties involve words. He has said that his identity is shaped by the "jumpy" feel of American language; this language makes up who he is. It is revealing, then, that he writes this scene in *Operation Shylock* so that the character Philip Roth likewise has a shatter-ing experience in a classroom devoted to the study of Hebrew. As we shall see, though, the scene in *Operation Shylock* leads us to believe tht Roth has found not his essential self but rather a new beginning—in the language of *The Facts*, yet another origin in a life of multiple origins. Given his antiessentialism it may strike many as

surprising that Roth would employ the sacred mystery that Jews associate with the Hebrew language (an association that English speakers, especially American English speakers, do not have with their language, except, in the case of the latter, perhaps through the Declaration of Independence) to confront his own identity. In the earlier "'I Always Wanted You to Admire My Fasting'; or, Looking at Kafka," though, Roth had imagined that Kafka had escaped his death and the Holocaust to become a Hebrew teacher in Newark. In other words, Kafka's arrival in New Jersey coincides with Roth's initiation into the Hebrew language. Roth's imaginary Kafka frightens him because what he teaches, the ancient language of Hebrew, compromises the root—the essence—of Jewish identity, insofar as essences can be said to exist in the Rothian universe. From this perspective, Henry's embrace of Hebrew is a projection of Roth-the-writer's worst nightmare: to be without his native language, to be self-less.

10  For excellent discussions of how Roth uses his invention of Zuckerman to confront both the meaning of the Holocaust and his own relation to European Jewish writers, see Wirth-Nesher and Hermione Lee.

11  That Roth allowed his essay to be published on the same page as the *Times*'s own review of *Operation Shylock* suggests how much he wanted his readers to make this connection.

12  Roth explains in the novel that among other effects Halcion causes one to believe that one's self is disintegrating.

13  The Hebrew term is the equivalent of "gossip" or "slander"; it might also be translated as "tongue of evil." It derives from Leviticus 19:16: "You shall not go about as a talebearer among thy people." Maimonides specifies in the first book of his *Mishneh Torah* that though it is not necessary to "give lashes in connection with this prohibition, it is a great sin and causes many people of Israel to be killed" (50). The Chofetz Chayyim, as he is often called, is a frequently mentioned authority among many contemporary Orthodox Jews. Roth's depiction of *loshon hora* and Chofetz Chaim is, predictably, double. On one hand, he mocks the Orthodox position through Smilesberger's reading of Chofetz Chaim by presenting it as a comic reductio ad absurdum; on the other hand, by suppressing the one chapter of the novel that details his spy mission for Israel, Roth slyly suggests that he is following the Orthodox position and has acquitted himself of any previous acts of *loshon hora*.

14  Hermione Lee has suggested that in the Zuckerman trilogy Roth projected "a complicated attitude, not simply the Jewish-American's writer's guilt for the sufferings of eastern European writers and, before that, for the Jews in Europe, but, with it, a kind of wistfulness, even envy, for the writer who has had more to sink his teeth into than books and relationships" (155). I agree that Roth's attitude is complicated, but I think that what wistfulness or envy he projects is, like everything else in Roth, highly fictionalized. What obsesses Roth is how these prior events impinge on the self-inventions his characters strive for. Indeed, Zuckerman's fantasy in *The Ghost Writer* that Anne Frank escaped death and reinvented herself as the American college student Amy Bellette, like Roth's fantasy about

Kafka, suggests the extent to which Roth cannot imagine a history for himself alternative to the one he has experienced. That is, he cannot imagine European Jews except as Americans. When the icons of Jewish literature Frank and Kafka are transported to Roth's America, they are no longer tragic figures; they are no longer—in our view—themselves. *Operation Shylock* pushes this sense of dislocation to its most extreme conclusion.

15  This scenario is not so outrageous. The Mossad often asks American Jews to do them small favors, such as agreeing to test whether planted material can bypass security at Ben Gurion airport in Tel Aviv.

16  Harold Bloom too says that the "fictive mission that 'Philip Roth' undertakes" is "a response to the potent myth of Shakespeare." Bloom concludes that *Operation Shylock*'s answer to Shakespeare's Shylock is "the mode of comedy practiced" by Aristophanes (48).

17  For a good discussion of how Roth's work projects itself "into the Holocaust through the image of the writer of silence," see Kartiganer, "Ghost Writing" (168).

18  The parallel with " 'I Always Wanted You to Admire My Fasting': Or, Looking at Kafka," where Roth also reminisces about his experience in Hebrew school, is, I imagine, intentional.

19  Regarding this point, it is intriguing to note that in one of his manuscripts Roth identified Smilesburger as "a friend of Singer's," presumably meaning I. B. Singer. I think Shostak is right to say that this "association suggests that Smilesburger is connected to the consummate Old-World Jewish storyteller, in a sense one of Roth's progenitors" (749).

## 5   Don't Be Cruel: Elvis Invents America Again

1  Mississippi blues singer Bukka White concurs, but suggests that the blues that began behind the mule just continued when the day's work was done. "That's where the blues start, back across them fields, you know, under them old trees, under them old log houses, you know. Guys will sit there at night—the moon was shining—and drink, you know. . . . It didn't start in no city, now. Don't ever get that wrong. It started behind one of them mules or one of them log houses, one of them log camps or the levee camp. That's where the blues sprung from. I know what I'm talking about" (quoted in Evans 43).

2  He replaced Robert Johnson with Big Joe Turner, whose style was very different from Johnson's.

3  The majority of the African American audience at this time was listening to Otis Redding or James Brown, soul artists who would have been embarrassed to be identified as blues singers.

4  See the video *Masters of the Country Blues: Son House/Bukka White* (Yazoo). No date is given. The compact disc *Delta Blues and Spirituals* (Columbia), recorded in 1970 before a live audience at London's 100 Club, also contains fascinating House monologues interspersed with blues and spirituals.

5  An additional irony to the history of "Hound Dog," which Walker does not choose to explore, is that it was written by two Jewish white boys, Jerry Leiber and Mike Stoller, in the hope that they could get a suitable black singer to perform it. For a full discussion of the many twists and turns the song took before finding fame and fortune with Elvis, including a reading of how Elvis radically reinterprets Thornton's original version, see Marcus, *Mystery* 155–56.

   Albert Goldman's biography *Elvis* portrays an ignorant "uncircumcised" hillbilly who crudely tries to ape the gestures of a culture he does not understand. Perhaps no other "critic" has done more to obscure the significance of Elvis's work than Goldman. Sympathetic with neither the southern culture that spawned Presley nor the achievement of his art, Goldman's book interests itself only with scandal—orgies, drugs, violence, and so forth. For a devastating critique of Goldman's *Elvis*, its shoddy research, and its lack of critical perspective, see Marcus, who aptly labels the book an "attempt at cultural genocide" (*Dead* 48, 47–59).

6  Marion Keisker, who was Phillips's close associate at Sun Records, told Elvis's 1971 biographer, Jerry Hopkins, that he said, "If I could find a white man who had the Negro sound and the Negro feel, I could make a billion dollars." Upon reading Goldman's biography, Greil Marcus phoned Keisker (who was not interviewed for Goldman's book) to get her version again. Keisker insisted that she never heard Phillips use the word "nigger" and that nothing would be more out of character (Marcus, *Dead* 52–53).

7  The logic of Handy's account is not so different from that of the "Empress of the Blues," Gertrude "Ma" Rainey. Rainey was a singer in a traveling vaudeville show working its way through Missouri when she heard a young woman sing "a strange and poignant song" about a man who had quit the singer. Rainey worked this "blues" into her act. When she discovered that this type of performing was what most moved rural black audiences, she began to look for more blues. She told John Work that she noticed many such songs afterward, noting that they were not then called blues (Work 32–33).

8  Elvis did cut a version of Water's "Got My Mojo Working," released posthumously on *Walk a Mile in My Shoes: The Essential 70's Masters.*

9  Nick Tosches reports seeing on the day Elvis died a sign outside a Baptist church in Orangeburg, South Carolina, declaring that "All That Hip Shaking Killed Elvis" (273).

10  Crudup himself articulated his own understanding of why theft is not a relevant term in discussing what Elvis supposedly did to black music. "People ask me about Elvis Presley, how do I feel about him. Ought to be mad with him, they say. For what? I said I don't even know the man. I said I know he's from Memphis, Tennessee, all right enough, but I've never met him. I didn't give him the songs. And he didn't steal them because I didn't write them on paper." Crudup is quoted in McKee and Chisenhall, 206.

11  Paul Simon's *Graceland* album, though widely admired, was also criticized for exploiting the African music it promoted.

12  See James, (*Writings* 509). I am quoting from the work *Pragmatism* (1907). My

abbreviated summary of pragmatism is obviously little more than a sketch, an evocation of the general aims that pragmatists share. For the best contemporary accounts of pragmatism, see the Rorty books elsewhere mentioned as well as Richard, *Poetry*, and West.

13  See also Michaels's "Race into Culture," an essay that he later worked into *Our America*.

14  The liner notes to Bear Family Records' definitive collection of Jimmie Rodgers's music shows a picture of the lyric sheet to "Blue Yodel #9" with Rodgers's hand-writing at the bottom noting that Armstrong and Harding accompanied him. For a solid discussion of Rodgers's life and music, see Nolan Porterfield's liner notes. For a more detailed examination of Rodgers, see Porterfield's *Jimmie Rodgers: The Life and Times of America's Blue Yodeler*.

15  See Guralnick, *Lost* 283 and *Feel* 163.

16  For an excellent discussion of other white country blues artists, see Wolfe "Lighter."

17  The then-president of CBS Records, Walter Yentikoff, threatened to remove all CBS artists from distribution if MTV would not agree to play videos from Jackson's *Thriller*. This near boycott broke MTV's color line. From its inception, MTV was criticized for its reluctance to play videos by black artists. As the success of *Yo! MTV Raps!* shows, however, once a market is proved to exist, even the most rigid color lines become fluid, washed over in the color of money (Marsh, *First* 204).

18  George acknowledges that rap poses a problem to his thesis, as his next two books admit. See *Buppies*.

19  At the time "Elvis Is Dead" was released, Little Richard could be seen and heard on Taco Bell commercials as well as during the theme song to television's *Friday Night Videos*. When he is given the chance to speak for himself, however, Richard makes it clear that he is the "originator" of rock and roll. After we offer the requisite apologies to Chuck Berry, Little Richard has a defensible claim, except for one thing: there was no originator to rock and roll any more than there was an original version of "Don't Be Cruel." In "Elvis Is Dead," Little Richard appears in the guise of the king who has survived, playing David to Elvis's Saul. Magnani-mous in his royalty, Little Richard preaches a sermon against the "vultures" who will not let Elvis rest in peace. That Little Richard could be speaking of Living Colour as one of those vultures is another nice irony the song allows.

20  Essentially, Brown was arrested and jailed for fleeing the police, who were fol-lowing him because of a misunderstanding. Details are jumbled, but apparently Brown had good reason to run. He drove six miles on wheel rims in a vehicle that by the end of the chase sported twenty-three bullet holes. For in-depth accounts of the sordid story that landed Brown in prison, see Marsh, "Prisoner" 269–83 and Booth 228–49.

21  Brown's interpretation of Elvis seems consonant with the view of Toni Morrison and other black intellectuals that President Clinton is culturally black. African Americans identify with Clinton, according to this argument, because they under-stand his treatment by the white establishment to be consonant with their experi-ence as African Americans.

22 White tells this story in the liner notes to the *CD of JBII* (1987).

23 It is appropriate that they first met each other at a Jackie Wilson concert. See Guralnick, *Careless* 238–39 and Brown, 165.

24 You can hear James Brown trying to overcome his debt to Little Richard on *The Federal Years Parts 1 and 2*.

25 Michael Brooks points out repeatedly in his liner notes to the nine-volume "Quintessential Billie Holiday" series on Columbia that Holiday was almost always given second-rate material. Of "Gloomy Sunday," he remarks: "If ever there was a song manufactured by the media this is it. It was imported from Hungary, given English lyrics and dubbed 'The Hungarian Suicide Song,' supposedly because distraught lovers made the air black with their flying bodies after hearing it, much the same way as financiers acted after the '29 Crash. The authenticity of both stories has yet to be verified." For Holiday's version of this song, see Holiday vol. 9.

26 Henry Louis Gates defines "signifying" as a practice crucial to African American culture, "a trope of a trope" that takes prior forms of discourse and reshapes them in a way that comments on the previous form of discourse while forging a new kind of language. This practice depends on the "symbiotic relationship between . . . black vernacular discourse and Standard English discourse" (*Signifying* 50).

27 Lomax, who was not inclined to appreciate cultural hybridity, was ambivalent in his account of Elvis. Noting a similarity between Elvis and the anonymous black blues singer Turner Junior Thompson, Lomax writes: "Turner was from Elvis Presley's hometown, the place where he learned from the blacks how to perform black style, his pelvis twisting, his left thigh swinging, his voice swooping into blue notes. The handsome young cracker from Tupelo put black and white singing styles together in a way that won over young white lovers and singers in the English-speaking world over to the black side. Elvis Presley sold more records than any other singer in history and ushered in the age of rock. And the haunting quality of Elvis's voice, the note that captures and holds you, echoes the dark and tragic history of Tupelo that sounded in every note Turner Junior Johnson sang" (*Land* 36).

28 Speaking of white jazz critics, Gerald Early argues that Davis saw "the white male presence as a hegemonic challenge to his right of self-definition" ("Lives" 129–46).

29 After playing Elvis's version of bluesman Arthur Crudup's "That's All Right, Mama," Dewey Phillips was besieged with phone calls questioning the identity of the new, and strange, singer. Elvis was immediately rushed to the studio so Phillips could ask, "What high school do you attend?" Elvis: "Humes High." The answer let the listeners know that Elvis was white.

30 See the video *Elvis: '68 Comeback Special*, dir. Steve Binder, Media Home Entertainment, 1984.

31 As we are more and more aware, and as southerners have always known, if not always admitted, the interaction between black and white cultures has been going on for a long time. For a detailed discussion of how white and black minstrels copied each other's styles near the turn of this century, see Sundquist, *To Wake* 294–323.

32 See Guralnick's account of this musical encounter (*Careless* 63).

33 Johnny Rivers told Elvis biographer Jerry Hopkins: "One of Elvis's idols when he was young was Jake Hess of the Statesmen Quartet. If you listen to some of their recordings, you'll hear some of that style is now Elvis Presley's style, especially in his ballad singing. He was playing some of their records one day and he said, 'Now you know where I got my style'" (18). See Charles Wolfe's liner notes to *Elvis Presley Amazing Grace: His Greatest Sacred Performances*.

34 Fifteen years later Elvis returned to "Little Cabin on the Hill" for his *Elvis Country* album (1971). Making what is hardly a traditional country album in any sense, Elvis takes country standards and—as he always did—makes them over in his own image. That version, too, begins with Elvis pretending to be Monroe before modulating into his own style. As for "Blue Moon of Kentucky," an alternate take exists where Elvis deconstructs it from the inside, as it were (*Sunrise*). This version is slow, respectful, but still utterly different from Monroe's. Marcus says it "sounds so primitive," "music out of the Mississippi woods a hundred years gone" (*Mystery* 165).

35 On the subject of royalties, Elvis's white band mates also got a raw deal. According to Scotty Moore, Elvis at one time suggested that they get 1% of his royalties, but the Colonel nixed the deal. Moore, Black, and Fontana were of course disappointed to be cut out of Elvis's financial success, and were unquestionably denied a lot of money. As the years progressed, it became clear that Elvis too was cheated out of a lot of money by the Colonel. The point here is that mixing art and money almost always makes for a dirty story, but that melancholy truth is not the same as saying that Elvis liked black music because singing it would make him rich. Elvis's skill at adapting the blues made a lot of people rich—and continues to make people rich with Elvis in the grave for nearly twenty-five years.

36 I have not been able to determine the exact date of the Letterman show Blackwell was on, though I am fairly certain it was sometime during 1986.

37 Actually, the version I am thinking of also belongs to Coleman Hawkins, who duetted with Rollins on this song and the album of the same name (RCA Bluebird).

38 Elvis's friend George Klein tells a story that, in a limited way, shows Elvis and one of his African American peers actually interacting. Klein apparently was present when the great rhythm-and-blues singer Ivory Joe Hunter paid a visit to Elvis's home, Graceland. Elvis was a great admirer of Hunter's work and had even recorded his "I Need You So." After swapping stories for a while, Elvis asked Hunter if he had any more songs he could record. Klein relates:

> Now Ivory Joe was a real friendly guy. Great big, 'Hey, baby, how you doing, baby?' kind of guy. You just immediately like him. And he said, 'Well, baby, I just have—I got one just for you.' So we went in the piano room, and he sang 'My Wish Came True,' and Elvis said, 'Shit, I'm cutting that at my next session!' Which he did, even though it didn't come out for a couple of years. And they sat there for hours, mostly singing Ivory Joe's songs, a few of Elvis'—man, I just wish I'd had a tape machine running. (Guralnick, *Last* 425)

We are lucky that Sam Phillips had one running the day that Elvis created Jackie Wilson's version of him.

39   Nat D. Williams, on the other hand, was disturbed by the "thousand black, brown and beige teen-age girls in the audience [who] blended their alto and soprano voices in one wild crescendo of sound that rent the rafters . . . and took off like scalded cats in the direction of Elvis" (McKee and Chisenhall 96).

40   I do not have the figures for how many saw this show. According to Neal and Janice Gregory, though, for the September 9, 1956, show "a record 82.6 percent of the population was watching, compared with 78.6 percent that had watched a few weeks earlier as President Eisenhower accepted his party's nomination for a second term" (61).

41   To view this performance of "Don't Be Cruel," see *This Is Elvis*, dir. Andrew Solt and Malcom Leo, Warner Brothers, 1981. As for Jackie Wilson, he awaits his hattie gosset to mythologize him. One of the most gifted of rhythm-and-blues singers, Wilson never caught on. Equipped with an operatic vocal range, he was shuffled from producer to producer while his career yielded a dozen or so hits, a handful of R & B classics, and a pile of string-soaked Mantovanniesque *dreck*. Most commentators view Wilson as a great rhythm-and-blues singer who, for some reason or other, never got to pursue his talent, an odd fate for one who was the boyhood friend of Berry Gordy, the founder of Motown. In a sense, Presley's career was as badly mismanaged as Wilson's. Both became the mute dupes of their handlers. The difference, of course, is that Elvis made a fortune.

42   Lansky Brothers catered mostly to African American clientele. It was where, says Stanley Booth, "the black pimps traded" (50). Nonetheless, white boys like Elvis Presley and Carl Perkins went there—as Perkins sang—"to put their cat clothes on," that is, to dress like blacks. Although classmates of Elvis would sometimes make fun of the way he dresssed, they also knew where (if not why) he was buying his clothes.

43   Consider this letter written by a "scion of an old Memphis family" to the Elvis biographer Elaine Dundy:

> I have only one overall impression about Mr. Presley's position and acceptance in Memphis. And that is naturally from the point of view of the world I was born and raised in, the world of the country club, etc. He was referred to then as a embarrassment to the community, as his art was vulgar and common, tacky and lower class.
>
> As the years passed and Presley's wealth as well as his fame began to benefit the Memphis charities, a transition occurred. He became known as "a fine young man." Of course, he was still secretly mocked as being tasteless and vulgar—all those many-colored Cadillacs, etc. And in the typical fashion of the hypocrisy people of that class and its culture, or I should say lack of culture, Presley was admired but you really wouldn't want him to marry "our daughters" or sit down at "our table," or belong to "our club." But it would be nice to have him present at some social event to add some "kickness" to the occasion. Or some fund-raising event where he would be valuable. (229)

Dundy's work provides an excellent analysis of the relation Elvis had with his mother.

44 For the Carters' debt to black music, see Barry O'Connell's moving essay on Lesley Riddle, the black guitar player from whom they learned so much. Autry's interesting Jimmie Rodgers–style country blues are collected on *Gene Autry: Blues Singer 1929–31* (Columbia). Wills's music is full of jazz and blues and just about any collection will do, but especially *Tiffany Transcriptions*, Vol. 9.

45 Elvis responded, "When I'm out there, I do what they want to hear—when I'm back here, I can do what I want to do," at which point Ira tried to strangle Elvis (Guralnick, *Last* 253). By the 1970s Elvis could do anything he wanted on stage since not only did he play "nigger trash," but he had also hired the most prominent white gospel group on the gospel circuit, J. D. Sumner and the Stamps, to perform with him. As a youth Elvis knew Sumner as the bass singer for the Blackwood Brothers. See Wolfe, "Presley."

46 According to Little Richard, the nonsense syllables filled in for obscenities.

47 When Elvis introduces "Ready Teddy" at the Mississippi-Alabama State Fair in 1956 by proclaiming it "one of the most beautiful songs ever written" and saying, "Friends, this is a sad song, really," he sounds loose, confident. Singing to a rural southern audience of blacks and whites, Elvis knows that he is in his element. His playful song introductions ooze with confidence and irony. Along with the Dorsey and Sullivan performances, this show is included in the indispensable *Elvis: A Golden Celebration*.

48 In 1969 when Elvis was in the recording studio to solidify the "comeback" he had made the previous year with his TV special, he was told that Roy Hamilton, the legendary blues singer and one of Elvis's heroes, was cutting a record in a nearby studio. He asked his producer to set up a meeting with Hamilton at Hamilton's convenience. Upon meeting his idol (one of many to be sure), Elvis did something that "totally floored" everyone in the studio, including Hamilton. Elvis gave to Hamilton "Angelica," one of the songs written by the top-notch songwriting team of Barry Weil and Cynthia Mann, which Elvis was going to record during his own sessions. "Man, he really loved that song," noted Elvis's longtime companion George Klein. Although "Angelica" likely would have been a hit as big as "In the Ghetto" or "Suspicious Minds," two songs Elvis had also recorded recently during that session, Elvis was eager to the point of desperation to express to Hamilton how much the older man's music had meant to him (Guralnick, *Careless* 333–34).

49 In perhaps the most prominent academic study which attempts to meld high culture with popular culture, literature with the blues, Houston A. Baker Jr. ignores the extent to which both "black" (blues) and "white" (hillbilly) culture overlapped and cross-pollinated. Baker rightly says that the mark for a railroad crossing, "X," is a peculiarly appropriate evocation of the blues since "the dominant blues syntagm in America is an instrumental imitation of *train-wheels-over-track-junctures.*" Therefore, "the blues figure at the crossing . . . became an expert at reproducing these locomotive energies." Though Baker is certainly right in linking the blues with trains and railroad crossings, he fails to realize that the locomo-

tive was as emblematic of hillbilly music, as country and western was called in its early, less reputable days, as it was of "blues." Jimmie Rodgers was not called "The Singing Brakeman" for nothing, and the sound of the steel guitar, perhaps hillbilly's most distinctive instrument, has always sought—even today—to hum like train wheels going down the track or pierce like a train's whistle. Thus, the railroad crossing "X," which Baker finds to be "a point of ceaseless input and output," actually demarcates a cultural crossroads of black and white culture, of American culture in whole and in part. See Baker, *Blues* 8, 11.

50  Only Gerri Hirshey and Bruce Tucker, Brown's co-writer for his autobiography, discuss the relationship, perhaps because they talked with Brown himself rather than surrendering to Brown's iconography.

# SELECTED DISCOGRAPHY
■■■■■■■

*I   Mississippi Delta Blues*

The following represents a selection of mostly available Delta blues recordings, including all of the ones mentioned in this book. I have taken some liberties with geography
and chronology. In order to suggest the range of Mississippi blues I have included
performers such as Mississippi Fred McDowell and Mississippi John Hurt, whose styles
are not limited only to that associated with the Delta. As I note in chapter 2, many great
Mississippi delta blues performers came from the adjoining regions of Louisiana,
Arkansas, and western Tennessee. Blues performers and their families rambled all
throughout these areas—Muddy Waters and Son House both spent their formative
years in Louisiana—and as a result local styles were shared freely. I have also included
the names of a few contemporary performers who still very obviously work out of the
Delta style. Fat Possum records, based in Oxford, Mississippi, has been releasing an astonishing series of recordings documenting this still living folk tradition. This list is not
meant to be a comprehensive or encyclopedic guide to Delta blues, but is intended as a
starting point for those interested in discovering this wonderful music for themselves.

INDIVIDUALS

R. L. Burnside (*Too Bad Jim; Come On In* Fat Possum 42082-2, 80317-2). Burnside is
    capable of making Delta blues records in the traditional acoustic style, but his
    electric blues are what make him truly noteworthy. These two albums are a stun-
    ning instance of how the blues can absorb the styles it inspired—from Jimi Hen-
    drix to heavy metal. Apocalyptic and foreboding, Burnside's blues are ready for the
    21st century. *Acoustic Stories* (MC 0034) contains an excellent version of "Walking
    Blues."
Honeyboy Edwards (*White Windows* Evidence ECD 26939-2). Edwards is perhaps best
    noted for frequently sharing "canned heat"—a brutal type of low-grade alcohol—
    with Tommy Johnson. Not a master like Johnson or Son House, his playing on
    this 1988 album is a moving instance of an old-time Delta performer still beau-
    tifully practicing his trade.

The Fieldstones (*Memphis Blues Today* High Water/HMG 6505). Recorded by folklorist David Evans in 1981–82, the Fieldstones play the country blues of Tommy Johnson, Robert Johnson, and Charlie Patton inflected through the groove of 1960s Memphis soul. What Tommy Johnson might have sounded like if he were backed by Booker T. and the MGs.

Buddy Guy and Junior Wells (*Alone and Acoustic* Alligator ALCD 4802). Guy and Wells grew up in Louisiana idolizing Chess recording legends such as Muddy Waters, Howlin' Wolf, and Little Walter Jacobs. Wells eventually replaced Little Walter in Muddy Waters's best band, and Guy also would get to play with all of his heroes. Along with B. B. King, Guy is now recognized as the Grand Seigneur of the blues. His recent records are electrified rock-blues of the sort that the white blues performers Eric Clapton and Stevie Ray Vaughan made popular, but in concert he will still give masterful lessons in blues history by working through the styles of his own mentors, Robert Johnson, John Lee Hooker, and Muddy Waters. On *Alone*, Guy and Wells trace the blues through Hooker and Johnson back to the levee camps and the birth of the blues.

John Lee Hooker (*Alternative Boogie: Early Studio Recordings*, 1948–52 Capitol CDP 7243; *The Legendary Blues Modern Recordings*, 1948–54 Flair 7243 8 39658 2 3). An essential Delta-based performer, Hooker is still releasing records with virtually anyone who wants to perform with him and has the cash to pay him. Even when he is tricked up with bands and celebrity guests, the force of his original style still comes through. Compared with R. L. Burnside or Junior Kimbrough, Hooker comes across as an archaeological discovery, perfectly preserved and still breathing. His most powerful work has been solo: Hooker alone with his pounding guitar, stamping foot, and stoic rage. His early recordings remain essential, but almost any record is representative. "Blues for Abraham Lincoln" is on *John Lee Hooker's 40th Anniversary Album* (DCC Compact Classics DZS 042).

Howlin' Wolf (*Howlin' Woof: The Chess Box* MCA CHD3-9332; *Howlin' Wolf: Memphis Days—The Definitive Editions Vols. 1 & 2*, Bear Family Records BCD 15460, 15500). Born Chester Burnett in West Helena, Arkansas, in 1910, Howlin' Wolf became part of the great migration from the South to Chicago. Along with Muddy Waters, Wolf was the biggest name in Chicago blues. *Memphis Days* is amplified blues straight from the cotton field—electric Chicago blues before it came to Chicago. His last album, *The Back Door Wolf* (MCA CHD 9358), was as topical as Wolf's music was resilient: it contained a blues about the moon landing ("Coon on the Moon") and Watergate ("Watergate Blues"). A fierce personality, Wolf never wavered in his commitment to play the blues he had learned as a young man. The Chess set nicely encapsulates his entire career; of special interest are the monologues in which Wolf puckishly discusses his music's origins. Sam Phillips once remarked that he had heard no voice as powerful as Howlin' Wolf's—it marked the spot where "the soul of man never dies."

Son House (*The Complete Library of Congress Sessions* Travelin' Man TM CD 02). Muddy Waters's master and one of the greatest of the Delta bluesmen, Son House is known more for his extraordinary singing than his guitar playing. House first recorded in the 1920s with Charlie Patton and by the 1940s was retired. He moved to Rochester, New York, and lived there in obscurity until he was rediscovered by Dick Waterman. Finding that he still had an audience—though one that had not been born at the time he first achieved his fame—House took up the guitar again and began playing folk concerts here and abroad. Recorded by Alan Lomax at Klacks's Store in Lake Cormorant, Mississippi, in 1941, the *Library of Congress Sessions* is one of the essential recordings in American music. *Father of the Delta Blues: The Complete 1965 Sessions* (Columbia CK 48867) and *Delta Blues and Spiritual* (Capitol Blues Collections D108935) prove that House remained a power performer even in his second career. Two amazing videos exist of House performing with other Delta legends: *Son House/Bukka White* (Yazoo 500) and *Devil Got My Woman: Blues at Newport 1966* (Vestapol 13409), which also includes White, Howlin' Wolf, Skip James, and Reverend Pearly Brown.

Mississippi John Hurt (*1928 Sessions* Yazoo 1065; *The Best of Mississippi John Hurt* Vanguard VCD 19/20). Another rediscovery, Hurt recorded in a wider variety of folk styles than conventional Delta blues players. Through Hurt we can imagine how other folk song forms became the blues. Compared with the other major figures, Hurt comes across as serene—even when singing about murder. His recordings in the 1960s are on par with his earlier ones. The Vanguard CD documents Hurt's sly mastery of both his material and his 1960s audience.

Little Walter Jacobs (*The Essential Little Walter* Chess CHD2-9342). Along with Sonny Boy (Rice Miller) Williamson, Little Walter is the greatest of Delta blues harmonica players. Through his collaboration with Muddy Waters, he was a major figure in transforming the acoustic country rhythms of the Delta to the explosive electricity of the city. A master of electronic distortion long before Jimi Hendrix, he also had the uncanny ability to make his harmonica sound like a saxophone—usually Louis Jordan's. It is impossible to imagine Chicago blues without his influence.

Elmore James (*The Sky Is Crying: The History of Elmore James* Rhino R2 71190; *Elmore James: The King of the Slide Guitar* Capricorn 9 42006-2). James is often said to have made a career out of electrifying Robert Johnson's "I Believe I'll Dust My Broom." Actually, though, his style was much more varied and nuanced than this familiar view suggests. He was also one of the first to translate the Delta idiom into an electric band format. His greatest recordings are included on *The King of the Slide Guitar*, and the Rhino set is an excellent one-disc overview of his career. *Sky* has the added benefit of a definitive essay by Robert Palmer.

Skip James (*The Complete Early Recordings* Yazoo 2009). The most idiosyncratic of the Delta masters, James played guitar and piano. Possessed of a high, keening wail, James nearly always pitched his voice in a register of pure terror. No recording in American music is as eerie or lonely as his chilling "Devil Got My Woman." Like Mississippi John Hurt, Bukka White, and Son House, James lived long enough to be rediscovered. His 1960s recordings (*Blues from the Delta* Vanguard VMD 75917-2) are as great as anything he ever did—to my mind the finest of the 1960s Delta blues recordings. *Skip's Piano Blues* (Genes GCD 9910), recorded in 1965 with James alone on piano, is equally astonishing.

Jelly Roll Kings (*Off Yonder Wall* Fat Possum/Capricorn 314 534 131-2). Lively contemporary Delta blues. Old pros led by Frank Frost, who, like Elvis, recorded for Same Phillip's Sun label, stomp through updated Delta standards, including a version of "That's Alright Mama" which recalls Elvis's version more than it does Arthur "Big Boy" Crudup's. The hilarious "Fishin' Musician" deserves special recognition.

Robert Johnson (*Robert Johnson: The Complete Recordings* Columbia C2K 46222). The archetype of the doomed bluesman—murdered by a jealous boyfriend before he reached the age of 30. Johnson's early death and amazing recordings have made him the most legendary of the Delta blues singers. Bob Dylan made sure his audience knew of his admiration for Johnson in 1965 by prominently displaying the album cover for Johnson's collected recordings (then recently reissued) on the album cover for his first electric album, *Bringing it All Back Home*. Eric Clapton and Keith Richards of the Rolling Stones have always said that Johnson was their key inspiration. Muddy Waters acknowledged having been influenced by his records. Son House said that Johnson sold his soul to the Devil to be able to play as well as he did. Certainly Johnson's technical mastery is astonishing, but it was his lyrics that made him legendary. Where the songs of Son House or Charlie Patton at times seemed almost randomly put together, Johnson crafted his lyrics with the precision of Cole Porter. To the belated, his blues performances come across as finished standards rather than fragments of a larger folk tradition. *The Roots of Robert Johnson* (Yazoo 1073) collects recordings by blues artists who either influenced Johnson or were dipping out of the same musical well. Recorded live at the 1991 Folklife Festival in Washington, D.C., *Roots of Rhythm and Blues: A Tribute to Robert Johnson* (Columbia CK 48584) presents Johnson's contemporaries (Johnny Shines, Henry Townsend, David "Honeyboy" Edwards) with present-day blues performers (Lonnie Pitchford, John Cephas, and Phil Wiggins) to pay tribute to Johnson's legacy.

Tommy Johnson (*Tommy Johnson 1928–29: Complete Recorded Works in Chronological Order* Document DOCD-5001). When H. C. Speir, a white man who owned a record store in Jackson, Mississippi, and served as a talent scout for the big record companies, first tried to record Tommy Johnson, he could only get him to record two different songs. Actually, they were basically the same song, composed of the fifteen or so verses that Johnson sang over and over—verses that reappeared countless times in countless other recordings over the years. Elvis was basically singing Tommy Johnson whenever he performed "C. C. Rider," as he liked to do late in his career. These tracks constitute perhaps the purest Delta blues recorded commercially. Rich, deeply poetic, a treasure.

Junior Kimbrough (*Sad Days, Lonely Nights; All Night Long; Most Things Haven't Worked Out* Fat Possum/Capricorn 42081-2, 42085-2, 314 534 510-2). Steeped in the tradition of the Delta blues, Kimbrough nonetheless plays them as if they were his invention. The rockabilly singer and Sun studios alumnus Charlie Feathers recalls hearing Junior around Holly Springs, Mississippi, in the 1950s and says that Kimbrough is "the beginning and end of music." Like all great blues musicians, Kimbrough is meant to be heard live. Indeed, his sense of timing depends on his audience's response. He performs regularly at his own Junior's Place just outside of Holly Springs, about an hour's drive southeast from Memphis.

Furry Lewis (*In His Prime* 1927–28 Yazoo 1050). Late in his life Lewis achieved notoriety by regularly cracking up Johnny Carson on *The Tonight Show* with tales of his sexual exploits. The comic irony that pervaded his blues also allowed him to steal the movie *W. W. and the Dixie Dancekings* from the star Burt Reynolds. *Fourth and Beale* (Lucky Seven CD 9202) was recorded in 1969 at Lewis's home, with Lewis singing from his bed. *Prime*, a beautiful collection of his early recordings, includes his widely copied version of "Casey Jones."

Robert Jr. Lockwood (*I Got to Find Me a Woman* Verve 314 537 448-2). At one point the stepson to Robert Johnson—hence the name Robert Jr.—Lockwood developed a guitar style that went beyond the Delta to include jazz and other forms of blues. He formed a partnership with Johnny Shines in the 1940s (see the very fine *Flyright Sessions* Paula Records PCD-14) that continued into the 1980s. He also played with Sonny Boy (Rice Miller) Williamson and was for a while B. B. King's guitar teacher. On *I Got* King joins his old teacher for a couple of duets, a generous gesture on King's part given that his mentor had told various researchers that King's sense of timing was "apeshit." This 1996 issue is noteworthy for its sublime version of the Mississippi Delta national anthem, "Walkin' Blues."

Mississippi Fred McDowell (*Mississippi Delta Blues* Arhoolie CD 304). First recorded in 1958 by Alan Lomax during one his field recording trips, McDowell quickly became one of the most revered of the Mississippi bluesmen. Except, perhaps, for his dabbling with an English rock band, McDowell never cut a side that was not exemplary.

Memphis Minnie (*Hoodoo Lady 1933–37* Columbia CK 46675). The only significant recorded female country blues performer, Memphis Minnie sold more records during her lifetime than any of her male contemporaries. Her magnificent "Nothing in Rambling" (*Memphis Minnie, Vol. 1* Blues Classics LP) might be viewed as a kind of protofeminist answer to the rambling, decidedly male ethos of most other country blues singers—that is if her "I'm Going Don't You Know" didn't suggest that Minnie too was a dedicated rambler. Represented here are her early recordings, but she also did some fine sides for Chess in the 1950s ("Lake Michigan" on *The Blues, Vol. 6* 50's Rarities MCA CHD 9330).

Robert (McCoy) Nighthawk (*Bricks in My Pillow* Delmark DD-711; *Live on Maxwell Street* Rounder CD 2022; *Robert Nighthawk Houston Stockhouse* Testament TCD 5010). Nighthawk first recorded for RCA Bluebird under the same of Robert McCoy. Some years later he resurfaced as Robert Nighthawk, and through the tutelage of Houston Stackhouse and Tampa Red he had mastered the slide guitar technique. After Robert Johnson, he may have been the best of the slide guitar players. Unfortunately, Nighthawk's legacy is not as great as it should be since he was underrecorded. *Bricks* collects his 1950s recordings; *Live* is a brutal electric set recorded in the 1960s in Chicago; the Testament disc is a lovely collection recorded in 1974 with his teacher, Houston Stackhouse, also contributing tracks.

Charlie Patton (*Founder of the Delta Blues: King of the Delta Blues* Yazoo 1020, 2001).

Born in 1891, Patton cut his first record in 1929 and was dead by 1934. Descended from Indians as well as slaves, Patton's blood ancestry was Faulknerian, and his music was equally rich. In terms of range and influence, he is the most important figure in the Delta blues tradition. Tommy Johnson, Son House, Bukka White, Muddy Waters, and Fred McDowell all sat at Patton's feet at one point or another. No one who heard him play forgot him. Despite being as influential as Louis Armstrong or Duke Ellington, we know virtually nothing about how Patton learned his art. The fact that Elvis developed his style in response to black music is no cultural crime; the fact that Charlie Patton is known only to blues scholars and a handful of blues fans is. One of the very greatest American artists.

Jimmy Rogers (*Chicago Bound* MCA CHD-93000). Another crucial figure in bringing the Delta blues to Chicago. With Little Walter, Rogers was a key figure in Muddy Waters's first great electric band. As these recordings prove, Rogers was also a great performer in his own right. "Chicago Bound" recounts the story of the blues' migration from the rural South to Chicago—in its way the perfect complement to the more well-known "Walkin' Blues."

Otis Rush (*His Cobra Recordings: 1956–58* Flyright FLYCD 01). Perhaps the most gifted musician of the second wave of Delta musicians, who moved to Chicago. Rush's career is not as well documented as it should be due to the indifference and outright exploitation he suffered from the recording industry. He remains a formidable live performer, though, when in the mood. In the last few years several live albums have appeared, each of which contains undeniable evidence of his continuing genius. The *Cobra Recordings*, though, remains his best recorded work to date: fierce, manic, almost murderous in their intensity. *Door to Door* (MCA CHLD 19169) contains, among other gems, Rush's great "So Many Roads" as well as several fine early cuts by the Indianola, Mississippi, native Albert King.

Johnny Shines (*Too Wet to Plow* Tomato 2696362). Shines traveled with Robert Johnson in the 1930s and has been able to provide some information about Johnson's obscure life. He was an excellent blues performer in his own right, though, and his work on this 1975 album vindicates Shines as a blues musician worthy to share the bill with Robert Johnson. His "Slavery Time Breakdown" can be heard on *Worried Blues Ain't Bad* (The Blues Alliance TBA 13004).

Dave Thompson (*Little Dave and Big Love* Fat Possum/Capricorn 42089-2). Cut in 1995 when Thompson was only 24, *Little Dave* was a stunning blues debut. Thompson and his band, Big Love, range freely over a variety of styles—blues shuffles, Sly Stone–James Brown–type funk, and even traces of Caribbean beats—without ever losing a Delta feel. The lyrics are rooted in contemporary Mississippi life. Proof that Delta blues tradition continues to be reinvented.

Muddy Waters (*The Complete Plantation Recordings: The Historic 1941–42 Library of Congress Field Recordings* Chess/MCA CHD 9344). Sharecropper, moonshine bootlegger, and occasional musician—Muddy Waters as he sounded before he moved to Chicago and changed the face of American music. Alan Lomax made these recordings on Stovall's plantation in Coahoma County, Mississippi, settling for Muddy Waters after he was unable to find the already dead Robert Johnson. They are a staggering document, both for the music captured and the hindsight view we get of Waters before he left the Delta. The dialogue between Waters and Lomax (and also John Work, Lomax's assistant) is priceless. Along with giving an invaluable glimpse into the process of blues creation, it allows you to hear how Muddy Waters actually spoke before he went to the city. The supple richness of Water's thick Mississippi speaking voice—as lovely in some ways as the blues he sings—calls to mind a young Elvis. Each speaks with the same mixture of diffident confidence and cautious respect for authority. Like Elvis, Waters never doubted his talent. Upon hearing a recording of his playing for the first time, his initial reaction was "man, this boy can play the blues." It would be seven years before he began recording in Chicago, where he would embark upon the career that is captured in *Muddy Waters: The Chess Box* (MCA CHD3-80002). A less expensive choice is *More Real Folk Blues* (MCA CHD 9298). *The London Muddy Waters Sessions*, recorded in 1970, contains a lovely acoustic version of "Walking Blues." The albums that he recorded with Johnny Winters on Blue Sky late in his life are also excellent. Perhaps his most lasting moment, though, came during Martin Scorcese's *The Last Waltz* (1976), when a sixty-year-old Waters absolutely stole the stage and the film from Bob Dylan, Van Morrison, Neil Young, and The Band. His eloquent face holds the screen like no one else has in the history of American film.

Bukka White (*The Complete Sessions* 1930–40 Travelin' Man TM CD 03). A student of mine once interviewed White's son, who professed embarrassment at his father's legend. His singing is a precisely modulated growl—a voice that seems to emanate out of the gravel roads of Mississippi. "He had such a terrible voice, you know," the son reportedly said. Another bluesman who went to have a second career during the 1960s revival, White learned much from Charlie Patton, but his style, as his son must have known, remained his own. Many of the songs on this set he wrote while in the state prison in Parchman, where he was serving time for allegedly having shot a man. According to Big Joe Williams, White broke bond to go to Chicago to record and was arrested there and brought back to Parchman by a Mississippi sheriff. White's 1960s records were also fine, including the interesting *Sky Songs* (Arhoolie CD 323).

Elmo Williams and Hezekiah Early (*Takes One to Know One* Fat Possum/Epitaph 80313–2). Early plays drums and harmonica (at the same time); Williams plays a screaming guitar that would be the envy of any heavy-metal wannabe. Manic, lunatic, and terrific fun.

Robert Pete Williams (*Robert Pete Williams Vols. 1 & 2* Arhoolie CD 394, 395). Convicted for murder in 1956, Williams was pardoned by Huey Long in 1964. Recorded at Angola State Penitentiary, Louisiana, in 1959, the Angola recordings are in a sense an extension of the prison ruminations of Bukka White. Against Williams's quiet, almost subdued reflections about the hardship of prison life and being wrongfully jailed, you can hear birds chirping. Williams relies less on traditional verses than other blues singers do, which means his blues were at times almost wholly improvised. His timing, wildly fluctuating lyric lines, and sense of percussion make him stand out from all other blues performers. A truly original musician.

Sonny Boy (Rice Miller) Williamson (*King Biscuit Time* Arhoolie CD 310). Arguably the greatest blues harmonica player of them all; certainly the funniest. (He needed his sense of humor to get through his 1960s recording sessions with British rock bands the Yardbirds and the Animals.) From 1941 to 1948 he performed live on KFFA in Helena, Arkansas, selling King Biscuit flour. The performances on *King Biscuit* were cut in Jackson, Mississippi, in the early 1950s before he moved to Chess in Chicago. Rougher than the Chess recordings, they reveal Sonny Boy to be in full possession of his talent. The disc also contains a sample from Sonny Boy's radio show. Any of the Chess records are exemplary. *Bummer Road* (MCA CHD93240) should be sought out for the argument Sonny Boy has with Leonard Chess over the proper definition of the word "village." Chess: "What's the name of this?" Sonny Boy: "Little Village. Little Village, motherfucker." Chess disputes the appropriateness of the title; Sonny Boy defends himself vigorously and continues his defense throughout the song.

Rev. Robert Wilkins (*The Original Rolling Stone* Yazoo 1077). Like Mississippi Fred McDowell's, Wilkins's blues were rooted not so much in the Delta style as that of the north Mississippi hill country. The blues in that region is characterized by its percussive, polyrhythmic quality. Wilkins's early recordings are richly varied and encompass a wide range of blues traditions. Wilkins eventually swore off the blues as "the Devil's music" to sing gospel music without losing either his percussive drive or fine sense of narrative song structure. The Rolling Stones recorded his "Prodigal Son" on their *Beggar's Banquet* album—a fitting tribute for a band whose name derives from Wilkins's own masterpiece "Rolling Stone." *Remember Me* (Genes GCD 9902), recorded in Memphis in 1971, is a beautiful collection of sacred material set to his inimitable blues rhythms.

## ANTHOLOGIES

*Blues in the Mississippi Night* (Rykodisc RCD 90155). With Alan Lomax playing the innocent to their blues experience, Big Bill Broonzy, Memphis Slim, and John Lee (Sonny Boy) Williamson commiserate about sharecropping, work farms, levee camps, chain gangs, casual hangings, and why they learned to ask for "Mister Prince Albert Tobacco" at the grocery store. "The blues come from slavery," Memphis Slim at one points remarks; on this remarkable document you can hear the journey. Conversation is interspersed with field recordings of railroad gangs chanting, churches humming, and prisoners hollering—meant to flesh out the history being told by the three men. For the original 1950s release, Lomax listed them as anonymous to protect their families from recriminations.

*Drop Down Mama* (MCA CHD 93002). A great collection of early Chess blues perched on the divide between country and urban styles—the sound of the Delta being moved to Chicago—this album contains some of Robert Nighthawk's finest recordings as well as outstanding efforts from Johnny Shines recording under the name of Shoe Shine Johnny. Arthur "Big Boy" Spires sings "Murmur Low" as if he were carrying a message to Tommy Johnson in his grave.

*Master of the Delta Blues: The Friends of Charlie Patton* (Yazoo 2002). The best anthology of Delta blues available on compact disc. It collects rare performances from Son

House, Bukka White, Tommy Johnson, Ishmon Bracey, and Willie Brown—the legendary running partner of both Charlie Patton and Robert Johnson, whose name appears frequently in Delta blues songs. The album includes Son House's great "My Black Mama" (parts 1 and 2), the arrangement of which Robert Johnson borrowed for his version of "Walkin' Blues." A nice bonus is the barrelhouse piano playing and bawdy singing of Louise Johnson.

*Mississippi Blues: Library of Congress Recordings* (Travelin' Man TM CD 07). Various recordings by John and Alan Lomax made in Natchez, Clarksdale, and Lake Cormorant, Mississippi, as well as at Sadie Beck's plantation in Arkansas across from Memphis. On some of the tracks you can hear the train that ran between Lake Cormorant and Robinsonville. The album includes a lovely version of the pre-blues "Make Me a Pallet on the Floor" performed by Willie Brown, probably at Lomax's request. It overlaps with LP *Walking Blues* (Flyright FLY LP 541), which contains additional interview material, including Willie Blackwell's assertion that he writes his blues *as an American.*

*Prison Songs Vols. 1 & 2: Murderous Home* (Rounder CD 1714). A perfect companion to *Blues in the Mississippi Night*, these two indispensable volumes delve deeper into the story that Memphis Slim, Broonzy, and Williamson tell. Track after track, this is the sound of Emerson's "fossil poetry" as it is being made. The album includes Bama's great rap, "What Makes Work Song Leader."

*Sun Blues* (Charly Sun Box 105 LP). Before happening upon Elvis, Sam Phillips recorded most of the Memphis area's great blues singers, including Howlin' Wolf, B. B. King, and Junior Parker. He told one interviewer that as he watched the Delta being taken over by great tractors and threshing machines, he knew that the type of blues that he had grown up loving was coming to an end. The music on this remarkable collection is a testament to the creativity of rural blacks in the first half of this century as well as to Sam Phillip's vision of what constituted lasting American culture.

## II  Elvis's Blues

Elvis was more than a blues singer. His talent for absorbing and transforming any singing style, from blues to opera, was so great that it is futile to try to say this or that singer was the one who made Elvis. We should rather say that Elvis made Elvis and one of the forms through which this marvelous invention was accomplished was the blues. By the time Elvis came to fame, the country blues was no longer the dominant musical form among African Americans—Muddy Waters's blues singles were listed by Billboard under the classification of "rhythm and blues." Even accounting for Elvis's admiration for country blues–style performers such as Arthur Drudup and Arthur Gunther, it is fair to say that Elvis probable thought of himself more as a rhythm-and-blues singer than a blues singer. Certainly, Waters's deep blues singing, though, differed greatly from that of the contemporary rhythm-and-blues and jump-blues singers that Elvis loved—Roy Brown, Big Joe Turner, Clyde McPhatter, Ray Charles, Laverne Baker, Little Willie John, and of course Jackie Wilson. Like these performers, Elvis was participating in the transformation of the blues into newer forms. That his involvement with African American musical forms was never static or idealized is reflected in Elvis's continuing admiration for his black contemporaries. His recording of Arthur Alexander's "Burning Love" in 1972 is as compelling as his recording of Roy Brown's "Good Rocking Tonight" in 1955. In the late 1960s and into the 1970s he was using the same back-up singers, the Sweet Inspirations, that Aretha Franklin sometimes used. In the following list I have tried to identify those recordings which were most clearly blues-derived. When singing Lowell Folsom's "Reconsider Baby," Roy Brown's "Good Rockin' Tonight," or anything by Arthur Crudup, Elvis is clearly working directly out of a blues tradition. Tracking down Elvis's blues sources and listing them cannot do his art justice, though, and is in some sense a distortion of it. Except for the posthumous collection *Reconsider Baby*, there is no Elvis recording devoted exclusively to the blues. Other than his gospel recordings, which are themselves a mixture of black and white styles, Elvis's catholic tastes prevented him from releasing records that represented only one style. The following list of "Elvis's Blues" is a record—by no means complete—of Elvis's life-long involvement with the many musical styles associated with African Americans.

*Amazing Grace* (RCA 66421). Elvis's gospel singing. As Charles Wolfe's excellent liner notes and essay show, Elvis's knowledge of African American gospel traditions in Memphis was as extensive as his knowledge of white southern gospel quartet traditions. More to the point, so does Elvis's magisterial singing.

*Elvis Is Back* (RCA 67737). In terms of Elvis's musical identity, there were three crucial moments in his career: 1954, 1960, and 1968. In 1954 he recorded his first record; in 1968 he made his "comeback" from years of cynical, desultory movie sound tracks. In 1960 he returned after two years in the army to face an uncertain audience. Each time in his career that Elvis was faced with the prospect of either having to prove or reinvent himself, he turned to the blues. The standout on this set is his version of "Reconsider Baby," which he knew from Lowell Fulsom's recording for Chess. Anyone who thinks that Elvis was merely an imitator of black singers should compare these two versions.

*Memories: The '68 Comeback Special* (RCA 67612). Proving that he was something more than a great cash cow, Elvis returned to his musical roots with a commitment that remains overpowering to this day. The first disc is made up of strong big-band studio numbers; the second has Elvis in the round with a few friends while playing electric lead guitar for the only time in his life. The performance is raw, spontaneous, yet seems to compress several musical lifetimes into a single hour. "Rock and roll music is basically rhythm and blues or gospel—or it sprang from that," Elvis asserts. Elvis then reaches for the blues to give this, his essential history lesson, in the ways of American music.

*The Million Dollar Quartet* (RCA 2023-2-r) Elvis, Jerry Lee Lewis, and Carl Perkins casually romp through a short but essential history of vernacular American music to that point. From Jelly Roll Morton to Chuck Berry, they hardly miss a beat. Best of all, though, is Elvis's impersonation of Jackie Wilson impersonating him.

*Reconsider Baby* (RCA PCD1-5418). The only self-conscious attempt by RCA to present Elvis as a blues singer. In terms of Elvis's career it stretches from 1954 to 1971. In terms of recorded blues, it goes from the 1920s (Lonnie Johnson's "Tomorrow Night") to the 1960s (Tommy Tucker's "Hi-Heel Sneakers"). An excellent and instructive compilation.

*Sunrise* (RCA 67675). What does it say that it took almost fifty years before Elvis's initial shattering, groundbreaking performances were released in their entirety? Including studio dialogue ("Damn, you sound like a nigger," Scotty Moore, the lead guitar player, can be heard to remark after one take) and muffed takes, you can hear how hard 19-year-old Elvis worked to achieve the mastery and grace that would reinvent America and send it reeling.

*Suspicious Minds* (RCA 67677). Along with the Sun sessions, Elvis's best studio recordings. With the exception of his brilliant reinterpretation of Percy Mayfield's "Stranger in My Own Home Town," nothing here would be classified in the record store as the blues. Nonetheless, Elvis's easy familiarity with contemporary soul—he covers Jerry Butler, Chuck Jackson, Della Reese, Percy Sledge, and Dionne Warwick—reveals how he continued to absorb and build on African American musical traditions. His searing version of Clyde McPhatter's "Without Love" manages to return a vintage 1950s rhythm and blues number to its gospel origin.

*Tiger Man* (RCA 67611). A companion to *Elvis/NBC-TV Special*, this record more obviously than any other reveals Elvis's deep affinity with the blues. From Lloyd Price's "Lawdy Miss Clawdy" to Jimmy Reed's "Baby, What You Want Me to Do," Elvis speaks the blues as if it were his only tongue. It isn't—but when you hear him sing Rufus Thomas's "Tiger Man" you may wonder why he ever sang anything else.

# WORKS CITED

■■■■■■■

Aarons, Victoria. *A Measure of Memory: Storytelling and Identity in American Jewish Culture*. Athens: U of Georgia P, 1996.

Adams, Henry. *Novels, Mont Saint Michel, The Education*. New York: Library of America, 1983.

Adell, Sandra. "The Big E(llison)'s Texts and Intertexts: Eliot, Burke, and the Underground Man." *College Language Association Journal* 37 (1994): 377–401.

Albrecht, James M. "Saying Yes and Saying No: Individualist Ethics in Ellison, Burke, and Emerson." *PMLA* 114.1 (Jan. 1999): 46–63.

Alter, Robert. "The Spritzer." Rev. of *Operation Shylock*, by Philip Roth. *New Republic* 5 April 1993: 31–34.

Anderson, Quentin. *The American Henry James*. New Brunswick, N.J.: Rutgers UP, 1957.

Andrews, William W., ed. *Critical Essays on Frederick Douglass*. Boston: G. K. Hall, 1991.

Antin, Mary. *From Plotzk to Boston*. Boston: W. B. Clarke, 1899.

———. "House of the One Father." *Common Ground* 1.3 (Spring 1941): 37–41.

———. *The Promised Land*. Boston: Houghton Mifflin, 1912.

———. *They Who Knock at Our Gates: A Complete Gospel of Immigration*. Boston: Houghton Mifflin, 1912.

Anzaldúa, Gloria. *Borderlands / La Frontera: The New Meztiza*. San Francisco: Aunt Lute, 1987.

Appelfeld, Aharon. "The Artist as a Jewish Writer." Milbauer and Watson 13–16.

Autry, Gene. *The Essential Gene Autry, 1933–46*. Columbia / Legacy, CK 48957, 1992.

Avery, Evelyn. "Oh My 'Mishpocha!' Some Jewish Women Writers from Antin to Kaplan View the Family." *Studies in American Jewish Literature* 5 (1986): 44–53.

Bailyn, Bernard. *The Ideological Origins of The American Revolution*. Cambridge: Harvard UP, 1967.

Baker, Houston A. Jr. "Autobiographical Acts." Andrews. 94–107.

———. *Blues, Ideology, and Afro-American Literature: A Vernacular Theory*. Chicago: U of Chicago P, 1984.

Barlow, William. *"Looking Up at Down": The Emergence of Blues Culture*. Philadelphia: Temple UP, 1989.

Basie, Count. *The Essential Count Basie: Volume 1.* Columbia, CK 40608, 1987.

Baudrillard, Jean. *America.* Trans. Chris Turner. London: Verso, 1988.

Bellow, Saul. *It All Adds Up.* New York: Viking, 1994.

——. "The Swamp of Prosperity." Rev. of *Goodbye, Columbus. Commentary* 28 (July 1959): 77.

Benert, Annette Larson. "Monsters, Bagmen, and Little Old Ladies: Henry James and the Unmaking of America." *Arizona Quarterly* 42 (1986): 331–43.

Benston, Kimberly W., ed. *Speaking for You.* Washington, D.C.: Howard UP, 1987.

Bercovitch, Sacvan. "Afterword." Bercovitch and Jehlen 418–42.

——. "Ambiguities of Dissent." *South Atlantic Quarterly* 89.3 (Summer 1990): 624–63.

——. *The American Jeremiad.* Madison: U of Madison P, 1978.

——. *The Puritan Origins of the American Self.* New Haven: Yale UP, 1975.

——. *The Rites of Assent: Transformations in the Symbolic Construction of America.* New York: Routledge, 1993.

——, ed. *Reconstructing American Literary History.* Cambridge: Harvard UP, 1986.

Bercovitch, Sacvan, and Myra Jehlen, eds. *Ideology and Classic American Literature.* Cambridge: Cambridge UP, 1986.

Berkson, Isaac P. *Theories of Americanization: A Critical Study with Special Reference to the Jewish Group.* 1920. New York: Arno Press, 1969.

Berry, Chuck. "Reeling and Rocking." *The Great Twenty-Eight.* MCA, CHD-92500, 1984.

Bigsby, C. W. "Improvising America: Ralph Ellison and the Paradox of Form." Benston 173–83.

Blackmur, R. P. *Studies in Henry James.* New York: New Directions, 1983.

Blackwell, Otis. "Don't Be Cruel." *Late Night with David Letterman.* 1986.

Blackwell, Willie "61." "Junior's a Jap Girl's Christmas for his Santa Claus." *Walking Blues.* Flyright, FLY LP 541, 1979.

Bloom, Harold. *The American Religion.* New York: Simon and Schuster, 1992

——. "Emerson: Power at the Crossing." Buell 148–58.

——, ed. *Philip Roth.* New York: Chelsea House, 1986.

——. "Operation Roth." Rev. of *Operation Shylock*, by Philip Roth. *New York Review of Books* 22 Apr. 1993: 45–48.

Boelhower, William. "The Making of Ethnic Autobiography in the United States." *American Autobiography: Retrospect and Prospect.* Ed. John Paul Eakin. Madison: U of Wisconsin P, 1991. 123–41.

——. *Through a Glass Darkly.* New York: Oxford UP, 1987.

Bone, Robert. "Ralph Ellison and the Use of Imagination." Hersey 95–112.

Boorstin, Daniel. *The Genius of American Politics.* Chicago: U of Chicago P, 1953.

Booth, Stanley. *Rythm Oil.* New York: Pantheon, 1992.

Bourne, Randolph. *The Radical Will.* Ed. Olaf Hansen. New York: Urizen, 1977.

——. "Trans-National America." *War and the Intellectuals.* Ed. Carl Resek. New York: Harper and Row, 1964. 107–23.

——. *War and the Intellectuals.* Ed. Carl Resek. New York: Harper and Row, 1964.

Brennan, Timothy. "Ellison and Ellison: The Solipsism of *Invisible Man*." *College Language Association Journal* 25.2 (Dec. 1982): 162–81.

Brent, Jonathan. "The Unspeakable Self: Philip Roth and the Imagination." Milbauer and Watson 180–200.

Brooks, Michael. Liner Notes. *The Quintessential Billie Holiday.* 9 vols. Columbia, 47301, 1987–91.

Brown, James. *The Federal Years: Part One.* Solid Smoke 8024. 1984.

——. *The Federal Years: Part Two.* Solid Smoke 8025. 1984.

——, with Bruce Tucker. *James Brown: The Godfather of Soul.* 1986. New York: Thunder's Mouth, 1990.

Buell, Lawrence, ed. *Ralph Waldo Emerson: A Collection of Critical Essays.* Englewood Cliffs, N.J.: Prentice-Hall, 1993.

Burke, Kenneth. *Attitudes toward History.* 1937. 3d ed. Berkeley: U of California P, 1984.

——. *Counter-Statement.* 1931. 3d ed. Berkeley: U of California P, 1968.

——. *A Grammar of Motives and A Grammar of Rhetoric.* 1945 and 1950. Cleveland: World, 1962.

——. *Language as Symbolic Action.* Berkeley: U of California P, 1966.

——. *Permanence and Change.* 1935. 3d ed. Berkeley: U of California P, 1984.

——. *The Philosophy of Literary Form.* 1941. 3d ed. Berkeley: U of California P, 1973.

——. "Ralph Ellison's Trueblooded *Bildungsroman*." Benston 349–59.

Butler, Thorpe. "What Is to Be Done? Illusion, Identity, and Action in Ralph Ellison's Invisible Man." *College Language Association Journal* 27.3 (Mar. 1984): 315–31.

Callahan, John F. "Frequencies of Eloquence." O'Meally 55–94.

Cameron, Sharon. *Thinking in Henry James.* Chicago: U of Chicago P, 1990.

Steve Cannon, Ishmael Reed, and Quincy Troupe. "The Essential Ellison: An Interview." *Y'Bird Reader* (Autumn 1977): 130–59.

Cavell, Stanley. *Conditions Handsome and Unhandsome: The Constitution of Emersonian Perfectionism.* Chicago: U of Chicago P, 1990.

——. *This New Yet Unapproachable America: Lectures after Emerson after Wittgenstein.* Albuquerque, N.M.: Living Batch, 1989.

——. *The Senses of Walden: An Expanded Edition.* San Francisco: North Point, 1981.

Chapman, John Jay. *The Selected Writings of John Jay Chapman.* Ed. Jacques Barzun. New York: Farrar, Strauss, and Cudahy, 1957.

Charters, Samuel. *The Blues Makers.* New York: Da Capo, 1991.

——. *The Legacy of the Blues.* New York: Da Capo, 1977.

——. *The Poetry of the Blues.* New York: Oak Productions, 1963.

Chase, Richard. *The American Novel and Its Tradition.* New York: Doubleday, 1957.

Cooper, Alan. *Philip Roth and the Jews.* Albany: State U of New York P, 1996.

Cox, James. "Recovering Literature's Lost Ground." Olney 123-45.

Creedence Clearwater Revival, *Cosmo's Factory.* Fantasy FCD 4516-2. 1970.

Crèvecoeur, Hector St. John de. *Letters from an American Farmer.* 1782. New York: Penguin, 1983.

Davis, Angela Y. *Blues Legacies and Black Feminism.* New York: Pantheon, 1998.

Davis, Charles T. "The Mixed Heritage of the Modern Black Novel: Ralph Ellison and Friends." Benston 272–82.

Davis, Miles, with Quincy Troupe. *Miles: The Autobiography*. New York: Simon and Schuster, 1989.

Deutsch, Leonard J. "Ralph Waldo Ellison and Ralph Waldo Emerson: A Shared Moral Vision." *College Language Association Journal* 16 (1972): 159–78.

Dewey, John. *Art as Experience*. 1934. New York: Perigee, 1980.

———. "Ralph Waldo Emerson." Konvitz and Whicher 24–30.

Diggins, John P. "Knowledge and Sorrow: Louis Hartz's Quarrel with American History." *Political Theory* 16.3 (August 1988): 355–76.

———. *The Lost Soul of American Politics*. 1984. Chicago: U of Chicago P, 1986.

———. *The Promise of Pragmatism*. Chicago: U of Chicago P, 1994.

Dixon, Willie, with Don Snowden. *I Am the Blues: The Willie Dixon Story*. New York: Da Capo, 1989.

Douglass, Frederick. *Narrative of the Life of Frederick Douglass*. Ed. Houston Baker. New York: Penguin, 1982.

Du Bois, W. E. B. *The Souls of Black Folk*. 1903. New York: Library of America, 1990.

———. *Writings*. New York: Library of America, 1986.

Dundy, Elaine. *Elvis and Gladys*. New York: St. Martin's, 1985.

Early, Gerald. "The Lives of Jazz." *American Literary History* 5.1 (Spring 1993): 129–46.

Edel, Leon. *The Master: 1901–1916*. New York: Avon, 1978.

Ellison, Ralph. *Going to the Territory*. 1986. New York: Vintage, 1987.

———. *Invisible Man*. 1952. New York: Modern Library, 1992.

———. *Shadow and Act*. 1964. New York: Vintage, 1972.

*Elvis: '68 Comeback Special*. Dir. Steve Binder. Media Home Entertainment, Inc., 1984.

Emerson, Everett, ed. *American Literature 1764–1789: The Revolutionary Years*. Madison: U of Wisconsin P, 1977.

Emerson, Ralph Waldo. *Emerson's Antislavery Writings*. Ed. Len Gougeon and Joel Myerson. New Haven: Yale UP, 1995.

———. *Emerson in His Journals*. Ed. Joel Porte. Cambridge: Belknap-Harvard UP, 1982.

———. *Essays and Lectures*. New York: Library of America, 1983.

———. *The Portable Emerson*. 1946. Ed. Carl Bode. New York: Penguin, 1981.

Evans, David. *Big Road Blues: Tradition and Creativity in Folk Blues*. Berkeley: U of California P, 1982.

Ezrahi, Sidra DeKoven. "The Grapes of Roth: Diasporism between Portnoy and Shylock." *Literary Strategies: Jewish Texts and Contexts*. Ed. Ezra Mendelsohn. New York: Oxford UP, 1996. 148–60.

Fabre, Genevieve, and Robert O'Meally, eds. *History and Memory in African-American Culture*. New York: Oxford UP, 1994.

Fabre, Michel. "From *Native Son* to *Invisible Man*: Some Notes on Ralph Ellison's Evolution in the 1950s." Benston 199–216.

Ferris, William. *Blues from the Delta*. Garden City, N.Y.: Anchor, 1978.

Feidelson, Charles. *Symbolism and American Literature*. Chicago: U of Chicago P, 1953.

Fiedler, Leslie. "The Image of Newark and the Indignities of Love: Notes on Philip Roth." Rev. of *Goodbye, Columbus*. *Midstream* 5 (Summer 1959): 96–99.

———. *Love and Death in the American Novel*. 1960. 2d ed. New York: Dell, 1966.

Firkins, O. W. *Ralph Waldo Emerson*. Boston: Houghton Mifflin, 1915.

Fish, Stanley. *Is There a Text in This Class?* Cambridge: Harvard UP, 1980.

Flippo, Chet. *Your Cheatin' Heart: A Biography of Hank Williams*. New York: Simon and Schuster, 1981.

Friedman, Allen. "The Jew's Complaint in Recent American Fiction: Beyond Exodus and Still in the Wilderness." Pinsker 149–63.

Friedman, Melvin J., and Ben Siegel, eds. *Traditions, Voices, and Dreams: The American Novel Since the 1960s*. Newark: U of Delaware P, 1995.

Frost, Robert. *Collected Poems, Prose, and Plays*. New York: Library of America, 1995.

Gates, Henry Louis Jr. *Loose Canons*. New York: Oxford UP, 1992.

———. *The Signifying Monkey: A Theory of African-American Literary Criticism*. New York: Oxford UP, 1988.

Gayle, Addison Jr., ed. *The Black Aesthetic*. Garden City, N.Y.: Doubleday, 1971.

Geismar, Maxwell. *Henry James and the Jacobites*. Boston: Houghton Mifflin, 1963.

Gellert, Lawrence. *Me and My Captain*. New York: Hours Press, 1939.

———. *Negro Songs of Protest*. New York: Carl Fischer, 1936.

Genovese, Eugene. *Roll, Jordan, Roll: The World That the Slaves Made*. New York: Vintage, 1976.

George, Nelson. *Buppies, B-Boys, Baps, and Bohos*. New York: HarperCollins, 1992.

———. *The Death of Rhythm & Blues*. New York: Dutton, 1989.

Gervais, David. "Deciphering America: The American Scene." *Cambridge Quarterly* 18.4 (1989): 349–62.

Girgus, Sam B., ed. *The American Self*. Albuquerque: U of New Mexico P, 1981.

———. *The New Covenant: Jewish Writers and the American Idea*. Chapel Hill: U of North Carolina P, 1984.

Glazer, Nathan, and Daniel Patrick Moynihan. *Beyond the Melting Pot*. Garden City, N.Y.: Anchor, 1975.

Gleason, Philip. "American Identity and Americanization." *Harvard Encyclopedia of Ethnic Groups*. Ed. Stephan Thernstrom, Ann Orlov, and Oscar Handlin. Cambridge: Belknap-Harvard UP 1980. 31–58.

———. *Speaking of Diversity*. Baltimore: Johns Hopkins UP, 1992.

Gougeon, Len. *Virtue's Hero: Emerson, Antislavery, and Reform*. Athens: U of Georgia P, 1990.

Goldman, Albert. *Elvis*. New York: Avon, 1982.

Gordon, Milton. *Assimilation in American Life*. New York: Oxford UP, 1964.

gosset, hattie. "billie lives! billie lives!" Moraga and Anzaldúa 109–12.

Greenway, John. *American Folksongs of Protest*. New York: Octagon, 1971.

Gregory, Neal, and Janice Gregory. *When Elvis Died*. New York: Pharos, 1980.

Gunn, Giles. *The Culture of Criticism and the Criticism of Culture*. New York: Oxford UP, 1987.

———. *Thinking across the American Grain*. Chicago: U of Chicago P, 1992.

Guralnick, Peter. *Careless Love: The Unmaking of Elvis Presley*. New York: Little, Brown, 1999.

——. "Elvis Sings the Blues." Liner notes. *Elvis Presley: Reconsider Baby*. RCA PCCD1-5418. 1985.

——. *Feel Like Going Home*. 1971. New York: Vintage, 1981.

——. *Last Train to Memphis: The Rise of Elvis Presley*. New York: Little, Brown, 1994.

——. Liner Notes. Elvis Presley. *Reconsider Baby*. RCA, PCD 1-5418, 1985.

——. *Lost Highway*. 1979. New York: Vintage, 1982.

Guttman, Allen. *The Jewish Writer in America: Assimilation and the Crisis of Identity*. New York: Oxford UP, 1971.

——. "Philip Roth and the Rabbis." Bloom, *Philip Roth* 53–62.

Handlin, Oscar. *The Uprooted*. New York: Grosset and Dunlap, 1951.

Handy, W. C. *Father of the Blues: An Autobiography*. 1941. New York: Da Capo, 1969.

Harap, Louis. *Creative Awakening: The Jewish Presence in Twentieth Century American Literature, 1900–1940s*. New York: Greenwood, 1987.

Hartz, Louis. *The Liberal Tradition in America: An Interpretation of American Political Thought since the Revolution*. New York: Harcourt, Brace, 1955.

Hawthorne, Nathaniel. *Novels*. New York: Library of America, 1983.

Hersey, John, ed. " 'A Completion of Personality': A Talk with Ralph Ellison." Benston 285–307.

——, ed. *Ralph Ellison: A Collection of Critical Essays*. Englewood Cliffs, N.J.: Prentice-Hall, 1974.

Higham, John. *Send These to Me*. 1975. Baltimore: Johns Hopkins UP, 1984.

——. *Strangers in the Land*. New York: Atheneum, 1967.

Hirshey, Gerri. *Nowhere to Run: The Story of Soul Music*. New York: Penguin, 1984.

Hocks, Richard A. *Henry James and Pragmatistic Thought*. Chapel Hill: U of North Carolina P, 1974.

Hofstadter, Richard. *The Progressive Historians*. 1968. Chicago: U of Chicago P, 1979.

Holiday, Billie. *The Quintessential Billie Holiday*. 9 vols. Columbia, 47301, 1987–91.

Holland, Laurence B. *The Expense of Vision*. 1964. Baltimore: Johns Hopkins UP, 1982.

——. Hollinger, David A. *In the American Province*. Baltimore: Johns Hopkins UP, 1985.

——. *Postethnic America: Beyond Multiculturalism*. New York: Basic Books, 1995.

Holte, James Craig. "The Representative Voice: Autobiography and the Ethnic Experience." *Melus* 9 (Summer 1982): 33–39.

Hook, Sidney, and Milton R. Konvitz, eds. *Freedom and Experience: Essays Presented to Horace M. Kallen*. Ithaca: Cornell UP, 1947.

Hooker, John Lee. "Blues for Abraham Lincoln." *John Lee Hooker's 40th Anniversary Album*. DCC Compact Classics, DZS 042, 1989.

——. "Boogie Chillen." *John Lee Hooker: The Ultimate Collection, 1948–90*. 2 vols. Rhino, R2 70572, 1991.

House, Son. "(Don't Mind People) Grinning in Your Face." *Delta Blues and Spirituals*. Capitol, Capitol Blues Collection D108935, 1970.

——. "How To Treat a Man." *Delta Blues and Spirituals*.

———. "My Black Mama." *Really! The Country Blues: 1927–33*. Origin Jazz Library, OJL 2, n.d.

———. "Walking Blues." *The Complete Library of Congress Recordings*. 1941–42. Recorded by Alan Lomax. Travelin' Man, TM CD 02, 1990.

Howe, Irving. "Black Boys and Native Sons." Hersey, *Ralph Ellison* 36–38.

———. *Celebrations and Attacks*. New York: Harcourt Brace, 1979.

———. Introduction. *The American Scene*. By Henry James. New York: Horizon Press, 1967. v–xvi.

———. "Philip Roth Reconsidered." Bloom, *Philip Roth* 71–88.

———. *World of Our Fathers*. New York: Harcourt Brace, 1976.

Hughes, Langston. *Famous Negro Music Makers*. New York: Dodd, Mead, 1955.

Hurston, Zora Neale. *Mules and Men*. 1935. New York: Perennial Library, 1990.

James, Henry. *The Ambassadors*. New York: Norton, 1964.

———. *The American Scene*. 1907. New York: Horizon, 1967.

———. *Autobiography*. 1956. Ed. F. W. Dupee. Princeton: Princeton UP, 1983.

———. *Hawthorne*. London: Macmillan, 1883.

———. *Letters*. Ed. Leon Edel. 4 vols. Cambridge: Harvard UP, 1974–84.

———. *Literary Criticism: American and English Writers*. New York: Library of America, 1984.

———. *Literary Criticism: European Writers*. New York: Library of America, 1984.

James, Henry, and Edith Wharton. *Letters: 1900–1915*. Ed. Lyall H. Powers. New York: Scribner's, 1990.

James, William. *The Letters*. Ed. Henry James III. 2 vols. Boston: Atlantic Monthly P, 1920.

———. *The Principles of Psychology*. 2 vols. 1890. New York: Holt, 1923.

———. *Talks to Teachers on Psychology*. New York: Holt, 1899.

———. *The Will to Believe and Other Essays in Popular Philosophy*. 1897. Cambridge: Harvard UP, 1979.

———. *Writings: 1902–1910*. Includes: *The Varieties of Religious Experience* (1902), *Pragmatism: A New Name for Some Old Ways of Thinking* (1907), *A Pluralistic Universe* (1909), *The Meaning of Truth* (1909), and *The Meaning of Truth* (1911). New York: Library of America, 1987.

Jay, Gregory S. "The End of 'American' Literature: Toward a Multicultural Practice." *College English* 53: 264–81.

Jay, Paul. *Contingency Blues: The Search for Foundations in American Criticism*. Madison: U of Wisconsin P, 1997.

Jefferson, Thomas. *Writings*. New York: Library of America, 1984.

Jehlen, Myra. "Precise Critics and Vague Poems." American Pragmatism and Richard Poirier. Paper presented at the annual meeting of the Modern Language Association, New York, 29 Dec. 1992.

Johnson, James Weldon. *The Autobiography of an Ex-Colored Man*. 1912. New York: Penguin, 1990.

———. *Black Manhattan*. New York: Knopf, 1930.

Johnson, Robert. *The Complete Recordings*. Columbia, C2K 46222, 1990.

Johnson, Tommy. "Big Fat Mama Blues." *Complete Recorded Works in Chronological Order.* Document, DOCD 5001, n.d.

——. "Big Road Blues." *Complete Recorded Works in Chronological Order.*

——. "Maggie Campbell Blues." *Complete Recorded Works in Chronological Order.*

Johnson, Stuart. "American Marginalia: James's *The American Scene.*" *Texas Studies in Language and Literature* 24 (Spring 1982): 83–101.

Jones, Leroi. *Blues People.* New York: Morrow, 1963.

Kallen, Horace. "Alain Locke and Cultural Pluralism." *Journal of Philosophy* 54.5 (28 February 1957): 119–27.

——. *Culture and Democracy in the United States.* New York: Boni and Liveright, 1924.

——. *Individualism: An American Way of Life.* New York: Liveright, 1933.

——. "Remarks on R. B. Perry's Portrait of William James." *William James Remembered.* Ed. Linda Simon. Omaha: U of Nebraska P, 1996. 240–51.

——. *William James and Henri Bergson: A Study in Contrasting Theories of Life.* Chicago: U of Chicago P, 1914.

Kaplan, Amy. " 'Left Alone with America': The Absence of Empire in the Study of American Culture." Kaplan and Pease 3–21.

Kaplan, Amy, and Donald E. Pease, eds. *Cultures of United States Imperialism.* Durham, N.C.: Duke UP, 1993.

Kartiganer, Donald. "Fictions of Metamorphosis: From *Goodbye, Columbus* to *Portnoy's Complaint.*" Milbauer and Watson 82–104.

——. "Ghost-Writing: Philip Roth's Portrait of the Artist." *Association for Jewish Studies Review* 13.1–2 (Spring–Fall 1988): 153–69.

Kauvar, Elaine M. "This Doubly Reflected Communication: Philip Roth's 'Autobiographies.' " *Contemporary Literature* 36.3 (1995): 412–46.

Kazin, Alfred. "The Vanity of Human Wishes." *Reporter* 16 Aug. 1962: 54.

Kent, George. "Ralph Ellison and the Afro-American Folk Tradition." Hersey, *Ralph Ellison* 160–70.

K[innard], J. Jr. "Who Are Our National Poets?" *Knickerbocker Magazine* 26 (1845): 338.

Kloppenberg, James T. *Uncertain Victory: Social Democracy and Progressivism in European and American Thought, 1870–1920.* New York: Oxford UP, 1986.

Konvitz, Milton R. "Horace Meyer Kallen (1882–1974): Philosopher of the Hebraic-American Idea." *American Jewish Yearbook* (1974–75): 55–80.

Konvitz, Milton R., and Stephen E. Whicher, eds. *Emerson: A Collection of Critical Essays.* Englewood Cliffs, N.J.: Prentice-Hall, 1962.

Kreibel, Henry Edward. *Afro-American FolkSongs.* New York: Schirmer, 1914.

Krupat, Arnold. *Ethnocriticism: Ethnography, History, Literature.* Berkeley: U of California P, 1992.

Krupnick, Mark. "Jewish Jacobites: Henry James's Presence in the Fiction of Philip Roth and Cynthia Ozick." Friedman and Siegel 89–107.

Kuklick, Bruce. *The Rise of American Philosophy.* New Haven: Yale UP, 1977.

Kundera, Milan. *The Art of the Novel.* Trans. Linda Asher. New York: Grove, 1988.

Larner, Jeremy. "The Conversion of the Jews." Pinsker 27–32.

Lawrence, D. H. *Studies in Classic American Literature*. 1923. New York: Viking, 1961.

Lee, Hermione. " 'You Must Change Your Life': Mentors, Doubles, and Literary Influences in the Search for Self." Bloom, *Philip Roth* 149–62.

Lee, Kun Jong. "Ellison's *Invisible Man*: Emersonianism Revised." *PMLA* 107 (1992): 331–44.

Lentricchia, Frank. *Criticism and Social Change*. Chicago: U of Chicago P, 1983.

———. "On the Ideologies of Poetic Modernism, 1890–1913: The Example of William James." Bercovitch, *Reconstructing* 220–49.

Levine, Lawrence. *Black Culture and Black Consciousness*. Oxford: Oxford UP, 1977.

———. *The Unpredictable Past*. New York: Oxford UP, 1993.

Lewis, Furry. *Fourth and Beale*. Lucky Seven, CD 9202, 1992.

———. *In His Prime 1927–28*. Yazoo, 1050, 1991.

1 Lewis, R. W. B. *The American Adam: Innocence, Tragedy, and Tradition in the Nineteenth Century*. Chicago: U of Chicago P, 1955.

——— *The Jameses: A Family Narrative*. New York: Farrar, Straus and Giroux, 1991.

Lewisohn, Ludwig. *Up Stream: An American Chronicle*. New York: Boni and Liveright, 1922.

Lipscomb, Mance. *I Say Me for a Parable*. New York: Norton, 1993.

Living Colour. "Elvis is Dead." *Time's Up*. CBS Records, EK 46202, 1990.

Locke, Alain. *The Negro and His Music*. 1936. Port Washington, N.Y.: Kennikat, 1968.

———. "The Negro Spirituals." Locke, *New Negro* 199–213.

———, ed. *The New Negro*. 1925. New York: Atheneum, 1968.

———. "Pluralism and Ideological Peace." Hook and Konvitz 63–69.

———. "Who and What is 'Negro.' " *The Philosophy of Alain Locke*. Ed. Leonard Harris. Philadelphia: Temple UP, 1989. 207–26.

Lomax, Alan. Transcript to *Blues in the Mississippi Night*. RykoDisc, RCD 90155, 1990.

———. *The Land Where the Blues Began*. New York: Pantheon, 1993.

———. Liner Notes. *Prison Songs: Historical Recordings from Parchman Farm Vol. One: Murderous Home*. Rounder, CD 1714, 1997.

———. *Mister Jell Roll*. 1949. New York: Pantheon, 1993.

Lovejoy, Arthur O. *The Thirteen Pragmatisms and Other Essays*. Baltimore: Johns Hopkins UP, 1963.

Lyons, Elizabeth. "Ellison and the Twentieth Century American Scholar." *Studies in American Fiction* 17.1 (Spring 1989): 93–106.

———. "Ellison's Narrator as Emersonian Scholar." Parr and Savery 75–78.

Lyons, Richard. "In Supreme Command." *New England Quarterly* 55 (1982): 517–39.

Mailer, Norman. *The Armies of the Night*. New York: New American Library, 1968.

Mann, Arthur. *The One and the Many*. Chicago: U of Chicago P, 1979.

Marcus, Greil. *Dead Elvis*. New York: Doubleday, 1991.

———. *Invisible Republic*. New York: Holt, 1997.

———. *Mystery Train*. 1975. 3d ed. New York: Dutton, 1990.

Marsh, Dave. *Elvis*. New York: Rolling Stone Press, 1982.

——. "Prisoner of Race." Epilogue. *James Brown: The Godfather of Soul.* By James Brown, with Bruce Tucker. 269–83.

——, ed. *The First Rock & Roll Confidential Report.* New York: Pantheon, 1985.

*Masters of the Delta Blues: The Friends of Charlie Patton.* Yazoo, 2002, 1991.

Matthiessen, F. O. *Henry James: The Major Phase.* New York: Oxford UP, 1963.

——, ed. *The James Family.* New York: Knopf, 1947.

McDermott, John J. *Streams of Experience.* Amherst: U of Massachusetts P, 1986.

McDowell, "Mississippi" Fred. "You Gonna Be Sorry." *Mississippi Delta Blues.* Arhoolie, CD 304, 1989.

McKee, Margaret, and Fred Chisenhall. *Beale Black & Blue: Life and Music on Black America's Main Street.* Baton Rouge: Louisiana State UP, 1981.

McPherson, James Alan. "Indivisible Man." Benston 15–29.

Memphis Slim (Peter Chatmon). Remarks in *Blues in the Mississippi Night.* Recorded by Alan Lomax. RykoDisc, RCD 90155, 1990.

Michaels, Walter Benn. *The Gold Standard and the Logic of Naturalism.* Berkeley: U of California P, 1987.

——. *Our America.* Durham, N.C.: Duke UP, 1995.

——. "Race into Culture." *Critical Inquiry* 18.4 (Summer 1992): 655–85.

Michaels, Walter Benn, and Stephen Knapp. "Against Theory." *Against Theory: Literary Studies and the New Pragmatism.* Ed. Michaels and Knapp. Chicago: U of Chicago P, 1985. 11–30.

Milbauer, Asher Z., and Donald G. Watson, eds. *Reading Philip Roth.* New York: St. Martin's, 1988.

Miller, Larry. "William James and Twentieth-Century Ethnic Thought." *American Quarterly* 31.4 (1979): 533–55.

Miller, R. Baxter. "A Deeper Literacy: Teaching *Invisible Man* from Aboriginal Ground." Parr and Savery 51–57.

Monoghan, David. "*The Great American Novel* and *My Life as a Man:* An Assessment of Philip Roth's Achievement." Pinsker 68–78.

Moraga, Cherie, and Gloria Anzaldúa, eds. *This Bridge Called My Back: Writings by Radical Women of Color.* New York: Kitchen Table: Women of Color Press, 1983.

Morrison, Toni. *Beloved.* New York: Knopf, 1987.

——. "Talk of the Town." *New Yorker* 5 Oct. 1998: 31–32.

Mumford, Lewis. *The Golden Day: A Study in American Literature and Culture.* Boston: Beacon, 1957.

Murray, Albert. *The Hero and the Blues.* Columbus: U of Missouri P, 1973.

——. *The Omni-Americans.* 1971. New York: Vintage, 1983.

——. *Stomping the Blues.* New York: McGraw-Hill, 1976.

Nadel, Alan. *Invisible Criticism.* Iowa City: U of Iowa P, 1988.

Neal, Larry. *Visions of a Liberated Future.* New York: Thunder's Mouth, 1989.

Nichols, William W. "Ralph Ellison's Black American Scholar." *Phylon* 31.1 (1970): 70–75.

O'Connell, Barry. " 'Step by Step': Lesley Riddle Meets the Carter Family: A Biographical Essay with Notes to His Recordings." Unpublished essay.

Odum, Howard. "Folk Songs and Folk Poetry as Found in the Secular Songs of Southern Negroes." *JAF* 24 (1911): 255–94.

———, and Guy B. Johnson, eds. *The Negro and His Songs.* 1925. New York: Negro Universities P, 1968.

Oliver, Paul. *Blues Fell This Morning.* New York: Cambridge UP, 1990.

Olney, James. *Autobiography: Essays Theoretical and Critical.* Princeton: Princeton UP, 1980.

O'Meally, Robert. *The Craft of Ralph Ellison.* Cambridge: Harvard UP, 1980.

———. "On Burke and the Vernacular: Ralph Ellison's Boomerang of History." Fabre and O'Meally 244–60.

O'Meally, Robert, ed. *New Essays on Invisible Man.* New York: Cambridge UP, 1988.

Ostendorf, Berndt. "Anthropology, Modernism, and Jazz." O'Meally, *New Essays* 95–122.

Ozick, Cynthia. *Metaphor and Memory.* New York: Knopf, 1989.

Packer, B. L. *Emerson's Fall.* New York: Continuum, 1982.

Palmer, Robert. *Deep Blues.* New York: Viking, 1981.

———. "James Brown." *The Rolling Stone Illustrated History of Rock & Roll.* Ed. Jim Miller. 1976. New York: Random House, 1980.

Parr, Susan Resnick, and Pancho Savery, eds. *Approaches to Teaching Ellison's Invisible Man.* New York: Modern Language Association of America, 1989.

Parrish, Timothy L. "Ralph Ellison, Kenneth Burke, and the Form of Democracy." *Arizona Quarterly* 52.3 (Autumn 1995): 117–48.

Patell, Cyrus. "Comparative American Studies: Hybridity and Beyond." *American Literary History* 11.1 (Spring 1999): 166–86.

Patterson, Orlando. *Ethnic Chauvinism.* New York: Stein and Day, 1977.

Peabody, Charles. "Notes on Negro Music." *Journal of American Folklore* 16 (1903): 148–52.

Pease, Donald. *Visionary Compacts.* Madison: U of Wisconsin P, 1987.

Pells, Richard. *The Liberal Mind in a Conservative Age.* New York: Harper and Row, 1985.

Pinsker, Sanford, ed. *Critical Essays on Philip Roth.* Boston: G. K. Hall, 1982.

Poirier, Richard. *Poetry and Pragmatism.* Cambridge: Harvard UP, 1992.

———. *The Renewal of Literature.* New York: Random House, 1987.

———. *A World Elsewhere: The Place of Style in American Literature.* New York: Oxford UP, 1966.

Porter, Carolyn. "Are We Being Historical Yet?" *South Atlantic Quarterly* 87 (1988): 743–86.

———. "What We Know That We Don't Know: Remapping Literary Studies." *American Literary History* 6 (1994): 467–526.

Porterfield, Nolan. *Jimmie Rodgers: The Life and Times of America's Blue Yodeler.* Champaign-Urbana: U of Illinois P, 1979.

———. Liner Notes. *The Singing Brakeman.* Bear Family Records, BCD 15540 FI, 1992.

Posnock, Ross. "Bourne, Dewey, Adorno: Reconciling Pragmatism and the Frankfurt School." *Center for Twentieth Century Studies* 21.1 (Apr. 1987): 31–54.

———. *Color and Culture.* Cambridge: Harvard UP, 1998.

———. "The Politics of Non-identity: A Genealogy." *Boundary 2* 19.1 (Spring 1992): 34–68.

———. "Pragmatism, Politics, and the Corridor." Putnam 343–62.

———. *The Trial of Curiosity.* New York: Oxford UP, 1991.

Pratt, Linda Ray. "Elvis, or the Ironies of Southern Identity." Quain 93–103.

———. "Don't Be Cruel." *The Million Dollar Quartet.* RCA, 2023-2-r, 1990.

———. "Got My Mojo Workin' / Keep Your Hands Off of It." *Walk a Mile in My Shoes: The Essential 70's Masters.* 5 vols. RCA, 07863 66670-2, 1995.

———. "Little Cabin on the Hill." *Elvis Country.* 1971. RCA, 07863 66279-2, 1992.

Presley, Elvis. "Ready Teddy." *A Golden Celebration.* 4 vols. 1985. RCA, 07863 67456-2, 1998.

———. *Sunrise.* RCA, 07863 67675-2, 1999.

Profreidt, William A. "The Education of Mary Antin." *Journal of Ethnic Studies* 17.4 (Winter 1990): 81–100.

Rev. of *The Promised Land,* by Mary Antin. *Bookman* 12 June 35: 419.

Public Enemy. "Fight the Power." *Music from "Do the Right Thing."* Motown, MOTD-6272, 1989.

Putnam, Ruth Anna, ed. *The Cambridge Companion to William James.* Cambridge: Cambridge UP, 1997.

Quain, Kevin, ed. *The Elvis Reader.* New York: St. Martin's, 1992.

Reilly, John M. "Discovering the Art of the Self in History: A Principle of Afro-American Life." Parr and Savery 37–42.

———. "The Testament of Ralph Ellison." Benston 49–62.

Reising, Russel. *The Unusable Past: Theory and the Study of American Literature.* New York: Methuen, 1986.

Reynolds, David. *Beneath the American Renaissance.* Cambridge: Harvard UP, 1988.

Rodgers, Jimmie. *The Singing Brakeman.* Bear Family Records, BCD 15540 FI, 1992.

Rogers, J. A. "Jazz at Home." Locke, *New Negro* 216–24.

Rodriguez, Richard. *Days of Obligation: An Argument with My Mexican Father.* New York: Viking, 1992.

———. *Hunger of Memory: The Education of Richard Rodriguez.* New York: Bantam, 1983.

Rogin, Michael. "Blackface, White Noise: The Jewish Jazz Singer Finds His Voice." *Critical Inquiry* 18.3 (Spring 1993): 417–53.

Roosevelt, Nicholas. "Professor Kallen Proposes to Balkanize America." *New York Times Book Review* 20 Apr. 1924: 3.

Rorty, Richard. "Americanism and Pragmatism." Pragmatism and the Politics of Culture. The Eighth Annual Comparative Literature Symposium. University of Tulsa, 26 March 1993.

———. *Consequences of Pragmatism.* Minneapolis: U of Minnesota P, 1982.

———. *Contingency, Irony, and Solidarity.* Cambridge: Cambridge UP, 1989.

———. *Objectivity, Relativism, and Truth: Philosophical Papers*, Vols. 1 and 2. Cambridge: Cambridge UP, 1991.

———. "Truth and Freedom: A Reply to Thomas McCarthy." *Critical Inquiry* 16 (Spring 1990): 633–43.

Rose, Cynthia. *Living in America: The Soul Saga of James Brown*. London: Serpent's Tail, 1990.

Roth, Philip. "A Bit of Jewish Mischief." *New York Times Book Review* 7 Mar. 1993: 1, 20.

———. "The Conversion of the Jews." *Goodbye Columbus and Five Short Stories*. 149–72.

———. *The Counterlife*. New York: Farrar, Straus, 1986.

———. *The Facts: A Novelist's Autobiography*. New York: Farrar, Straus, 1988.

———. *The Ghost Writer*. New York: Farrar, Straus, 1979.

———. *Goodbye Columbus and Five Short Stories*. Boston: Houghton Mifflin, 1959.

———. " 'I Always Wanted You to Admire My Fasting'; or, Looking at Kafka." *Reading Myself and Others*. 303–26.

———. *My Life as a Man*. New York: Holt, 1974.

———. *Operation Shylock: A Confession*. New York: Simon and Schuster, 1993.

———. *Patrimony: A True Story*. New York: Simon and Schuster, 1991.

———. *Reading Myself and Others: A New Expanded Edition*. New York: Penguin, 1985.

———. *Zuckerman Bound*. New York: Farrar, Straus, 1985.

Roth, Philip, and George J. Searles. *Conversations with Philip Roth*. Jackson: UP of Mississippi, 1992.

Rowe, John Carlos. *At Emerson's Tomb: The Politics of Classic American Literature*. New York: Columbia UP, 1997.

———. *The Theoretical Dimensions of Henry James*. Madison: U of Wisconsin P, 1984.

Rovit, Earl H. "Ralph Ellison and the American Comic Tradition." Hersey, *Ralph Ellison* 151–59.

Rubin, Steven J. "Style and Meaning in Mary Antin's *The Promised Land*: A Reevaluation." *Studies in American Jewish Literature* 5 (1986): 35–43.

Rueckert, William H. *Encounters with Kenneth Burke*. Urbana-Chicago: U of Illinois P, 1994.

Russell, Bertrand. *A History of Western Philosophy*. 1945. New York: Simon and Schuster, 1972.

———. *Philosophical Essays*. London: Allen and Unwin, 1966.

Saldívar, Ramón. *Chicano Narrative: The Dialectics of Difference*. Madison: U of Wisconsin P, 1990.

Santayana, George. *Character and Opinion in the United States*. 1920. New York: Doubleday, 1956.

Savery, Pancho. " 'Not like an arrow, but a boomerang': Ellison's Existential Blues." Parr and Savery 65–74.

Schaub, Thomas. *American Fiction in the Cold War*. Madison: U of Wisconsin P, 1991.

Schechner, Mark. "Philip Roth." Pinsker 117–32.

Schlesinger, Arthur M. *The Disuniting of America*. New York: Norton, 1992.

Schmidt, Sara L. "Horace Kallen and the Americanization of Zionism." Diss. U of Maryland, 1973.

Schultz, Elizabeth A. "The Illumination of Darkness: Affinities between *Moby Dick* and *Invisible Man.*" *College Language Association Journal* 32.2 (Dec. 1988): 170–200.

Scruggs, Charles. *Sweet Home: Invisible Cities in the Afro-American Novel.* Johns Hopkins UP, 1993.

Seltzer, Mark. *Henry James and the Art of Power.* Ithaca: Cornell UP, 1984.

Shines, Johnny. "Slavery Time Breakdown." *Worried Blues Ain't Bad.* 1974. The Blues Alliance, TBA 13004, 1996.

———. "This Morning." *Worried Blues Ain't Bad.*

Shostak, Debra. "The Diaspora Jew and the 'Instinct of Impersonation': Philip Roth's *Operation Shylock.*" *Contemporary Literature* 38.4 (1997): 726–54.

Sollors, Werner. *Beyond Ethnicity.* New York: Oxford UP, 1986.

———. "A Critique of Pure Pluralism." Bercovitch, *Reconstructing* 250–79.

———. "National Identity and Ethnic Diversity: 'Of Plymouth Rock and Jamestown and Ellis Island'; or, Ethnic Literature and Some Redefinitions of America." Fabre and O'Meally 92–121.

———. "Of Mules and Mares in a Land of Difference; or, Quadrupeds All?" *American Quarterly* 42.2 (June 1990): 167–90.

Solotaroff, Theodore. "Philip Roth: A Personal View." Bloom, *Philip Roth* 35–51.

Spengemann, William. *A Mirror for Americanists.* Hanover, N.H.: UP of New England, 1987.

Spires, Arthur "Big Boy." "Murmur Low." *Drop Down Mama.* 1970. MCA, CHD-93002, 1990.

Steinberg, Stephen. *The Ethnic Myth: Race, Ethnicity, and Class in America.* 1981. Boston: Beacon, 1989.

Stepto, Robert. *From Behind the Veil.* 1979. Urbana: U of Illinois P, 1991.

Stone, Albert E. Introduction *Letters from an American Farmer.* By Hector St. John de Crèvecoeur. 1782. New York: Penguin, 1983. 7–25.

Strout, Cushing. "'An American Negro Idiom': *Invisible Man* and the Politics of Culture." Parr and Savery. 79–85.

———. "Paradoxical Puritans." *American Scholar* 45 (Autumn 1976): 602–4.

Suckiel, Ellen Kappy. *The Pragmatic Philosophy of William James.* South Bend, Ind.: U of Notre Dame P, 1982.

Sundquist, Eric J., ed. *American Realism.* Baltimore: Johns Hopkins UP, 1982.

———. "The Country of the Blue." *American Realism.* Sundquist 3–24.

———. *To Wake the Nations: Race in the Making of American Literature.* Cambridge: Belknap-Harvard UP, 1993.

Tanner, Tony. "The Music of Invisibility." Ed. Hersey. 80–94.

Taylor, Gordon O. "Chapters of Experience: *The American Scene.*" *Genre* 12 (1979): 93–116.

———. "Learning to Listen to Lower Frequences." Parr and Savery 43–50.

*This is Elvis.* Dir. Andrew Solt and Malcom Leo. Warner Bros., 1981.

Thayer, H. S. *Meaning and Action: A Critical History of Pragmatism.* Indianapolis: Bobbs Merrill, 1981.

Thomas, D. M. "Face to Face with His Double." Rev. of *Operation Shylock*, by Philip Roth. *New York Times Book Review* 7 Mar. 1993: 1, 20.

Titon, Jeffrey Todd. *Early Downhome Blues: A Musical and Cultural Analysis*. Urbana: U of Illinois P, 1977.

Tocqueville, Alexis de. *Democracy in America*. Trans. Henry Reeve. Ed. Phillips Bradley. 2 vols. New York: Knopf, 1945.

Toll, William. "Horace M. Kallen: Pluralism and Jewish Identity." *American Jewish History* 85.1 (Mar. 1997): 57–74.

Trachtenberg, Alan. "The American Scene: Some Versions of the City." *Massachusetts Review* 8 (Summer 1967): 281–95.

Tracy, Steven C., ed. *Write Me a Few of Your Lines: A Blues Reader*. Amherst: U of Massachusetts P, 1999.

Tucker, Martin. "The Shape of Exile in Philip Roth, or the Part That Is Always Apart." Milbauer and Watson 33–49.

Tuerk, Richard. "The Youngest of America's Children in *The Promised Land*." *Studies in American Jewish Fiction* 5 (1986): 29–34.

Tosches, Nick. "Elvis in Death." Quain 272–80.

Tumlin, Melvin. "The Cult of Gratitude." *The Ghetto and Beyond: Essays on Jewish Life in America*. Ed. Peter I. Rose. New York: Random House, 1969. 69–82.

Updike, John. "Recruiting Raw Nerves." Rev. of *Operation Shylock*, by Philip Roth. *New Yorker* 15 Mar. 1993: 109–12.

Vaughan, Leslie J. "Cosmopolitanism, Ethnicity, and American Identity: Randolph Bourne's 'Trans-National America.'" *Journal of American Studies* 25.3 (1991): 443–59.

Wald, Priscilla. *Constituting Americans: Cultural Anxiety and Narrative Form*. Durham: Duke UP, 1995.

Walker, Alice. *You Can't Keep a Good Woman Down*. New York: Harcourt Brace, 1981.

Wallace, Michelle. *Invisibility Blues*. Verso: New York, 1990.

Walzer, Michael. "What Does It Mean to Be an American?" *Social Research* 57.3 (Fall 1990): 591–614.

———. *What It Means to Be an American*. New York: Marsilo, 1992.

Waters, Muddy. *The Complete Plantation Recordings*. Recorded by Alan Lomax and John Work. Chess/MCA, CHD-9344, 1993.

Watts, Jerry Gafio. *Heroism and the Black Intellectual: Ralph Ellison, Politics, and Afro-American Life*. Chapel Hill: U of North Carolina P, 1994.

Webb, Walter Prescott. "Notes to Folk-Lore of Texas." *Journal of American Folklore* 28 (1915): 290–99.

Wendell, Barret. *Barret Wendell and His Letters*. By M. A. De Wolfe Howe. Boston: Atlantic Monthly P, 1924.

West, Cornel. *The American Evasion of Philosophy: A Genealogy of Pragmatism*. Madison: U of Wisconsin P, 1989.

Westbrook, Robert B. *John Dewey and American Democracy*. Ithaca: Cornell UP, 1991.

Whitaker, Thomas R. "Spokesman for Invisibility." Benston 386–403.

White, Bukka. "Parchman Farm Blues." *The Complete Sessions 1939–40.* Travelin' Man,
 TM CD 03, 1990.

White, Cliff. Liner Notes. *CD of JB II.* By James Brown. Polydor, 831 700-2, 1987.

White, Hayden, and Margaret Brose, eds. *Representing Kenneth Burke.* Baltimore: Johns
 Hopkins UP, 1982.

Whitman, Walt. *Poetry and Prose.* New York: Library of America, 1982.

Wilkins, Robert. "Alabama Blues." *The Original Rolling Stone.* Yazoo, 1077, 1989.

Wills, Bob. "In the Mood." *The Tiffany Transcriptions.* Vol. 9. Kaleidoscope, K-35
 Mono, 1990.

Wills, Garry. *Lincoln at Gettysburg.* New York: Touchstone, 1992.

Wirth-Nesher, Hanna. "From Newark to Prague: Roth's Place in the American-Jewish
 Literary Tradition." Milbauer and Watson 17–32.

Wolfe, Charles. "A Lighter Shade of Pale: White Country Blues." Tracy 514-30.

———. Liner Notes. *Elvis Presley Amazing Grace: His Greatest Sacred Performances.* RCA,
 07863 66421-2, 1994.

———. "Presley and the Gospel Tradition." Quain 13–28.

Work, John. W. *American Negro Songs and Spirituals.* New York: Bonanza, 1940.

Wright, John. "Shadowing Ellison." Benston 63–88.

Wright, John S. "The Conscious Hero and the Rites of Man: Ellison's War." O'Meally,
 *New Essays* 157–86.

# INDEX

■■■■■■